# Sounds and their patterns in Indic languages

## Volume 2: Phonological Sketches

Pramod Pandey



FOUNDATION® BOOKS

Bengaluru • Chennai • Delhi • Hyderabad • Kolkata • Mumbai • Pune • Thiruvananthapuram

FOUNDATION®
BOOKS

Foundation Books is an imprint of Cambridge University Press India Pvt. Ltd.

Cambridge House, 4381/4 Ansari Road, Daryaganj, New Delhi 110 002

www.cambridgeindia.org



First published 2014

Printed in India at Bhavish Graphics, Chennai

ISBN 978-93-82993-93-3 Paperback

Mātā me Nirmalā Devī pitā devo Maheśwarah
Bāndhawāh Nirmalā bhaktāśca swadeśo bhuwanatrayam

# Contents

# Introductory Remarks

A detailed discussion on the issues related to the sketches has been presented in Chapter 1, Section 1.3 of Volume 1. Each sketch contains a total of maximally six sections: Section 1 includes consonant phonemes and their distribution in the word. Section 2 contains vowel phonemes, sub-grouped as Short, Long, Diphthongs, and Nasal vowels, as well as their distribution. Section 3 contains the consonant allophones and their distribution. Section 4 contains the vowel allophones and their distribution. General allophonic distributional facts are stated separately from specific allophonic facts. Section 5 contains statements of canonical syllable structure, and permitted consonant clusters in three positions in the word- initial, medial and final. Up to this point, all the sketches share a common format. Tonal languages have an additional section 6, of suprasegmentals, in which the tonemes and, where available, allotonic facts are stated.

The charts follow the general practice of arranging voiceless consonants on the left-hand side and voiced consonants on the right-hand side in a slot. The vowels are presented following the standard IPA practice of placing the unrounded ones on the left and the rounded ones on the right of a vertical line for Front, Central and Back vowels. A parenthesis in a phonemic chart or table stands for the marginal status of a phoneme. For example, the phoneme /q/ is enclosed in parentheses for Hindi, in which it has a marginal status, but not for Urdu, in which it is assumed to be a regular phoneme. In a chart or table for allophones, however, a parenthesis stands for the phoneme from which the allophone is assumed to be derived. Thus, the allophonic tables for Hindi and Urdu consonants contain the voiced retroflex flap allophone of the voiced retroflex plosive phoneme in the form- [ɽ] (ɖ), as a simplified version of [ɽ] (</ɖ/). In a statement of the canonical syllable structure, the parentheses stand for the optionality of a C/V element, following a general practice. For certain languages, especially of the Dravidian and Austro-Asiatic groups, the statement about the canonical syllable structure is divided into two, according to the relevant parametric variation (see the discussion in 5.1.2).

Every sketch contains the main reference(s) used as a basis for presentation. Other references are listed in section C of the Bibliography in Volume I.

Chapter 1

# AUSTRO-ASIATIC

# Bhumij

**Ethnologue code:** [muw][1].
**Language classification:** Austro-Asiatic, Munda
**Alternate names:** Not available
**Main region:** Orissa, Bihar, Andhra Pradesh

## 1 Consonant Phonemes

### 1.1 Inventory

| | Bilabial | | Dental | | Alveolar | Retro-flex | | Palatal | | Velar | | Glot-tal |
|---|---|---|---|---|---|---|---|---|---|---|---|---|
| Plosive | p<br>pʰ | b<br>bʱ | t<br>tʰ | d<br>dʱ | | ʈ<br>ʈʰ | ɖ<br>ɖʱ | | | k<br>kʰ | g<br>gʱ | ʔ |
| Nasal | | m | | | n | | ɳ | | | | ŋ | |
| Trill | | | | | r | | | | | | | |
| Flap | | | | | | | ɽ | | | | | |
| Fricative | | | | | s | | | | | | | h |
| Approx | | w | | | | | | | j | | | |
| Lat. Approx. | | | | | l | | | | | | | |
| Affricate | | | | | | | | ʧ<br>ʧʰ | ʤ<br>ʤʱ | | | |

[1] Ethnologue 14th edition language code.

## 1.2 Distribution

a. Consonants occur in all positions.

b. Aspirated stops /pʰ bʱ tʰ dʱ ʈʰ ɖʱ ʧʰ ʤʱ kʰ gʱ/ and /ʧ ɖ/ do not occur finally.

c. /pʰ bʱ ʧʰ ʤʱ/ do not occur medially.

d. /ʔ ɽ ŋ/ do not occur initially.

e. Geminate consonants occur rarely: /tt/

# 2 Vowel phonemes

## 2.1 Inventory

a. **Short**

| | FRONT | CENTRAL | BACK |
|---|---|---|---|
| Close | i | | u |
| Close-mid | e | | o |
| Open-mid | | | ɔ |
| Open | | a | |

b. **Long**

| | FRONT | CENTRAL | BACK |
|---|---|---|---|
| Close | iː | | uː |
| Close-mid | eː | | oː |
| Open-mid | | | ɔː |
| Open | | aː | |

c. **Nasal**

| | FRONT | CENTRAL | BACK |
|---|---|---|---|
| Close-mid | ẽ | | õ |
| Open | | ã | |

## 2.2 Distribution

a. Short oral vowels occur in all positions.

b. The long vowels and the nasal vowel / ã / do not occur finally.

c. /ẽ õ/ occur only medially.

d. Vowel sequences of two occur in all positions. Sequences of three vowels do not occur.

# 3 Consonant allophones

## 3.1 Inventory and distribution

**General:**

a. Plosives have tense allophones, [p̂ b̂ t̂ d̂ ʈ̂ ɖ̂ k̂ ĝ] </p b t d ʈ ɖ k g/ intervocalically.

**Specific:**

b. [ɲ] < /ŋ/ occurs before a following /i/ or a palatal consonant.

# 4 Vowel allophones

## 4.1 Inventory

[ɪ]: / i /

[ɛ]: / e /

[ʊ]: / u /

[o̞]: / o /

[ɐ]: / a /

## 4.2 Distribution

a. The lowered allophones of non-low vowels and the raised allophone of the low vowel [ɪ ɛ ʊ o̞ ʌ] < / i e u o a/ occur word-medially.

# 5 Syllable structure

## 5.1 Canonical syllable structure

(C) (C) V (C) (C)

## 5.2 Consonant clusters

Two-consonant clusters:

| | | |
|---|---|---|
| Initial | : | /pr-, pɹ-, sʈ-, sr-, sw-/ |
| Final | : | /-ʔp, -ʔt, -nt/ |
| Medial | : | general |

Three-consonant clusters:

| | | |
|---|---|---|
| Initial | : | Nil |
| Final | : | Nil |
| Medial | : | /-ʔtt- -ʔtk- / |

Four-consonant clusters:

| | | |
|---|---|---|
| Initial | : | Nil. |
| Final | : | Nil |
| Medial | : | -ʔmpɽ- |

**Reference:** Ramaswami (1989)

# Bonda

**Ethnologue code:** ISO 639-3: bfw
**Language classification:** Austro-Asiatic, Munda
**Alternate names:** Remo, Remosum, Poraja Katha, Bhonda Bhasha, Bondo-Poraja, Nanqa Poroja
**Main region:** Orissa.

## 1 Consonant Phonemes

### 1.1 Inventory

| | Bilabial | Alveolar | Retroflex | Palatal | Velar | Glottal |
|---|---|---|---|---|---|---|
| Plosive | p b<br>p$^{h}$ b$^{ɦ}$ | t d<br>t$^{h}$ d$^{ɦ}$ | ʈ ɖ<br>ʈ$^{h}$ ɖ$^{ɦ}$ | | k g<br>k$^{h}$ g$^{ɦ}$ | ʔ |
| Nasal | m | n | ɳ | ɲ | ŋ | |
| Trill | | r | | | | |
| Fricative | | s | | | | h |
| Approx | w | | | j | | |
| Lat Appr | | l | ɭ | | | |
| Affricate | | | | ʧ ʤ<br>ʧ$^{h}$ ʤ$^{ɦ}$ | | |

### 1.2 Distribution

a. The following sounds occur only in the initial and medial positions: /p$^{h}$ b$^{ɦ}$ d$^{ɦ}$ k$^{h}$ ɳ ɽ w /.

b. The following sounds occur only in the initial position: /g$^{ɦ}$ ʧ$^{h}$ ʤ$^{ɦ}$ ʈ$^{h}$ h/.

c. The following sounds occur only in the medial position: /ɭ ɳ/.

# 2 Vowel Phonemes

## 2.1 Inventory

**a. Short**

| | FRONT | CENTRAL | BACK |
|---|---|---|---|
| Close | i | | u |
| Close-mid | e | | o |
| Open-mid | ɛ | ə | ɔ |
| Open | | a | |

**b. Long**

| | FRONT | CENTRAL | BACK |
|---|---|---|---|
| Close | i: | | u: |
| Close-mid | e: | | |
| Open | | a: | |

**c. Nasal**

| | FRONT | CENTRAL | BACK |
|---|---|---|---|
| Close | ĩ | | ũ |
| Close-mid | ẽ | | õ |
| Open-mid | | | |
| Open | | ã | |

## 2.2 Distribution

a. The following vowels occur in the initial and medial positions: /ə ʊ u ː/.

b. The following vowels occur in the medial and final positions: / ɛ o /.

c. The following vowels occur only in the medial position: / ɪ e ː/.

d. Vowel sequences are common.

e. The vowels /ɪ ʊ ɛ ə/ are shorter than other short vowels in duration.

# 3 Consonant Allophones

Information not available.

# 4 Vowel Allophones

Information not available.

# 5 Syllable Structure

## 5.1 Canonical syllable structure

(C) (C) (C) V (C) (C)

## 5.2 Consonant clusters

Consonant Cluster:

Two-consonant clusters:

| | | |
|---|---|---|
| Initial | : | kr-, kl-, gl-, lr- sr-, ŋk-, ns-, ɳɖ -, mb- |
| Final | : | -nd, -nm, -rt, -ʔŋ |
| Medial | : | General |

Three-consonant clusters:

| | | |
|---|---|---|
| Initial | : | ntl-, ndr-, slɟ-, ŋŋk-, ɳɖɖ |
| Final | : | Nil |
| Medial | : | (1) CʔC |
| | | (2) -ndr- -ɳɖr- -nɖk- -mpr- -rɳɖ- |

**Reference:** Ramchandrarao (1986 b)

# Didayi[2]

**Ethnologue code:** ISO 639-3: gaq
**Language classification:** Austro-Asiatic, Munda, South Munda
**Alternate names:** Gta?, Geta?, Gataq, Getaq, Gta Asa, Didei, Didayi, Dire
**Main region:** Orissa.

## 1 Consonant Phonemes

### 1.1 Inventory

| | BILABIAL | DENTAL | ALVEOLAR | RETROFLEX | PALATAL | VELAR | GLOTTAL |
|---|---|---|---|---|---|---|---|
| Plosive | p b bʱ | t d (tʰ) | | ʈ ɖ ɖʱ | | k g (kʰ) | ʔ |
| Nasal | m | n | | | | ŋ | |
| Trill | | r | | | | | |
| Fricative | | | s | | | | h |
| Appr | w | | | | (j) | | |
| Lat Appr | | | l | | | | |
| Affricate | | | | | ʧ ʤ | | |

2 'Gta?' means 'man'. 'Didayi', meaning 'the wild people', has come from Oriya. Gta?, along with Bonda (or Remo) and Gutob, forms the lower Munda group. The people are found in Malkangiri district of Orissa, and in the Sojankanta police station area of Andhra Pradesh.

## 1.2 Distribution

a. Consonants occur in all positions, with the following restriction:
   i. /p b t d ʈ ɖ ʧ ʤ h m l w/ do not occur word- finally in native vocabulary.
   ii. /ʔ/ does not occur initially.

b. Geminates of /p t ɖ k g ʧ m n l r s h/ occur. Of these, /pp/ occur only medially, /rr/ and /nn/ medially and initially, and others only initially.

# 2 Vowel Phonemes

## 2.1 Inventory

a. **Short**

| | FRONT | CENTRAL | BACK |
|---|---|---|---|
| Close | i | | u |
| Close-mid | e | | o |
| Open-mid | ɛ | | |
| Open | | a | |

b. **Nasal**

| | FRONT | CENTRAL | BACK |
|---|---|---|---|
| Close | (ĩ) | | (ũ) |
| Close-mid | (ẽ) | | (õ) |
| Open-mid | (ɛ̃) | | |
| Open | | (ã) | |

## 2.2 Distribution

a. Vowels occur in all positions.

b. Vowel sequences of two occur, but they are realized as diphthongs: /ia ei ai ui oi ae ua oa ao oe ue eo eu/; either the first or the second vowel is stressed, and the other is desyllabified.

c. Nasal counterparts of oral vowels occur, independent of the context of a nasal consonant, but have not been established as phonemes for lack of sufficient data.

# 3 Consonant Allophones

a. Pregottalized allophones of velar plosives [ʔk̚ ʔɡ̚] < /k ɡ/ occur in the coda position in borrowed words.

b. [ɽ] < /ɖ/ occurs in the intervocalic position.

# 4 Vowel allophones

## 4.1 Inventory

[ɪ]: /i/
[ɛ]: /e/
[æ]: /ɛ/
[ʊ]: /u/
[ɔ]: /o/
[ə]: /a/

## 4.2 Distribution

a. [ɪ ɛ æ ə ɔ ʊ], allophones of /i e ɛ ə o u/, occur in unstressed syllables (other than the final ones) in polysyllabic words; [æ] also occurs word-finally.

# 5 Syllable structure

## 5.1 Canonical syllable structure

(C)(C)V(C)

## 5.2 Consonant clusters

Two-consonant clusters:

Initial : A large number of initial consonant clusters is found in Didayi, e.g. /ph pl bt btʃ bk bn bs br bl tm tn tr ɖl tʃn tʃr dʒn ŋk ŋtʃ kl kr gn gl gr mb mn ml mr nt nl ɳɖ lg lh sm sr ʂ ɖ sl rk hm hn hr/

E.g. /gnoʔ/ 'spear', /btʃweʔ/ 'sour', /bsa/ 'uncle', /tmuʔ/ 'his mouth', /gnalwa/ 'ant', /mbaŋ/ 'elder sister's husband', etc.

Final : Nil

Medial : /pr tb tl tr kn ŋk ŋg kr gb gk gm gd ml nd nt ŋt ŋl ŋs ŋɖ ŋr lk ls st rp rt rk rh rm/

Three-consonant clusters:

Initial : Nil

Final : Nil

Medial : Only one found: /ɳɖr/.

**References:** Ghosh (1996), Ashirvadam (1992)

# Gadaba–Gutob[3]

**Ethnologue code:** ISO 639-3: gau
**Language classification:** Dravidian, Central
**Alternate names:** Gutob, Gadaba
**Main region:** Orissa, Andhra Pradesh (Srikakulam district)

## 1 Consonant Phonemes

### 1.1 Inventory

| | Bilabial | Dental | Alveolar | Retroflex | Palatal | Velar | Glottal |
|---|---|---|---|---|---|---|---|
| Plosive | p b<br>pʰ bʱ | t d<br>tʰ dʱ | | ʈ ɖ<br>ʈʰ ɖʱ | | k g<br>kʰ gʱ | |
| Nasal | m | | n | ɳ | | ŋ | |
| Trill | | | r | | | | |
| Fricative | | | s | | | | h |
| Approx | w | | | | j | | |
| Lat Appr | | | l | | | | |
| Affricate | | | | | ʧ ʤ<br>ʧʰ | | |

### 1.2 Distribution

a. Consonants occur in all positions, with the following restrictions:

   i. /pʰ bʱ dʱ ʈʰ ɖ ɖʱ ʧʰ gʱ ʔ ɳ h w j/ do not occur word-finally.

[3] The data being described here are of Koraput district in Orissa. Of the three varieties of Gadaba, this variety is assumed to belong to the Austro-Asiatic group, and differs in many features from Konekor Gadaba and Ollari, both Dravidian varieties.

ii. /dʱ gʱ ʔ ɳ ŋ w/ do not occur initially.
iii. /bʱ tʰ ʈʰ ʧʰ gʱ ŋ h j/ do not occur medially.

b. Geminates of consonants are not attested.

# 2 Vowel Phonemes

## 2.1 Inventory

a. **Short**

| | FRONT | CENTRAL | BACK |
|---|---|---|---|
| Close | i | | u |
| Close-mid | e | | o |
| Open-mid | | ɞ | |
| Open | | a | |

b. **Nasal**

| | FRONT | CENTRAL | BACK |
|---|---|---|---|
| Close | ĩ | | ũ |
| Close-mid | ẽ | | õ |
| Open-mid | | ɞ̃ | |
| Open | | ã | |

## 2.2 Distribution

a. All vowels occur in all positions.

b. Vowel sequences of two are common. A three vowel sequence is also attested /eiɔ/.

# 3 Consonant allophones

Data on consonant allophones are not available.

# 4 Vowel allophones

Data on vowel consonant allophones are not available.

# 5 Syllable structure

## 5.1 Canonical syllable structure

a. **Final:** (C) V (C)

b. **Non-final:** (C (L/j)) V (C)

## 5.2 Consonant clusters

Two-consonant clusters:

Initial : C+L/j

Final : Nil

Medial : General

Three-consonant clusters:

Initial : Nil

Final : Nil

Medial : /-ŋtj-, ɳɖr-, -ɳɖl-, ndr-, -bɖr-, -str-/. (These can be generalized as N/b/s + t/d/ɖ + L/j.

**Reference:** Gaud (1980)

# Gorum[4]

**Ethnologue code:** ISO 639-3: pcj
**Language classification:** Austro-Asiatic, Munda
**Alternate names:** Pareng, Parenga Parja, Parenji, Poroja, Gorum, Gorum Sama
**Main region:** Orissa (Koraput District), Andhra Pradesh.

## 1 Consonant Phonemes

### 1.1 Inventory

| | BILABIAL | DENTAL | ALVEOLAR | RETROFLEX | PALATAL | VELAR | GLOTTAL |
|---|---|---|---|---|---|---|---|
| Plosive | p b | t d | | ʈ ɖ | | k g | ʔ |
| Nasal | m | n | | | | ŋ | |
| Trill | | | r | | | | |
| Fricative | | | s | | | | |
| Approx | w | | | | j | | |
| Lat Approx | | | l | | | | |
| Affricate | | | | | ʧ ʤ | | |

### 1.2 Distribution

a. Consonants occur in all positions, with the following restriction:

   i. /ʔ/ does not occur in the initial position.

[4] The present sketch is based on the description in Oriya. The name Gorum has been chosen in place of Parengi on the grounds of the wider use of the alternative name. The inventories of phonems and allophones are drawn from the data transcibed in phonetic script.

# 2 Vowel Phonemes

## 2.1 Inventory

a. **Short**

| | FRONT | CENTRAL | BACK |
|---|---|---|---|
| Close | i | | u |
| Close-mid | e | | o |
| Open-mid | | ɐ | |
| Open | | a | |

b. **Long**

| | FRONT | CENTRAL | BACK |
|---|---|---|---|
| Close | | | uː |

c. **Nasal:** The nasal vowels /ɔ̃/ and /ũ/ are attested in the context surrounding non-nasal sounds. In a sequence of nasal and oral vowels, nasalization does not spread.

## 2.2 Distribution

a. Vowels occur in all positions.

b. Sequences of up to three vowels occur.

# 3 Consonant Allophones

## 3.1 Inventory

| | BILABIAL | DENTAL | ALVEOLAR | RETROFLEX | VELAR |
|---|---|---|---|---|---|
| Plosive | pʰ (p) | t̪ʰ (t̪) | | ʈʰ (ʈ) | kʰ (k) |
| Flap | | | ɾ (ɖ) | | |

## 3.2 Distribution

a. The aspirated allophones of the voiceless plosives occur word-initially.

b. [ɽ] < /ɖ/ occurs inter-vocalically and word-finally.

# 4 Vowel allophones

Data not available.

# 5 Syllable structure

## 5.1 Canonical syllable structure

(C) V (C)

## 5.2 Consonant clusters

Two-consonant clusters:

| | |
|---|---|
| Initial | : Nil |
| Final | : Nil. |
| Medial | : General. |

Three-consonant clusters: Nil

**Reference:** Mahapatra (1994)

# Ho

**Ethnologue code:** ISO 639-3: hoc
**Language classification:** Austro-Asiatic, Munda
**Alternate names:** Lanka Kol, Bihar Ho
**Main region:** Jharkhand; Orissa; West Bengal.

## 1 Consonant phonemes

### 1.1 Inventory

| | BILABIAL | DENTAL | ALVEOLAR | RETROFLEX | PALATAL | VELAR | GLOTTAL |
|---|---|---|---|---|---|---|---|
| Plosive | p b (pʰ) (bʱ) | t d (tʰ) (dʱ) | | ʈ ɖ (ʈʰ) (ɖʱ) | | k g (kʰ) (gʱ) | |
| Nasal | m | | n | ɳ | ɲ | ŋ | |
| Trill | | | r | | | | |
| Tap/Flap | | | | ɽ | | | |
| Fricative | | | s | | | | h |
| Approx | w | | | | j | | |
| Lat Appr | | | l | ɭ | | | |
| Affricate | | | | | ʧ ʤ | | |

### 1.2 Distribution

a. Consonants occur in all positions, with the following restrictions:
   i. / ɳ ɲ ŋ w j ɭ ɽ / do not occur initially.
   ii. / bʱ dʱ dʒʱ gʱ ɲ h w / do not occur finally.

# 2 Vowel Phonemes

## 2.1 Inventory

a. **Short**

| | FRONT | CENTRAL | BACK |
|---|---|---|---|
| Close | i | | u |
| Close-mid | e | | o |
| Open-mid | | | ɔ |
| Open | | a | |

b. **Diphthongs** (Burrows 1980):

ai au ɔĩ

## 2.2 Distribution

a. Vowels occur in all positions.

b. Vowels occur in sequences of two and three: / ɔa ɔe ɔu aɔ ae au ea ei eu ia iu ua ui ue ie iɔ /, /aea uia oia oio / etc. Most of these remain separate on the surface, and stress can be placed on any one of them.

c. Burrows (1931) notes three of the vowel sequences as diphthongs:

ai̯ au̯ ɔĩ.

# 3 Consonant allophones

Data not available.

# 4 Vowel allophones

Data not available.

# 5 Syllable structure

## 5.1 Canonical syllable structure

(C)V(C)

## 5.2 Consonant clusters

Two-consonant clusters:

Initial : Nil

Final : Nil

Medial : General

Three-consonant clusters: Not attested.

**References:** Bhattacharya (1984), Burrows (1980 [1915]).

# Juang[5]

**Ethnologue code:** ISO 639-3: jun
**Language classification:** Austro-Asiatic, Munda
**Alternate names:** Juango, Puttooas, Patua, Patra-Saara
**Main region:** Orissa.

## 1 Consonant phonemes

### 1.1 Inventory

| | BILABIAL | DENTAL | ALVEOLAR | RETROFLEX | PALATAL | VELAR | GLOTTAL |
|---|---|---|---|---|---|---|---|
| Plosive | p b (pʰ) (bʱ) | t d (tʰ) (dʱ) | | ʈ ɖ (ʈʰ) (ɖʱ) | | k g (kʰ) (gʱ) | |
| Nasal | m | n | | (ɳ) | (ɲ) | ŋ | |
| Trill | | | r | | | | |
| Flap | | | | ɽ (ɽʱ) | | | |
| Fricative | | | s | | | | (h) |
| Lat Appr | | | l | (ɭ) | | | |
| Affricate | | | | | ʧ ʤ (ʧʰ) (ʤʱ) | | |

[5] The data being described here are of Keonjhar district in Orissa. Data from Dhenkanal and Pal Lahara are also considered.

## 1.2 Distribution

a. Consonants occur in all positions, with the following restrictions: /p b t d k/

   i. /p t d ʈ ɖ ɳ l ɭ/ do not occur word-finally.

   ii. / ɳ ɲ ŋ ɭ ɽ / do not occur word-medially.

b. The aspirates /pʰ bʱ tʰ dʱ tʰ dʱ ʧʰ ʤʱ kʰ gʱ/ freely vary with the homorganic non-aspirates. They occur in Oriya loan words.

c. /ɳ/ and /n/ show a lot of free variation.

d. Geminates of the following consonants occur inter-vocalically: /p b t d k ʧ s/.

# 2 Vowel Phonemes

## 2.1 Inventory

a. **Short**

| | FRONT | CENTRAL | BACK |
|---|---|---|---|
| Close | i | | u |
| Close-mid | e | | (o) |
| Open-mid | (ɛ) | | ɔ |
| Open | | a | |

b. **Nasal**

Deasgupta (1976) notes that non-contextual nasal vowels alone and in sequences occur in Juang, but there were no minimal pairs in his data to establish them as phonemes. As noted for the AN languages, minimal pairs are hard to come by for many of these endangered languages, because of the relatively small size of their lexicons. The non-contextual nasal vowels found in the data produced by Dasgupta are the following: [ĩ ũ ẽ ɔ̃ ã].

## 2.2 Distribution

a. All vowels occur in all positions.

b. /ɛ/ and /o/ are free variant forms of /e/ and /ɔ/.

c. Sequences of two and three vowels occur commonly.

# 3 Consonant allophones

## 3.1 Inventory

a. [ʔ] < /t k/

## 3.2 Distribution

a. In fast speech, /k/ and /t/ may be realized as [ʔ].

# 4 Vowel Allophones

## 4.1 Inventory and Distribution

a. Vowels are lengthened before /m n ŋ s r ɽ/ in the coda position.

b. In a sequence of two vowels, the higher one is desyllabified, e.g., ai̯ u̯a etc.

# 5 Syllable structure

## 5.1 Canonical syllable structure

(C) (r) V (C)

## 5.2 Consonant clusters

Two-consonant clusters:

Initial : S+r

Final : Nil

Medial : General

Three-consonant clusters:

Initial : Nil

Final : Nil

Medial : Only the following attested: N + S + Tr: -ndr-, -ɳɖr-, -ŋgr-.

**References:** Matson (1964), Dasgupta (1976)

# Kharia

**Ethnologue code:** ISO 639-3: khr
**Language classification:** Austro-Asiatic, Munda, South Munda
**Alternate names:** Haria, Kharvi, Khatria, Kheria, Khadia, Khariya
**Main region:** Jharkhand; Chhattisgarh; Orissa.

## 1 Consonant Phonemes

### 1.1 Inventory

| | Bilabial | Dental | Alveolar | Retroflex | Palatal | Velar | Glottal |
|---|---|---|---|---|---|---|---|
| Plosive | p b<br>(p$^h$) b$^ɦ$ | t d<br>t$^h$ d$^ɦ$ | | ʈ ɖ<br>ʈ$^h$ ɖ$^ɦ$ | | k g<br>k$^h$ g$^ɦ$ | (ʔ) |
| Nasal | m | n | | (ɳ) | ɲ | ŋ | |
| Trill | | | r | | | | |
| Tap/Flap | | | | ɽ | | | |
| Fricative | | s | | | | | h |
| Approx | w | | | j | | | |
| Lat Appr | | l | | | | | |
| Affricate | | | | | ʧ ʤ<br>ʧ$^h$ ʤ$^ɦ$ | | |

### 1.2 Distribution

a. Consonants occur in all positions, with the following restrictions:

i. /ɳ ŋ ɽ w ʔ/ do not occur word initially.

ii. /p$^h$ b$^ɦ$ t$^h$ d d$^ɦ$ ʧ$^h$ ʤ$^ɦ$ g$^ɦ$ ɳ ɽ h j w/ do not occur finally.

b. Tautomorphemeic geminate consonants are rare, with an attested instance of inter-vocalic /tt/. Geminates of consonants across morphemes are common.

# 2 Vowel Phonemes

## 2.1 Inventory

a. **Short**

| | FRONT | CENTRAL | BACK |
|---|---|---|---|
| Close | i | | u |
| Close-mid | e | | o |
| Open-mid | ɛ | | ɔ |
| Open | | a | |

b. **Nasal**

| | FRONT | CENTRAL | BACK |
|---|---|---|---|
| Close | ĩ | | ũ |
| Close-mid | ẽ | | õ |
| Open-mid | ɛ̃ | | ɔ̃ |
| Open | | ã | |

## 2.2 Distribution

a. Vowels occur in all positions.

b. Vowels also occur in sequences of two. Identical vowels remain syllabic. One of the non-identical vowels is desyllabified.

# 3 Consonant Allophones

## 3.1 Inventory

| | **Bilabial** | **Labio-dental** | **Dental** | **Retro-flex** | **Pala-tal** | **Glot-tal** |
|---|---|---|---|---|---|---|
| Plosive | b$^{ʔ}$ (b) | | d$^{ʔ}$ (d) | | ʤ$^{ʔ}$ (ʤ) | ʔ (g) |
| Tap/Flap | | | | ɽ$^{ɦ}$ (ɖ$^{ɦ}$) | | |
| Fricative | | f (p$^{h}$) | | | | |

## 3.2 Distribution

a. [b$^{ʔ}$ d$^{ʔ}$ ʤ$^{ʔ}$ g$^{ʔ}$] < / b d ʤ g / occur before a consonant or pause.

b. [ɽ$^{h}$] < /ɖ$^{ɦ}$/ occurs intervocalically. Post-consonantly, it occurs freely with /ɖ$^{ɦ}$/.

c. [f] is a free variant of [p$^{h}$].

# 4 Vowel allophones

## 4.1 Inventory

| | |
|---|---|
| [i:] [ ĭ ] : | / i / |
| [u:] [ ʊ̆ ] [u$^{j}$]: | / u / |
| [e:][ ɛ̆ ] [e$^{j}$]: | /e/ |
| [o:] [ ŏ ] [ɔ$^{j}$]: | /o/ |
| [ ə ] [ ə̆ ] [ə$^{j}$] [ɑ·$^{j}$] [ɑ·]: | / a / |

## 4.2 Distribution

a. Vowels are lengthened in three contexts: (i) in the word-final position, (ii) in the penultimate position, if open, and if the final is also open, and (iii) in closed monosyllables.

b. The extra-short allophones, [ĭ ŭ ɛ̆ ɔ̆ ə̆] < /i u e o a /, occur before /b ɖ ʤ g/.

c. [ə ɑˑ] are free allophones of /a/ before /j w/.

d. Vowels (except i) have a j – glide before /j/.

# 5 Syllable Structure

## 5.1 Canonical syllable structure

(C)V(C)

Note: Peterson (2006) mentions -$p^h$ŋg-, -lŋg-, -rŋg- as medial consonant sequences, but assumes that the nasal is syllabic: *laphŋga* 'cave' [lə.$p^h$ŋ.ga].

## 5.2 Consonant clusters

Two-consonant clusters:

Initial : Nil.
Final : Nil.
Medial : General

Three-consonant clusters:

Initial : Nil
Final : Nil.
Medial : -kʧ$^h$j-, -gtr-, jgn-.

**References:** Biligiri (1965), Peterson (2006).

# Khasi

**Ethnologue code:** ISO 639-3: kha
**Language classification:** Austro-Asiatic, Mon-Khmer
**Alternate names:** Kahasi, Kassi, Khasa, Khashi, Khasiyas, Khuchia
**Main region:** Meghalaya, Assam

## 1 Consonant Phonemes

### 1.1 Inventory

| | BILABIAL | LABIO-DENTAL | POST-DENTAL | ALVE-OLAR | PALA-TAL | VELAR | GLOT-TAL |
|---|---|---|---|---|---|---|---|
| Plosive | p b<br>pʰ | | t d<br>tʰ | | | k g<br>kʰ | ʔ |
| Nasal | m | | | n | ɲ | ŋ | |
| Trill | | | | r | | | |
| Fricative | | f | | s | ʃ | | h |
| Approx | w | | | | j | | |
| Lateral Appr | | | | l | | | |
| Affricate | | | | | dʒ | | |

### 1.2 Distribution

a. Consonants occur in all positions, with the following restrictions:
   i. / g f / do not occur word-initially.
   ii. /b d g pʰ tʰ kʰ ʤ f s ʃ h l/ do not occur word-finally. /l/ occurs only in loan-words.
b. /pʰ/ and /f/ are frequently in free variation.
c. Geminates do not occur.

# 2 Vowel Phonemes

## 2.1 Inventory

a. **Short**

| | FRONT | CENTRAL | BACK |
|---|---|---|---|
| Close | ɪ | | ʊ |
| Mid | e | | o |
| Open | | a | |

b. **Long**

| | FRONT | CENTRAL | BACK |
|---|---|---|---|
| Close | i : | | u : |
| Mid | e : | | o : |
| Open | | a : | |

c. **Diphthongs:** /ia ie uo/

## 2.2 Distribution

a. Vowels occur in all positions, with the following exceptions:
   i. The long mid vowels /e : o : / do not occur finally.

b. Sequences of two vowels occur.

# 3 Consonant Allophones

## 3.1 Inventory

**General:** All liquids and nasals except /ɲ/ have two novel allophones: (i) all are syllabic between two consonants: [m̩ n̩ ŋ̩ r̩ l̩], and (ii) all have vocalic release before CV:[mᵊ nᵊ ŋᵊ lᵊ rᵊ].

**Specific:**

[ʔᵊ]: /ʔ/
[u̯]: /w/
[i̯]: /i/
[tʃ]: /ʤ/

## 3.2 Distribution

a. The released glottal stop [ʔᵊ] < /ʔ/ occurs before a liquid or nasal.

b. The desyllabified high vocalic allophones [i̯ u̯] < /j w/ occur before and after a vowel.

c. The voiceless palatal affricate [tʃ] </ʤ/ occurs word-finally.

# 4 Vowel Allophones

## 4.1 Inventory

**General:** All vowels have an [i̯] off-glide before the palatal consonants [tʃ] and [ɲ].

**Specific:**

[i̞], [i] : /iː/
[ɪ], [e̞] : /i/
[u·], [u] : /uː/
[o̞], [ʊ] : /u/
[ɛ ː] : /e ː/
[ɛ] : /e/
[ɔ ː] : /o ː/
[ɔ] : /o/
[ĭă] : /ia/
[e̞e̯] : /ie/
[o̞o̯] : /uo/

## 4.2 Distribution

a. [i̝̞], [ e̝], [u·], [o̝] < /i :/, /i/, /u :/, /u/ occur word-finally.

b. [i], [ɪ], [ɛ], [ɔ], [ɔ:], [u], [ĭă], [e̝e̯], [o̝o̯] < /i:/, /i/, /e/, /o/, /o:/, /u:/, /ia/, /ie/, /uo/ occur in closed syllables.

# 5 Syllable Structure

## 5.1 Canonical syllable structure

Rabel (1961) proposes two types of syllables in Khasi, with two types of nuclei and minimal word requirements:

**Major syllable** (with a vocalic nucleus in a minimum monosyllabic word): C (C) V(C).

**Minor syllable** (with a syllabic nasal or liquid as nucleus in a minimum bisyllabic word): C C̩.

## 5.2 Consonant clusters

Two-consonant clusters:

Initial : $C_1C_2$ (where $C_1C_2$ are non-identical)
Final : Nil
Medial : General.

Three-consonant clusters: Nil

**Reference:** Rabel (1961)

# Kisan[6]

**Ethnologue code:** None
**Language classification:** Austro-Asiatic, Munda
**Alternate names:** Not available
**Main region:** Orissa

## 1 Consonant Phonemes

### 1.1 Inventory

| | Bilabial | Dental | Alv. | Retro-flex | Pala-tal | Velar | Glot-tal |
|---|---|---|---|---|---|---|---|
| Plosive | p b<br>$p^{h}$ $b^{ɦ}$ | t d<br>$t^{h}$ $d^{ɦ}$ | | ʈ ɖ<br>$ʈ^{h}$ $ɖ^{ɦ}$ | | k g<br>$k^{h}$ $g^{ɦ}$ | ʔ |
| Nasal | m | | n | ɳ | | ŋ | |
| Trill | | | r | | | | |
| Flap | | | | ɽ | | | |
| Fricative | | | s | | | | h |
| Appr | (w) | | | | j | | |
| Lat. Approx. | | | l | | | | |
| Affricate | | | | | ʧ ʤ<br>$ʧ^{h}$ $ʤ^{ɦ}$ | | |

[6] There is no definite information about the classification of Kisan, as belonging to either the A-A or the Dravidian group. It is included here as belonging to A-A group on the basis of its closeness to Korku and some other Munda languages

## 1.2 Distribution

a. Consonants occur in all positions, with the following restrictions:

   i. / pʰ bʱ dʱ tʰ ʈʰ ɖʱ tʃtʃʰ ʤʱ kʰ gʱ h/ do not occur finally.

   ii. / ɳ ŋ ɽ / do not occur initially.

b. Geminates of /b ʧ ʤ t m n l r s/ are attested word medially and finally.

# 2 Vowel Phonemes

## 2.1 Inventory

a. **Short**

| | FRONT | CENTRAL | BACK |
|---|---|---|---|
| Close | i | | u |
| Close-mid | e | | o |
| Open-mid | | | ɔ |
| Open | | a | |

b. **Nasal**

| | FRONT | CENTRAL | BACK |
|---|---|---|---|
| Close | ĩ | | ũ |
| Close-mid | ẽ | | õ |
| Open-mid | | | ɔ̃ |
| Open | | ã | |

## 2.2 Distribution

a. Vowels occur in all positions.

b. Sequences of two syllabic vowels are common.

# 3 Allophones

Data not available.

# 4 Syllable Structure

## 4.1 Canonical Syllable Structure

(C) V (C) (C)

## 4.2 Consonant Clusters

Two-consonant clusters:

Initial : Nil
Final : -ɳʈ, -ŋk
Medial : General

Three-consonant clusters: Not attested.

**Reference:** Goswami (1989)

# Korku[7]

**Ethnologue code:** ISO 639-3: kfq
**Language classification:** Austro-Asiatic, Munda
**Alternate names:** Bondeya, Bopchi, Korki, Kurku, Kuri, Ramekhera, Kurku-Ruma
**Main region:** Southern Madhya Pradesh; northern Maharashtra.

## 1 Consonant Phonemes

### 1.1 Inventory

| | BILABIAL | | DENTAL | | ALVEOLAR | | RETROFLEX | | PALATAL | | VELAR | | UVULAR | GLOTTAL |
|---|---|---|---|---|---|---|---|---|---|---|---|---|---|---|
| Plosive | p<br>pʰ | b<br>bʱ | t<br>tʰ | d<br>dʱ | | | ʈ<br>ʈʰ | ɖ<br>ɖʱ | | | k<br>kʰ | g<br>gʱ | q | |
| Nasal | | m | | | | n | | | | | | ŋ | | |
| Trill | | | | | | r | | | | | | | | |
| Flap | | | | | | | | ɽ | | | | | | |
| Fricative | | | | | s | | | | | | | | | h |
| Appr | | (w) | | | | | | | | j | | | | |
| Lat. Appr | | | | | | l | | ɭ | | | | | | |
| Affricate | | | | | | | | | ʧ<br>ʧʰ | ʤ<br>ʤʱ | | | | |

### 1.2 Distribution

a. Consonants occur in all positions, with the following restrictions:

[7] The two descriptions differ in details, especially with regard to tone. Nagaraja (p.c.) has not found the presence of tone in any variety of Korku.

i. /ɽ ɭ/ do not occur initially.
ii. /pʰ bʱ tʰ d dʱ ʈʰ ɖʱ ʧ ʧʰ ʤʱ k kʰ gʱ h s/ do not occur finally.

b. Geminates of consonants occur inter-vocalically, except for the following: /ɲ ɽ w/.

# 2 Vowel Phonemes

## 2.1 Inventory

a. Short

| | FRONT | CENTRAL | BACK |
|---|---|---|---|
| Close | i | | u |
| Close-mid | e | | o |
| Open-mid | | ə | |

b. Long

| | FRONT | CENTRAL | BACK |
|---|---|---|---|
| Close | i : | | u : |
| Close-mid | e : | | o : |
| Open | | a : | |

c. Nasal

| | FRONT | CENTRAL | BACK |
|---|---|---|---|
| Open | | ã : | |

## 2.2 Distribution

a. Vowels occur in all positions, with the following restriction:
   i. /i: e:/ do not occur finally.

b. Sequences of two and three syllabic vowels are found.

# 3 Consonant Allophones

## 3.1 Inventory

[ʔ] : /h/
[ʃ] : /s/
[ŵ] : /w/
[ĵ] : /ɹ/

## 3.2 Distribution

a. [ʔ] < /h/ occurs inter-vocalically.

b. [ʃ] < /s/ occurs before /i/.

c. [ŵ ĵ ] < /w j/ occur initially and inter-vocalically.

# 4 Vowel Allophones

## 4.1. Inventory

**General:** Long vowels

**Specific:**

[ɛ] [ɨ] : /e/

[ɜ] : /ɐ/

[ʊ] : /u/

## 4.2 Distribution

**General:**

Vowels are lengthened before /r ɽ/ in monosyllables.

**Specific:**

a. [ɛ] < /e/ occurs before /e/.

b. [ ɨ ] < /e/ occurs before / ɐ u/.

c. [ʊ] < /u/ occurs when the preceding syllable has /o/.

d. [ɜ]< /ɐ/ occurs between consonants in a few morphemes.

# 5 Syllable Structure

## 5.1 Canonical syllable structure

(C) (G) V (C) (C)

## 5.2 Consonant clusters

Two-consonant clusters:

Initial : C+w/ȷ
Final : /nɖ ɲʤ ng ȷʧ/.
Medial : General.

Three-consonant clusters:

Initial : Nil.
Final : Nil.
Medial : One of the members must be a N/G/L.

Four-consonant clusters:

One instance in the medial position: /ngkl/.

**References:** Nagaraja (1999), Zide (1960).

# Mundari

**Ethnologue code:** ISO 639-3: muw
**Language classification:** Austro-Asiatic, Munda
**Alternate names:** Mandari, Munari, Munda, Mondari, Horo, Colh, Killi
**Main region:** Jharkhand, Assam, Orissa, West Bengal.

## 1 Consonant Phonemes

### 1.1 Inventory

| | BILABIAL | LABIODENTAL | DENTAL | ALVEOLAR | RETROFLEX | PALATAL | VELAR | GLOTTAL |
|---|---|---|---|---|---|---|---|---|
| Stop | p b | | t d | | ʈ ɖ | | k g | |
| Nasal | m | | n | | ɳ | (ɲ) | ŋ | |
| Trill | | | | r | | | | |
| *Flap* | | | | ɾ | | | | |
| Fricative | | | | s | | | | h |
| Appr | | ʋ | | | | j | | |
| Lat Appr | | | | l | | | | |
| Affricate | | | | | | ʧ ʤ | | |

### 1.2 Distribution

a. Consonants occur in all positions, with the following restrictions:
   i. / ŋ / does not occur initially.
   ii. / p t ʈ ɖ k ʧ ʤh ɳ/ do not occur word finally.

b. Aspirated stops borrowed from Hindi freely vary with unaspirated stops.

# 2 Vowel Phonemes

## 2.1 Inventory

a. **Short**

| | FRONT | CENTRAL | BACK |
|---|---|---|---|
| Close | i | | u |
| Close-mid | ɛ | | ɔ |
| Open-mid | | a | |

## 2.2 Distribution

a. Vowels occur in all positions.

b. Vowels also occur in sequences of two and three in all positions.

# 3 Consonant allophones

| | |
|---|---|
| [ʔb], [ʔb$^{m}$] | : /b/ |
| [ʔd], [ʔd$^{n}$] | : /d/ |
| [ʔ] | : /g/ |
| [ɽ] | : /ɖ/ |

## 3.1 Distribution

a. /b d/ are preglottalized [ ʔb ʔd ] in the coda position, with nasal release in monosyllables [ ʔb$^{m}$ ʔd$^{n}$ ].

b. [ɽ] < /ɖ and [ʔ] < /g/ occur in the coda position.

# 4 Vowel Allophones

## 4.1 Inventory

[iː] [ĩ] [ĩː]: / i /

[uː] [ũ] [ũː] : / u /

[ɛː] [ɛ̃] [ɛ̃ː]: / ɛ /

[ɔː] [ɔ̃] [ɔ̃ː]: / ɔ /

[aː] [ã] [ãː] [ɐ]: / a /

## 4.2 Distribution

a. Long vowels occur in open syllables.

b. Vowels are nasalized:
   i. after /m n/.
   ii. before /ŋ/ and NC.
   iii. before and after /ɳ/.
   iv. before and after nasalized vowels.

c. Obstr +C sequences give rise to an intermittant extra-short vowel that is a copy of the preceding vowel , e.g., /epraŋ/ > [epᵉraŋ] 'to fight together', /aʈkar/ > [aʈᵃkar] 'to feel'.

# 5 Syllable structure

## 5.1 Canonical syllable structure

(C)V(C)

## 5.2 Consonant clusters

Two-consonant clusters:

Initial: Nil.

Medial:

Stop + C : dc dk dl ds ʔs

Stop + liquid : pl pɽ bt tr tk tk kl kr kɽ gr

Liquid + C : rp rb rt rd rtʃ rd rk rg rl

Final: Nil

Three-consonant clusters:

Initial: Nil

Medial: rare: -ngr- > -ngVr-; -mbɽ > mbVɽ; mbr > mbVr.

Final: Nil.

**References:** Osada (1992), Sinha (1975), Cook (1965), Pandey (1989)

# Nancowry-Nicobarese

**Ethnologue code:** ISO 639-3: ncb
**Language classification:** Nicobar, Nancowry
**Alternate names:**Nicobar
**Main region:** Nicobar Islands, Katchal, Camorta, Nancowry, and Trinket islands.

## 1 Consonant Phonemes

### 1.1 Inventory

| | BILABIAL | LABIO-DENTAL | ALVEOLAR | PALA-TAL | VELAR | GLOTTAL |
|---|---|---|---|---|---|---|
| Plosive | p | | t | | k | ʔ |
| Nasal | m | | n | ɲ | ŋ | |
| Trill | | | r | | | |
| Fricative | | f | s | | | h |
| Approx | | ʋ | | j | | |
| Lat. Approx | | | l | | | |
| Affricate | | | | ʧ | | |

### 1.2 Distribution

a. Words must begin with a consonant.

b. Consonants also occur medially and finally with the following restriction:

   i. /f/ and /r/ do not occur finally.

# 2 Vowel Phonemes

## 2.1 Inventory

a. **Short**

| | FRONT | CENTRAL | BACK |
|---|---|---|---|
| Close | i | ɨ | u |
| Close-mid | e | | o |
| Open-mid | ɛ | ə | (ɔ) |
| Open | æ | a | |

b. **Nasal**

| | FRONT | CENTRAL | BACK |
|---|---|---|---|
| Close | ĩ | ɨ̃ | ũ |
| Close-mid | ẽ | | õ |
| Open-mid | ɛ̃ | ə̃ | ɔ̃ |
| Open | æ̃ | ã | |

c. **Diphthongs:** ia ua ɨa

## 2.2 Distribution

a. Vowels occur medially and finally.

b. Stressed vowels and nasal vowels occur in the root morpheme.

c. / ɔ / is found to occur only in three forms.

d. Vocalic sequences are found with / i u ɨ / as the first member and /a/ as the second member.

# 3 Consonant Allophones

## 3.1 Inventory

| | DENTAL | ALVEOLAR |
|---|---|---|
| Plosive | t̪ (t) | d(r) |
| Nasal | n̪ (n) | |
| Trill | | dr(r) |

## 3.2 Distribution

a. [t̪] < /t/ occurs in syllable initial position.

b. [dr] < /r/ occurs initially in stressed syllables.

c. [d] < /r/ occurs in unstressed syllables.

# 4 Vowel allophones

## 4.1 Inventory

[i] [i ː iː] [e]: /i/

[e ˑ ] [e ː ]: /e/

[ɛ ˑ ] [ɛ ː ]: /ɛ/

[æ ˑ ][æ ː ]: /æ/

[a ˑ ] [a ː ] [ə]: /a/

[ə ˑ ] [ə ː ]: /ə /

[u ˑ ] [u:] : /u /

[o ˑ ] [o ː ]: /o/

[ɨ ˑ ] [ɨ ː ]: /ɨ/

## 4.2 Distribution

a. [e]< /i/ and [ə]</a/ occur in unstressed positions after a vowel.

b. All stressed vowels have half length in closed syllables and full length in open syllables.

# 5 Syllable structure

## 5.1 Canonical syllable structure[8]

CV(C)

## 5.2 Consonant clusters

Two-consonant clusters:

Initial : Nil

Final : Nil

Medial : General

Three-consonant clusters: Nil

**Reference:** Radhakrishnan (1981)

---

[8] (a) A word must begin with a consonant.

(b) Syllable division is kept between consonants. There is no consonantal assimilation observed between adjacent syllables.

# Nicobarese-Car

**Ethnologue code:** caq
**Language classification:** Austro-Asiatic, Mon-Khmer, Nicobarese
**Alternate names:** Pu
**Main region:** Car islands

## 1 Consonant Phonemes

### 1.1 Inventory

| | BILABIAL | LABIO-DENTAL | ALVE-OLAR | RETRO-FLEX | PALA-TAL | VELAR | GLOT-TAL |
|---|---|---|---|---|---|---|---|
| Plosive | p | | t | ʈ | | k | |
| Nasal | m | | n | | ɲ | ŋ | |
| Trill | | | r | | | | |
| Tap | | | ɾ | | | | |
| Fricative | | f | s | | | | h |
| Approx | w | | | | | | |
| Lat Appr | | | l | | | | |
| Affricate | | | | | ʧ | | |

### 1.2 Distribution

a. Consonants occur in all positions, with the following restrictions:
   i. / r ɾ / do not occur finally.
   ii. /v/ alternates freely with /w/, especially in the initial and final positions.
   iii. Geminates of the following consonants are attested: /t k m n l/.

# 2 Vowel Phonemes

## 2.1 Inventory

a. **Short**

| | FRONT | CENTRAL | BACK |
|---|---|---|---|
| Close | i | | ɯ u |
| Close-mid | e | | o |
| Open-mid | ɛ | | ɔ |
| Open | | | ɒ |

b. **Long**

| | FRONT | CENTRAL | BACK |
|---|---|---|---|
| Close | i: | | ɯ: u: |
| Close-mid | e: | | o: |
| Open-mid | ɛ: | ə: | ɔ: |
| Open | | | ɒ: |

c. **Nasal**

| | FRONT | CENTRAL | BACK |
|---|---|---|---|
| Close-mid | | | (õ) |
| Open-mid | | | (ɔ̃) |
| Open | | (ã) | |

## 2.2 Distribution

a. Vowels occur commonly in non-initial positions. Initially their occurrence is rare.

b. A large number of two vowel sequences are found in Car-Nicobarese:

| | | | | | | | | | |
|---|---|---|---|---|---|---|---|---|---|
| ei | e:i | ɛ:i | ɒi | ɒ:i | əi | oi | o:i | ɯi | ui |
| oe | o:e | ɒe | ɒ:e | uɛ | ɒɛ | uɒ | iɒ | oɒ | ɛ : ɒ |
| iə | uə | iɔ | ɛɔ | ɛ : ɔ | e : o | ɛo | iu | ɒu | |

These have the second vowel short and non-syllabic, leading to phonetic diphthongs.

c. Inherent nasalized vowels are attested, but their phonemic status has not been established.

# 3 Consonant allophones

## 3.1 Inventory

| | **LABIO-DENTAL** | **DENTAL** | **RETROFLEX** |
|---|---|---|---|
| Plosive | | d(r) | ʈ(t) |
| Fricative | v (w) | | |

## 3.2 Distribution

a. [ ʈ ] < /t/ occurs finally.

b. [d] < /r/ occurs after /n/ or /l/.

c. [v] alternates freely with /w/, especially in the initial and medial positions.

# 4 Vowel Allophones

## 4.1 Inventory

[ ị̯ ẹ̯ ɛ̣̯ ụ̯ ọ̯ ə̣̯ ạ̯ ] < / i e ɛ u o ə a /

## 4.2 Distribution

a. A short vowel occurring as the second member of a vowel sequence is realized as non-syllabic leading to phonetic diphthongs.

# 5 Syllable structure

## 5.1 Canonical syllable structure

(C)V(C)

## 5.2 Consonant clusters

Two-consonant clusters:

Initial : Nil in native words; restricted to a few borrowings from English and Hindi, e.g., /tram/ 'drum'.

Final : Nil.

Medial : General.

Three-consonant clusters: Nil.

**References:** Braine (1970), Das (1972)

# Santali[9]

**Ethnologue code:** ISO 639-3: sat
**Language classification:** Austro-Asiatic, Munda
**Alternate names:** Hor, Har, Satar, Santhali, Sandal, Sangtal, Sentali, Samtali, Santhiali
**Main region:** Jharkhand, Assam, Orissa, West Bengal.

## 1 Consonant Phonemes

### 1.1 Inventory

| | Bilabial | Dental | Alveolar | Retroflex | Palatal | Velar | Glottal |
|---|---|---|---|---|---|---|---|
| Plosive | p b<br>pʰ bʱ | t̪ d̪<br>t̪ʰ d̪ʱ | | ʈ ɖ<br>ʈʰ ɖʱ | | k g<br>kʰ gʱ | |
| Nasal | m | | n | ɳ | ɲ | ŋ | |
| Trill | | | r | | | | |
| Flap | | | | ɽ | | | |
| Fricative | | | s | ʂ | | | h |
| Approx | w | | | | | | |
| Lat. Approx. | | | l | | | | |
| Affricate | | | | | tʃ dʒ | | |

[9] Santali has two main varieties- the northern, known as Deumka, and the southern, known as Bugri, according to the communities settled north or south of the river Damodar. Several phonemic systems of Santali have been presented from time to time. The vocalic system, more controversial than the consonantal system, is as presented in De (1996).

## 1.2 Distribution

a. Consonants occur in all positions, with the following restriction:

   i. The following consonants do not occur finally: / bʱ d dʱ ɖ ɖʱ g gʱ /.

b. Geminates are not attested.

# 2 Vowel Phonemes

## 2.1 Inventory

a. **Short**

| | FRONT | CENTRAL | BACK |
|---|---|---|---|
| Close | i | | u |
| Close-mid | e | | o |
| Open | | a | |

## 2.2 Distribution

a. Vowels occur in all positions.

b. Sequences of two and three vowels are found.

c. Nasal vowels, although noted in earlier descriptions, are not found to have significant contrast with oral vowels.

# 3 Consonant allophones

## 3.1 Inventory

[pˀ] : /p/

[tˀ] : /t/

[kˀ] : /k/

[tʃˀ] : /tʃ/

## 3.2 Distribution

a. The voiceless stop allophones with a glottal catch occur word-finally ("Checked deliberately and suddenly in the middle of being pronounced", McPhail 1957).

# 4 Vowel Allophones

## 4.1 Inventory

[ɛ] : /e/

[ɔ] : /o/

[ə] : /a/

## 4.2 Distribution

a. [ɛ]</e/ occurs in (a) monosyllables, and (b) in bisyllables, if there is a vowel other than /e/ in the second syllable, e.g., [ɛr]'to sow', [ɛgɛr] 'to scold', but [era] 'wife'.

b. [ɔ]</o/ occurs in (a) monosyllables, and in (b) bisyllables with /o/ in both the syllables, e.g. [ɔl] 'to write', [hɔpɔn] 'child', but [oka] 'what'.

c. [ə]</a/ occurs in (a) monosyllables, except when the final sound is not /m/, e.g. [ətˀ] 'opportunity', but [am] 'you', (b) disyllables, when one of the syllables has a high vowel, e.g. [əgu] 'to bring', [bidə] 'to give a send-off'.

# 5 Syllable structure

## 5.1 Canonical syllable structure

(C) V (C)

## 5.2 Consonant clusters

Two-consonant clusters:

Initial: Nil

Final: Nil

Medial: General.

Three-consonant clusters: Nil.

**References**: Suresh (1986), De (1996), Macphail (1957)

Chapter 2

# DRAVIDIAN

## Ave[1]

**Ethnologue code:** None
**Language classification:** Dravidian, South
**Alternate names:** Kondh
**Main region:** Kalhandi and Koraput districts of Orissa.

## 1 Consonant Phonemes

### 1.1 Inventory

| | BILA-BIAL | LABIO-DENTAL | DENTAL | ALVE-OLAR | RETRO | PALA-TAL | VELAR | GLOT-TAL |
|---|---|---|---|---|---|---|---|---|
| Plosive | p b | | t d | | ʈ ɖ | | k g | |
| Nasal | m | | | n | ɳ | | ŋ | |
| Trill | | | | r | | | | |
| Flap | | | | | ɽ | | | |
| Fricative | | | | s | | | | h |
| Approx | | ʋ | | | | j | | |
| Lat. Approx | | | | l | | | | |
| Affricate | | | | | | ʧ ʤ | | |

[1] Spoken in Kalahandi and Koraput districts of Orissa; also known as 'Kondh'; 'Ave' is preferred.

### 1.2 Distribution

a. Consonants occur in all positions, with the following restrictions:
   i. /ɳ ŋ j/ do not occur word-initially.
   ii. /ɖ g/ do not occur word-finally.
   iii. /ŋ/ does not occur inter-vocalically.

b. Geminate consonants do not occur within a morpheme. Geminates occur inter-morphemically on account of word-formation.

## 2 Vowel phonemes

### 2.1 Inventory

a. **Short**

| | Front | Central | Back |
|---|---|---|---|
| Close | i | | u |
| Close-mid | e | | o |
| Open | | a | |

b. **Long**

| | Front | Central | Back |
|---|---|---|---|
| Close | iː | | uː |
| Close-mid | eː | | oː |
| Open | | aː | |

### 2.2 Distribution

a. Vowels occur in all positions, with the following restriction:
   i. Phonemic long vowels do not occur in non-initial syllables.

b. Vowel sequences do not occur. Across morphemes, either the first vowel, if it is short, or the second vowel otherwise, is deleted.

c. Word-initially, front and back vowels have [j] and [w] on-glides respectively.

# 3 Consonant allophones

## 3.1 Inventory

| | Bilabial | Alveolar |
|---|---|---|
| Fricative | | s (ʧ) |
| Approx | w (ʋ) | |
| Affricate | | ts (ʧ)   d (ʤ) |

## 3.2 Distribution

a. [w] < /ʋ/ occurs either before or after /u/.

b. [ts d] < /ʧ ʤ/ occur before non-front vowels /a o  u a : o : u : /.

c. /s/ and /tʃ/ freely vary in lexical items.

# 4 Vowel Allophones

Details not available.

# 5 Syllable Structure

## 5.1 Canonical syllable structure

(C) (C) V (C)

## 5.2 Consonant clusters

Two-consonant clusters:

Initial : S/m + ɳ/r/ɽ/j
Final : Nil.
Medial : General.

Three-consonant clusters:

Intial : Nil
Medial : N+SH+L/G; n+S+S; L+N+S
Final : Nil

**Reference:** Ramanaiah (1982)

# Badaga

**Ethnologue code:** ISO 639-3: bfq
**Language classification:** Dravidian, Southern, Tamil-Kannada
**Alternate names:** Badag, Badagu, Badugu, Baduga, Vadagu
**Main region:** Tamil Nadu.

## 1 Consonant phonemes

### 1.1 Inventory

| | Bila-bial | Labio-dental | Dental | Alveo-lar | Retr. | Pala-tal | Velar | Glot-tal |
|---|---|---|---|---|---|---|---|---|
| Plosive | p b | | t d | | ʈ ɖ | | k g | |
| Nasal | m | | n | | ɳ | | | |
| Trill | | | | r | | | | |
| Fricative | | | | s | | | | h |
| Approx | ʋ | | | | | j | | |
| Lat. Appr | | | | l | ɭ | | | |
| Affricate | | | | | | ʧ ʤ | | |

### 1.2 Distribution

a. Consonants occur in all positions, with the following restrictions:
   i. / ɳ j ɭ / do not occur initially.
   ii. /j/ occurs finally.

b. Geminate consonants occur medially, except for the following: /r s h/.

# 2 Vowel phonemes

## 2.1 Inventory

a. **Short**

| | FRONT | CENTRAL | BACK |
|---|---|---|---|
| Close | i | | u |
| Close-mid | e | | o |
| Open | | a | |

b. **Long**

| | FRONT | CENTRAL | BACK |
|---|---|---|---|
| Close | i: | | u: |
| Close-mid | e: | | o: |
| Open | | a: | |

## 2.2 Distribution

a. Vowels occur in all positions in words.

b. Sequences of vowels do not occur.

# 3 Consonant Allophones

## 3.1 Inventory

a. [ɽ] </ɖ/ occurs intervocalically.

# 4 Vowel Allophones

## 4.1 Inventory

[ ï ] : /i/

[ɛ] : /e/

[ɔ] : /o/

[ i̯ ] : /j/

## 4.2 Distribution

a. [ï] < /i/ occurs medially when adjacent to a non-back vowel.

b. [ɛ ɔ] < /e o / occur finally.

c. [ i̯ ] < /j/ occurs intervocalically.

# 5 Syllable structure

## 5.1 Canonical syllable structure[2]

Word-finally: (C) (C) V (j)

Non-finally: (C) (C) V(C)

## 5.2 Consonant clusters

Two-consonant clusters:

Initial : C + r, s + t/n/ʋ

Final : Nil.

Medial : General.

---

[2] The complex onset in medial syllables is of restricted type: C + r, s + t/n/ʋ

Three-consonant clusters:

Initial : Nil

Final : Nil

Medial : -ŋgd-, -jŋg-, -jnd-, ʋɳɖ-, -ʋnd-, -str-.

**References:** Balakrishnan (1999).

# Gadaba-Konekor[3]

**Ethnologue code:** ISO 639-3: gau
**Language classification:** Dravidian, Central, Parji-Gadaba
**Alternate names:** Gadaba, Kondekar, Kondkor
**Main region:** Andhra Pradesh (Mundli, Poya, Salur in Srikakulam district).

## 1 Consonant phonemes

### 1.1 Inventory

| | Bilabial | Labiodental | Dental | Alveolar | Retr. | Palatal | Velar | Glottal |
|---|---|---|---|---|---|---|---|---|
| Plosive | p b | | t d | | ʈ ɖ | | k g | |
| Nasal | m | | n | | ɳ | | ŋ | |
| Trill | | | | r | | | | |
| Flap | | | | | ɽ | | | |
| Fricative | | | | s z | | | | h |
| Approx | w | | | | | j | | |
| Lat. Appr | | | | l | | | | |
| Affricate | | | | | | ʧ ʤ | | |

[3] According to Bhaskararao (1980), Konekor Gadaba and Ollari (Bhattacharya 1957) are the same language, as also admitted by Bhattacharya and Burrow (1962–63). We have kept the two varieties here, as there are noticeable differences in the data and the descriptions. The data for the present variety have come from Panukuvalesa village near Salur in the Srikakulam district of Andhra Pradesh.

## 1.2 Distribution

a. Consonants occur in all positions, with the following restrictions:
   i. / ɳ ŋ j/ do not occur initially.
   ii. /ʧ/ does not occur finally.

b. Geminate consonants occur, except for the following: /ɳ ŋ s/.

# 2 Vowel Phonemes

## 2.1 Inventory

a. **Short**

| | FRONT | CENTRAL | BACK |
|---|---|---|---|
| Close | i | | u |
| Close-mid | e | | o |
| Open | | a | |

b. **Long**

| | FRONT | CENTRAL | BACK |
|---|---|---|---|
| Close | iː | | uː |
| Close-mid | eː | | oː |
| Open | | aː | |

c. **Nasal**

| | FRONT | CENTRAL | BACK |
|---|---|---|---|
| Open | | ãː | |

## 2.2 Distribution

a. Vowels occur in all positions in words.

b. Long vowels occur more frequently in initial syllables.

c. Sequences of vowels do not occur.

# 3 Consonant Allophones

## 3.1 Inventory

| | |
|---|---|
| [z] | : /dʒ/ |
| [dʒ ] | : /g/ |
| [pf] | : /p/ |
| [bv] | : /b/ |
| [ts] | : /ʧ/ |
| [dz] | : /ʤ / |
| [ʋ] | : /w/ |

## 3.2 Distribution

a. [z] < /dʒ/ occurs finally and before /g/.

b. [ʧ] < /g/ occurs inter-vocalically.

c. [pf] < /p/ occurs before a heterorganic stop.

d. [bv] < /b/ occurs inter-vocalically and before a heterorganic stop.

e. [ts], [dz] < /ʧ/, /ʤ / occur before non-front vowels.

f. [ʋ] < /w/ occurs before unrounded vowels.

# 4 Vowel Allophones

## 4.1 Inventory

**General:**

a. Long vowels

b. High vowels

## 4.2 Distribution

a. Short vowels in closed final syllables in polysyllabic words are longer than in other positions.

b. Vowels are relatively higher if the following syllable has a higher vowel.

# 5 Syllable Structure

## 5.1 Canonical syllable structure[4]

**Initial:** (C) V (C)

**Non-Initial:** (C) (C) V(C) (C)

## 5.2 Consonant clusters[5]

Two-consonant clusters:

Initial : Nil.

Final : Nil.

Medial : General.

Three-consonant clusters:

Initial : Nil

Final : Nil

Medial : N+C+C, j+C+C

**Reference:** Bhaskararao (1980).

---

[4] a. The complex onset in medial syllables is of a restricted type: C+r.
b. Bhaskararao's analysis assumes that the syllable division between medial 3 consonant clusters is as follows:
If $C_3$ is /r/ then the division is between $C_1$ and $C_2$. Otherwise, the syllable divides between $C_2$ and $C_3$.

[5] Stems may end in 2 consonant clusters, e.g., /va : rp/- 'to filter', /ve ṭ p-/ 'to cause to run'.

# Gadaba-Ollari[6]

**Ethnologue code:** ISO 639-3: gdb
**Language classification:** Dravidian, Central, Parji-Gadaba
**Alternate names:** Ollar Gadaba, Ollari, Ollaro, Hallari, Allar, Hollar Gadbas
**Main region:** Andhra Pradesh, Orissa.

## 1 Consonant Phonemes

### 1.1 Inventory

| | BILA-BIAL | LABIO-DENTAL | DENTAL | ALV | RETR. | PALA-TAL | VELAR |
|---|---|---|---|---|---|---|---|
| Plosive | p b | | t d | | ʈ ɖ | | k g |
| Nasal | m | | | n | ɳ | (ɲ) | ŋ |
| Trill | | | | r | | | |
| Flap | | | | | ɽ | | |
| Fricative | | v | | s z | | | |
| Approx | | | | | | j | |
| Lat. Appr | | | | l | | | |
| Affricate | | | ts dz | | | ʧ ʤ | |

### 1.2 Distribution

a. Single consonants begin and end words; but medial heterorganic sequences are found abundantly.

[6] Ollari is spoken by the Ollars, a subcommunity of the Gadaba people. "ola' means 'leaf' in Gadaba. Ollars are to be found in Koraput district of Orissa.

b. Geminate consonants occur inter-vocalically for the following attested consonants: /t ʈ n s ʤ l/.

c. Stems can end in up to three consonant clusters, e.g., [kaɳɖp-], [kaɳɖt-] 'to scratch'.

# 2 Vowel Phonemes

## 2.1 Inventory

a. **Short**

| | FRONT | CENTRAL | BACK |
|---|---|---|---|
| Close | i | | u |
| Close-mid | e | | o |
| Open | | a | |

b. **Long**

| | FRONT | CENTRAL | BACK |
|---|---|---|---|
| Close | i: | | u: |
| Close-mid | e: | | o: |
| Open | | | ɑ: |

## 2.2 Distribution

a. Vowels occur in all positions in words.

b. Nasal vowels occur rarely as also surface diphthongs.

c. Long vowels occur mostly in monosyllabic words or in the first syllable of polysyllabic words. Compound words can have non-initial long vowels.

d. Vowel sequences do not occur (except in some loan words).

# 3 Consonant Allophones

a. [z] < / dʒ/ or </s/ occurs following a nasal.

# 4 Vowel Allophones

Inadequate data available.

# 5 Syllable Structure

## 5.1 Canonical syllable structure

Ollari has two canonical syllable structures:

Word: (C) V (C) (C)[7]

Stem: (C) V (C) (C) (C)

Most stem and affix combinations give rise to anaptyctic vowels, e.g. /kaɳɖp/- 'to search'> /kaɳɖupmen/ 'do not search'.

## 5.2 Consonant clusters

Two-consonant clusters:

| | |
|---|---|
| Initial | : Nil. |
| Final | : Rare; the only cluster is /ɳɖ/ in loan words from Oriya. |
| Medial | : general. |

Three-consonant clusters:

| | |
|---|---|
| Initial | : Nil |

[7] Because of medial three consonant clusters in some words, coda clusters have to be posited.

Final : Nil
Medial : -rɳɖ- -ɳɖz- etc.

**Reference:** Bhattacharya (1956)

# Gondi[8]

**Ethnologue code:** ISO 639-3: gno
**Language classification:** Dravidian, South-Central, Gondi-Kui
**Alternate names:** Gondi, Gaudi, Gondiva, Gondwadi, Goondile, Goudwal, Ghond, Godi, Gondu, Goudi
**Main region:** Madhya Pradesh; Maharashtra (Amravati, Wardha, Nagpur, Bhandara, Yavatmal districts).

## 1 Consonant Phonemes

### 1.1 Inventory

| | BILA-BIAL | LABIO-DENTAL | DEN-TAL | ALVE-OLAR | RETR. | PAL-ATAL | VELAR | UVU | GLO-TTAL |
|---|---|---|---|---|---|---|---|---|---|
| Plosive | p b | | t d | | ʈ ɖ | | k g | | |
| Nasal | m | | n | | | | ŋ | | |
| Trill | | | | r | | | | ʀ | |
| Fricative | | | | s | | | | | h |
| Approx | | ʋ | | | | j | | | |
| Lat. Appr. | | | | l | | | | | |
| Affricate | | | | | | ʧ ʤ | | | |

### 1.2 Distribution

a. Consonants occur in all positions, (however, an enunciative vowel is often added at the end of words;), with the following restriction:
   i. /ŋ ɽ ʀ/ do not occur word-initially.

b. All consonants except /ŋ/ have geminate forms word-medially.

[8] The variety being described is largely of the variety of Muria Gondi dialect spoken in Narayanpur tehsil of Bastar district in Madhya Pradesh.

# 2 Vowel Phonemes

## 2.1 Inventory

a. **Short**

| | FRONT | CENTRAL | BACK |
|---|---|---|---|
| Close | i | | u |
| Close-mid | e | | o |
| Open | | a | |

## 2.2 Distribution

a. Vowels occur in all positions in the word.

b. Vowel sequences do not occur intra-morphemically. Vowel sequences on account of word-formation are reduced to one, with the second vowel in the sequence deleted.

# 3 Consonant Allophones

## 3.1 Inventory

[p] : /b/

[p$^h$] : /p/

[t] : /d/

[t$^h$] : /t/

[t̲ ] : /t/, /ʈ/

[d̲ ] : /d/, /ɖ/

[ʈ] : /ɖ/

[ʈ$^h$] : /ʈ/

[k] : /g/

[kʰ] : /k/

[ʔ] : /h/

[tʃ] : /ʤ/

[tʃʰ] : /ʧ/

[ɳ] : /n/

[ʀ̥] : /ʀ/

[β] : /ʋ/

[ɭ] : /l/

## 3.2 Distribution

a. The voiceless aspirated stop allophones occur in the Onset position in the syllable.

b. The alveolar stops [ t̠ d̠ ] have two sources [t ʈ] and [d ɖ] respectively. [t̠ʰ] < /t/ occurs before non-low back vowels /o u/. [t̠ʰ] < /ʈ/, and [d̠] < /ɖ/ occur before front vowels /i e/.

c. The voiced stops /b d ɖ ʤ g/ and the uvular trill /ʀ/ have voiceless allophones [p t ʈ tʃ k] and [ʀ̥] word-finally. Thus there is no voicing contrast for the stops in the word-final position.

d. [β] /ʋ/ occurs when adjacent to a non-low back vowel /o u/, or before /β ʋ/ in geminates.

e. [ʔ] /h/ occurs before /h/: /ahhe/ > [aʔhe] 'just like that'.

f. [ɭ] /l/ occurs after /u/: /goʈʈul/ > [goʈ˺ʈu:ɭ] 'a dormitory for young people'.

# 4 Vowel Allophones

## 4.1 Inventory

[i:] [i:ᵊ] : / i /

[e:] [e:ᵊ] [e˙] [ɛ] : / e /

| | |
|---|---|
| [u:] [u : ᵊ] [u ˑ ] | : / u / |
| [o : ] [o :ᵊ] [o ˑ ] | : / o / |
| [a : ] [a ˑ ] | : / a / |

## 4.2 Distribution

a. The long vowel allophones of all the short vowel phonemes occur in open syllables.

b. The slightly diphthongized allophones of the non-low vowels occur before /ʀ/, and for the mid vowels also before /h/.

c. The half-long allophones (of the vowels /u e o a/) occur in open medial syllables of trisyllabic or longer words. (E. g., /alosa/ > [a : o ˑ sa : ] (a feminine name), /sarkari/ > [sarka ˑ ri : ] 'government (Adj.)'

# 5 Syllable Structure

## 5.1 Canonical syllable structure

(C)V(C)

## 5.2 Consonant clusters

Two-consonant clusters:

Initial : Nil
Final : Nil
Medial : General.

Three-consonant clusters: Nil

**References:** Andres (1977), Steever (1998)

# Gondi-Abujhmaria[9]

**Ethnologue code:** ISO 639-3: ggo
**Language classification:** Dravidian, South-Central, Gondi-Kui
**Alternate names:** Koi Gondi, Telugu Gondi.
**Main region:** Andhra Pradesh (Adilabad District); Maharashtra (southern Yavatmal, southern Chandrapur and southeastern Garhchiroli)

## 1 Consonant Phonemes

### 1.1 Inventory

| | Bila-bial | Labio-dental | Den-tal | Alve-olar | Retro | Pal-atal | Velar | Uvu | Glo-ttal |
|---|---|---|---|---|---|---|---|---|---|
| Plosive | p b | | t d | | ʈ ɖ | | k g | | |
| Nasal | m | | | n | | | ŋ | | |
| Trill | | | | r | | | | ʀ | |
| Fricative | | | | s | | | | | (h) |
| Approx | | ʋ | | | | j | | | |
| Lat Appr | | | | l | | | | | |
| Affricate | | | | | | tʃ dʒ | | | |

### 1.2 Distribution

a. Consonants occur in all positions, with the following restriction:
   i. /ŋ ɽ/ do not occur initially.

b. eminate consonants, except for / h ɽ ŋ w/ occur in the medial position, in the environment V _ V or V _ V: (but not *V: _ V).

[9] The variety being described is spoken in Abujhmar Hills, Bastar district of Chhatisgarh state.

# 2 Vowel Phonemes

## 2.1 Inventory

a. **Short**

| | FRONT | CENTRAL | BACK |
|---|---|---|---|
| Close | i | | u |
| Close-mid | e | | o |
| Open | | a | |

b. **Long**

| | FRONT | CENTRAL | BACK |
|---|---|---|---|
| Close | iː | | uː |
| Close-mid | eː | | oː |
| Open | | aː | |

## 2.2 Distribution

a. Vowels occur in all positions in the word.

b. The contrast between long and short vowels is neutralized word-finally, where only vowels with half-length occur. These are treated as allophones of long vowels.

c. Vowel sequences do not occur.

# 3 Consonant Allophones

## 3.1 Inventory

General:

Tense plosive allophones

Specific:

[ʀ] : /r/

## 3.2 Distribution

a. The stops are articulated tense, [p̂ b̂ t̂ d̂ ʈ̂ ɖ̂ ʤ̂ k̂ ĝ] < /p b t d ʈ ɖ ʧ ʤ k g/, in the word-initial position.

b. A strong mid-palatal voiced trill allophone [ʀ <] < /r/ occurs finally after non-low vowels.

# 4 Vowel Allophones

## 4.1 Inventory

| | |
|---|---|
| [ɨ], [ʲi] | : /i / |
| [ i ˑ ], [ʲi : ] | : / i : / |
| [ʔa] [ə] | : /a/ |
| [a ˑ ], [ʔa : ] | : /a : / |
| [ʔe ] | : /e / |
| [e ˑ ], [ʔe : ] | : /e : / |
| [ʔu ] | : / u/ |
| [u ˑ ], [ʔu : ] | : /u : / |
| [o ˑ ], [ʔo : ] | : /o : / |
| [ i̯ ] | : /j/ |
| [ u̯ ] | : /w/ |

## 4.2 Distribution

a. Final long vowels are pronounced half-long finally.

b. [ ʲi ʲi : ] < / i i : / occur in the initial position.

c. The allophones with a glottal catch (of vowels other than /i iː/) occur word-initially.

d. [ɨ] < / i/ occurs medially when preceded by a retroflex or a flap consonant.

e. [ə] < / a/ occurs in monosyllables or in the penultimate position when the final has /a/.

f. [ i̯ u̯ ] < / j w/ respectively occur before vowels.

# 5 Syllable Structure

## 5.1 Canonical syllable structure[10]

(C) (r/j) V (C) (C) (C)

## 5.2 Consonant clusters

Two-consonant clusters:

Initial : Only two instances found: /tr/ /gj/
Final : Restricted heterogeneous types.
Medial : General.

Three-consonant clusters:

Initial: Nil.
Final: $C_1$ $C_2$ $C_3$, where either $C_1$ $C_2$ or $C_2$ $C_3$ are homorganic.
Medial: $C_1$ $C_2$ $C_3$, where (i) $C_1$ $C_2$ are homorganic
(ii) $C_2$ $C_3$ are homorganic
(iii) $C_3$ is /k/.

**Reference:** Natarajan (1985)

[10] A syllable must have an Onset or a Coda in a monosyllabic morpheme.

# Irula

**Ethnologue code:** ISO 639-3: iru
**Language classification:** Dravidian, Southern
**Alternate names:** Eravallan, Erukala, Irava, Irulan, Irular, Irular Mozhi, Irulavan, Iruliga, Iruligar, Kad Chensu
**Main region:** Tamil Nadu; Karnataka; Kerala, Andhra Pradesh.

## 1 Consonant Phonemes

### 1.1 Inventory

| | Bilabial | | Dental | | Alveolar | | Retr. | | Palatal | | Velar | |
|---|---|---|---|---|---|---|---|---|---|---|---|---|
| Plosive | p | b | t | d | t̠ | d̠ | ʈ | ɖ | | | k | g |
| Nasal | | m | | n | | | | ɳ | | | | |
| Trill | | | | | | r | | ʀ̣ | | | | |
| Approx | | w | | | | | | | | j | | |
| Lat. Appr | | | | | | l | | ɭ | | | | |
| Affricate | | | | | | | | | ʧ | ʤ | | |

### 1.2 Distribution

a. Consonants do not occur word-finally.

b. All consonants except /r/ have geminates.

# 2 Vowel Phonemes

## 2.1 Inventory[11]

a. **Short**

| | FRONT | | CENTRAL | | BACK | |
|---|---|---|---|---|---|---|
| Close | i | ï | | | ü | u |
| Close-mid | e | ë | | | ö | o |
| Open-mid | | | | | | ɔ |
| Open | | | ä | a | | |

b. **Long**

| | FRONT | | CENTRAL | | BACK | |
|---|---|---|---|---|---|---|
| Close | iː | ïː | | | üː | uː |
| Close-mid | eː | ëː | | | öː | oː |
| Open | | | äː | aː | | |

## 2.2 Distribution

a. Vowels occur in all positions, with the following restriction:

   i. / öː üː / do not occur word-finally.

b. Vowel sequences are not attested.

---

[11] The centralized low vowels / ä äː / have front realizations [æ̈ ɛ̈<] respectively.

# 3 Consonant Allophones

## 3.1 Inventory

| | **Bilabial** | **Labiodental** | **Dental** | **Alveolar** | **Post Alv** | **Retroflex** | **Velar** |
|---|---|---|---|---|---|---|---|
| Plosive | p̂ (p) | | t̂ (t)<br>tt (R R)<br>d(R) | | | ʈ̂ (ʈ) | k̂ (k)<br>$k^j$ (k) |
| Flap | | | | | ɽ(ɖ) | | |
| Fricative | β(b) | v(w) | ð(d) | s (tʃ) | | ʂ(tʃ) | ɣ (g) |

## 3.2 Distribution

a. The tense allophones of plosives [p̂ t̂ ʈ̂ k̂] < /p t ʈ k/ occur non-initially (in medial geminates, post-nasally).

b. [β ð ɣ] < /b d g/ occur inter-vocalically.

c. [s] < /tʃ/ occurs initially.

d. [ʂ] < /tʃ/ occurs before retroflex plosives.

e. [ɽ] < /ɖ/ occurs inter-vocalically.

f. [$k^j$] < /k/ occurs before front vowels.

g. The retroflex trill /R/ is realized as voiceless alveolar plostive [t], when geminated, i.e. /R R/ is realized as [tt].

h. [d] < /R/ occurs post-nasally.

i. [v] < /w/ occurs when preceded by a vowel.

# 4 Vowel Allophones

## 4.1 Inventory

[ɪ]: /i /

[ɪ̈]: / ï/

[ɛ]: /e/  
[ɛ̈]: /ë/  
[ɔ]: /o/  
[ɔ̈]: /ö/  
[ɨ] [ʊ̈] [ʊ]: /u/  
[u̯]: /w/

## 4.2 Distribution

a. Non-low short vowels / i ï u ü e ë o ö/ have lower realizations [ɪ ɪ̈ ʊ ʊ̈ ɛ ɛ̈ ɔ ɔ̈] than their long counterparts.

b. [ɨ] < /u/ occurs non-initially.

c. [u̯] < /w/ occurs in the C – V environment.

# 5 Syllable Structure

## 5.1 Canonical syllable structure

(C)(C)V(C)

## 5.2 Consonant clusters

Two-consonant clusters:

Initial : $C_2$ = a) r/ l/ w; b) n if C1 is [tʃ] < /s/.  
Final : Nil  
Medial : General

Three-consonant clusters:

Initial : Nil  
Final : Nil  
Medial : -kʈr-, -jɳɖ-, -ɳɖr-.

**References:** Perialwar (1979), Zvelebil (1973)

# Kadar[12]

**Ethnologue code:** ISO 639-3: kej
**Language classification:** Dravidian, Southern
**Alternate names:** Kada
**Main region:** Kerala (Thrissur District, Palakkad District), Tamil Nadu (Coimbatore District)

## 1 Consonant Phonemes

### 1.1 Inventory

| | BILA-BIAL | LABIO-DENTAL | DENTAL | ALVE-OLAR | RETRO-FLEX | PAL-ATAL | VELAR |
|---|---|---|---|---|---|---|---|
| Plosive | p b | | t | | ʈ | | k |
| Nasal | m | | n | n̠ | ɳ | ɲ | ŋ |
| Trill | | | | r | | | |
| Approx | | ʋ | | | | j | |
| Lat. Approx | | | | l | ɭ | | |
| Affricate | | | | | | tʃ | |

### 1.2 Distribution

a. Consonants occur in all positions, with the following restrictions:
   i. Plosives and nasals do not occur word-finally, except for the dental nasal /n/.
   ii. Consonants other than plosives and nasals occur only after the vowels /a aː/.

[12] Kadar is closely related to Malayalam.

iii. The following consonants do not occur initially in words: /ʈ ɳ ŋ lɭ w j/.

b. Geminate consonants occur inter-vocalically.

# 2 Vowel Phonemes

## 2.1 Inventory

a. **Short**

| | FRONT | CENTRAL | BACK |
|---|---|---|---|
| Close | i | | u |
| Close-mid | e | ə | o |
| Open | | a | |

b. **Long**

| | FRONT | CENTRAL | BACK |
|---|---|---|---|
| Close | i: | | u: |
| Close-mid | e: | ə : | o: |
| Open | | a: | |

## 2.2 Distribution

a. Vowels occur in all positions, with the following restrictions:

   i. vowels do not occur before and after /b/.

b. Vowel sequences do not occur.

# 3 Consonant Allophones

| | Bilabial | Dental | Alveolar | Retroflex | Palatal | Velar | Glottal |
|---|---|---|---|---|---|---|---|
| Plosive | b(p) | d(t) | d̲(r, t) | ɖ (ʈ)<br>ḍ (ʈ) | | g(k) | |
| Nasal | | | | | | ŋʲ (ŋ) | |
| Tap/Flap | | | ɾ (r) | ɽ (ʈ) | | | |
| Fricative | β(p) | ð(t) | | | | | h(k) |
| Affricate | | | | | ʤ(ʧ) | | |

## 3.1 Distribution

a. The voiced allophones [b d ɖ ʤ g] < /p t ʈ ʧ k/ occur after a homorganic nasal.

b. The voiced fricative allophones [ß ð] </p t / occur inter-vocalically.

c. The voiceless retroflex stop /ʈ/ has a voiced lenis retroflex allophone [ḍ] inter-vocalically.

d. [h] < /k/ occurs inter-vocalically.

e. [d̲]< /r/ occurs after a homorganic nasal.

f. [ɾ] < /r/ occurs word-finally.

# 4 Vowel Allophones

## 4.1 Inventory

[ʲi] : /i/

[ʲe], [ɛ] : /e/

[ɜ] : /ə/

[ɐ], [ʌ] : /ɑ/
[ʷu], [ɯ] : /u/
[ʷo] : /o/

## 4.2 Distribution

a. The high and mid vowels with palatal and labial on-glides [ʲi ʲe ʷu ʷo] initially in words.

b. [ɛ] < /e/ occurs initially before /l/.

c. [ɜ] < /a/ occurs before a nasal consonant.

d. [ɐ] < /a/ occurs in the initial and final positions.

e. [ɯ] < /u/ occurs finally.

# 5 Syllable Structure

## 5.1 Canonical syllable structure

(C (L)) V (C)

## 5.2 Consonant Clusters

Two-consonant clusters:

Initial : C+L
Final : Nil
Medial : Nil

Three-consonant clusters:

Initial : Nil.
Final : Nil
Medial : N/L/j+Ci+Ci.

**Reference:** Indira (1976).

# Kannada

**Ethnologue code:** ISO 639-3: kan
**Language classification:** Dravidian, Southern
**Alternate names:** Kanarese, Canarese, Banglori
**Main region:** Karnataka; Andhra Pradesh; Tamil Nadu; Maharashtra.

## 1 Consonant Phonemes

### 1.1 Inventory

| | BILABIAL | LABIODENTAL | DENTAL | ALVEOLAR | RETROFLEX | PRE-PALATAL | PALATAL | VELAR | GLOTTAL |
|---|---|---|---|---|---|---|---|---|---|
| Plosive | p b<br>(p$^{h}$) (b$^{ɦ}$) | | t̪ d̪<br>(t̪$^{h}$) (d̪$^{ɦ}$) | | ʈ ɖ<br>(ʈ$^{h}$) (ɖ$^{ɦ}$) | | | k g<br>(k$^{h}$) (g$^{ɦ}$) | |
| Nasal | m | | | n | ɳ | | | | |
| Tap/Flap | | | | r | | | | | |
| Fricative | | (f) | | s (z) | ʂ | ś | | | h |
| Approx | | ʋ | | | | | j | | |
| Lat Appr | | | | l | ɭ | | tʃ dʒ<br>(tʃ$^{h}$) (dʒ$^{ɦ}$) | | |

### 1.2 Distribution

a. Consonants occur in all positions, with the following restrictions:
   i. /ɭ ɳ ŋ/ do not occur initially.
   ii. /ś/ is frequently substituted by /ʂ/.

b. The sounds in parentheses occur in lexical loanwords. They do not occur in function words.

c. Geminates of all consonants can occur word medially.

# 2 Vowel Phonemes

## 2.1 Inventory

a. **Short**

| | FRONT | CENTRAL | BACK |
|---|---|---|---|
| Close | ɪ | | ʊ |
| Mid-close | e | | o |
| Mid-open | (æ) | | |
| Open | | a | |

b. **Long**

| | FRONT | CENTRAL | BACK |
|---|---|---|---|
| Close | i: | | u: |
| Mid-close | e: | | o: |
| Open | | a: | |

## 2.2 Distribution

a. Vowels occur in all positions, with the following restrictions:
   i. /a :/ does not occur initially in words.
   ii. The long vowels /i: e: o: u:/ do not occur finally, except for /u:/ in clitics, and /e: o:/ in vocatives.

b. /u/ occurs as the enunciative vowel word finally. The enunciative vowel is /i/ in words ending in /j/.

c. Forms beginning with /e e:/ and /o o:/ have /j/ and /ʋ/ on-glide, when preceded by a vowel or pause.

d. Sequences of syllabic vowels do not occur, giving rise to vowel deletion (usually of the following vowel) and approximate insertion (/j/ before front vowels and /ʋ/ before non-front vowels).

# 3 Consonant Allophones

**General:**

a. Degemination: Geminate consonants are degeminated when a consonant follows them as a consequence of vowel loss.

**Specific:**

a. [t] < /d/ occurs before /t/, and when not preceded by a nasal.

b. [l] < /ɭ/ occurs following retroflex consonants.

c. [ɭ] < /l/ occurs after dental plosives /t d/.

# 4 Vowel Allophones

Data not available.

# 5 Syllable Structure

## 5.1 Canonical syllable structure

(C) (C) (C) V (C) (C) (C)

## 5.2 Consonant clusters

Two-consonant clusters:

Initial : C+ Son, C+ /h/, Sib + HS, /s/ + S, /kʂ/
Final : a. Word Final: Nil, except in English loan words.
b. Stem Final : Son+ C.
Medial : General.

Three-consonant clusters:

Initial : s+S+Son

Final : Word Final: Nil, except in a few loan words.

Stem Final: /ʋ/ +Son + C.

Medial : /s/ +S+ -non-nasal Son.

More than three consonants:

Initial : Nil.

Final : Nil

Medial : In complex words, up to five consonants occur across morphemes (e.g., /tiɾg.sdɾu/ 'they turned it', /mulg.sdʋu/ 'we drowned him'). "No regular restrictions have been found."

**References:** Bright (1958), Sridhar (1990)

# Kattunaicka

**Ethnologue code:** None
**Language classification:** Dravidian, southern
**Alternate names:**
**Main region:** Tamil Nadu

## 1 Consonant Phonemes

### 1.1 Inventory

| | Bilabial | Labiodental | Dental | Alveolar | Post Alveolar | Retroflex | Palatal | Velar |
|---|---|---|---|---|---|---|---|---|
| Plosive | p b | | t d | | | ʈ ɖ | | k g |
| Nasal | m | | n | | | ɳ | ɲ | ŋ |
| Tap | | | | ɾ | | | | |
| Trill | | | | | r | | | |
| Flap | | | | | | ɽ | | |
| Fricative | | | | s z | | ʂ | | |
| Approx | | ʋ | | | | | j | |
| Lat. Approx. | | | | l | | ɭ | | |
| Affricate | | | ts dz | | | | tʃ dʒ | |

### 1.2 Distribution

a. Consonants occur initially and medially, with the following restrictions:
   i. /ɲ ŋ ɭ/ do not occur initially in words.

b. Geminates of consonants, except the following /ʦ ʣ ɲ ŋ ɾ r ʂ/, occur inter-vocalically.

# 2 Vowel Phonemes[13]

## 2.1 Inventory

a. **Short**

| | Front | Central | Back |
|---|---|---|---|
| Close | i | ɨ | u |
| Close-mid | e | | o |
| Open-mid | | ɐ | |

b. **Long**

| | Front | Central | Back |
|---|---|---|---|
| Close | iː | ɨː | uː |
| Close-mid | eː | | oː |
| Open | | aː | |

c. **Nasal**

| | Front | Central | Back |
|---|---|---|---|
| Close | ĩː ĩ | ɨ̃ | ũː ũ |
| Close-mid | ẽ | ɘ̃ | õ |
| Open-mid | | ɐ̃ | |
| Open | | ãː | |

## 2.2 Distribution

a. Vowels occur in all positions.

b. Sequences of vowels do not occur.

[13] Non-low short vowels are lower in quality than their long counterparts. The low short vowels (oral and nasal) are higher in quality than their long counterparts.

# 3 Consonant Allophones

## 3.1 Inventory[14]

a. [v] : /ʋ/

b. [jᶻ] : /j/

## 3.2 Distribution

a. [v jᶻ] < /ʋ j/ occur in geminate forms.

# 4 Vowel Allophones

## 4.1 Inventory

| | | |
|---|---|---|
| [ˀə] | : | /ə/ |
| [ˀɐ] | : | /ɐ/ |

## 4.2 Distribution

[ˀə ˀɐ] < /ə ɐ/ occur word-initially.

# 5 Syllable Structure

## 5.1 Canonical syllable structure

(C)(C)V(C)

---

14 [jᶻ] is a fricative approximate.

## 5.2 Consonant clusters[15]

Two-consonant clusters:[16]

| | | |
|---|---|---|
| Initial | : | C+r/j, s+t/ʋ |
| Final | : | Nil |
| Medial | : | General |

Three-consonant clusters:

| | | |
|---|---|---|
| Initial | : | Nil |
| Final | : | Nil |
| Medial | : | NH + P + ʈ/c/s/r, rtj, rʂʈ. |

**Reference:** Natanasabapathy (1986)

[15] The consonant clusters are highly restricted.

[16] Instances of C are restricted to /p b k g m ɳ/.

# Kodagu

**Ethnologue code:** ISO 639-3: kfa
**Language classification:** Dravidian, Southern, Tamil-Kannada
**Alternate names:** Coorge, Kadagi, Khurgi, Kotagu, Kurja, Kurug, Kodava Thak
**Main region:** Karnataka.

## 1 Consonant Phonemes

### 1.1 Inventory

| | BILA-BIAL | LABIO-DENTAL | DEN-TAL | ALVE-OLAR | POST ALVEOLAR | RETRO | PALA-TAL | VELAR | GLO-TTAL |
|---|---|---|---|---|---|---|---|---|---|
| Plosive | p b | | t d | | | ʈ ɖ | | k g | |
| Nasal | m | | | n | | ɳ | ɲ | | |
| Trill | | | | r | | | | | |
| Fricative | | (f) | | s | (ʃ) | | | | (h) |
| Approx | | ʋ | | | | | j | | |
| Lat Appr | | | | l | | ɭ | | | |
| Affricate | | | | | | | ʧ ʤ | | |

### 1.2 Distribution

a. Consonants do not occur finally.

b. /ʈ ɖ ɳ ɭ l j/ do not occur initially in native words.

c. Geminates of all consonants can occur medially before short vowels[17].

[17] Balakrishnan (1976) gives only /p b t d ʈ ɖ ʧ ʤ k g/ in the V-V position.

# 2 Vowel Phonemes

## 2.1 Inventory

a. **Short**

| | FRONT | CENTRAL | BACK |
|---|---|---|---|
| Close | i | | u ɯ |
| Close-mid | e | | o ɤ |
| Open-mid | ɛ | | |
| Open | | a | |

b. **Long**

| | FRONT | CENTRAL | BACK |
|---|---|---|---|
| Close | i: | | u: ɯ : |
| Close-mid | e: | | o: ɤ : |
| Open-mid | ɛ: | | |
| Open | | a: | |

## 2.2 Distribution

a. Vowels occur in all positions, with the following restrictions:
   i. / i : u : / do not occur finally.
   ii. The back unrounded vowels /ɯ ɤ/ do not occur after /ʧ ʤ/.
   iii. The vowels /i e/ do not occur before retroflex consonants. (Historically, the vowels in that position became / u o / after labials, and /ɯ ɤ/ elsewhere).
   iv. Final short /u a/ are rare; they occur only when accompanied by the identical vowel in the preceding syllable.

b. Vowel sequences occur, but with glide insertion, /j/ after front vowels, and /w/ after back vowels.

c. "Euphonic k is inserted between roots ending in a vowel or n and a following a. After n the inserted consonant is voiced." (Ebert, p.9)

d. "Two identical vowels at word boundaries are contracted rather than separated by an extra consonant", e.g., /awa maŋgal a : ci/ 'Let's drink!' (Ebert p.9)

# 3 Consonant Allophones

## 3.1 Distribution

a. [ð] < /d/ occurs (a) inter-vocalically, and (b) after /r v j/.

b. [ɽ] < /ɖ/ occurs inter-vocalically.

# 4 Vowel Allophones

## 4.1 Inventory

| | |
|---|---|
| [ɪ] [ɨ]: | / i/ |
| [ɛ] [ɛː] [ɛ̝]: | /e / |
| [ɐ] [ɑ]: | /a / |
| [o̝]: | /o / |
| [ ʊ ] [ʉ]: | /u / |
| [ɨ]: | /ɯ/ |
| [ə]: | /ɤ/ |

**Semivowels:**

| | |
|---|---|
| [ i̯ ] : | / j/ |
| [ u̯ ]: | / ʋ/ |

## 4.2 Distribution

a. [ɪ ɛ ʊ] < /ieu/ occur medially in open syllables.

b. [ɛ̝ o̝] < /e o/ occur medially when the final contains /e/.

c. [ɐ] < /a/ occurs non-finally.

d. [ɑ] < /a/ occurs finally when preceded by velar and glottal consonants.

e. The centralized allophones occur
   i. Finally, [ɨ ə] < /ɯ ɤ/ ; [ə] is preceded by VV.
   ii. Medially in unstressed position, [ɨ] < /i/ and /ɯ/ , [ʉ] < /u/; the vowels cannot be discriminated in that position (Ebert p. 7); [ə] < /a/ in the same position, making it indistinguishable from /ɤ/.

f. [ i̯ ] < /j/ occurs inter-vocalically and finally. [u̯ ] < / ʋ/ occurs between a vowel and a consonant other than /w/.

# 5 Syllable Structure

## 5.1 Canonical syllable structure

a. Word-final: CV(C) or (C)VV.

b. Non-final: (C)V(C) or (C)VV

## 5.2 Consonant clusters

Inadequate data available.

**References:** Ebert (1996), Emeneau (1970), Balakrishnan (1976)

# Kolami

**Ethnologue code:** ISO 639-3: nit
**Language classification:** Dravidian, Central, Kolami-Naiki
**Alternate names:**
**Main region:** Andhra Pradesh; Maharashtra.

## 1 Consonant Phonemes

### 1.1 Inventory

| | BILA-BIAL | LABIO-DENTAL | DENTAL | POST DENTAL | RETRO | PALATAL | VELAR | GLO-TTAL |
|---|---|---|---|---|---|---|---|---|
| Plosive | p b | | t d | | ʈ ɖ | | k g | |
| Nasal | m | | n | | | | ŋ | |
| Trill | | | | r | | | | |
| Fricative | | v | | s z | | ʝ | | (ɦ) |
| Lat. Approx. | | | | l | (ɭ) | | | |
| Affricate | | | (ts) | | | tʃ ʤ | | |

### 1.2 Distribution

a. Consonants occur in all positions, with the following restrictions:
   i. /ŋ ʝ/ do not occur initially.
   ii. /tʃ ʤ/ do not occur inter-vocalically.
   iii. /b tʃ ʤ / do not occur finally.

b. Geminates of consonants except /ŋ ɻ z/ occur inter-voclly.

c. /ts ɭ ɦ/ are found to occur in Marathi loan-words.

# 2 Vowel Phonemes

## 2.1 Inventory

a. **Short**

| | FRONT | CENTRAL | BACK |
|---|---|---|---|
| Close | i | | u |
| Close-mid | e | | o |
| Open-mid | | (ə) | |
| Open | | | ɑ |

b. **Long**

| | FRONT | CENTRAL | BACK |
|---|---|---|---|
| Close | i: | | u: |
| Close-mid | e: | | o: |
| Open-mid | | (ə:) | |
| Open | | | ɑ: |

## 2.2 Distribution

a. Short vowels occur in all positions.

b. Long vowels occur in stressable positions, in a monosyllable and in the first syllable of a polysyllable.

c. Vowel sequences do not occur.

# 3 Consonant Allophones

## 3.1 Inventory

[ç] : /s/

[ḷ] : /l/

[ṛ ] : /r/

[dz] : /z/

## 3.2 Distribution

a. [ç] < /s/ occurs before /i/; e.g. /posia/ 'ball of fool'.

b. [ḷ ṛ] < /l r/ occur following retroflex consonants.

c. [dz] < /z/ occurs when single in all positions. [z] occurs in a cluster.

# 4 Vowel Allophones

## 4.1 Inventory

[ë ] : /e/

[ë :] [ i̯ e] : / e : /

[ᵛu:] : /u:/

## 4.2 Distribution

a. [ë ë :] < / ee : / occur following a retroflex consonant.

b. [i̯ e] < / e : / occurs phrase initially or word initially, when the preceding word ends in /a:/, e.g. /a: e: ḍ/ 'two years before last'> [a: i̯ e ḍ].

c. [ᵛu:] < /u:/ occurs word initially in a phrase, when preceded by a vowel; e.g. /a:u:r/ > [a:ᵛu:r] 'that village'.

# 5 Syllable Structure

## 5.1 Canonical syllable structure[18]

a. Initial: C V (:)

b. Final in Bisyllabic words: C V (N) (C) (C) (C)

c. Final in Tri- or polysyllabic words: C V (C)

## 5.2 Consonant clusters

Two-consonant clusters:

Initial : Nil

Final : N + C, vlS/s + t

Medial : General

Three-consonant clusters:

Initial : Nil

Final : -nḻt, -ṭlt, -ḍlt, -ṭln, -ḍln.

Medial : General

Four-consonant clusters:

Final : e.g. -nḍln (as in /malanḍln/ 'barbers (ACC.)'

**Reference:** Emeneau (1955)

[18] Minimal word requirement in Kolami is: CV: / CVC

# Konda

**Ethnologue code:** ISO 639-3: kfc
**Language classification:** Dravidian, South-Central, Gondi-Kui, Konda-Kui, Konda
**Alternate names:** Porja
Main region: Andhra Pradesh, Orissa.

## 1 Consonant Phonemes

### 1.1 Inventory

| | BILA-BIAL | LABIO-DENTAL | DENTAL | ALVE-OLAR | RETRO-FLEX | PALA-TAL | VELAR | GLO-TTAL |
|---|---|---|---|---|---|---|---|---|
| Plosive | p b | | t d | | ʈ ɖ | | k g | ʔ |
| Nasal | m | | | n | ɳ | | ŋ | |
| Trill | | | | r̥ r | | | | |
| Tap | | | | ɾ | | | | |
| Flap | | | | | ɽ | | | |
| Fricative | | | | s | (ʂ) | | | (h) |
| Approx | | (ʋ) | | | | (j) | | |
| Lat Appr | | | | l | | | | |
| Affricate | | | | | | (ʧ) ʤ | | |

### 1.2 Distribution

a. Consonants occur in all positions, with the following restriction:

   i. / ʔ r̥ ɳ ŋ / do not occur initially.

b. Geminates of consonants occur inter-vocalically (adequate data not available).

# 2 Vowel Phonemes

## 2.1 Inventory

**a. Short**

| | FRONT | CENTRAL | BACK |
|---|---|---|---|
| Close | i | | u |
| Close-mid | e | | o |
| Open | | a | |

**b. Long**

| | FRONT | CENTRAL | BACK |
|---|---|---|---|
| Close | i: | | u: |
| Close-mid | e: | | o: |
| Open | | a: | |

## 2.2 Distribution

a. Vowels occur in all positions.

b. Vowel length contrast is maintained in the initial syllable only. Non-initially short vowels are longer.

c. Vowel sequences occur only across word boundaries.

d. Word-final short /u/ tends to get deleted.

e. Non-low short vowels are lower in height than their long counterparts. The low short vowel is higher than the long counterpart, as in a majority of the Indian languages.

# 3 Consonant Allophones

Details not available.

# 4 Vowel Allophones

a. Short vowels are half-long word-finally.

b. /u/ has an occasional free variant [ï].

c. The front vowels /i iː e eː/ have a j-onglide[ji jiː je jeː] and the vowels /u uː o oː/ have a ʋ-onglide [ʋu ʋuː ʋo ʋoː] in words beginning with them.

# 5 Syllable Structure

## 5.1 Canonical syllable structure

(C) V (C) (C)

## 5.2 Consonant clusters

Two-consonant clusters:[19]

| | |
|---|---|
| Initial | : Rare |
| Final | : Obs + Obs, Son + Obs, Son + Son, Obs + Son |
| Medial | : General. |

Three-consonant clusters: [20]

| | |
|---|---|
| Initial | : Nil |
| Final | : Nil |
| Medial | : Son + Obs + Son. |

**Reference:** Krishnamurti and Benham (1998)

---

[19] a. Obs + Obs clusters have identical voicing word-internally. (Across words, they can have disparate voicing.)

b. /r̥/ is never the second member of a cluster.

c. /ʔ/ is never the first member of a cluster.

[20] 3-consonant clusters usually occur across morphemes, as many affixes have an onset.

# Koraga

**Ethnologue code:** ISO 639-3: kfd
**Language classification:** Dravidian, Southern, Tulu, Koraga
**Alternate names:** Koragar, Koragara, Korangi, Korra
**Main region:** Karnataka; Kerala; Tamil Nadu.

## 1 Consonant Phonemes

### 1.1 Inventory

| | Bilabial | Dental | Alv | Post-Alv | Retr. | Palatal | Velar | Glottal |
|---|---|---|---|---|---|---|---|---|
| Plosive | p b | t d | | | ʈ ɖ | | k g | |
| Nasal | m | n | | | ɳ | ɲ | ŋ | |
| Trill | | | r | | | | | |
| Flap | | | | | ɽ | | | |
| Fricative | | | s | ʃ | | | | h |
| Approx. | w | | | | | j | | |
| Lat. Approx. | | | l | | | | | |
| Affricate | | | | | | ʧ ʤ | | |

### 1.2 Distribution

a. Consonants do not occur finally.

b. /ɳ ŋ/ do not occur initially.

c. All the consonants have geminates inter-vocalically.

# 2 Vowel Phonemes

## 2.1 Inventory

a. **Short**

| | FRONT | CENTRAL | BACK |
|---|---|---|---|
| Close | i | ɨ | u |
| Close-mid | e | | o |
| Open-mid | ɛ | | |
| Open | | a | |

b. **Long**

| | FRONT | CENTRAL | BACK |
|---|---|---|---|
| Close | iː | ɨː | uː |
| Close-mid | eː | | oː |
| Open-mid | ɛː | | |
| Open | | aː | |

## 2.2 Distribution

a. Vowels occur in all positions, with the following restrictions:
   i. / ɛ ɛː ɨ / do not occur initially.
   ii. /eː ɛː o/ do not occur finally.
   iii. /ɨ u/, /u ɨ/ and /ɨ ɛː/ do not occur in consecutive syllables in the word.

b. Vowel sequences do not occur.

# 3 Consonant Allophones

## 3.1 Inventory[21]

| | BILABIAL | DENTAL | RETROFLEX | PALATAL | VELAR |
|---|---|---|---|---|---|
| Plosive | p̂ˈ (p)<br>p̆ (p) | t̂ˈ (t)<br>t̆ (t) | ʈ̂ˈ (ʈ) | tʃ̆ (tʃ) | k̂ˈ (k)<br>k̆ (k) |
| Flap | | | ɽ(ɖ) | | |

## 3.2 Distribution

a. The tense and slightly aspirated allophones [p̂ˈ t̂ˈ ʈ̂ˈ k̂ˈ] < /p t ʈ k/ occur word-initially.

b. The lax allophones [ p̆ t̆ tʃ̆ k̆ ] < /p t tʃ k/ occur inter-vocalically.

c. [ɽ] < /ɖ/ occurs inter-vocalically.

# 4 Vowel Allophones

## 4.1 Inventory

| | |
|---|---|
| [ʲi : ]: | /i :/ |
| [i ˑ] [ʲi ] [i̞]: | /i/ |
| [e ] [ʲe] [e̞]: | /e/ |
| [je : ]: | /eː/ |
| [ə] [a ˑ ]: | /a/ |
| [ʲɛ :]: | /ɛ :/ |
| [ɛ ˑ] [ʲɛ]: | /ɛ/ |
| [ o ] [ʷo] [ o̞ ]: | /o/ |
| [ʷo : ]: | /o : / |

[21] The superscript [ˈ] is used for weak aspiration.

[ u ] [ʷu] [ u̞ ]: /u/

[ʷu : ]: /u :/

## 4.2 Distribution

a. The half-long allophones of short vowels occur word-finally.

b. The lowered allophones of short vowels occur when followed by /a a:/ in the following syllable.

c. The allophones with j-onglide and w-onglide occur word-initially before Front and Back vowels respectively.

d. [ə ] < / a/ occurs in closed syllables.

# 5 Syllable Structure

## 5.1 Canonical syllable structure

(C)(r)V

## 5.2 Consonant clusters

Two-consonant clusters:[22]

Initial : C+r

Final : Nil

Medial : General.

Three-consonant clusters:

Initial : Nil.

Final : Nil.

Medial : (a) N+ C+C; (b) C+N+C, (c) C1 C1+j ; (d) j/r/l + N+C.

**Reference:** Shetty (1978)

22 The fact that there are no word-final clusters may be interpreted to imply that there is no coda in Koraga. Word-medial clusters should thus go as onsets.

# Kota

**Ethnologue code:** ISO 639-3: kfe
**Language classification:** Dravidian, Southern, Tamil-Kannada,
**Alternate names:** Kotta, Kowe-Adiwasi, Kother-Tamil
**Main region:** Tamil Nadu.

## 1 Consonant Phonemes

### 1.1 Inventory

| | Bilabial | Labio-dental | Dental | Alveolar | Retro | Palatal | Velar |
|---|---|---|---|---|---|---|---|
| Plosive | p b | | t d | t̠ d̠ | ʈ ɖ | | k g |
| Nasal | m | | | n | ɳ | | ŋ |
| Trill | | | | r | | | |
| Flap | | | | | ɽ | | |
| Fricative | | v | | | | | |
| Approx. | | | | | | j | |
| Lat. Appr. | | | | l | ɭ | | |
| Affricate | | | | | | ʧ ʤ | |

### 1.2 Distribution

a. Consonants occur in all positions, with the following restriction:
   i. /t d n ŋ ɽ j/ do not occur initially.

b. Geminate consonants do not occur.

# 2 Vowel Phonemes

## 2.1 Inventory

a. **Short**

| | FRONT | CENTRAL | BACK |
|---|---|---|---|
| Close | i | | u |
| Close-mid | e | | o |
| Open | | a | |

b. **Long**

| | FRONT | CENTRAL | BACK |
|---|---|---|---|
| Close | i: | | u: |
| Close-mid | e: | | o: |
| Open | | a: | |

## 2.2 Distribution

a. Vowels occur in all positions, with the following restriction:

   i. /e o a u u:/ do not occur finally.

b. Sequences of the following two vowels occur: /uo uo : ua/. Vowel sequences with /i u/ as the second member are realized as diphthongs on the surface.

# 3 Consonant Allophones

## 3.1 Inventory

[s] : /tʃ/

[z] : /ʤ/

[ʃ] : / tʃ/

## 3.2 Distribution

a. [s z] < / tʃ ʤ/ occur word-initially before back vowels. ([s z] are described as 'alveolar grooved fricatives'.)

b. [ʃ] < /tʃ/ occurs medially before /ɽ/.

# 4 Vowel Allophones

## 4.1 Inventory

| | |
|---|---|
| [ ɪ ] [ i̯ ]: | /i / |
| [ ʊ ] [ u̯ ]: | /u/ |
| [ɛ]: | / e / |
| [ɐ]: | /a/ |
| [ ɔ ]: | / o / |

## 4.2 Distribution

a. [ɪ ʊ ɛ ɔ ɐ] < /i u e o a/ occur medially i.e. when preceded by a consonant (an onset), and followed by a consonant or a syllable.

b. [i̯ u̯ ] < /i u/ occur following vowels, leading to phonetic diphthongs.

# 5 Syllable Structure

## 5.1 Canonical syllable structure[23]

(C) (L) V (C) (C) (C)

[23] There is an instance of a five-consonant final cluster cited - /oɳʈjgn/ 'male pig'.

## 5.2 Consonant clusters

Two-consonant clusters:

| | | |
|---|---|---|
| Initial | : | C + r/l |
| Final | : | (i) C + m/l/n/ɭ/tʃ/k |
| | | (ii) N + S |
| | | (iii) r/ɽ + C |
| Medial | : | N+S, N+ N, L + C, Tr + C, ɽ+k. |

Three-consonant clusters:

| | | |
|---|---|---|
| Initial | : | Nil |
| Final | : | must have a nasal as $C_2$ or $C_3$ |
| Exceptions | : | -rktʃ-, -rltʃ-, -njp-. |
| Medial | : | -dnk-, -glv-, -ŋgl-, -lrtʃ-, -rpt-, -rjk-. |

Four-consonant clusters:

| | | |
|---|---|---|
| Initial | : | Nil |
| Final | : | Nil |
| Medial | : | /ɖjlv/ |

Five-consonant clusters:

| | | |
|---|---|---|
| Initial | : | Nil |
| Final | : | /ɳʈjgn/ |
| Medial | : | Nil |

**Reference:** Subbiah (1986)

# Koya[24]

**Ethnologue code:** ISO 639-3: kff
**Language classification:** Dravidian, South-Central, Gondi-Kui
**Alternate names:** Koi, Koi Gondi, Kavor, Koa, Koitar, Koyato, Kaya, Koyi, Raj Koya
**Main region:** Andhra Pradesh, Maharashtra, Chhattisgarh, Orissa.

## 1 Consonant Phonemes

### 1.1 Inventory

| | Bila-bial | Labio-dental | Dental | Alv. | Retro-flex | Pala-tal | Velar | Glo-ttal |
|---|---|---|---|---|---|---|---|---|
| Plosive | p b | | t d | | ʈ ɖ | | k g | |
| Nasal | m | | | n | ɳ | | | |
| Tap | | | | ɾ | | | | |
| Fricative | | | | s | | | | ɦ |
| Appr | | ʋ | | | | j | | |
| Lat. Approx. | | | | l | | | | |
| Affricate | | | | | | tʃ dʒ | | |

### 1.2 Distribution

a. Consonants occur in all positions, with the following restrictions:

   i. /p b t ʈ tʃ dʒ k g ɳ ɦ/ do not occur finally.

---

[24] "1. This description of Koya is of Gommu dialect. The other well-known dialects of Koya are Gutta, basa, Livgn and Dorla. Gommu Koya has been more influenced by Telugu than other dialects."

"2. t d n [i.e.ʈ ɖ ɳ- PP] are not true retroflexes. The tip of the tongue is extended to the roof of the mouth, but it is not curled back as it would be for retroflexion. I have described these as post-alveolar or as cacuminal, but otherwise will refer to them as retroflex in accordance with accepted usage." (Tyler 1969:17)

ii. / ʧ ʤ ɳ/ do not occur initially.
iii. /ʧ ʤ/ occur only when geminated inter-vocalically preceded by a short vowel.

b. All consonants except /ɦ/ can be geminated inter-vocalically.

# 2 Vowel Phonemes

## 2.1 Inventory

a. **Short**

| | FRONT | CENTRAL | BACK |
|---|---|---|---|
| Close | i | | u |
| Mid | e | | o |
| Open | | a | |

b. **Long**

| | FRONT | CENTRAL | BACK |
|---|---|---|---|
| Close | i: | | u: |
| Mid | e: | | o: |
| Open | | a: | |

## 2.2 Distribution

a. Vowels occur in all positions, with the following exception:

i. /u:/ does not occur finally in words. /o:/ and /e:/ are also rare finally.

b. Vowel sequences do not occur intra-morphemically.

c. Inter-morphemically vowel sequences have intervening semivowels /j/ or /w/ for Front or Back vowels respectively.

# 3 Allophones

## 3.1 Inventory

| | BILA-BIAL | DENTAL | ALVE-OLAR | POST ALVEOLAR | RETRO-FLEX | PALA-TAL | VELAR | GLO-TTAL |
|---|---|---|---|---|---|---|---|---|
| Plosive | p̆(p)<br>b̆(b)<br>bʷ(b) | t̆(t)<br>d̆(d) | | | | | k̆ (k)<br>kʷ(k)<br>ğ (g)<br>gʷ(g) | |
| Nasal | m̆ (m) | | | | | | | |
| Trill | | r̤ (r) | | | | | | |
| Fricative | β (ʋ) | | | ʃ(s) | ʂ(s) | | | h(ɦ) |
| Approx | | | | | | jˀ (j) | | |
| Lat Appr | | | ɮˠ (l)<br>ɬ (l) | | | | | |
| Affricate | | ʦ (ʧ)<br>ʣ (ʤ) | | | | | | |

## 3.2 Distribution

a. The stops /p b t d k g/ and the nasal /m/ have lax allophones [p̆ b̆ t d k̆ ğ m̆] in inter-vocalic position.

b. /b k g/ have labialised allophones [ bᵂ kᵂ gᵂ ] before [o̩].

c. [ ʃ ] < /s/ occurs before front vowels / i e /.

d. [ʂ] < /ʂ/ occurs before /ʈ/.

e. [ɮˠ] < /l/ occurs before velar stops /k g/

f. [ɬ] < /l/ occurs before stops other than velar, /h/, /l/ and word finally.

g. [h] < /ɦ/ occurs before consonants.

h. [ʦ dz] < /ʧ ʤ/ occur before back vowels; [ʦ] also occurs before /m t k/.

i. [r̤ ] < /r/ occurs before dental stops.

j. [ β ] < /ʋ/ occurs before back vowels and inter-vocalically.

k. [ j$^{ʔ}$ ] < /j/ occurs before /j/ and word finally.

# 4 Vowels

## 4.1 Inventory and distribution

a. The short vowels have checked allophones / i$^{ʔ}$ e$^{ʔ}$ a$^{ʔ}$ o$^{ʔ}$ / word-finally.

b. All vowels except /e e: u u:/ have retroflexed allophones / ị̥ ị̥ : ạ̥ ọ̥ ọ̥ : / before retroflex consonants.

c. All vowels undergo modifications on the height or backness parameter in different contexts as given below:

| **Allophone** | **Modifications** |
|---|---|
| /i/ > [ɪ]/---C $\left\{\begin{matrix}(c)\\ i\\ a\end{matrix}\right\}$ | Back and lowered |
| /u/ > [ɨ]/C---# | Centralized and unrounded. |
| /u:/ > [ ɨ̞ ]/---Ca | Centralized, somewhat lowered and unrounded. |
| /e/ > [ɛ̈]/---C $\left\{\begin{matrix}(c)\\ i\\ \#\end{matrix}\right\}$ | Lowered and centralized. |
| /e/ > [æ̈]/---C $\left\{\begin{matrix}a\\ o\end{matrix}\right\}$ | Considerably lowered and centralized. |
| /o/ > [ɤ]/---C(C)$_{i}$ | Unrounded |
| /o/ > [ọ : ]/---Ca | Lowered |
| /o/ > [ ɤ : ]/---j | Unrounded |
| /o/ > [ọ :]/---Ca | Lowered |
| /a/ > [ɐ : ]/(C)---j# | Raised |

/a:/ > [ɐ :]/j — Raised

j-C

/a:/ > [ɑ:]/---Cu — Lowered, backed.

# 5 Syllables

## 5.1 Canonical syllable structure[25]

a. Word: (C) V (C)

b. Stem: (C) V (C) (C) (C)

## 5.2 Consonant clusters

Two-consonant clusters:

Initial : Nil
Final in B type: e.g. –rl, sk, -ŋg, etc
Medial : General.

Three-consonant clusters:

Initial : Nil

Final in B type: rsk-, -ndt- etc.

Medial : -ptk-, -ʧtk-, -rtk-, -ktk-, -ʋtk-, -stk-, -ltk-, -dkt-, -rsk- (O/L/ʋ/s + O + k)

-mpt-, -ŋgt-, -ndt-, -ɳɖt-, -ntr-, -mbr-, -ŋgt-, -ŋkt-. (N + Pl + Pl/r)

**Reference:** Tyler (1969)

[25] Initial Consonant clusters are found in loan words from English, e.g. /gre:ɖ/ 'grade'.

# Kui

**Ethnologue code:** ISO 639-3: kxu
**Language classification:** Dravidian, South-Central, Gondi-Kui
**Alternate names:** Kandh, Khondi, Khond, Khondo, Kanda, Kodu, Kodulu, Kuinga, Kuy
**Main region:** Orissa; Andhra Pradesh; Madhya Pradesh; Tamil Nadu.

## 1 Consonant Phonemes

### 1.1 Inventory

| | BILA-BIAL | LABIO-DENTAL | DENTAL | ALV. | RETRO | PALA-TAL | VELAR | GLO-TTAL |
|---|---|---|---|---|---|---|---|---|
| Plosive | p b | | t d | | ʈ ɖ | | k g | ʔ |
| Nasal | m | | | n | ɳ | | ŋ | |
| Tap | | | | ɾ | | | | |
| Flap | | | | | ɽ | | | |
| Fricative | | | | s | (ʂ) | | | h |
| Approx | | (ʋ) | | | | (j) | | |
| Lat Appr | | | | l | | | | |
| Affricate | | | | | | (ʧ) ʤ | | |

### 1.2 Distribution

a. Consonants occur in all positions, with the following restrictions:
   i. /p b t d ɽ ʧ ʤ k n ɳ ʂ h l ɽ ʋ j/ do not occur finally.
   ii. /ʔ ɳ h ʋ j/ do not occur initially.
   iii. /ɳ/ is found to occur only when geminated inter-vocalically preceded by a short vowel.

b. All consonants except /ŋ r ʋ h ʂ ʔ/ can be geminated inter-vocalically.

# 2 Vowel Phonemes

## 2.1 Inventory

a. **Short**

| | FRONT | CENTRAL | BACK |
|---|---|---|---|
| Close | i | | u |
| Close-mid | e | | o |
| Open | | a | |

b. **Long**

| | FRONT | CENTRAL | BACK |
|---|---|---|---|
| Close | i: | | u: |
| Close-mid | e: | | o: |
| Open | | a: | |

## 2.2 Distribution

a. Vowels occur in all positions, with the following restriction:

   i. Long vowels do not occur finally.

b. Vowel sequences occur intra-morphemically in all positions (with restrictions on the sequences).

c. Word-initially, front and back vowels have [j] and [w] on-glides respectively.

# 3 Consonant Allophones

Details not available (apart from nasal allophones homorganic with following stops)

# 4 Vowel Allophones

a. Short vowels are lengthened word-finally.

b. The front /ɪ e/ and the back /ʊ o/ vowels have [j] and [w] on-glides word-initially.

# 5 Syllable Structure

## 5.1 Canonical syllable structure

Non-final: (C) (C) V (C) (C)

Final: (C) (C) V (GS)

## 5.2 Consonant clusters

Two-consonant clusters:

Initial : C+ L/ɽ/j.
Final : -ɳɖ, -ŋg.
Medial : General.

Three-consonant clusters:

Initial : Nil
Medial : N+S+C, C+C+ʔ
Final : Nil

**Reference:** Maheswaran (1989)

# Kurux

**Ethnologue code:** ISO 639-3: kru
**Language classification:** Dravidian, Northern
**Alternate names:** Uraon, Oraon, Urang, Kurukh, Kunrukh, Kadukali, Kurka, Kunha, Kunhar, Kunuk, Kunna, Kuda, Kora, Koda,
**Main region:** Bihar; Chhattisgarh; Jharkhand; Orissa,

## 1 Consonant Phonemes

### 1.1 Inventory

| | Bilabial | Dental | Alveolar | Retroflex | Palatal | Velar | Glottal |
|---|---|---|---|---|---|---|---|
| Plosive | p b<br>$p^h$ $b^ɦ$ | t d<br>$t^h$ $d^ɦ$ | | ʈ ɖ<br>$ʈ^h$ $ɖ^ɦ$ | | k g<br>$k^h$ $g^ɦ$ | ʔ |
| Nasal | m | | n | | | | |
| Trill | | | r | | | | |
| Flap | | | | ɽ | | | |
| Fricative | | | s | | | x | h |
| Approx | w | | | | j | | |
| Lat. Approx. | | | l | | | | |
| Affricate | | | | | ʧ ʤ<br>$ʧ^h$ $ʤ^ɦ$ | | |

### 1.2 Distribution

a. Consonants occur in all positions, with the following restrictions:
   i. /ʔ ɖ $ɖ^ɦ$/ do not occur finally.
   ii. /ɽ/ does not occur initially.

b. All consonants have geminates except /ɽ/ intervocalically.

# 2 Vowel Phonemes

## 2.1 Inventory

a. **Short**

| | FRONT | CENTRAL | BACK |
|---|---|---|---|
| Close | ɪ | | ʊ |
| Close-mid | ɛ | | ɔ |
| Open | | | ɑ |

b. **Long**

| | FRONT | CENTRAL | BACK |
|---|---|---|---|
| Close | iː | | uː |
| Close-mid | eː | | oː |
| Open | | | ɑː |

c. **Nasal**

| | FRONT | CENTRAL | BACK |
|---|---|---|---|
| Close | ĩː ɪ̃ | | ũː ʊ̃ |
| Close-mid | ẽː | | õː |
| Open-mid | ɛ̃ | | ɔ̃ |
| Open | | | ɑ̃ ɑ̃ː |

## 2.2 Distribution

a. Vowels occur in all positions, with the following restrictions:
   i. /ɪ̃ ũ ʊ̃/ do not occur initially
   ii. /o ĩː ũː õː ɑ̃ː/ do not occur finally

b. Sequences of two and three vowels occur in all positions.

# 3 Consonant Allophones

No significant allophones noted, apart from the usual nasal consonant ones.

# 4 Vowel Allophones

## 4.1 Inventory

| | |
|---|---|
| [ i ] [ ɪ̯ ]: | /ɪ/ |
| [ ĩ ] [ ɪ̃ ]: | /ɪ̃/ |
| [e] [ ɛ̯ ]: | /ɛ/ |
| [ẽ ] [ ɛ̯̃ ]: | /ɛ̃/ |
| [a̬ a]: | /ʌ/ |
| [ã]: | /ʌ̃/ |
| [o] [ ɔ̯ ]: | /ɔ/ |
| [õ] [ ɔ̯̃ ]: | /ɔ̃/ |
| [o] [ ʊ̯ ]: | /ʊ/ |
| [õ] [ ʊ̯̃ ]: | /ʊ̃/ |

## 4.2 Distribution

a. The short higher vowel allophones [i u e o] < /ɪ ʊ ɛ ɔ/ and their nasal counterparts [ĩ ũ ẽ õ] < /ɪ̃ ʊ̃ ɛ̃ ɔ̃/ occur finally.

b. [a̬] < /ɐ/ also occurs finally.

c. [ɪ̯ ɛ̯ u̯ o̯] < /ɪ ɛ ʊ o/ occur after syllabic vowels. In a sequence of three vowels only the middle vowel is non-syllabic. /ʌ ɪ ɔ/ > [a̯ i̯ o].

# 5 Syllable Structure

## 5.1 Canonical syllable structure[26]

a. Initial : (C) V (C) (C)

b. Non-initial : (C) (C) V (C) (C)

## 5.2 Consonant clusters

Two-consonant clusters:

| | |
|---|---|
| Initial in A type | : Nil |
| Initial in B type | : C+r, C+ʔ, r+n/d/k etc. |
| Final | : -js, -jtʃ, -jr, -wɽ, -nd, - nɽ, -ndʒ, -ŋk |
| Medial | : general |

Three-consonant clusters:

| | |
|---|---|
| Initial | : Nil |
| Final | : Nil |
| Medial | : general |

**Reference:** Ekka (1985)

[26] Monosyllabic words have the structure of the initial syllable.

# Kuvi

**Ethnologue code:** ISO 639-3: kxv
**Language classification:** Dravidian, South-Central, Gondi-Kui, Konda-Kui, Manda-Kui, Kui-Kuvi
**Alternate names:** Kuwi, Kuvinga, Kuvi Kond, Kond, Khondi, Khondh, Jatapu
**Main region:** Orissa; Andhra Pradesh.

## 1 Consonant Phonemes

### 1.1 Inventory

| | Bilabial | Labiodental | Dental | Alveolar | Retroflex | Palatal | Velar | Glottal |
|---|---|---|---|---|---|---|---|---|
| Plosive | p b | | t d | | ʈ ɖ | | k g | ʔ |
| Nasal | m | | | n | ɳ | | ŋ | |
| Trill | | | | r | | | | |
| Flap | | | | | ɽ | | | |
| Fricative | | v | | s | | | | h |
| Approx | | | | | | j | | |
| Lat Appr | | | | l | | | | |
| Affricate | | | ts dʑ | | | | | |

### 1.2 Distribution

a. Consonants do not occur finally, except in loan words and in bound morphemes.

b. Geminate consonants occur medially, except for / ŋ ɾ h ʔ/.

# 2 Vowel Phonemes

## 2.1 Inventory

a. **Short**

| | FRONT | CENTRAL | BACK |
|---|---|---|---|
| Close | i | | u |
| Close-mid | e | | o |
| Open | | a | |

b. **Long**

| | FRONT | CENTRAL | BACK |
|---|---|---|---|
| Close | i: | | u: |
| Close-mid | e: | | o: |
| Open | | a: | |

c. **Nasal**

| | FRONT | CENTRAL | BACK |
|---|---|---|---|
| Close | ĩ: ĩ | | ũ: ũ |
| Close-mid | ẽ ẽ: | | õ õ: |
| Open | | ã ã: | |

## 2.2 Distribution

a. Vowels occur in all positions, with the following restrictions:
   i. Long oral vowels do not occur finally except in verbal roots.
   ii. The long nasal vowels /ĩ: ẽ: õ: ã:/ do not occur finally.
   iii. /ũ:/ does not occur medially.

b. Sequences of vowels do not occur, except in a few borrowed words, e.g., /bilei/ 'cat'.

# 3 Consonant Allophones

## 3.1 Inventory

[tʃ] : /ts/

[dʒ] : /dz/

[w] : /v/

## 3.2 Distribution

a. [tʃ dʒ] < / ts dz/ occur after /n/.

b. [w] < /v / occurs inter-vocalically when the following vowel is non-front i.e. back or central.

# 4 Vowel Allophones

a. There are no significant allophonic alternants of vowel segments.

# 5 Syllable Structure

## 5.1 Canonical syllable structure[27]

(C)(C)V(C)

## 5.2 Consonant clusters

Two-consonant clusters:

Initial : C + r/ɽ/ɳ (C = a) unaspirated plosive, b) /m/

---

[27] a. A coda consonant can be posited for bound morphemes and word medial syllables.

b. Monosyllabic words are rare in Kuvi.

Final : Nil

Medial : General

Three-consonant clusters:

Initial : Nil.

Final : Nil

Medial : (a) N+S+C (b) r+ C+C

**References:** Reddy (1979), Israel (1979)

# Malayalam[28]

**Ethnologue code:** ISO 639-3: mal
**Language classification:** Dravidian, Southern
**Alternate names:** Alealum, Malayalani, Malayali, Malean, Maliyad, Mallealle, Mopla
**Main region:** Kerala, Lakshadwip Islands, and neighboring states.

## 1 Consonant Phonemes

### 1.1 Inventory

| | Bila-bial | Labio dental | Dental | Alv | Post Alv | Retr | Pala-tal | Vel-ar | Glo-ttal |
|---|---|---|---|---|---|---|---|---|---|
| Plosive | p b<br>pʰ bʱ | | t d<br>tʰ dʱ | t̲ | | ʈ ɖ<br>ʈʰ ɖʱ | | k g<br>kʰ gʱ | |
| Nasal | m | | n | n̠ | | ɳ | ɲ | ŋ | |
| Trill | | | | r | | | | | |
| Tap | | | | ɾ | | | | | |
| Fricative | | f | | s | ʃ | ʂ | | | h |
| Approx | | ʋ | | ɹ | | | j | | |
| Lat. Appr. | | | | l | | ɭ | | | |
| Affricate | | | | | | | tʃ ʤ<br>tʃʰ ʤʱ | | |

### 1.2 Distribution

a. Consonants occur in all positions, with the following restrictions:

   i. /ɳ ŋ ɭ ɹ/ do not occur initially; /ʈ/ does not occur initially in native words.

[28] Malayalam has a vigorous borrowed sub-component of Sanskrit vocabulary. The aspirated consonants belong to its borrowed sub-system. Two of the segments /f/ and /æ/ are found in words from English.

ii. Only /m n/ occur finally without an enunciative final /ə/; the enunciative /ə/ may be optionally dropped after /ɳ l ɭ r ɾ j/

b. Consonants except /ʈh ʤʱ gʱ r ʂ h ɻ/ have geminates word-medially.

# 2 Vowel Phonemes

## 2.1 Inventory

a. **Short**

| | FRONT | CENTRAL | BACK |
|---|---|---|---|
| Close | i | | u |
| Close-mid | e | | o |
| Open-mid | (æ) | ə | |
| Open | | a | |

b. **Long**

| | FRONT | CENTRAL | BACK |
|---|---|---|---|
| Close | i: | | u: |
| Close-mid | e: | | o: |
| Open | | a: | |

**Vocalic consonant:** /r̩/

## 2.2 Distribution

a. Vowels occur in all positions, with the following restrictions:
   i. /ə/ does not occur word-initially.
   ii. The front vowels /i i: e e:/ and the back vowels /u u: o o:/ take /j/ and /ʋ/ on-glides word-initially.
   iii. The short medial vowels /e o/ do not occur in medial syllables.

iv. Word-finally, many vowels have restricted occurrenc: /o/ does not occur there; the other mid vowels /e e: o:/ occur only in grammatical morphemes; and /a: i: u:/ also occur in a few grammatical and lexical subsets.

b. Sequences of syllabic vowels do not occur. In complex words, in the context of contiguous vowels, the constraint is resolved either by an epenthetic /j/ or /ʋ/ glide or by the deletion of the stem-final vowel.

# 3 Consonant Allophones

## 3.1 Inventory

| | BILA-BIAL | DENTAL | ALVE-OLAR | RETR-OFLEX | PALA-TAL | VELAR |
|---|---|---|---|---|---|---|
| Plosive | b (p) | t(r) | d̠ (r)<br>d̠ (t) | ʈ (k) ɖ (ʈ) | | k$^j$ (k)<br>g(k) |
| Nasal | | | | | | ŋ$^j$ (ŋ) |
| Tap / Flap | | | | ɽ (ʈ) | | |
| Fricative | β (p) | ð (t) | | | | ɣ (k) |
| Approx | | | | | | |
| Affricate | | | | | tʃ (tʃ)<br>ʤ (tʃ) | |

## 3.2 Distribution

a. [β ð ɽ ʤ ɣ] < /p t ʈ ʧ k/ occur inter-vocalically, in fast speech.

b. [b d ɖ g ʤ] < /p t ʈ k ʧ/ occur following a nasal consonant. [d] < /r/ occur in the same environment, resulting in the contextual neutralization of /t/ and /r/.

c. [t] < /r/ occurs as a member of the geminate /r/: [tt] < /rr/.

d. [k$^j$ ŋ$^j$] < /k ŋ/ occur following a front vowel /i/ or /e/.

e. [t] < /k/ occurs before /ʃ/: [tʃ$^h$i:ɳəm] < /kSi:ŋəm/ 'tiredness'.

# 4 Vowel Allophones

## 4.1 Inventory

Details about significant allophones not available. It may be noted, however, that owing to a large number of nasal consonants, there is a preponderance of nasal vowels in Malayalam speech.

**Semivowels:**

[ i̯ ]: /j/

[ɐ]: /ə/

[ u̯ ]: /ʋ/

## 4.2 Distribution

a. [ i̯ ] < /j/ occurs after /a e o/, and [ u̯ ]< /ʋ/ occurs after /a/. This gives rise to the following phonetic diphthongs: [ ai ei oi au ].

b. [ɐ] < /ə/ occurs in stressed positions.

# 5 Syllable Structure

## 5.1 Canonical syllable structure[29]

(C)(C)(C)V(C)

## 5.2 Consonant clusters

Two-consonant clusters:

| | |
|---|---|
| Initial | : In assimilated loans from Sanskrit and English |
| Final | : In assimilated loans from Sanskrit and English, but vary freely with preferred forms having a final enunciative /ə/. |

[29] Asher and Kumari (1997: 429-30) give exhaustive rules of syllable division in Malayalam.

Medial : These include: (a) geminate consonants (except ɟɦ ʈ$^{h}$ ɡɦ), (b) C + N/S, (c) C + L/Fr.

Three-consonant clusters:

Initial : In assimilated loans from Sanskrit and English.

Final : Nil

Medial : In assimilated loans from Sanskrit and English.

**References:** Asher & Kumari (1997), Mohanan & Mohanan (1984)

# Malto

**Ethnologue code:** ISO 639-3: mjt
**Language classification:** Dravidian, Northern
**Alternate names:** Malto, Malti, Maltu, Maler, Sawriya Malto, Malatri
**Main region:** Jharkhand, West Bengal

## 1 Consonant Phonemes

### 1.1 Inventory

| | Bilabial | Interdetal | Dental | Alv | Retro | Palatal | Velar | Uvular | Glottal |
|---|---|---|---|---|---|---|---|---|---|
| Plosive | p b | | t d | | ʈ ɖ | | k g | q ɢ | |
| Nasal | m | | | n | | ɲ | ŋ | | |
| Trill | | | | r | | | | | |
| Tap / Flap | | | | | ɽ | | | | |
| Fricative | | θ | | s | | | | ɣ | h |
| Approx | w | | | | | j | | | |
| Lat Appr | | | | l | | | | | |

### 1.2 Distribution

a. Consonants occur in all positions, with the following restrictions:
   i. /θ ɽ ɣ/ do not occur word-initially.
   ii. /ɢ/ occurs only word-medially.
   iii. /q ɣ/ do not occur before /i iː/ unless a juncture intervenes.

b. Geminates of the following consonants occur word-medially: /p b t ɖ c ɟ k q s n ɽ l j/

# 2 Vowel Phonemes

## 2.1 Inventory

a. Short

| | Front | Central | Back |
|---|---|---|---|
| Close | i | | u |
| Close-mid | e | | o |
| Open | | a | |

b. Long

| | Front | Central | Back |
|---|---|---|---|
| Close | i: | | u: |
| Close-mid | e: | | o: |
| Open | | a: | |

## 2.2 Distribution

a. Vowels occur in all positions, with the following restriction:
   i. Long vowels do not occur finally.

b. Vowel sequences do not occur.

# 3 Consonant Allophones

## 3.1 Inventory and distribution

a. [ɲ] < / ŋ / occurs before palatal consonants, or finally in monosyllables.

b. [ʀ] < / r / occurs before the uvular plosives /q ɢ/.

# 4 Vowel Allophones

Data not available.

# 5 Syllable Structure

## 5.1 Canonical syllable structure

Root: (C)V(C) (C)

Final of complex word: (C) (C) V

## 5.2 Consonant clusters

Two-consonant clusters:

Initial : Nil (One borrowed item has [kristanin]

Final : Nil. (Roots, however, may end in -ɽp, -ld, -nj, -mθ, -ŋg, -rɢ, -ɽs)

Medial : General.

Three-consonant clusters: [30]

Initial : Nil

Final : Nil

Medial : General

**References:** Das (1973), Steever (1998)

[30] Syllable division is between the last consonant and the penultimate in a sequence CCC.C, unless the final is a /r/ or a /j/, in which case the division is between the penult and the antepenult.

# Manda

**Ethnologue code:** ISO 639-3: mha
**Language classification:** Dravidian-south Central
**Alternate names:** Nil
**Main region:** Orissa, Kalahandi district, Thuamul Rampur subdivision.

## 1 Consonant Phonemes

### 1.1 Inventory

| | Bilabial | Dental | Retroflex | Palatal | Velar | Glottal |
|---|---|---|---|---|---|---|
| Plosive | p b | t d | ʈ ɖ | | k g | |
| Nasal | m | n | ɳ | | ŋ | |
| Trill | | r | | | | |
| Flap | | | ɽ | | | |
| Fricative | | s | | | | h |
| Approx | | ʋ | | j | | |
| Lat Approx | | l | | | | |
| Affricate | | | | ʤ | | |

### 1.2 Distribution

a. Consonants occur in all positions, with the following restriction:
   i. /ɳ ŋ j/ do not occur initially.

b. Geminates of the following consonants occur inter-vocalically: /p t ʈ d ɖ ʤ s n r l/

c. Consonant clusters occur in all positions.

# 2 Vowel Phonemes

## 2.1 Inventory

a. **Short**

| | FRONT | CENTRAL | BACK |
|---|---|---|---|
| Close | i | | u |
| Close-mid | e | | o |
| Open | | a | |

b. **Long**

| | FRONT | CENTRAL | BACK |
|---|---|---|---|
| Close | i: | | u: |
| Close-mid | e: | | o: |
| Open | | a: | |

## 2.2 Distribution

a. All the vowels occur in all the positions.

b. Vowel sequences do not occur.

# 3 Consonant Allophones

Data not available.

# 4 Vowel Allophones

Data not available.

# 5 Syllable Structure

## 5.1 Canonical syllable structure

(C (C) V (C) (C))

## 5.2 Consonant clusters

Two-consonant clusters:

Initial : Pl/m + r/ɽ/ɳ

Final : N+ HVdC (-mb, -nd, ɳɖ, ŋg)

Medial : General.

Three-consonant clusters:

Initial : Nil

Final : Nil

Medial : N/r + voiced Pl/N/s + C (k g ʈ ɖ r l n ɳ j)

**Reference:** Reddy & Reddy (1986)

# Naiki

**Ethnologue code:** ISO 639-3:nit
**Language classification:** Dravidian, Central, Kolami-Naiki
**Alternate names:** Southeastern Kolami
**Main region:** Andhra Pradesh, Adilabad district; Maharashtra, Chandrapur, Nanded districts.

## 1 Consonant Phonemes

### 1.1 Inventory

| | BILA-BIAL | LABIO DENTAL | DEN-TAL | ALV. | RETR. | PAL.-ALV. | PAL. | VELAR | GLO-TTAL |
|---|---|---|---|---|---|---|---|---|---|
| Stop | p b (pʰ) (bʱ) | | t d (tʰ) (dʱ) | | ʈ ɖ (ʈʰ) (ɖʱ) | | | k g (kʰ) (gɦ) | |
| Nasal | m | | n | | | | | ŋ | |
| Trill | | | | r | | | | | |
| Fricative | | | | s | | | | | h |
| Approx | | ʋ | | | | | j | | |
| Lat Appr | | | | l | | | | | |
| Affricate | | | | | | tʃ ʤ (tʃʰ) (ʤʱ) | | | |

### 1.2 Distribution

a. Consonants occur in all positions, with the following restrictions:
   i. /ŋ/ does not occur initially.
   ii. The marginal aspirated plosives and affricates do not occur medially and finally. (They occur word-initially and contrast with the unaspirated counterparts in that position.)
   iii. /h/ does not occur finally.

b. Geminate consonants except / **ʧ ʤ h ŋ** / occur in the medial position.

# 2 Vowel Phonemes

## 2.1 Inventory

a. **Short**[31]

| | FRONT | CENTRAL | BACK |
|---|---|---|---|
| Close | i | | u |
| Mid | e | | o |
| Open | | | ɑ |

b. **Long Vowels**

| | FRONT | CENTRAL | BACK |
|---|---|---|---|
| Close | i: | | u: |
| Close-mid | e: | | o: |
| Open | | | ɑ : |

## 2.2 Distribution

a. All the vowels occur in all the positions.

b. Vowel sequences do not occur morpheme internally; across morphemes, either the following vowel is deleted or there is semi-vowel insertion between them in different cases.

# 3 Consonant Allophones

## 3.1 Inventory

| | POST- ALV. | RETROFLEX |
|---|---|---|
| Trill / Flap | r<(r) | ɽ (ɖ) |
| Lat Appr | l<(l) | |

[31] The low central vowel is phonetically closer to being back than central.

## 3.2 Distribution

a. The post-alveolar trill and lateral allophones [r> l>] < /r l/ occur before retroflex consonants.

b. The retroflex flap allophone [ɽ] < /ɖ/ occurs inter-vocalically and adjacent to a consonant.

## 3.3 Vowel Allophones

**General:**

a. Word-final half long vowels.

b. Non-initial lowered and raised vowels.

**Specific:**

c. [ɯ]: /u/

## 3.4 Distribution

a. The half long allophones [iˑ eˑ ɑˑ uˑ oˑ] < /iː eː ɑː uː oː/ occur word-finally.

b. The lowered allophones [ɪ ɛ ʊ ɔ] < /i e u o/ and the raised allophone [ʌ]< /ɑ/ occurs non-initially.

c. The unrounded back vowel allophone [ɯ] < /u/occurs finally following a labial consonant.

# 4 Syllables

## 4.1 Canonical syllable structure

(C) (r) V (C) (C) (C)[32]

---

32 There is only one instance of a three-consonant coda /jŋg/

## 4.2 Consonant clusters

Two-consonant clusters:

Initial : Nil[33]

Final : -O+Son, -Son +Son, -tt.

Medial : General.

Three-consonant clusters:

Initial : Nil

Medial : -jŋg-

Final : Nil

Four-consonant clusters:

Initial : Nil

Medial : -jŋg+C

Final : Nil

**References:** Krishnamoorthy (1984)

---

[33] Initial clusters with /r/ and /v/ occur in a few words, all borrowing from Indo-Aryan.

# Pengo

**Ethnologue code:** ISO 639-3: peg
**Language classification:** Dravidian, South-Central, Gondi-Kui
**Alternate names:** Pengu, Hengo, Hengo Poraja, Jani, Muddali, Paraja, Pango, Pengua, Pango Paraja
**Main region:** Orissa.

## 1 Consonant Phonemes

### 1.1 Inventory

| | BILA-BIAL | DENTAL | RETR-OFLEX | PAL.-ALV. | PALA-TAL | VELAR | GLO-TTAL |
|---|---|---|---|---|---|---|---|
| Plosive | p b | t d | ʈ ɖ | | | k g | |
| Nasal | m | n | ɳ | | | ŋ | |
| Trill | | r | | | | | |
| Flap | | | ɽ | | | | |
| Fricative | | | s z | | | | h |
| Approx | w | | | | j | | |
| Lat. Approx. | | l | | | | | |
| Affricate | | | | tʃ ʤ | | | |

### 1.2 Distribution

a. Consonants occur in all positions, with the following restriction:

   i. /z ɽ/ do not occur in the initial position.

b. /ɟ/ alternates with /j/ in certain dialects.

c. /h/ is widely distributed in Pengo, a feature which is uncommon in Dravidian languages. It occurs in all positions, including medial clusters.

d. Geminates of the following consonants occur intervocalically: /k g ʧ ʤ t d p b n m s z/. However, they "are always morphologically motivated, and they arise from the combination of stem final and suffix initial" (p. 6), in for example, the past stem, the future stem, the gerund, and the intensive. In the case of the palatal stops, /c ɟ/ gemination arises on account of assimilation, e.g., -ʧ + t- > -ʧʧ-, -ʧ + d- > -j j-, -j + d- > -j j-.

# 2 Vowel Phonemes

## 2.1 Inventory

a. **Short**

| | FRONT | CENTRAL | BACK |
|---|---|---|---|
| Close | i | | u |
| Close-mid | e | | o |
| Open | | a | |

b. **Long**

| | FRONT | CENTRAL | BACK |
|---|---|---|---|
| Close | i: | | u: |
| Close-mid | e: | | o: |
| Open | | a: | |

c. **Diphthongs:** /aj uj ej oj/ are attested.

## 2.2 Distribution

a. Vowels occur in all positions.

b. Sequences of vowels occur. Across morphemes, identical vowels coalesce (a + a > a:, u + u > u:, but dissimilar vowels remain separate usually with a glide insertion (e.g., ija, eja, owa, uwa, etc.) .

# 3 Consonant Allophones

## 3.1 Inventory

| | DENTAL | ALVEOLAR | RETROFLEX |
|---|---|---|---|
| Flap | | | ɽ (ʈ/ɖ) |
| Fricative | | s(z) | |
| Affricate | ʥ (ɟ) | | |

## 3.2 Distribution

**General:**

Voice assimilation:

a. Voiced stops are voiceless before voiceless stops, and vice versa.

**Specific:**

b. [s] < /z/ occurs before voiceless stops.

c. [ʥ] < /ɟ/ occurs before front vowels.

d. [ɽ] < /ʈ ɖ/ occurs before the voiceless dental stop.

# 4 Vowel Allophones

Data not available.

# 5 Syllable Structure

## 5.1 Canonical syllable structure

(C (C) V (C) (C)

## 5.2 Consonant clusters

Two-consonant clusters:

Initial : S+r/ṛ

Final : N+S.

Medial : General.

Three-consonant clusters: [34]

Initial : Nil

Final : Nil

Medial : N+SH+S

**Reference:** Burrow and Bhattacharya (1970)

[34] The three consonant clusters in the medial position are found in morphologically complex forms.

# Tamil[35]

**Ethnologue code:** ISO 639-3: tam
**Language classification:** Dravidian, Southern, Tamil-Kannada
**Alternate names:** Tamalsan, Tambul, Tamili, Tamal, Damulian
**Main region:** Tamil Nadu and neighboring states.

## 1 Consonant Phonemes

### 1.1 Inventory

| | BILABIAL | LABIODENTAL | DENTAL | ALVEOLAR | POST-ALV | RETR | PALATAL | VELAR |
|---|---|---|---|---|---|---|---|---|
| Plosive | p b | | t d | t̠ | | ʈ ɖ | | k g |
| Nasal | m | | n | n̠ | | ɳ | ɲ | |
| Trill | | | | r | ṛ | | | |
| Flap | | | | | | ɽ | | |
| Fricative | | f | | s | | ʂ | | |
| Approx | w | ʋ | | | | ɻ | j | |
| Lat. Appr. | | | | l | | ɭ | | |
| Affricate | | | | | | tʃ dʒ | | |

### 1.2 Distribution

a. Consonants occur in all positions, with the following restrictions:
   i. Only sonorants occur word-finally.
   ii. The retroflex consonants /ʈ ɖ ɳ ʂ ɽ ɻ ɭ/ and the alveolar plosive and nasal /t̠ n̠ / do not occur word-initially.
   iii. The palatal nasal phoneme /ɲ / occurs only initially.

[35] Tamil has considerable amount of variation even in standard spoken variety. A consensus, however, may be found regarding certain aspects of its sound structure. Only what has been commonly noted in the descriptions is being included here.

b. Geminates of consonants except the rhotics / r ṟ ɽ / occur inter vocalically.

c. The rhotics / r ṟ ɽ / and /j/ and no other consonant can occur before geminate consonants.

d. Sonorant geminates do not occur after long vowels.

e. /j ʋ/ do not occur before /i u/ respectively, morpheme-initially.

# 2 Vowel Phonemes

## 2.1 Inventory

**a. Short**

| | Front | Central | Back |
|---|---|---|---|
| Close | i | | u |
| Close-mid | e | | o |
| Open | | a | |

**b. Long**

| | Front | Central | Back |
|---|---|---|---|
| Close | i: | | u: |
| Close-mid | e: | | o: |
| Open | | a: | |

**c. Nasal**

| | Front | Central | Back |
|---|---|---|---|
| Close-mid | ẽ: ẽ | | õ: õ |
| Open | | ã: ã | |

## 2.2 Distribution

a. Vowels occur in all positions, with the following restrictions:
   i. Short vowels /e o / occur only in initial position.
   ii. Long vowels except /a:/ rarely occur in non-initial position.
   iii. The nasal vowels  occur finally in polysyllabic words. They are all derived from a final nasal consonant which is elided.

b. /ʊ/ is epenthesized in monosyllabic stems ending in consonants except /j/.

c. Sequences of vowels of different qualities do not occur.

# 3 Consonant Allophones

## 3.1 Inventory

| | **Bilabial** | **Labiodental** | **Dental** | **Alveolar** | **Retroflex** | **Palatal** | **Pre-Velar** | **Velar** |
|---|---|---|---|---|---|---|---|---|
| Plosive | b(p) | | d(t) | | ɖ(ʈ) | | k̟ (k)<br>g̟ (g)<br>g (k) | |
| Nasal | | | | r̲(t) | | | | ŋ(n) |
| Fricative | | | | s(tʃ) | | | | x(k) |
| Approx. | | ʋ(p, Ø) | | | | j(Ø) | | |
| Affricate | | | | | | ʤ (tʃ) | | |

## 3.2 Distribution

a. [ʋ d r̲ ɖ s x ] < / p t t̲ ʈ tʃ k / occur intervocalically.

b. [ b d d̲ ɖ ʤ g ] < / p t t̲ ʈ tʃ k / after nasal consonants.

c. Prevelar consonants [k̟ g̟] occur after front vowels.

d. Onglides [ʋ j] occur at the beginning in words beginning with the back vowels /u u: o o:/ and /i i: e e:/ respectively.

# 4 Vowel Allophones

## 4.1 Inventory

| | |
|---|---|
| [ɯ]: | /u/ |
| [ʌ : ]: | /aː/ |
| [ɜ] [ʌ] [ɔ]: | /a/ |

## 4.2 Distribution

a. [ɯ] < /u/ occurs non-initially.

b. [ɜ] < /a/ occurs finally except before /m/

c. [ɔ] < /a/ occurs finally before /m/.

d. [ɐ] < /a/ occurs non-finally.

e. [ ɐ : ] < /aː/ occurs finally.

# 5 Syllable Structure

## 5.1 Canonical syllable structure

(C) (C) V (C) (C)

## 5.2 Consonant clusters

Two-consonant clusters:

| | |
|---|---|
| Initial | : P + L/j, s + p/t/k/l/n, v + j |
| Final | : Only in loan words<br>Close to Native English clusters, e.g. JN + Pl, s + t, l + t, l + f, r + k, r + f<br>Innovated, e.g. v + s /blavs/ 'blouse', v + ɳ 'tavɳ/ 'town', j + l /majl/ 'mail', ɖ + dʒ / dʒaɖdʒ/ 'judge'. |
| Medial | : General |

Three-consonant clusters:

| | |
|---|---|
| Initial | : Nil |
| Final | : Nil |
| Medial | : -mpl-, -mpr̩-, -ntr-, -rɭɭ-, -rcc-, -rkk-, -r̩kk-, -r̩pp-, -r̩tt-, -r̩kk-, -vr̩ɳ-, -jbr̩-, -jtt-, -jnt-. |

**References:** Vasanthakumari (1989), Christdas (1988) Schiffman (1999)

# Telugu

**Ethnologue code:** ISO 639-3: tel
**Language classification:** Dravidian, South-Central, Telugu
**Alternate names:** Telegu, Andhra, Gentoo, Tailangi, Telangire, Telgi, Tengu, Terangi, Tolangan
**Main region:** Andhra Pradesh and neighboring states.

## 1 Consonant Phonemes

### 1.1 Inventory

| | Bila-bial | Labio dental | Den-tal | Alv. | Post-Alv | Retr | Pala-tal | Vel-ar | Glo-ttal |
|---|---|---|---|---|---|---|---|---|---|
| Plosive | p b<br>pʰ bʱ | | t d<br>tʰ dʱ | | | ʈ ɖ<br>ʈʰ ɖʱ | | k g<br>kʰ gʱ | |
| Nasal | m | | n | | | ɳ | | | |
| Trill | | | | r | | | | | |
| Fricative | | f | | s | ʃ | ʂ | | | h |
| Approx | w | | | | | | j | | |
| Lat. Appr. | | | | l | | ɭ | | | |
| Affricate | | | | | | | tʃ ʤ<br>tʃʰ ʤʱ | | |

### 1.2 Distribution

a. Consonants occur in all positions, with the following restrictions:
   i. Only / m w j / occur word-finally.
   ii. /ɭ ɳ/ do not occur word-initially.

b. Geminate consonants occur inter-vocalically, except for the following: /pʰ bʰ dʰ ʈʰ ɖʰ tʃʰ dʒʰ kʰ gʰ ʂ h /.

# 2 Vowel Phonemes

## 2.1 Inventory

**a. Short**

| | FRONT | CENTRAL | BACK |
|---|---|---|---|
| Close | i | | u |
| Close-mid | e | | o |
| Open-mid | æ | ɐ | |

**b. Long**

| | FRONT | CENTRAL | BACK |
|---|---|---|---|
| Close | i: | | u: |
| Close-mid | e: | | o: |
| Open | | a: | |

## 2.2 Distribution

a. Vowels occur in all positions. Finally, they occur obligatorily, except when the final consonant is /m w j/.

b. Long vowels occur initially, only rarely non-initially.

c. Of the short vowels, /o/ does not occur finally.

d. Final /e/ freely varies with /i/ and /a/.

e. /u/ has the largest occurrence. It is also the vowel commonly epenthesized in loan words, e.g., 'purse' [parusu]; 'film' [filum].

f. The epenthetic vowel has harmony with the following vowel, in native vocabulary, e.g., /gurtu/ [gurutu] 'mark'; /ra:tri/ [ratiri] 'night'.

g. Initial /i e/ and /u o/ have /j-/ and /w-/ on-glides respectively.

h. Vowel sequences do not occur morpheme-internally.

# 3 Consonant Allophones

## 3.1 Inventory

| | Bilabial | Labio-dental | Alveolar | Retroflex | Velar |
|---|---|---|---|---|---|
| Plosive | | | | | ǩ (k) ğ (g) |
| Tap / Flap | | | ɾ (r) | ɽ (ɖ) ɽʰ (ɖʰ) | |
| Fricative | | v(w) | | | |
| Approx. | w̃ (m) | | | | |
| Affricate | | | | | |

## 3.2 Description

a. [w̃ ] < /m/, [ɽ] </ɖ/, [ɽʰ] < /ɖʰ/, [ǩ ] < /k/, [ğ] < /g/, [ɾ] < /r/ occur inter-vocalically.

b. [v]< /w/ occurs before /i e/ and occasionally before /u/.

c. [t s] < /tʃ/, [dz] < /ʤ/ occur before non-front vowels.

d. The distinction between an alveo-palatal and an alveolar voiceless fricative is often blurred, both being pronounced as alveolar, except before /æ/, where the alveopalatal is pronounced as such.

# 4 Vowel Allophones

## 4.1 Inventory

| | |
|---|---|
| [ə] [a] : | /ɐ / |
| [ɐ ː] [ɒ]: | /a ː / |
| [ɪ] : | /i/ |
| [ ï ː ]: | / i ː/ |

| | |
|---|---|
| [ ʊ]: | /u / |
| [ ʊ : ]: | / u :/ |
| [ɛ] : | /e / |
| [əi]: | /æ : / |
| [ɔ ]: | /o / |
| [ ɔ :]: | / o :/ |

## 4.2 Distribution

a. [ ə ɐ : ]< /ɐ a : / occur following /tʄ dʒ ʃ j/.

b. [ a ɒː ɪ ï : ʊ ʊ : ɛ ɔ ɔ : ] < / ɐ a : i iː u u : e o o : / respectively occur before / ɐ a : / in the following syllable.

c. [əi] < / æː / is found to occur sometimes in medial and final syllables.

# 5 Syllable Structure

## 5.1 Canonical syllable structure

(C) (L/G) V (N) (C)

## 5.2 Consonant clusters

Two-consonant clusters:

Initial : C+L/G (limited to loan-words from Sanskrit and English.)
Final : Nil
Medial : general.

Three-consonant clusters:

Medial : general. (More commonly with a nasal)

**References:** Krishnamurti (1998), Subrahmanyam (1974), K. N. Reddy (forthcoming), Rao (1987).

# Toda

**Ethnologue code:** ISO 639-3: tcx
**Language classification:** Dravidian, Southern, Tamil-Kannada
**Alternate names:** Todi, Tuda
**Main region:** Tamil Nadu: Nilgiri Hills, Kunda Hills.

## 1 Consonant Phonemes

### 1.1 Inventory

| | Bilabial | Labiodental | Interdental | Dental | Post dental | Alveolar | Alveopalatal | Retro | Palatal | Velar |
|---|---|---|---|---|---|---|---|---|---|---|
| Plosive | p b | | | t d | | t̠ d̠ | | ʈ ɖ | ʧ ʤ | k g |
| Nasal | m | | | | | n | | ɳ | | (ŋ) |
| Trill | | | | | r | r̠ | | | | |
| Flap | | | | | | | | ɽ | | |
| Fricative | | f | θ | | s z | s̠ z̠ | ʃ ʒ | ʂ ʐ | | x |
| Approx | w | | | | | | | j | | |
| Lat. Approx. | | | | | l̥ l | | ɭ̊ ɭ | | | |
| Affricate | | | | | ts ʣ | | | tʃ ʤ | | |

### 1.2 Distribution

a. Consonants occur in all positions, with the following restriction:
   i. Only /p t k m n w j s r l/ occur initially in words, the last three only in borrowed words.
b. Geminate consonants occur cross-morphemically, but tend to be reduced to a single consonant in fast speech.
c. Cluster simplification is common in fast Toda speech, in general leading to the deletion of the first consonant in two consonant clusters.
d. Longer clusters occur finally than initially.

# 2 Vowel Phonemes

## 2.1 Inventory

a. **Short**

| | Front | Central | Back |
|---|---|---|---|
| Close | i ʏ | | u ɯ |
| Close-mid | e | ɵ | o |
| Open | | | ɑ |

b. **Long**

| | Front | Central | Back |
|---|---|---|---|
| Close | iː ʏː | | uː ɯː |
| Close-mid | eː | ɵː | oː |
| Open | | | ɑː |

## 2.2 Distribution

a. Vowels occur in all positions.

b. Vowel sequences do not occur.

# 3 Consonant Allophones

## 3.1 Inventory

| | Bila-bial | Labio dental | Den-tal | Post dental | Alv | Alveo-palatal | Retr | Pala-tal | Vel-ar |
|---|---|---|---|---|---|---|---|---|---|
| Plosive | | | $\mathrm{t}^{\theta}$ (t)<br>$\mathrm{d}^{\eth}$ (d) | | | | | | |
| Nasal | m̥ (m) | | | | n̥ (n) | | ɳ̊ (ɳ) | | |

| Trill | | | | | r̠̥ (r̠) | | | | |
|---|---|---|---|---|---|---|---|---|---|
| Tap / Flap | | | | | | | ɽ̥ (ɽ) | | |
| Fricative | | v (f) | ð (θ) | z (s) | z̠ (s̠) | ʒ(ʃ) | ʐ(ʂ) | | ɣ (x) |
| Approx | | | | | | | | j̊ (j) | |

## 3.2 Distribution

**General:**

a. Voiceless stops are strongly aspirated word-finally before pause. In most other positions, for example, initially, they are weakly aspirated.

b. Identical consonants occurring cross-morphemically tend to get reduced to a single consonant in fast speech.

c. Nasals do not assimilate in place to following consonants.

**Specific:**

a. Voiced allophones of voiceless fricatives, trills and laterals, [v ð z z̠ ʒ ʐ ɣ l ɭ] < /f θ s s̠ ʃ ʂ x l̥ ɭ̥/, occur inter-vocalically.

b. Voiceless allophones of nasals and the palatal glide, [m̥ n̥ ɳ̊ j̊] < / m n ɳ j/ occur finally, and before or after the voiceless consonants that do not have voiced allophones.

c. The affricated allophones of the dental stops, [$t^{\theta}$ ] < /t/, [ $d^{ð}$] < /d/ occur before sibilant fricatives.

# 4 Vowel Allophones

## 4.1 Inventory

| | |
|---|---|
| [$i^j$]: | / i/ |
| [i : $^j$]: | /i : / |
| [ɛ]: | /e / |
| [ɛ :]: | /e : / |

| | |
|---|---|
| [ɐ ] [ʌ]: | /ɑ / |
| [ɐ : ] [ʌ :]: | /ɑ : / |
| [ ɔ ]: | /o / |
| [ ɔ : ] | /o : / |
| [ɞ]: | /θ/ |
| [ɞ : ]: | /θ : / |

## 4.2 Distribution

**General:**

a. Vowels are longer in the first syllable of the word, than in the other syllables.

b. Vowels are retroflexed before retroflex consonants.

**Specific:**

a. The low vowel raised and fronted allophones [ɐ] < /ɑ/, [ɐ :] < /ɑ : / occur before the post-dental tap /ɾ/.

b. The low vowel raised and back allophones [ʌ] < /ɑ/, [ʌ :] < /ɑ : / occur before /w/.

c. The opener allophones of the mid vowels occur before voiceless consonants and word-finally.

# 5 Syllable Structure

## 5.1 Canonical syllable structure[36]

(C) (G) V (C) (C) (C) (C).

---

[36] a. The initial consonant cluster is of a restricted type, as can be seen below.

b. Emeneau (1957, 1984: 27-28) notes that the multiple final consonant clusters have historically arisen from the loss of short vowels, and can be treated as syllables in themselves. Saktivel (1976) too presents an analysis of Toda syllables based on this assumption.

## 5.2 Consonant clusters

Two-consonant clusters:

Initial : C+ G

Final : General

Medial : General.

Three-consonant clusters:

Initial : Nil

Final : CC+j/m

Medial : restricted[37]

Four-consonant clusters:

Final : five instances found: -rkjm, -rkjn, -f ɖkj, -ɳkjm, -jtjm.

**References:** Emeneau (1984), Nara and Bhaskararao (2002), Ladefoged and Bhaskararao (1996)

[37] As for the final syllables, consonant clusters occur word medially as 'isolated syllables', with open or close transitions between them.

# Tulu

**Ethnologue code:** ISO 639-3: tcy
**Language classification:** Dravidian, Southern, Tulu
**Alternate names:** Tal, Tallu, Thalu, Tilu, Tuluva Bhasa, Tullu, Thulu
**Main region:** Karnataka; Andhra Pradesh; Kerala.

## 1 Consonant Phonemes

### 1.1 Inventory[38]

| | Bilab | Labio dental | Den- tal | Alv | Post- Alv | Retr | Pala- tal | Vel- ar | Pha- ryn | Glo- ttal |
|---|---|---|---|---|---|---|---|---|---|---|
| Plosive | p b<br>p$^h$ b$^ɦ$ | | t d<br>t$^h$ d$^ɦ$ | | | ʈ ɖ<br>ʈ$^h$ ɖ$^ɦ$ | | k g<br>k$^h$ g$^ɦ$ | | |
| Nasal | m | | n | | | ɳ | ɲ | ŋ | | |
| Trill | | | | | r | | | | | |
| Tap | | | | | ɾ | | | | | |
| Fricative | | | | s | ʃ | ʂ | | | ʕ | ɦ |
| Approx | | ʋ | | | | ɻ | j | | | |
| Lat. Appr. | | | | l | | ɭ | | | | |
| Affricate | | | | | | | tʃ ʤ<br>tʃ$^ɦ$ ʤ$^ɦ$ | | | |

### 1.2 Distribution

a. Consonants do not occur finally, except /j m/.

b. /ɳ ŋ ɭ/ do not occur initially.

c. All the consonants except /ʃ ʂ ʕ/ have geminates inter-vocalically. /ss/ occurs rarely.

[38] Bhat (1967) describes [ʕ] as a voiced velar fricative and uses the symbol [h]. We have verified it as a voiced pharyngeal fricative.

# 2 Vowel Phonemes

## 2.1 Inventory

a. **Short**

| | FRONT | CENTRAL | BACK |
|---|---|---|---|
| Close | i | | ɯ[38]<br>u |
| Close-mid | e | | o |
| Open-mid | ɛ | ə | |

b. **Long**

| | FRONT | CENTRAL | BACK |
|---|---|---|---|
| Close | i: | | u: |
| Close-mid | e: | | o: |
| Open-mid | ɛ: | | |
| Open | | a: | |

c. **Nasal**

| | FRONT | CENTRAL | BACK |
|---|---|---|---|
| Open | | ã | |

## 2.2 Distribution

a. Vowels occur in all positions, with the following restrictions:
   i. The vowels /e e: ɯ/ do not occur in the word-initial position.
   ii. The vowel /o/ does not occur in the word-final position.

b. Sequences of vowels do not occur.

---

[38] Shetty (2001) has the unrounded high central short vowel /ɨ/ in place of the unrounded high back short vowel /ɯ/.

# 3 Consonant Allophones

## 3.1 Inventory

[ħ]: /ʕ/

[w]: /ʋ/

## 3.2 Distribution

**General:**

a. Consonants are lengthened before /rjʋ/.

b. Lightly aspirated phones [ $p^{ˈ}$ $t^{ˈ}$ $k^{ˈ}$ $b^{ˈ}$ $d^{ˈ}$ $g^{ˈ}$ ] occur initially as allophones of the unaspirated stops / p t k b d g /, and medially of the aspirated stops /$p^{h}$ $t^{h}$ $k^{h}$ $b^{ɦ}$ $d^{ɦ}$ $g^{ɦ}$/.

Specific:

a. [w ] < /ʋ/ occurs before any segment and after rounded vowels.

b. [ħ] < /ʕ/

# 4 Vowel Allophones

## 4.1 Inventory

[i ˑ ]: /i/

[e ˑ ] [$^{j}$e]: /e/

[o ˑ ] [$^{w}$o] [ʊ]: /o/

[u ˑ ]: /u/

[ɨ]: /ɯ/

[ɐ] [a ˑ ]: /ə/

## 4.2 Distribution

a. The short vowels have half-long allophones finally.

b. The mid vowels /e o/ have /j/ and /w/ onglides word-initially, in which position /e/ is lower and /o/ has varying degrees of height depending on the vowel in the following syllable.

c. [ɨ] < /ɯ/ occurs after a /r/, occurring alone or in a cluster as a second member.

d. [ɐ] < /ə/ occurs initially in words if there is /ə/ in the following syllable.

e. [ʊ] < /o/ occurs if there is an /i/ or /u/ in the following syllable or an /e/ or /a/ in the following non-final syllable.

# 5 Syllable Structure

## 5.1 Canonical syllable structure[39]

(C) (C) V(C)

## 5.2 Consonant clusters

Two-consonant clusters:

| | |
|---|---|
| Initial | : a) C+L/G; b) nd-, nt-. |
| Final | : Nil. |
| Medial | : General. |

Three-consonant clusters:

| | |
|---|---|
| Initial | : Nil |
| Final | : Nil |
| Medial | : a) The first consonant tends to be a N/r/j/s; b) If the first is /ɖ/ then the third is L/g. |

**Reference:** Bhat (1967)

[39] There is one occurrence of a CCV syllable. CV, CVC type are the commonest.

# Yerava

**Ethnologue code:** ISO 639-3: yea
**Language classification:** Dravidian, Southern, Tamil-Kannada, Tamil-Kodagu, Tamil-Malayalam, Malayalam
**Alternate names:** Adiya, Adiyan, Yoruba, Yerava, Panjiri Yerava, Iryavula. Ravula
**Main region:** Karnataka; Kerala.

## 1 Consonant Phonemes

### 1.1 Inventory

| | Bilabial | Labio-dental | Dental | Alv | Retro | Palatal | Velar | Glottal |
|---|---|---|---|---|---|---|---|---|
| Plosive | p b | | t d | | ʈ ɖ | | k g | |
| Nasal | m | | | n | ɳ | ɲ | ŋ | |
| Trill | | | | r | | | | |
| Flap | | | | | ɽ | | | |
| Fricative | | v | | | | | | |
| Approx | | ʋ | | | | j | | |
| Lat Appr | | | | l | ɭ | | | |
| Affricate | | | | | | tʃ ʤ | | |

### 1.2 Distribution

a. Consonants do not occur word-finally.

b. / ʈ ɖ ɳ l ɭ j/ do not occur word-initially.

c. All consonants have geminates inter-vocalically.

# 2 Vowel Phonemes

## 2.1 Inventory

a. **Short**

| | FRONT | CENTRAL | BACK |
|---|---|---|---|
| Close | i | | u |
| Close-mid | e | | o |
| Open | | a | |

b. **Long**

| | FRONT | CENTRAL | BACK |
|---|---|---|---|
| Close | i: | | u: |
| Close-mid | e: | | o: |
| Open | | a: | ɑ: |

## 2.2 Distribution

a. Vowels occur in all positions in words.

b. Vowel sequences do not occur.

# 3 Consonant Allophones

## 3.1 Inventory

Inadequate data available.

## 3.2 Distribution

a. [s] < /c/ occurs inter-vocalically.

# 4 Vowel Allophones

## 4.1 Inventory

| | |
|---|---|
| [ ɪ ]: | /i/ |
| [ɛ ]: | /e/ |
| [ ɛ : ]: | /eː/ |
| [ ə ] [ ɐ ]: | /a/ |
| [ ɔ ]: | /o/ |
| [ ɔ : ]: | /o :/ |
| [ ʊ ]: | /u/ |

## 4.2 Distribution

a. [ɪ ʊ] < /i u/ occur before consonant clusters.

b. [ə] < /a/ occurs before retroflex stops.

c. [ɐ] < /a/ occurs before consonant clusters of non-retroflex stops.

d. [ɛ] < /e/ occurs medially before /r/.

e. [ɛ ː] < /eː/ occurs medially before /r m/.

f. [ɔ ɔ ː] < /o oː/ occur medially before /r/ and retroflex stops.

# 5 Syllable Structure

## 5.1 Canonical syllable structure

a. Word: (C) V (C)

b. Stem: (C) V (C) (C) (C)

## 5.2 Consonant clusters

Two-consonant clusters:

Initial : Nil.

Final for B type:

Medial : general.

Three-consonant clusters:

Initial : Nil

Final : Nil

Medial : -jŋg-, -jmb-, -rnd-.

**Reference:** Mallikarjun (1993)

Chapter 3

# INDO-ARYAN

# Assamese

**Ethnologue code:** ISO 639-3: asm
**Language classification:** Indo-Aryan, Eastern zone, Bengali-Assamese
**Alternate names:** Asambe, Asami, Asamiya
**Main region:** Assam, West Bengal, Meghalaya, Arunachal Pradesh

## 1 Consonant Phonemes

### 1.1 Inventory[1]

| | BILABIAL | ALVEOLAR | POST ALVEOLAR | PALATAL | VELAR | GLOTTAL |
|---|---|---|---|---|---|---|
| Plosive | p b<br>$p^h$ $b^ɦ$ | t̲ d̲<br>$t̲^h$ $d̲^ɦ$ | | | k g<br>$k^h$ $g^ɦ$ | |
| Nasal | m | n | | | ŋ | |
| Fricative | | s z | | | x | ɦ |
| Approx | w | | ɹ | j | | |
| Lat Appr | | l | | | | |

[1] Goswami (1966) has a trill, which I do not find attested in the standard Assamese speech around Nowgong and Dibrugarh, where the approximant is found.

## 1.2 Distribution

a. Consonants occur in all positions, with the following restrictions:
   i. /ŋ/ does not occur initially.
   ii. /w j/ do not occur as single segments, but in a cluster, as the second member, and contrast in that position with vowels /o u/ and /i/.

b. Geminates of the following consonants occur inter-vocalically: /p t̪ k b d̪ n ŋ l s z/.

# 2 Vowel Phonemes

## 2.1 Inventory

a. **Short**

| | FRONT | CENTRAL | BACK |
|---|---|---|---|
| Close | i | | u |
| Close-mid | e | | o |
| Open-mid | ɛ | | ɔ |
| Open | | a | ɒ |

b. **Nasal**

| | FRONT | CENTRAL | BACK |
|---|---|---|---|
| Close | ĩ ỹ | ʉ̃ | ũ |
| Close-mid | ẽ | ɵ̃ | õ |
| Open-mid | ɛ̃ | | ɔ̃ |
| Open | | ã | ɒ̃ |

## 2.2 Distribution

a. Vowels occur in all positions.

b. /ɛ ɒ o/ have restricted distribution:
   i. /ɛ/ occurs in closed syllables.

ii. /ɛ ɒ o/ freely vary with /e ɞ u/ in open syllables, when followed by /i u/ in the following syllable.

c. Sequences of two and three vowels occur commonly. Sequences of up to five vowels are attested in complex forms: /baiuei/ 'even air (Nom. Emph.)'.

# 3 Consonant Allophones

## 3.1 Inventory

| | Bilabial | Alveolar | Retroflex | Palatal | Glottal |
|---|---|---|---|---|---|
| Plosive | | | ʈ(t) ɖ(d)<br>ʈ$^{h}$ (t$^{h}$)<br>ɖ$^{ɦ}$ (d$^{ɦ}$) | | |
| Tap / Flap | | ɾ (r) | ɽ (r) | | |
| Fricative | ɸ(p$^{h}$)<br>β(b$^{ɦ}$) | | ʂ(s) | ç (x)<br>ś (s) | h(ɦ) |
| Approx | | ɹ (r) | ɭ~(l) | | |
| Affricate | p$^{\phi}$ (p$^{h}$)<br>b$^{\beta}$ (b$^{ɦ}$) | d·z(z)<br>dz$^{j}$(z) | | | |

## 3.2 Distribution

a. All consonants except /ŋ w x ɦ / are lengthened before /j r/ and after /r/.

b. Alveolar consonants except /s z/ are retroflexed after /r/.

c. Alveolar stops have pre-alveolar allophones before and after certain vowels.

d. Consonants have lip rounding when preceded or followed by Back vowels /ɔ o u/.

e. [ɸ β] < /p$^{h}$ b$^{ɦ}$/ occur word-finally, where they freely vary with affricates [p$^{\phi}$ b$^{\beta}$].

f. [dzʲ ] occurs before /j/.

g. [ d ˑ z ] < /z/ occurs after /r/.

h. [ç] </x/ occurs after /i e/.

i. [h]< /ɦ/ occurs after /x/.

j. [ɹ]< /r/ occurs utterance initially.

k. [ɾ] < /r/ occurs inter-vocalically.

l. [ɽ] < /r/ occurs before another consonant.

m. [ɭ] freely varies with /l/ between /r/ and a vowel.

# 4 Vowel Allophones

## 4.1 Inventory

| | |
|---|---|
| [ˀi] [i˃] : | / i / |
| [ei̯ ] [ˀe] [ë] : | / e / |
| [ɛe̯] [ˀɛ] [ɛ̈]: | /ɛ / |
| [ue̯] [ˀu] [ü]: | / u / |
| [oe̯] [ˀo] [ö]: | / o / |
| [ɞe̯] [ˀɞɔ] [ɞ̈]: | /ɞ/ |
| [ɒe̯] [ˀɒ] [ɒ̈]: | / ɒ / |
| [ae̯] [ˀa] [ä̞]: | / a / |

## 4.2 Distribution

a. All vowels except /i/ are diphthongized with [e̯] as the second member before Cj clusters.

b. All Front and Back vowels are slightly centralized after Cr cluster; /a/ is raised in that position.

c. Vowels are preglottalized word-initially.

# 5 Syllable Structure

## 5.1 Canonical syllable structure

(C)(C)(C)V(C)(C)

## 5.2 Consonant clusters

Two-consonant clusters:

Initial : (i) C + L/G; (ii) s + C.

Final : -mp –nt -nd -nd$^{ɦ}$ -ns -rt -rs -rz -rɦ

Medial : General.

Three-consonant clusters:

Initial : -spr -str -skr -smr

Final : Nil

Medial : N + C + r/j

**Reference:** Goswami (1966)

# Bagri

**Ethnologue code:** ISO 639-3: bgq
**Language classification:** Indo-European, Indo-Iranian, Indo-Aryan, Central zone, Rajasthani,
**Alternate names:** Bagari, Bagria, Bagris, Bahgri, Baorias
**Main region:** Punjab, Rajasthan, Haryana

## 1 Consonant Phonemes

### 1.1 Inventory

| | Bilabial | Dental | Alv | Post-Alv | Retroflex | Palatal | Velar | Glottal |
|---|---|---|---|---|---|---|---|---|
| Plosive | p b<br>$p^{h}$ $b^{ɦ}$ | t d<br>$t^{h}$ $d^{ɦ}$ | | | ʈ ɖ<br>$ʈ^{h}$ $ɖ^{ɦ}$ | | k g<br>$k^{h}$ $g^{ɦ}$ | |
| Nasal | m | | n | | ɳ | | | |
| Tap | | | r | | | | | |
| Flap | | | | | ɽ | | | |
| Fricative | | | s | | | ʃ | | h |
| Approx | w | | | | | j | | |
| Lat Appr | | | l | | ɭ | tʃ ʤ<br>$tʃ^{h}$ $ʤ^{ɦ}$ | | |

### 1.2 Distribution

a. Consonants occur in all positions, with the following restrictions:
   i. /ɳ ɭ ɽ/ do not occur initially.
   ii. /h/ does not occur medially and finally.

b. Geminates of consonants (e.g. /p t k n l/ etc.) occur; details not available.

# 2 Vowel Phonemes

## 2.1 Inventory

a. **Short**

| | FRONT | CENTRAL | BACK |
|---|---|---|---|
| Close | ɪ | | ʊ |
| Open-mid | | ə | |

b. **Long**

| | FRONT | CENTRAL | BACK |
|---|---|---|---|
| Close | iː | | uː |
| Close-mid | eː | | oː |
| Open-mid | ɛː | aː | ɔː |

c. **Nasal**

| | FRONT | CENTRAL | BACK |
|---|---|---|---|
| Close | ĩː ɪ̃ | | ũː ʊ̃ |
| Close-mid | ẽː | | õː |
| Open-mid | ɛ̃ː | ə̃ | ɔ̃ː |
| Open | | ãː | |

## 2.2 Distribution

a. Vowels occur in all positions.
b. Vowel sequences occur.

# 3 Consonant Allophones

**General:** a. Consonants are pronounced tense in the intervocalic position.
b. Aspiration is weaker in medial and final positions.

**Specific:** a. [ʋ] < /w/ occurs before front vowels.

# 4 Vowel Allophones

Allophonic details of vowels not available.

# 5 Syllable Structure

## 5.1 Canonical syllable structure

(C) (G)V(C) (C)

## 5.2 Consonant clusters

Two-consonant clusters:

| | | |
|---|---|---|
| Initial | : | C+G |
| Final | : | -N/r/s+S |
| Medial | : | General. |

# 6 Suprasegmentals

## 6.1 Tone

**Tonemes:**

a. High (H): ( ′ )

b. Low (L): ( ` )

c. Mid (M): (Unmarked)

E.g., /pér/ ‘put on’, /pèr/ ‘duration’, /per/ ‘leg’

**Reference:** Gusain (2000)

# Bengali

**Ethnologue code:** ISO 639-3: ben
**Language classification:** Indo-Aryan, Eastern zone, Bengali-Assamese
**Alternate names:** Banga-Bhasa, Bangala, Bangla
**Main region:** West Bengal, Assam, Jharkhand, Bihar, Delhi

## 1 Consonant Phonemes

### 1.1 Inventory[2]

| | BILABIAL | DENTAL | ALVEOLAR | POST-ALVEOLAR | RETROFLEX | PALATAL | VELAR | GLOTTAL |
|---|---|---|---|---|---|---|---|---|
| Plosive | p b<br>pʰ bʱ | t d<br>tʰ dʱ | | | ʈ ɖ<br>ʈʰ ɖʱ | | k g<br>kʰ gʱ | |
| Nasal | m | n | | | | | ŋ | |
| Tap | | | ɾ | | | | | |
| Fricative | | | | ʃ | | | | h |
| Approx | w | | | | | j | | |
| Lat Appr | | | l | | | | | |
| Affricate | | | | | | ʧ ʤ<br>ʧʰ ʤʱ | | |

### 1.2 Distribution

a. Consonants occur in all positions.

b. Geminates of consonants other than /ŋ h r/ occur inter-vocalically.

c. Homorganic voiced and voiceless consonants do not occur adjacently.

---

[2] The affricates and the fricative have been described with different places

# 2 Vowel Phonemes

## 2.1 Inventory

a. **Short**

| | FRONT | CENTRAL | BACK |
|---|---|---|---|
| Close | i | | u |
| Close-mid | e | | o |
| Open-mid | æ | ɞ | |
| Open | | a | |

b. **Nasal**

| | FRONT | CENTRAL | BACK |
|---|---|---|---|
| Close | ĩ | | ũ |
| Close-mid | ẽ | | õ |
| Open-mid | æ̃ | ɞ̃ | |
| Open | | ã | |

## 2.2 Distribution

a. Many occurrences of /ɞ/ and /o/ are unstable, i.e., they freely vary.

b. / ɞ̃ / freely varies with /ɞn/ : /pɞ̃tʃasi/ ~ /pɞntʃasi/ 'eighty five'.

c. Vowel sequences of two and three occur:

/ɞe ɞo æe̯ .../

/ae̯a̯ ae̯o ɞe̯o ɞe̯a ai̯a oi̯e ao̯a au̯a/

# 3 Consonant Allophones

## 3.1 Inventory

| | BILABIAL | DENTAL | RETROFLEX | VELAR |
|---|---|---|---|---|
| Plosive | p:(p) b:(b)<br>p$^{h}$: (p$^{h}$) b$^{ɦ}$: (b$^{ɦ}$) | t: (t) d: (d)<br>t$^{h}$: (t$^{h}$) d$^{ɦ}$ : (d$^{ɦ}$) | | |
| Nasal | m: (m) | n: (n) | | ŋ: (ŋ) |
| Tap / Flap | | | ɽ (ɖ) | |
| Fricative | ɸ (p$^{h}$) β(b$^{ɦ}$) | s(ʃ) | | |

## 3.2 Distribution

a. [ɽ] / < /ɖ / occurs inter-vocalically and in the Coda position when not preceded by /n/.

b. [s] < /ʃ/ occurs before / t t$^{h}$ n r /.

c. [ɸ β] < / p$^{h}$ b$^{h}$/ tend to occur inter-vocalically.

d. Bilabial and dental stops and nasals, and velar nasal are lengthened [p: p$^{h}$: b: b$^{ɦ}$: t: t$^{h}$: d: d$^{ɦ}$: m: n: ŋ: ] in the context of a single vowel preceding and /r/ following.

# 4 Vowel Allophones

## 4.1 Inventory

[e] : /æ /

[o] : /ɞ/

## 4.2 Distribution

a. Mid low vowels /æ ɞ / have raised allophones [e o] in the following contexts:

   i. When the following syllable has a high vowel / i u /:
   /æk/ 'one', [ekṭ u] 'a little'.

   ii. When they occur in non-initial syllables:
   /mɞl/ 'dirt' [ɞmol] 'pure', / æk/ 'one' [ɞnek] 'many'.

# 5 Syllable Structure

## 5.1 Canonical syllable structure[3]

(C)(C)(C)V(C)

## 5.2 Consonant clusters

Two-consonant clusters:

| | | |
|---|---|---|
| Initial | : | (i) S/N+r/l; (ii) s+S/n/r/l. |
| Final | : | Nil. |
| Medial | : | General. |

Three-consonant clusters:

| | | |
|---|---|---|
| Initial | : | /str/ |
| Final | : | Nil |
| Medial | : | General. |

**References:** Ferguson & Chowdhary (1960), Klaiman (1987)

[3] Three-consonant onset cluster is restricted to str-.

# Bhili[4]

**Ethnologue code:** ISO 639-3: bhb
**Language classification:** Indo-Aryan, Central zone, Bhil
**Alternate names:** Bhilbari, Bhilboli, Bhilla,Bhilodi, Vil, Bhagoria, Lengotia
**Main region:** Madhya Pradesh, Gujarat, Rajasthan, Maharashtra, Andhra Pradesh, Karnataka

## 1 Consonant Phonemes

### 1.1 Inventory

| | BILABIAL | LABIODENTAL | DENTAL | ALVEOLAR | RETROFLEX | PRE-PALATAL | PALATAL | VELAR | GLOTTAL |
|---|---|---|---|---|---|---|---|---|---|
| Plosive | p b<br>$p^h$ $b^ɦ$ | | t d<br>$t^h$ $d^ɦ$ | | ʈ ɖ<br>$ʈ^h$ $ɖ^ɦ$ | | | k g | |
| Nasal | m<br>$m^h$ | | n | | | | | | |
| Trill | | | | r | | | | | |
| Fricative | | | | s | | $ç^<$ | | | h |
| Approx | | ʋ | | | | | j | | |
| Lat Appr | | | | l | ɭ | | | | |
| Affricate | | | | ʦ ʣ<br>$ʣ^ɦ$ | | ʧ ʤ<br>$ʤ^ɦ$ | | | |

### 1.2 Distribution

a. Consonants occur in all positions, with the following restriction:

i. / ɭ / does not occur word-initially.

[4] Kulkarni (1976) posits $l^h$ $r^h$ $n^h$ as phonemes. As these, unlike $m^h$, do not occur word-initially, but only medially, we treat them as clusters i.e. l + h, r + h, n + h.

[ʷo ː ] [ʷo ˑ ] [ʷo] [o ː ] [o ˑ ]: /o/

[ə ː ] [ə ˑ ]: /ə/

[ɨ ː ] [ɨ ˑ ]: /ɨ/

[a̟ ː ] [a̟ ː ] [a̟] [a ː ] [a ˑ ]: /a/

## 4.2 Semivowels

[ i̯ ]: /j/

[ u̯ ]: /ʋ/

## 4.3 Distribution

a. Vowels are fully long in closed monosyllables.

b. Vowels are half long in final closed syllables in polysyllables.

c. The allophones with palatal and labial onglides [ ʲi ʲi ː ʷo̟ ː ʷo ˑ ʷo] < /i o/ occur in syllables without onsets.

d. The fronted allophones [e̟ e̟ˑ e̟ː a̟ a̟ˑ a̟ː] < /e a/ occur after palatal consonants /j, tʃ, dʒ/.

e. [ i̯ u̯ ] < /j ʋ/ occur in the coda position.

# 5 Syllable Structure

## 5.1 Canonical syllable structure

Initial: (C)V(C)(C)

Non-Initial: (C) (C)V(C)(C)

## 5.2 Consonant clusters

Two-consonant clusters:

Initial : Nil.

Final : Only the following 2 Consonant clusters are attested: (i) -nC (ii) -jC.

Medial : general

Three-consonant clusters:

Initial : Nil

Final : Nil

Medial : (i) –nCC-, -CCj-, -rndʒ-, -ɭmb-.

Four-consonant clusters:

Initial : Nil

Final : Nil

Medial : -nCCj-

**Reference:** Kulkarni (1976)

# Bhojpuri

**Ethnologue code:** ISO 639-3: bho
**Language classification:** Indo-Aryan, Eastern zone, Bihari
**Alternate names:** Bhojapuri, Bhozpuri, Bajpuri, Bihari, Deswali, Khotla, Piscimas
**Main region:** Bihar; Eastern Uttar Pradesh; Assam; Delhi; Madhya Pradesh; West Bengal. Also spoken in Mauritius, Nepal.

## 1 Consonant Phonemes

### 1.1 Inventory

| | Bilabial | Labiodental | Dental | Alveolar | Retroflex | Palatal | Velar | Glottal |
|---|---|---|---|---|---|---|---|---|
| Plosive | p b<br>pʰ bʱ | | t d<br>tʰ dʱ | | ʈ ɖ<br>ʈʰ ɖʱ | | k g<br>kʰ gʱ | |
| Nasal | m<br>mʱ | | n<br>nʱ | | | | ŋ | |
| Tap | | | | ɾ<br>ɾʱ | | | | |
| Fricative | | | s | | | | | h |
| Approx | | ʋ | | | | j | | |
| Lat Appr | | | | l<br>lʱ | | | | |
| Affricate | | | | | | ʧ ʤ<br>ʧʰ ʤʱ | | |

### 1.2 Distribution

a. Consonants occur in all positions with the following restrictions:
   i. Aspirated sonorants /mʱ nʱ ɾʱ lʱ/ and the velar nasal /ŋ/ do not occur word-initially.
   ii. /ŋ/ tends to occur with /g/.

b. Geminates of consonants other than /h/ occur inter-vocalically.

# 2 Vowel Phonemes[5]

## 2.1 Inventory

a. **Short**

| | FRONT | CENTRAL | BACK |
|---|---|---|---|
| Close | i | | u |
| Close-mid | e | | o |
| Open-mid | | ə | |

b. **Long**

| | FRONT | CENTRAL | BACK |
|---|---|---|---|
| Open | | aː | |

c. **Nasal**

| | FRONT | CENTRAL | BACK |
|---|---|---|---|
| Close | ĩ | | ũ |
| Close-mid | ẽ | | õ |
| Open-mid | ə̃ĩ | ə̃ | ə̃ũ |
| Open | | ãː | |

d. **Diphthongs /əi əu/**

## 2.2 Distribution

a. Vowel sequences occur.

Sufficient details not available.

[5] Vowel length distinction is neutralized in Bhojpuri, as in Magahi. Most vowels have slightly long realizations.

# 3 Consonant Allophones

## 3.1 Inventory

[b]: /w/

[ɟ]: /j/

## 3.2 Distribution

a. [b] < /w/ and [ɟ] < /j/ occur word-initially.

# 4 Vowel Allophones

**General:**

Vowels are reduced in length non-finally in unstressed positions.

**Specific:**

a. /əj/ and /əw/ are realized as [əi̯] and [əu̯] before a vowel.

Adequate allophonic details of vowels are not available.

# 5 Syllable Structure

## 5.1 Canonical syllable structure

(C)V (C) (C)

## 5.3 Consonant clusters

Two-consonant clusters:

Initial : Nil

Final : N+ S, s+S

Medial : General.

Three-consonant clusters: Nil

**Reference:** Verma (2003)

# Brokskat

**Ethnologue code:** ISO 639-3: bkk
**Language classification:** Indo-Aryan, Northwestern zone, Dardic
**Alternate names:** Brokpa, Brokpa of Dah-Hanu, Dokskat, Kyango
**Main region:** Jammu and Kashmir

## 1 Consonant Phonemes

### 1.1 Inventory

| | BILABIAL | LABIODENTAL | DENTAL | ALV. | ALV. PALATAL | RETR. | PAL | VELAR | PHAR | GLOT |
|---|---|---|---|---|---|---|---|---|---|---|
| Plosive | p b $p^h$ | | t d $t^h$ | t̠ d̠ $\underline{t}^h$ | | | | k g $k^h$ | q | |
| Nasal | m | | n | | | | | ŋ | | |
| Trill | | | r | | | | | | | |
| Fricative | | f v | s z | | ʃ ʒ | ʂ ʐ | | x ɣ | | h |
| Approx | | | | | | | j | | | |
| Lat Appr. | | | l | | | | | | | |
| Affricate | | | | ts | | | | | | |

### 1.2 Distribution

a. Consonants occur in all positions, with the following restrictions:
   i. Aspirated stops and / f z ts g x ɣ ʃ ʒ / do not occur in the final position.

b. Lexical free variation is attested between [$t^h$] ~ [ʈʂ], [r] ~ [ʒ], and [l] ~ [$l^ɦ$].

# 2 Vowel Phonemes

## 2.1 Inventory

a. **Short**

| | FRONT | CENTRAL | BACK |
|---|---|---|---|
| Close | i | | u |
| Close-mid | e | | o |
| Open-mid | | a | |

b. **Long**

| | FRONT | CENTRAL | BACK |
|---|---|---|---|
| Close | iː | | uː |
| Close-mid | eː | | oː |
| Open-mid | | aː | |

## 2.2 Distribution

a. Vowels occur in all positions, with the following restrictions:

   i. Length distinction is neutralized word-finally: Half-long vowels occur in the final position.

b. Vowel sequences are found to occur restrictedly: /ei aːi/ are attested.

# 3 Consonant Allophones

## 3.1 Inventory

| | BILABIAL | RETROFLEX |
|---|---|---|
| Plosive | | ʈ (t)<br>ɖ (d) |

| | | |
|---|---|---|
| Approx | w (v) | |
| Lat Approx | | ɭ (l) |

## 3.2 Distribution

a. The retroflex allophones [ʈ ɖ] < /t d/ occur following retroflex consonants.

b. The retroflex lateral allophone [ɭ] < /l/ occurs following retroflex and palatal consonants.

c. The bilabial allophone [w] < /v/ occurs word-finally.

# 4 Vowel Allophones

a. Word-finally length distinction among vowels is neutralized, with only half-long vowels occurring in that position.

b. [ɐ] < /a/ occurs when flanked by consonants (in open or closed syllables).

# 5 Syllable Structure

## 5.1 Canonical syllable structure

(C) (C) (C) V (C) (C)

Words of up to seven syllables are attested.

## 5.2 Consonant clusters

Two-consonant clusters:

Initial : S + r/ʃ/ʂ/ʐ; s + S/N; L + d/c/z/g

Final : b/k/g/h/m/ŋ (all single instances) +s

Medial : General.

Three-consonant clusters:

Initial : C1 = s/z/r; C2 = Pl; C3 = r (and single instances of v/j)

Final : Nil

Medial : General

Four-consonant clusters:

Initial : Nil

Final : Nil

Medial : -ksbr-, -qskj-, -mskj-.

**References:** Ramaswamy (1982, 1975)

# Chakma

**Ethnologue code:** ISO 639-3: ccp
**Language classification:** Indo-European, Indo-Iranian, Indo-Aryan, Eastern zone, Bengali-Assamese
**Alternate names:** Sangma, Sakma, Takam
**Main region:** Southeast Chittagong Hills area, and Chittagong City. (Also spoken in Bangladesh)

## 1 Consonant Phonemes

### 1.1 Inventory

| | Bilabial | Dental | Alv. | Post-Alv. | Palatal | Velar | Glottal |
|---|---|---|---|---|---|---|---|
| Stop | p b<br>$p^h$ $b^{ɦ}$ | t d<br>$t^h$ $d^{ɦ}$ | | | | k g<br>$k^h$ $g^{ɦ}$ | |
| Nasal | m | | n | | | ŋ | |
| Trill | | | | ɾ | | | |
| Fricative | | | | ʃ | | | h |
| Approx | w | | | | j | | |
| Lat. Approx. | | | l | | tʃ dʒ<br>$tʃ^h$ $dʒ^{ɦ}$ | | |

### 1.2 Distribution

a. Consonants occur in all positions with the following restrictions:
   i. / k $k^h$ tʃ $tʃ^h$ ŋ/ does not occur initially.
   ii. /ʃ/ does not occur medially.
   iii. /b $b^{ɦ}$ d $d^{ɦ}$ g $g^{ɦ}$ ʃ h j w/ do not occur finally.

b. Geminates of the following consonants occur inter-vocalically: /p $p^h$ t $t^h$ tʃ $tʃ^h$ k $k^h$/.

# 2 Vowel Phonemes

## 2.1 Inventory

a. **Short**

| | FRONT | CENTRAL | BACK |
|---|---|---|---|
| Close | ɪ | | ʊ |
| Mid | ɛ | | o |
| Open | æ | | ɒ |

b. **Long**

| | FRONT | CENTRAL | BACK |
|---|---|---|---|
| Open | | | ɑː |

c. **Diphthongs:** /ɛɪ aɪ ɒɪ oɪ uɪ/

## 2.2 Distribution

a. All the vowels occur in all the positions.

b. Vowel sequences are allowed morpheme internally, but not across morphemes, following derivational affixes and some inflections, except for case suffixation and compounding.

# 3 Consonant Allophones

## 3.1 Inventory

General: Single voiceless stops are geminated intervocalically.

# 4 Vowel Allophones

Data not available.

# 5 Syllable Structure

## 5.1 Canonical syllable structure: (C) (G) V (C)

Conditions: a. $C_1$ is any consonant other than /k kʰ ʧ ʧʰ ŋ/.

## 5.2 Consonant Clusters

Two-consonant clusters:

Initial : C+G (subject to the above condition about $C_1$)

Final : Nil

Medial : General.

Three-consonant clusters:

Medial : Nil (data not available in the source)

# 6 Suprasegmentals

## 6.1 Tones

Data not available.

**Reference:** Bardhan (1999)

# Dogri

**Ethnologue code:** ISO 639-3: dgo
**Language classification:** Indo-Aryan, Northern zone, Western Pahari
**Alternate names:** Dhogaryali, Dogari, Dongari, Dogri, Tokkaru
**Main region:** Jammu and Kashmir; Chandigarh

## 1 Consonant Phonemes

### 1.1 Inventory

| | BILABIAL | LABIO-DENTAL | DENTAL | RETRO-FLEX | PALATAL | VELAR | GLOTTAL |
|---|---|---|---|---|---|---|---|
| Plosive | p b<br>pʰ | | t d<br>tʰ | ʈ ɖ<br>ʈʰ | | k g | |
| Nasal | m | | n | ɳ | (ɲ) | ŋ | |
| Trill | | | r | | | | |
| Flap | | | | ɽ | | | |
| Fricative | | (f) | s(z) | | | x ɣ | h |
| Approx | w | | | | j | | |
| Lat Approx | | | l | | | | |
| Affricate | | | | | tʃ dʒ<br>tʃʰ | | |

### 1.2 Distribution

a. Consonants occur in all positions, with the following restrictions:
   i. /ɳ ɽ/ do not occur in the initial position.
   ii. /w j/ do not occur finally.
b. All consonants except /s ɾ ɽ ɳ/ can be geminated inter-vocalically.

# 2 Vowel Phonemes

## 2.1 Inventory

a. **Short**

| | FRONT | CENTRAL | BACK |
|---|---|---|---|
| Close | ɪ | | ʊ |
| Open-mid | | ə | |

b. **Long**

| | FRONT | CENTRAL | BACK |
|---|---|---|---|
| Close | i: | | u: |
| Close-mid | e: | | o: |
| Open-mid | ɛ: | | ɔ: |
| Open | | a: | |

c. **Nasal**

| | FRONT | CENTRAL | BACK |
|---|---|---|---|
| Close | ĩ : | | ũ: |
| Close-mid | (ẽ:) | | (õ:) |
| Open-mid | ɛ̃: | | ɔ̃: |
| Open | | ã: | |

## 2.2 Distribution

a. Vowels occur in all positions, with the following restriction:
   i. /ɪ ʊ ə/ occur rarely in the final position.

b. Sequences of two or three vowels occur, with the following restriction:
   i. /ɛ/ does not occur as the first member of the sequence, and /e/ occurs as the first member only with /i/.

c. /i/ freely varies with /e/ when accompanied with Low-Rising tone.

d. / ẽ: / and / ɛ̃: / and / õ: / and / ɔ̃: / vary freely.

# 3 Consonant Allophones

## 3.1 Inventory

| | LABIODENTAL | RETROFLEX | PALATAL | VELAR |
|---|---|---|---|---|
| Flap | | ɽ (ɖ) | | |
| Fricative | f (p) | | ʤ (ʧ) | ɣ (k) |

## 3.2 Distribution

a. [f] < /p/ and [ʤ] < /ʧ/ occur in word-final position.

b. [ɽ] < /ɖ/ and [ɣ] < /k/ occur in the intervocalic position.

# 4 Vowel Allophones

## 4.1 Inventory

/e/ : [ ĕ ]
/ɛ/ : [ ɛ̆ ], [ɛ̞ : ˑ ]
/a:/ : [ ă̞ ]
/ɔ:/ : [ ɔ̝ :]
/o:/ : [ o̝ :]
/ʊ/ : [ u̝ ]
/i:/ : [i ˑ]

## 4.2 Distribution

a. The shortened allophones [ĕ ɛ̆ ă] occur word-finally. [ĕ] also occurs following a vowel.

b. The shortened allophone [i ˑ] occurs with Low-Rising tone.

c. The raised allophones [ɔ̝ : o̝ :] occur with High tone

d. The raised allophone [ ʊ̝ ] occurs with Low and Mid tones.

e. The lowered and extra-long allophone [ɛ̞ : ˑ] occurs with Low tone.

# 5 Syllable structure

## 5.1 Canonical syllable structure[6]

(C) (C) V (C) (C)

## 5.2 Consonant Clusters

Two-consonant clusters:

Initial : s+S/L, S + ɽ/l/Retr, N + ɽ , Sib + N

Final : a. Monosyllables: l+S/F, r+S/F/N, s+S/N, N+ SH

b. Polyyllables: Rare, e.g. r+g/d/t, s + t.

Medial : General.

Three-consonant clusters:

Medial : General

# 6 Suprasegmentals

## 6.1 Tone

a. Low-Rising : LH

b. High-Falling : HL

c. Mid tone : M

E.g., /sàːɽiː/ 'ours', /sáːɽiː/ 'saree', /sāːɽiː/ 'burnt'

**References:** Ghai (1991), Bahri (2001), Kaul (2012)

[6] 1. Words of up to four syllables are found to occur.

2. Final consonant clusters in polysyllabic words are much more restricted than in monosyllabic words.

# Garhwali

**Ethnologue code:** ISO 639-3: gbm
**Language classification:** Indo-Aryan, Northern zone, Garhwali
**Alternate names:** Gadhavali, Gadhawala, Gadwahi, Gashwali, Godauli, Gorwali, Gurvali, Girwali
**Main region:** Uttaranchal; Himachal Pradesh.

## 1 Consonants Phonemes

### 1.1 Inventory[7]

| | Bilabial | Dental | Alveolar | Retroflex | Alveo-Palatal | Palatal | Velar | Glottal |
|---|---|---|---|---|---|---|---|---|
| Stop | p b<br>pʰ bʱ | t d<br>tʰ dʱ | | ʈ ɖ<br>ʈʰ ɖʱ | | | k g<br>kʰ gʱ | |
| Nasal | m | | n | ɳ | | | | |
| Trill | | | r | | | | | |
| Fricative | | | s | | | | | h |
| Approx | w | | | | | j | | |
| Lat Appr | | | l | | | | | |
| Affricate | | | | | | tʃ dʒ<br>tʃʰ dʒʱ | | |

[7] Chandrasekahar (1970) treats voiceless and voiced aspirated stop phones as clusters of voiceless stops and /h/, but does not provide adequate data. As there are limited data for complex onsets, we resort to the non-cluster analysis here. The retroflex nasal /ɳ/ has been added on the basis of evidence from data collection reported in fn. 10.

## 1.2 Distribution

a. Consonants occur in all positions, with the following restrictions:
   i. /h/ does not occur in the word-final position.
   ii. /ɳ/ does not occur in the word-initial position.

b. Geminates of consonants occur; examples for /b n l/ are attested; but the data are inadequate.

# 2 Vowel phonemes

## 2.1 Inventory[8]

**a. Short:**

| | FRONT | CENTRAL | BACK |
|---|---|---|---|
| Close | i | | u |
| Mid | e | | o |
| Open | | a | |

**b. Long:**

| | FRONT | CENTRAL | BACK |
|---|---|---|---|
| Close | iː | | uː |
| Open | | aː | |

**c. Nasal:**

| | FRONT | CENTRAL | BACK |
|---|---|---|---|
| Close | ĩ ĩː | | ũ ũː |
| Mid | ẽ | | õ |
| Open | | ã ãː | |

[8] The mid vowels /e o/ are phonetically long, but do not have contrastive length. Besides, there is evidence that Garhwali has surface diphthongs; however, there is need for further analysis to establish surface diphthongs as phonemes.

## 2.2 Distribution

a. Vowels occur in all positions.

b. Vowel sequences occur.

# 3 Consonant allophones

## 3.1 Inventory

**General:** Consonants tend to be geminated following stressed vowels.

**Specific:**

| | BILABIAL | RETROFLEX | VELAR | GLOTTAL |
|---|---|---|---|---|
| Stop | | | | ʔ(k) |
| Nasal | | ɳ(n) | | |
| Flap | | ɽ (ɖ)[9]<br>ɽ$^h$ (ɖ$^h$) | | |
| Fricative | ɸ(p)<br>β(b) | | x (k)<br>ɣ(g) | |
| Lat Appr | | ɭ(l) | | |

## 3.2 Distribution

a. The bilabial fricative allophones [ɸ β] < /p b/ occur inter-vocalically.

b. The velar fricative allophones [x ɣ] < /k g/ tend to occur word-finally and inter-vocalically.

c. The glottal stop allophone [ʔ] < /k/ tends to occur in the coda position when followed by the trill /r/.

d. The retroflex nasal allophone [ɳ] < /n/ occurs word-finally and inter-vocalically (in addition to the pre-retroflex stop position).

[9] The flap allophones are based on observed data and analysis of Garhwali carried out at the Centre for Linguistics, Jawaharlal Nehru University, New Delhi 2006-07.

e. The retroflex lateral allophone [ɭ] < /l/ occurs when geminated (in stressed syllables).

# 4 Vowel allophones

## 4.1 Inventory

| | |
|---|---|
| [ï] [i̯]~[j] [ʏ] | : /i/ |
| [ü] [u̯]~[w] | : /u/ |
| [e:] [ɛ:] | : /e/ |
| [o̯] [ɒ:] [ɔ:] | : /o/ |
| [aɐ] [ɐ] [æ] [ə] | : /a/ |

## 4.2 Distribution:

a. The 'elsewhere' full vowel allophones of the five vowels occur in stressed positions.
b. Non-final unstressed vowels are realized as centralized [ï ü ɛ: ɐ] < /i u e a/; The desyllabified mid back vowel allophone [o̯] </o/ occurs when unstressed and immediately preceded by another vowel, and the lowered and lengthened allophone [ɒ:] < /o/ occurs when unstressed and in the context h_i.
c. The rounded high front vowel allophone [ʏ] < /i/ occurs when followed by /n/ in monosyllabic words.
d. The low-mid back allophone [ɔ:] < /o/ occurs when immediately followed by one of the following: /u m d ɖ/.

# 5 Syllables

## 5.1 Canonical Syllable Structure

(C) V (C) (C)

## 5.2 Consonant Clusters[10]

Two-consonant clusters:

Initial : Nil

Final : N+S, L+S

Medial : General.

Three-consonant clusters:

Initial : Nil

Medial : Final + initial consonants

Final : Nil.

**Reference:** Chandrasekhar (1970).

[10] The statement about the canonical syllable structure is based on the data on Garhwali collected at the Centre for Linguistics, Jawaharlal Nehru University, in 2006, from Mr Ramanand at J. N. U. and at village Thalisan, District Pauri, Uttaranchal. I have access to the data from a field report by Radhika Gopalkrishnan.

# Gojri

**Ethnologue code:** ISO 639-3: gju
**Language classification:** Indo-Aryan, Central zone, Rajasthani
**Alternate names:** Gujuri, Gujer, Gujar, Gujjari, Gurjar, Gogri, Gujuri
**Main region:** Jammu and Kashmir; Himachal Pradesh; Uttaranchal.

## 1 Consonant phonemes

### 1.1 Inventory

| | BIL. | LABIO-DENTAL | DENTAL | ALV. | POST-ALV. | RETR. | PAL. | VELAR | GLOT |
|---|---|---|---|---|---|---|---|---|---|
| Plosive | p b<br>p$^{h}$ | | t d<br>t$^{h}$ | | | ʈ ɖ<br>ʈ$^{h}$ | | k g<br>k$^{h}$ | |
| Nasal | m | | n | | | ɳ | | | |
| Trill | | | | r | | | | | |
| Nasal Flap | | | | | | ɽ̃ | | | |
| Flap | | | | | | ɽ | | | |
| Fricative | | f | | s z | ʃ | | | x ɣ | h |
| Approx | w | (ʋ) | | | | | j | | |
| Lat Appr | | | | l | ɭ | | | | |
| Affricate | | | | | | | tʃ dʒ<br>dʒ$^{h}$ | | |

### 1.2 Distribution

a. Consonants occur in all positions, with the following restrictions:
   i. /h w j/ do not occur word-finally.

ii. /ŋ ɳ ɽ ɭ/ do not occur word-initially.
iii. /h/ does not occur medially.

b. All the stops except /q/, the nasals /m n /, /s/ and /j/ can be geminated following the short vowels /ɪ ə ʊ/ and preceding any vowel.

# 2 Vowel phonemes

## 2.1 Inventory

a. **Short:**

| | FRONT | CENTRAL | BACK |
|---|---|---|---|
| Close | ɪ | | ʊ |
| Open-mid | | ə | |

b. **Long:**

| | FRONT | CENTRAL | BACK |
|---|---|---|---|
| Close | i: | | u: |
| Close-mid | e: | | o: |
| Open-mid | ɛ: | | ɔ: |
| Open | | a: | |

c. **Nasal:**

| | FRONT | CENTRAL | BACK |
|---|---|---|---|
| Close | ɪ̃ ĩ: | | ũ ʊ̃: |
| Close-mid | ẽ: | | õ: |
| Open-mid | ɛ̃ : | | ɔ̃: |
| Open | | ã: | |

## 2.2 Distribution

a. Vowels occur in all positions, with the following restriction:

The short vowels /ɪ ʊ ə/ do not occur word-finally.

b. Two vowel sequences occur with the following restrictions:
   i. /ɛ:/ and /ɔ:/ do not occur in vowel sequences.
   ii. /ɪ/ does not occur as the first member.
   iii. /ə a/ do not occur as the second member.

# 3 Consonant allophones

## 3.1 Inventory

**General:**

a. Half-long and long allophones.

**Specific:**

[g<] < /g/

[ɳ] < /ɽ̃/

## 3.2 Distribution

**General:**

a. All the consonants except [q ɽ̃ f ʃ h z x ɣ r ɭ w j/ have half-long and fully long allophones. The half-long allophones occur after long vowels /i: u: e: ɛ: o: œ a:/ in polysyllables. The long allophones occur after short vowels /ɪ ʊ ə/ in polysyllables.

b. The voiced post-velar [g<] < /g/ occurs between back vowels.

c. [ɳ] < /ɽ̃/ occurs before homorganic retroflex stops.

# 4 Vowel allophones

## 4.1 Inventory

Details not available.

# 5 Syllable structure

## 5.1 Canonical syllable structure

(C) (G/r) V (C) (C)

## 5.2 Consonant Clusters

Two-consonant clusters:

Initial : C + r/G

Final : (i) N/ Fr + S

(ii) r/l + Stop/N/Fr

(iii) Y/L¹ɳ + n/k

(iv) f/x + t.

Medial : General

Three-consonant clusters:

Initial : Nil
Final : Nil

Medial : $C_1$ $C_2$ $C_3$

(1) $C_{1\,=\,\alpha}$Place, $C_{2\,=\,\alpha}$Place, $C_3 = r/j$ (2) $C_1C_2$ are as in the word-final position.

# 6 Suprasegmentals

## 6.1 Tone

Tonemes:

High: H ( ´ )

Low: L ( ` )

Mid: M (unmarked)

E.g., /tə́ki:/ 'slope', /tèki:/ 'covered', /teki:/ 'raised' and between two rivers',

**References:** Sharma (1979)

# Gujarati

**Ethnologue code:** ISO 639-3: guj
**Language classification:** Indo-Aryan, Central zone, Gujarati
**Alternate names:** Gujrathi, Gujerati, Gujerathi
**Main region:** Gujarat; Maharashtra; Rajasthan.

## 1 Consonant phonemes

### 1.1 Inventory

| | BILABIAL | DENTAL | ALV. | POST-ALV. | RETROFLEX | PALATAL | VELAR | GLOTTAL |
|---|---|---|---|---|---|---|---|---|
| Plosive | p b<br>p$^{h}$ b$^{ɦ}$ | t d<br>t$^{h}$ d$^{ɦ}$ | | | ʈ ɖ<br>ʈ$^{h}$ ɖ$^{ɦ}$ | | k g<br>k$^{h}$ g$^{ɦ}$ | |
| Nasal | m | | n | | ɳ | ɲ | ŋ | |
| Tap | | | ɾ | | | | | |
| Fricative | | | s (z) | ʃ | | | | ɦ |
| Approx | w | | | | | j | | |
| Lat Appr | | | l | | ɭ | | | |
| Affricate | | | | | | tʃ dʒ<br>tʃ$^{h}$ dʒ$^{ɦ}$ | | |

### 1.2 Distribution

a. Consonants occur in all positions in the word, with the following restriction:
   i. /ɭ ɳ/ do not occur initially.

b. Geminates occur medially (inter-vocalically) except /ɳŋ ɭ ʃ ɦ/.

c. Consonant clusters are found mainly in loanwords from Sanskrit, English, Arabic and Persian.

d. / z / occurs in the borrowed vocabulary of some speakers.

e. / z / ~ /dʒ/ or / dʒʱ/ variation is found in the speech of some speakers.

f. /ʃ/ ~ / s / variation occurs in some dialects.

g. / s / ~ / ɦ/ variation occurs in some dialects.

# 2 Vowel phonemes

## 2.1 Inventory

**a. Short**

| | FRONT | CENTRAL | BACK |
|---|---|---|---|
| Close | i | | u |
| Close-mid | e | | o |
| Open-mid | (ɛ) | ə | (ɔ) |
| Open | | a | |

**b. Nasal**

| | FRONT | CENTRAL | BACK |
|---|---|---|---|
| Close | ĩ | | ũ |
| Close-mid | ẽ | | õ |
| Open-mid | (ɛ̃) | ə̃ | (ɔ̃) |
| Open | | ã | |

## 2.2 Distribution

a. Vowels occur in all positions, with the following restriction:

i. /ɛ ɔ/ do not occur finally in monosyllables and occur infrequently in general.

b. Murmur vowels show contrast in some varieties. They have allophonic status in all varieties.

c. Most speakers do not show a contrast between /e/ and /ɛ/ and between /o/ and /ɔ/.

d. Vowel sequences of two and three occur in all positions.

# 3 Consonant allophones

## 3.1 Inventory

[ v ] < /w/

[ ɽ ] < /ɖ/

## 3.2 Distribution

a. [ v ] < /w/ occurs before vowels and after / r j /.

b. [ɽ] < /ɖ/ occurs inter-vocalically, and in the coda position, provided there is no nasal consonant before and any of the following consonants after: /ɖ ɳ ɭ r/.

# 4 Vowel allophones

## 4.1 Inventory

[ɪ] [i:] : /i/

[e̞] [e:] : /e/

[ʊ] [u:] : /u/

[o̞] [o:] : /o/

[ɜ] [ə:] : /ə/

[a:] : /a/

## 4.2 Distribution

a. Vowels are lower in open syllables [ɪ e̞ ɜ o̞ ʊ] </ i e ə o u /.

b. Vowels are longer in final syllables and when nasalized:

/ i: e: ə: a: o: u: /. E.g.,

| | | | |
|---|---|---|---|
| [pəɖo:ʃ] | 'neighbourhood' | [ pəɖo ʃ i: ] | 'neighbour' |
| [kadʒi:] | 'judge' | [ kã:dʒi: ] | 'porridge' |

# 5 Syllable structure

## 5.1 Canonical syllable structure

(C)(C)(C)V(C)(C)

## 5.2 Consonant Clusters

Two-consonant clusters:

Initial : (i) sp- st- sk- sp$^h$- st$^h$- sk$^h$ (st
(ii) sm- sn- sw- sr-
(iii) C+ w / j / l / r

Final : S+ S, r +s / ʃ, S + HS.
Medial : general.

Three-consonant clusters:

Initial : str-, spr-, smr-.

Final : Nil

Medial : General (inadequate data available).

# 6 Suprasegmentals

The presence of murmur in Gujarati vowels may be treated as a suprasegmental (Modi 1989). As Mistry (1997) notes, the loss of h leads to the emergence of murmured vowels in casual and rapid speech. E.g.

| Formal | Colloquial | |
|---|---|---|
| / hisab / | [i̤ sa : b] | 'account' |
| / humlo: / | [ṳmlo] | 'attack' |
| / hat$^{h}$ / | [a̤ : t $^{h}$] | 'hand' |
| / wəhelũ/ | [vɛ̤ lũ] | 'early' |
| / pəholũ/ | [pɔ̤ lũ] | 'broad' |
| / bəhar/ | [ba̤r] | 'outside' |
| / ʃ ahukar/ | [ ʃɑ̤wkar] | 'banker' |
| / məhino / | [mə̤ jno] | 'month' |

There are morphological exceptions to the loss of / h /.

The loss of aspiration in voiced stops also leads to murmured vowels, e.g.

| | |
|---|---|
| /ɖag$^{h}$ / ~ vs [ɖa̤g] | 'blot' |
| /lab$^{h}$ / ~ /la̤b] | 'gain' |

**References:** Mistry (1999), Modi (1983), Pandit (1975)

# Haryanvi

**Ethnologue code:** ISO 639-3: bgc
**Language classification:** Indo-Aryan, Central zone, Western Hindi
**Alternate names:** Bangri, Bangru, Haryani, Desari, Chamarwa, Jatu
**Main region:** Haryana; Punjab

## 1 Consonant phonemes

### 1.1 Inventory

| | Bilabial | Dental | Alveolar | Retroflex | Palatal | Velar | Glottal |
|---|---|---|---|---|---|---|---|
| Plosive | p b<br>pʰ bʱ | t d<br>tʰ dʱ | | ʈ ɖ<br>ʈʰ ɖʱ | | k g<br>kʰ gʱ | |
| Nasal | m | n | | ɳ | | ŋ | |
| Tap/ Flap | | | ɾ | ɽ | | | |
| Fricative | | | s | | | | ɦ |
| Approx | w | | | | j | | |
| Lat Appr | | | l | ɭ | | | |
| Affricate | | | | | tʃ dʒ<br>tʃʰ dʒʱ | | |

### 1.2 Distribution

a. Consonants occur in all positions, with the following restriction:
   i. /ɳ ŋ ɭ ɽ/ do not occur initially.
   ii. /j w/ do not occur finally.

b. Geminates of consonants other than /ɳ ŋ ɭ ɽ/ occur inter-vocalically.

# 2 Vowel phonemes

## 2.1 Inventory

a. **Short**

| | FRONT | CENTRAL | BACK |
|---|---|---|---|
| Close | ɪ ï | | ü ʊ |
| Open -mid | | ə | |

b. **Long**

| | FRONT | CENTRAL | BACK |
|---|---|---|---|
| Close | i: | | u: |
| Close-mid | e: | | o: |
| Open-mid | æ:[11] | | ɔ: |
| Open | | a: | |

c. **Nasal:**

| | FRONT | CENTRAL | BACK |
|---|---|---|---|
| Close | ĩ: ĩ | | ʊ̃ ũ: |
| Close-mid | ẽ: | | õ: |
| Open-mid | æ̃: | ə̃ | ɔ̃: |
| Open | | ã: | |

## 2.2 Distribution

a. Long vowels occur in all positions.

b. Short vowels do not occur finally.

c. Vowel sequences of two occur medially and finally. Sequences having short vowels in the final position do not occur. Vowel sequences of

[11] The vowel is below open-mid.

three to five vowels occur finally. These vowel sequences result from word-formation. /a:ɪ e:/ /ɔ: ɪ e:/ /a:ɪ ɔ:/ /ʊa: ɪe:/ /ʊa: ɪɔ:/ /ʊa: ɪe:e:/ /ʊa: ɪɔ:e/.

# 3 Consonant allophones

## 3.1 Inventory

| | ALVEOLAR | RETROFLEX | GLOTTAL |
|---|---|---|---|
| Fricative | ɾʱ (ɾ) | ɽʱ (ɾ) | h (ɦ) |

## 3.2 Distribution

**General:**

a. Word finally,
   i. Aspiration is weakened.
   ii. Voicing in voiced consonants is partially lost.

b. Before / ï / consonants are palatalized: [kʲila] 'fort', [sʲira] 'end'.

c. Before back vowels consonants are slightly labialized [sʷu:r] 'pig' [sʷo:r] 'noise' /tʷük/ 'a little'.

d. Consonants are released in the coda position, except when followed by /j h / or by homorganic consonants.

e. Consonants are slightly lengthened inter-vocalically following long vowels: - e.g. [si:p ˑ i:] 'shell', [la:k ˑ əɽ] 'wood'.

**Specific:**

a. / ɾ / is pronounced as a 'fricativized' tap [ ɾʱ ] inter-vocalically and a retroflexed 'fricative' [ɽʱ] before retroflex stops, e.g. [a:ɾʱa:] 'a saw'; [kəɽʱa:] 'hard'.

b. [h]</ɦ/ occurs finally and after voiceless consonants, e.g. [goh] 'lizard'; [pətᵊho:r] 'leaves for fodder'.

# 4 Vowel allophones

## 4.1 Inventory

[ï ]: /ɨ/
[ ü̞ ]: /ü /
[ɛ]: /ə/
[o̞:] /o:/

## 4.2 Distribution

a. [o̞:] /o:/ occurs before /n ɳ/ optionally preceded by /ɦ/.
b. [ ü̞ ] < /ü/ occurs before /ɦ/ optionally preceded by /s/.
c. [ɛ] < /ə/ occurs before /ɦ/ in the coda position or when it (/ɦ/) is followed by /ə/. [kɛh] 'say (Imp.)'; [nɛhər] 'canal'.

# 5 Syllable structure

## 5.1 Canonical syllable structure[12]

(C) (C) (C) V (C) (C) (C)

## 5.2 Consonant clusters[13]

Two-consonant clusters:

| | | |
|---|---|---|
| Initial | : | Cj- Ch- (pj nh etc.) |
| Final | : | -Cj, -Ch, N + S (lj tj nh nt mp etc.) |
| Medial | : | general. |

[12] The onset and coda clusters are restricted consonant clusters.

[13] a. Initial consonants in medial clusters are released except when followed by /j/ or /h/ or homorganic consonants (in N + S or S + hom. S. /mp ŋk/ or /tt gg/ etc.). b. Medially disallowed sequences: Aspirate+Aspirate; Flap + Flap.

Three-consonant clusters:

| | | |
|---|---|---|
| Initial | : | Crj- Chj- |
| Final | : | Chj e.g., /ka: lhj/ 'tomorrow/ yesterday'. |
| Medial | : | General. (These result from word-formation processes. E.g. /sa:ʈ ʰjma:/ 'sixteen'). |

**References:** J. D. Singh (1970)

# Hindi[14]

**Ethnologue code:** ISO 639-3: hin
**Language clasiification:** Indo-European, Western Hindi, Hindustani
**Alternate names:** Khari Boli, Khadi Boli
**Main region: Throughout northern India, Rajasthan; Punjab; Madhya Pradesh**

## 1 Consonant Phonemes

### 1.1 Inventory[15]

| | Bilabial | Lab-Dental | Dental | Alv | Post-Alv | Retroflex | Palatal | Velar | Uvu. | Glottal |
|---|---|---|---|---|---|---|---|---|---|---|
| Plosive | p b<br>pʰ bʱ | | t d<br>tʰ dʱ | | | t d<br>tʰ dʱ | | k g<br>kʰ gʱ | (q) | |
| Nasal | m | | | n | | | | (ŋ) | | (ŋ) |
| Nasal Flap | | | | | | ɽ̃ | | | | |
| Tap | | | | ɾ | | | | | | |
| Fricative | | f (v) | | s (z) | ʃ | | | x<br>(ɣ) | | h |
| Approx | | | | | | | j | | | |
| Lat Appr | | | | l | | | | | | |
| Affricate | | | | | | | ʧ ʤ<br>ʧʰ ʤʱ | | | |

[14] In addition to the references cited some facts have been added by the present author.

[15] Hindi has a retroflex nasal flap in lieu of a simple nasal consonant.

## 1.2 Distribution

a. Consonants occur in all positions, with the following restrictions:
   i. /ɽ̃ ŋ/ do not occur word-initially
   ii. /ŋ/ tends to occur with /g/.

b. Geminate consonants occur, except for the following: [bʱ ʃ h j] inter-vocalically. Of these, /bʱ ʃ/ have allophonic gemination before /j r w/, after a general process, e.g., /səbʱjə/ > [səb.bʱjə] 'cultured'; /miʃrə/ > [miʃ.ʃrə] (a last name), /əʃwə/ > [əʃ.ʃwə] 'horse'.

c. There is considerable variation between the following fricatives and stops (i.e. plosives and affricates) such as z ~ ʤ, x ~ kʰ, ɣ ~ g.

# 2 Vowel Phonemes

## 2.1 Inventory

a. **Short**

| | FRONT | CENTRAL | BACK |
|---|---|---|---|
| Open | ɪ | | ʊ |
| Open-mid | | ə | |

b. **Long**

| | FRONT | CENTRAL | BACK |
|---|---|---|---|
| Close | i: | | u: |
| Close-mid | e: | | o: |
| Open-mid | ɛ: (æ:) | | ɔ: |
| Open | | a: | |

c. Nasal

| | FRONT | CENTRAL | BACK |
|---|---|---|---|
| Close | i: ĩ | | ũ: ʊ̃ |
| Close-mid | ẽ: | | õ: |

| Open-mid | ɛ̃: | ə̃ | əʊ̃: |
|---|---|---|---|
| Open | | ã: | |

## 2.2 Distribution

a. In most varieties of Hindi, word-finally, the short vowels /ɪ ʊ/ are lengthened to /i: u:/, and /ə/ does not occur.

b. In western Hindi, /e:/ is pronounced as /ɛ:/.

c. /æ:/ occurs in borrowed vocabulary from English. It does not contrast with /ɛ:/.

d. [e o] are in free variation with /ɪ ʊ/ in many lexical items of Perso-Arabic origin.

e. The Hindi /əʊ̃:/ is phonetically different from the IPA /ɔ/ in having a delayed rounding, and a glide from the open-mid central to close-mid back position.

# 3 Consonant Allophones

## 3.1 Inventory

| | Bilabial | Dental | Alveolar | Post-alveolar | Retro-flex | Palatal | Glottal |
|---|---|---|---|---|---|---|---|
| Nasal | m̤ (m) | | n̤ (m) | | | ɲ | |
| Trill | | r̪ (ɾ) | | ɾ̠ >(ɾ) | ɽ̃ | | |
| Flap | | | | | ɽ (ɖ)<br>ɽʰ (ɖʰ) | | |
| Fricative | | | | | ʂ(s) | | |
| Lat Appr | | | | l̠ >(l)<br>l̤ (l) | | | |

## 3.2 Distribution

**General:**

a. Consonants are lengthened before /j w r/. Aspirated plosives and affricates have their plosive parts lengthened, e.g., [ p:ʰ t:ʃ ] etc.

b. [ɽ ɽʰ] < / ɖ ɖʰ / occur between vowels, and in syllable Coda positions, except in loan-words.

c. [ m̤ n̤ l̤ ] < /m n l/ occur before /h/.

d. [ ʂ ] < / s / occurs before retroflex consonants.

e. The post-alveolar lateral allophone [ l˃ ] < / l / occurs before retroflex consonants, e.g., [ ʊ | ˃ʈa:] < / ʊ | ʈa:/ 'inverted'.

f. [ ɦ ] < / h / occurs non-finally.

g. The dental [ r̪ ] and the post-alveolar [r̠˃] allophones of the tap /ɾ/ occur after dental and retroflex consonants. E. g., /tritija:/ 'the third day of the fortnight', / ɖrəm / 'drum'.

# 4 Vowel Allophones

## 4.1 Inventory

[ e ] [ ə ]: /e:/

[ ə i̯ ]: /ɛ:/

[ o: ]: /o:/

[ ə u̯ ]: /əo:/

[e]: [ɐ]: /ə/

## 4.2 Distribution

a. [e]< /ə/ occurs when followed by /h/, and a vowel other than /ə a:/ in the next syllable.

b. [e o]< /e: o:/ occur before /h/, e.g., /ko:hra:/ >[kohra:] 'fog'; /me:hta:/ >[mehta:] (a last name)

c. [ ə i̯ ]: < /ɛ:/ə and [ə u̯]< /æ: / occur before vowels and semivowels, e.g., /b$^{h}$ɛja:/ > [b$^{h}$əija:] 'brother' (mainly vocative).

# 5 Syllable Structure

## 5.1 Canonical syllable structure

(C)(C)(C)V(C)(C)(C)

E.g., /ʃa:str/ 'learned book'; /stri:tʋə/ 'womanhood'.

## 5.2 Consonant clusters

Two-consonant clusters:

Initial : (i) C+L/G; (ii) s+C.

Final : general

Medial : general.

Three-consonant clusters:

Initial : /spr-, str-, smr-/

Final : / -NPlr (e.g. -ntr, -ndr), -NPlAx (e.g. -ntj, ŋk$^{h}$j), -str, -ʂʈr, -rdr, -tsj)

Medial : general.

**References:** Kelkar (1968) Ohala (1983)

# Jaunsari

**Ethnologue code:** ISO 639-3: jns
**Language classification:** Indo-Aryan, Northern zone, Western Pahari
**Alternate names:** Jansauri, Jaunsauri, Pahari
**Main region:** Uttarakhand (Dehra Dun District, Jaunsar-Bawar Division)

## 1 Consonant phonemes

### 1.1 Inventory

| | Bilabial | Dental/ Alveolar | Post-alv. | Retro-flex | Pala-tal | Velar | Glo-ttal |
|---|---|---|---|---|---|---|---|
| Plosive | p b<br>p$^h$ b$^ɦ$ | t d<br>t$^h$ d$^ɦ$ | | ʈ ɖ<br>ʈ$^h$ ɖ$^ɦ$ | | k g<br>k$^h$ g$^ɦ$ | |
| Nasal | m | n̥ n | | ɳ | | | |
| Trill | | r | | | | | |
| Flap | | | | ɽ | | | |
| Fricative | | s | ʃ | | ç | | h |
| Approx | w | | | | j | | |
| Lat Approx | | l | | | | | |
| Affricate | | | ts ʥ<br>ts$^h$ | | ʧ ʤ<br>ʧ$^h$ ʤ$^ɦ$ | | |

### 1.2 Distribution

a. Consonants occur in all positions, with the following restrictions:
   i. /ɳ ɽ/ do not occur initially in words.

b. Geminate of the following consonants occur inter-vocalically: /p b t d ʈ ɖ k g ʧ ʤ m n s ʃ l w j/.

# 2 Vowel phonemes

## 2.1 Inventory

a. **Short**

| | FRONT | CENTRAL | BACK |
|---|---|---|---|
| Close | ɪ | | ʊ |
| Open | | a | |

b. **Long**

| | FRONT | CENTRAL | BACK |
|---|---|---|---|
| Close | i: | | u: |
| Close-mid | e: | | o: |
| Open-mid | ɛ: | | ɔ: |
| Open | | a: | |

c. **Nasal:**

| | FRONT | CENTRAL | BACK |
|---|---|---|---|
| Close | ɪ̃ ĩ: | | ʊ̃ ũ: |
| Close-mid | ẽ: | | õ: |
| Open-mid | ɛ̃: | | ɔ̃: |
| Open | | ã ã: | |

d. **Diphthongs:** /ai̯ au̯ i̯u u̯a/

## 2.2 Distribution

a. Vowels occur in all positions.

b. Vowel sequences occur.

# 3 Consonant allophones

a. /h/ is pronounced as voiced [ɦ] between vowels and when followed by a nasal or a liquid.

# 4 Vowel allophones

## 4.1 Inventroy

[ i̥ ː ] : /i/

[ɪ̥ ] : /ɪ/

[ɐ] : /a/

[ʊ̥] : /ʊ/

[u̥ ː] : /u

## 4.2 Distribution

a. [ɐ] < /a/ occurs between consonants.

b. [ɪ̥] < /ɪ/ occurs after a consonant cluster (and therefore its distribution is limited).

c. [ʊ̥] < /ʊ/ occurs initially and medially followed by consonant cluster.

d. [i̥ ː] < /i ː/ and [u̥ ː] < /u ː/ occur initially and finally in monosyllabic words.

# 5 Syllable structure

## 5.1 Canonical syllable structure

(C (L/G)) V ((C) C)

Cond.: The coda clusters are highly restricted.

## 5.2 Consonant clusters

Two-consonant clusters:

Initial : (a) S/L + G/L, (b) Obs + w, (c) S + r
Final : st, nd, n̪ḍ, nc.
Medial : General

Three-consonant clusters:

Initial : Nil
Final : Nil
Medial : (a) C + C + r, (b) s + C + j.

**References:** Sharma (1972, 1990)

# Kacchi

**Ethnologue code:** ISO 639-3: kfr
**Language classification:** Indo-Aryan, Northwestern zone, Sindhi
**Alternate names:** Kachchhi, Kutchchi, Cuchi
**Main region:** Gujarat, Rann of Kachchh Area.

## 1 Consonant phonemes

### 1.1 Inventory

| | BILA-BIAL | LABIO-DENTAL | DEN-TAL | POST-ALVEOLAR | RETRO-FLEX | PALA-TAL | VELAR | GLO-TTAL |
|---|---|---|---|---|---|---|---|---|
| Plosive | p b $p^h$ | | t d $t^h$ | | ʈ ɖ $ʈ^h$ | | k g $k^h$ | |
| Nasal | m | | n | | ɳ | | ŋ | |
| Trill | | | | r | | | | |
| Tap | | | | ɾ | | | | |
| Flap | | | | | ɽ | | | |
| Fricative | | | | s | | | | ɦ |
| Approx | | ʋ | | | | j | | |
| Lat. Appr | | | | l | ɭ | | | |
| Affricate | | | | | | tʃ dʒ $tʃ^h$ | | |
| Imalosive | ɓ | | | ɗ | | | | |

### 1.2 Distribution

a. Consonants occur in all positions , with the following restrictions:

   i. /ɳ ŋ ɽ / do not occur initially.

ii. /ŋ/ occurs only after a short vowel.
iii. /ɦ/ occurs only initially in words.

b. Geminate consonants occur inter-vocalically.

# 2 Vowel phonemes

## 2.1 Inventory

a. **Short**

| | FRONT | CENTRAL | BACK |
|---|---|---|---|
| Close | ɪ | | ʊ |
| Mmid | | ə | |

b. **Long**

| | FRONT | CENTRAL | BACK |
|---|---|---|---|
| Close | i: | | u: |
| Close-mid | e : | | o : |
| Open-mid | ɛ : | | ɔ : |
| Open | | a : | |

c. **Nasal:**

| | FRONT | CENTRAL | BACK |
|---|---|---|---|
| Close | ĩ : | | ũ: |
| Close-mid | ẽ : | | õ : |
| Open-mid | ɛ̃ : | ə̃ | ɔ̃ : |
| Open | | ã : | |

## 2.2 Distribution

a. Vowels occur in all positions, with the following restrictions:
   i. The short vowels do not occur word finally. /ə/ occurs only in a few numerals and a few Sanskrit loan words.
   ii. Vowel sequences are permitted except for /ɪ ɛ ɔ/.

b. Sequences of two and three vowels occur in all positions.

c. /ɪ ʊ/ do not have nasal counterparts as phonemes. /ə̃/ occurs when not flanked by a plosive.

# 3 Consonant allophones

Data are not available.

# 4 Vowel allophones

Data are not available.

# 5 Syllable structure

## 5.1 Canonical syllable structure

(C) V (C)

## 5.2 Consonant clusters

Two-consonant clusters:

Initial : Nil
Final : Nil
Medial : General.

Three-consonant clusters: Nil

**References:** Rohra (1966)

# Kashmiri

**Ethnologue code:** ISO 639-3: kas
**Language classification:** Indo-Aryan, Northwestern zone, Dardic, Kashmiri
**Alternate names:** Keshur, Cashmiri
**Main region:** Jammu and Kashmir; Punjab; Uttar Pradesh; Delhi; Kashmir Valley.

## 1 Consonant phonemes

### 1.1 Inventory

| | BILA-BIAL | LABIO-DENTAL | DEN-TAL | ALV. | PAL.-ALV. | RETR. | PALA-TAL | VEL-AR | GLO-TTAL |
|---|---|---|---|---|---|---|---|---|---|
| Plosive | p b<br>pʰ | | t d<br>tʰ | | | ʈ ɖ<br>ʈʰ | | k g<br>kʰ | |
| Nasal | m | | | n | | | | | |
| Trill | | | | r | | | | | |
| Flap | | | | | | (ɽ) | | | |
| Fricative | | | | s z | ʃ | | | | h |
| Approx | | ʋ | | | | | j | | |
| Lat Appr | | | | l | | | | | |
| Affricate | | | ts<br>tsʰ | | | | tʃ dʒ<br>tʃʰ | | |

### 1.2 Distribution

a. Consonants occur in all positions, with the following restriction:
   i. /t/ does not occur initially.
b. Geminate consonants do not occur.

# 2 Vowel phonemes

## 2.1 Inventory

**a. Short**

| | FRONT | CENTRAL | BACK |
|---|---|---|---|
| Close | ɪ | ɨ | ʊ |
| Close-mid | e | | o |
| Open-mid | | ə | |
| Open | | ɐ | ɒ |

**b. Long**

| | FRONT | CENTRAL | BACK |
|---|---|---|---|
| Close | iː | ɨː | uː |
| Close-mid | eː | | |
| Open-mid | ɛː | əː | ɔː |
| Open | | aː | |

**c. Nasal:**

| | FRONT | CENTRAL | BACK |
|---|---|---|---|
| Close | ɪ̃ ɪ̃ ː | ɨ̃ ɨ̃ː | ʊ̃ ũː |
| Close-mid | ẽ ẽː | | õ |
| Open-mid | ɛ̃ː | ə̃ ə̃ː | ɔ̃ː |
| Open | | ɐ̃ ãː | |

**d. Diphthongs:**

/ʊɪ uːɪ oə ɒa ː/

## 2.2 Distribution

a. Vowels occur in all positions, with the following restrictions:
   i. /ɨ ɔː ɒ/ do not occur initially.
   ii. /ɨː əː uː o ɔː ɒ/ do not occur finally.

b. Vowel sequences have intervening glides /j ʋ/.

c. Diphthongs /ʊɪ uːɪ oə/ occur medially and in contrast with monophthongs. E.g. /gʊr/ 'horse'; /gʊIr/ 'mare'.

# 3 Consonant allophones

## 3.1 Inventory

| | Bilabial | Labio-Dental | Dental | Retro-flex | Palatal | Velar | Glottal |
|---|---|---|---|---|---|---|---|
| Plosive | p (~pʰ) | | t (~tʰ) | ʈ (~ʈʰ) | | k (~kʰ)<br>k̟ g̟<br>k̟ʰ | |
| Fricative | | f (~pʰ) | | | | | ɦ (h) |
| Affricate | | | | | ʧ̟ ʤ̟<br>ʧ̟ʰ | | |

## 3.2 Distribution

a. All the consonants are labialised when followed by either a High or a Low Back vowel /ʊ uː ɒ/; e.g. /gur/ [gʷur] 'horse'.

b. All the consonants are palatalized before /i/.

c. Aspirated stops /pʰ tʰ ʈʰ ʧʰ kʰ/ are optionally deaspirated /p t ʈ ʧ k/.

d. /pʰ/ freely varies with [f].

e. Palatal and velar consonants are fronted [ʧ̟ ʤ̟ ʧ̟ʰ k̟ g̟ k̟ʰ] before front vowels: /ɪ iː e ɛː /.

f. [ɦ] < /h/ occurs inter-vocalically.

# 4 Vowel allophones

## 4.1 Inventory

/ i: / : [ʲi:]
/ ɪ / : [ʲɪ]
/ ɛ: / : [ɛ:ʲ]
/ ɔ: / : [ɔ:ə]

## 4.2 Distribution

a. [ʲi: ʲɪ] < /i: ɪ/ occur word-initially.
b. [ɛ:ʲ] < /ɛ:/ occurs everywhere.
c. [ɔ:ə] < /ɔ:/ occurs non-finally.

# 5 Syllable structure

## 5.1 Canonical syllable structure

(C) (r) V (C) (C)

## 5.2 Consonant clusters

Two-consonant clusters:

Initial : C + r
Final : (i) N + S (ii) sibilant + S.
Medial : general.

Three-consonant clusters:

Initial : Nil
Final : Nil
Medial : /-ndr-, -ndk-, -ndg-, -ŋgt-, -ŋgz-, -ŋgh-, -nzr-/

**References:** Kelkar & Trishal (1964), Bhat (1987), Wali & Koul (1997), Raina (1990).

# Konkani

**Ethnologue code:** ISO 639-3: knn
**Language classification:** Indo-Aryan, Southern zone
**Alternate names:** Bankoti, Concorinum, Cugani, Konkanese, Konkani, Kunabi
**Main region:** North and central coastal strip of Maharashtra; Karnataka; Dadra and Nagar Haveli.

## 1 Consonant phonemes

### 1.1 Inventory

| | Bilabial | Labiodental | Dental | Alv | Retr. | Palato-Alv. | Palatal | Velar | Glottal |
|---|---|---|---|---|---|---|---|---|---|
| Plosive | p b<br>b$^{ɦ}$ | | t d<br>t$^{h}$ d$^{ɦ}$ | | ʈ ɖ<br>ʈ$^{h}$ ɖ$^{ɦ}$ | | | k g<br>k$^{h}$ g$^{ɦ}$ | |
| Nasal | m<br>m$^{ɦ}$ | | | n<br>n$^{ɦ}$ | ɳ | | ɲ | ŋ | |
| Tap | | | | ɾ | | | | | |
| Fricative | | f v<br>v$^{ɦ}$ | | s | | ʃ | | | h |
| Approx | | | | | | | j | | |
| Lat Appr | | | | l<br>l$^{ɦ}$ | ɭ | | | | |
| Affricate | | | ts ʣ<br>ʣ$^{ɦ}$ | | | | tʃ ʤ<br>tʃ$^{h}$ ʤ$^{ɦ}$ | | |

### 1.2 Distribution

a. Consonants occur in all positions, with the following exceptions:
   i. /b$^{ɦ}$ t$^{ɦ}$ d$^{ɦ}$ ʈ$^{ɦ}$ ɖ$^{ɦ}$ k$^{ɦ}$ g$^{ɦ}$ v$^{ɦ}$ ɭ$^{ɦ}$/ do not occur finally.
   ii. /ɳ ɲ ŋ ɳ$^{ɦ}$ ɭ/ do not occur initially.

b. Geminates of the following consonants occur inter-vocalically: /p t ʈ k d ɖ m n ɳ s ʃ ts ʣ ʧ ʤ l ɭ/.

# 2 Vowel phonemes

## 2.1 Inventory

a. **Short**

| | FRONT | CENTRAL | BACK |
|---|---|---|---|
| Close | ɪ | | ʊ |
| Close-mid | e | ə | o |
| Open-mid | ɛ | | ɔ |
| Open | | a | |

b. **Long**

| | FRONT | CENTRAL | BACK |
|---|---|---|---|
| Close | i : | | uː |
| Open | | a : | |

c. **Nasal:**

| | FRONT | CENTRAL | BACK |
|---|---|---|---|
| Close | ĩ ĩ : | | ũ ũ : |
| Close-mid | ẽ | | õ |
| Open-mid | ɛ̃ | ə̃ | ɔ̃ |
| Open | | ã ã : | |

d. **Diphthongs: /əi əu ai au ei eu oi ou ui iu//**

## 2.2 Distribution

a. Vowels occur in all positions.

b. Vowel sequences occur, but not so frequently.

# 3 Consonant allophones

## 3.1 Inventory

| | LABIO-DENTAL | ALV | RETROFLEX | PALATO-ALV. | GLOTTAL |
|---|---|---|---|---|---|
| Tap/ Flap | | | ɽ (d) | | |
| Nasal | ɱ(m) | | | | |
| Fricative | | z(ʥ) | | ʒ(ʤ) | ɦ(h) |
| Approx | ʋ(v) | | | | |

## 3.2 Distribution

a. [ɱ] < /m/ occurs between /u/ and a fricative.

b. [ɽ] < /ɖ/ occurs inter-vocalically and word-finally

c. [z ʒ] < [ʥ ʤ] occur inter-vocalically and word-finally.

d. [ɦ] < /h/ occurs after voiced consonants and inter-vocalically.

e. [ʋ] < /v/ occurs before non-front vowels.

# 4 Vowel allophones

## 4.1 Inventory

**General:**

a. The non-high peripheral short vowels have half-long allophones; the low-mid ones are also lowered: [eˑ æˑ oˑ ɒˑ] < /e ɛ o ɔ/

**Specific:**

| | | |
|---|---|---|
| [ə̞] [ə̝ ] | : | /ə/ |
| [ɪ̆] | : | /i/ |
| [ʊ̆] | : | /u/ |

## 4.2 Distribution

a. The half-long allophones [eˑ æˑ oˑ ɒˑ] < /e ɛ o ɔ/ occur in closed syllables.

b. The raised and lowered allophones of /ə/ occur before high and low vowels respectively.

c. The extra-short allophones of the short high vowels occur before consonant clusters word-medially.

# 5 Syllable structure

## 5.1 Canonical syllable structure[15]

(C)V(C)

## 5.2 Consonant clusters

Two-consonant clusters:

Initial : Nil

Final : Nil.

Medial : General.

Three-consonant clusters: Nil

**References:** Almeida (1989)

[15] Consonant onset and coda clusters occur in borrowed vocabulary.

# Lahndi

**Ethnologue code:** ISO 639-3: pnb
**Language classification:** Indo-Aryan, Northwestern zone, Lahnda
**Alternate names:** Hindki, Western Punjabi, Lahnda, Lahanda, Lahndi
**Main region:** Jammu and Kashmir, Delhi, Haryana.

## 1 Consonant phonemes

### 1.1 Inventory

| | BILABIAL | LABIODENTAL | DENTAL | ALVEO | POST-ALV | RETR. | PALATAL | VELAR | UVU. | GLOTTAL |
|---|---|---|---|---|---|---|---|---|---|---|
| Plosive | p b<br>$\text{p}^{\text{h}}$ $\text{b}^{\text{ɦ}}$ | | t d<br>$\text{t}^{\text{h}}$ $\text{d}^{\text{ɦ}}$ | | | ʈ ɖ<br>$\text{ʈ}^{\text{h}}$ $\text{ɖ}^{\text{ɦ}}$ | | k g<br>$\text{k}^{\text{h}}$ $\text{g}^{\text{h}}$ | | |
| Nasal | m | | | n | | ɳ | ɲ | ŋ | | |
| Tap | | | | ɾ | | | | | | |
| Flap | | | | | | ɽ | | | | |
| Fricative | | f v | | s z | ʃ | | | x ɣ | χ (ʁ) | h |
| Approx | | | | | | | j | | | |
| Lat Appr | | | | l | | ɭ | | | | |
| Affricate | | | | | | | ʧ ʤ<br>$\text{ʧ}^{\text{h}}$ $\text{ʤ}^{\text{ɦ}}$ | | | |

### 1.2 Distribution

a. Consonants occur in all positions, with the following restrictions:
   i. The long consonants /b: ɖ: dʒ:  g:/ only occur word initially.
   ii. /j/ does not occur finally.

iii. /ɳ/ does not occur initially.

iv. /h/ occurs initially and at the beginning of stressed syllables /heva:z/ 'sound', /lehɜo: r/ 'Lahore'.

v. /ʁ/ occurs rarely.

b. /dʒ/ replaces /z/ in many words in Lahndi.

c. / h / may be inserted at the beginning of vowel-initial words. e.g. /hus / 'he', /his/ 'that' (Punjabi has /u s/ /i s/)

d. Geminates occur in the following environments:

i. inter-vocalically, of most consonants.

ii. Initially, of /b d g ʄ/, especially in the Multani dialects.

# 2 Vowel phonemes

## 2.1 Inventory

a. **Short**

| | FRONT | CENTRAL | BACK |
|---|---|---|---|
| Close | i | | u |
| Open-mid | | ɐ | |

b. **Long**

| | FRONT | CENTRAL | BACK |
|---|---|---|---|
| Close | i: | | u: |
| Close-mid | e: | | o: |
| Open-mid | æ:[16] | | ɜo: |
| Open | | | ɑ: |

[16] The vowel is below open-mid.

c. **Nasal:**

| | FRONT | CENTRAL | BACK |
|---|---|---|---|
| Close | ĩ: ĩ | | ũ ũ: |
| Close-mid | ẽ: | | õ: |
| Open-mid | æ̃: | | ɔ̃: |
| Open | | | ɑ̃: |

## 2.2 Distribution

a. Vowels in Lahndi are associated with different pitch levels:
   /i i: u u:/ are pronounced with a high pitch;
   /e: ɐ o/ are pronounced with mid pitch, and
   /æ: ɔ: a:/ are pronounced with low pitch.
b. Vowels occur in all positions in the word, with the following restrictions:
   i. /i/ occurs in the unstressed first syllable in a word.
   ii. /æ: a u/ occur in monosyllabics and initially in bisyllabics.
   iii. /o:/ occurs medially and finally.
c. All vowels have nasalized counter-parts.
d. Vowel sequences are found to occur within and across words.

# 3 Consonant allophones

Details not available.

# 4 Vowel allophones

## 4.1 Inventory

[ə]: /ɐ/
[ə̃]: /ɐ̃/
[ə]: /u/
[ə̃]: /ũ/

## 4.2 Distribution

a. /u/ and /ɐ/ and their nasalized counterparts are realized as [ə] and its nasalized counterpart in unstressed syllables. [ə] and [ə̃] are pronounced with mid level of pitch.

# 5 Syllable structure

## 5.1 Canonical syllable structure[17]

(C)V(C)

## 5.2 Consonant clusters

Two-consonant clusters:

Initial : Nil

Final : Nil

Medial : General

Three-consonant clusters: Nil

# 6 Suprasegmentals

## 6.1 Tone

Tonemes:

Lahndi has two tones:

a. Level: M
b. Rising: LH

[17] As noted in 1.2, long consonants appear word-initially.

Tones affect the segments in certain ways:

a. All vowels become shorter, high vowels become higher, and low vowels become lower.
b. Consonants are pronounced fortis.

**References:** Smirnov (1975), Bahri (1962)

# Lamani[18]

**Ethnologue code:** ISO 639-3: lmn
**Language classification:** Indo-Aryan, Central zone, Rajasthani,
**Alternate names:** Lamani, Lamadi, Lambani, Labhani, Lambara, Lavani, Lemadi, Lumadale, Banjara, Banjari, Banjori, Banjuri, Brinjari, Gohar-Herkeri, Goola, Gurmarti, Gormati, Kora, Singali, Sugali, Sukali, Tanda, Vanjari, Wanji
**Main region:** Andhra Pradesh; Madhra Pradesh; Himachal Pradesh; Gujarat; Tamil Nadu; Maharashtra; Karnataka; Orissa; West Bengal.

## 1 Consonant phonemes

### 1.1 Inventory

| | Bila-bial | Dental | Alv. | Post-alv | Retro-flex | Pala-tal | Velar | Glo-ttal |
|---|---|---|---|---|---|---|---|---|
| Plosive | p b<br>pʰ bʱ | t d<br>tʰ dʱ | | | ʈ ɖ<br>ʈʰ ɖʱ | | k g<br>kʰ gʱ | |
| Nasal | m | | n | | ɳ | | ŋ | |
| Tap | | | ɾ | | | | | |
| Fricative | | | s | ʃ | | | | h |
| Approx | w | | | | | j | | |
| Lat Appr | | | l | | ɭ | | | |
| Affricate | | | | | | ʧ ʤ<br>ʧʰ ʤʱ | | |

[18] Lamani is spoken by a nomadic community known by various names, the name Gormati and Gorwat  preferred by them. The community is scattered in central and southern India, especially Maharashtra, Karanataka and Andhra Pradesh. The present description is one based on the dialect spoken around Pune.

## 1.2 Distribution

a. Consonants occur in all positions, with the following restrictions:
   i. /ɳɭŋ/ do not occur initially.
   ii. /h tʃ ʃ/ do not occur finally and in the coda position.

b. / ŋ h tʃ ʃ/ do not occur in onset position in the middle of the word.

c. Geminates of the following consonants occur inter-vocalically: /t d ʈ ɖ k g s n ɳ l ɭ w j/.

# 2 Vowel phonemes

## 2.1 Inventory

a. **Short**

| | FRONT | CENTRAL | BACK |
|---|---|---|---|
| Close | i | | u |
| Close-mid | e | | o |
| Open -mid | | ə | |

b. **Long**

| | FRONT | CENTRAL | BACK |
|---|---|---|---|
| Open-mid | | | ɔ: |
| Open | | | ɑ: |

c. **Nasal:**

| | FRONT | CENTRAL | BACK |
|---|---|---|---|
| Close | ĩ | | ũ |
| Close-mid | ẽ | | õ |
| Open-mid | | ə̃ | |
| Open | | | ɑ̃: |

## 2.2 Distribution

a. Vowels occur in all positions.

b. Vowel sequences occur freely in two's, and form separate syllabic nuclei:

/ ii iu ie io iə iɑ: /

/ ui uu ue uo uə uɑ: /

/ oi ou oe oo oə/

/ ɑ:i ɑ:u ɑ:e ɑ:o/

/ ei eu /

/ əi /

# 3 Consonant allophones

## 3.1 Inventory

| | Labio-dental | Dental | Retroflex |
|---|---|---|---|
| Tap/ Flap | | | ɽ (ɖ) |
| Fricative | v(w) | | |
| Approx | | | ɭ̥ (ɭ) |
| Affricate | | ts (t ʃ)<br>dz (ʤ) | |

## 3.2 Distribution

a. [ɽ] < /ɖ/ occurs word finally and medially with /ʈ/ and non-homorganic consonants.

b. [ts dz ] < /tʃ ʤ / occur finally and freely with [tʃ ʤ] before non-front vowels.

c. [ɭ̥] < /ɭ/ occurs before / r / and homorganic consonants.

d. [v] /w/ occurs before the front vowels /i e/.

# 4 Vowel allophones

## 4.1 Inventory

/ i / : [ i: ]

/ e / : [ e: ]

## 4.2 Distribution

a. [i: e:] < /i e/ occur in open syllables, and before /r/ in the coda position.

# 5 Syllable structure

## 5.1 Canonical syllable structure

(C) (G) V (C) (C)

## 5.2 Consonant clusters

Two-consonant clusters:

| | | |
|---|---|---|
| Initial | : | Cj (C excludes / p $p^h$ b b꜀ m w ŋ h j / ), kw gw. |
| Final | : | -N + Plosive; -st, -jl, -jn, -ks, -ɖɖ , -nn. |
| Medial | : | General. |

**References:** Trail (1968)

# Magahi

**Ethnologue code:** ISO 639-3: mag
**Language classification:** Indo-Aryan, Eastern zone
**Alternate names:** Magadhi, Magaya, Maghai, Maghaya, Maghori, Magi, Bihari
**Main region:** Bihar; Jharkhand.

## 1 Consonant phonemes

### 1.1 Inventory

| | Bilabial | Dental | Alv. | Retroflex | Palatal | Velar | Glottal |
|---|---|---|---|---|---|---|---|
| Stop | p b<br>p$^{h}$ b$^{ɦ}$ | t d<br>t$^{h}$ d$^{ɦ}$ | | ʈ ɖ<br>ʈ$^{h}$ ɖ$^{ɦ}$ | | k g<br>k$^{h}$ g$^{ɦ}$ | |
| Nasal | m<br>m$^{ɦ}$ | n<br>n$^{ɦ}$ | | | | ŋ | |
| Tap/ Flap | | | ɾ<br>ɾ$^{ɦ}$ | | | | |
| Fricative | | s | | | | | h |
| Approx | w | | | | j | | |
| Lat Appr | | | l<br>l$^{ɦ}$ | | | | |
| Affricate | | | | | ʧ ʤ<br>ʧ$^{h}$ ʤ$^{ɦ}$ | | |

## 1.2 Distribution

a. Consonants occur in all positions, with the following restrictions:
   i. Aspirated sonorants ( /mʱ nʱ ɽʱ lʱ/) and /ŋ/ do not occur word-initially.
   ii. (/ŋ/) tends to occur with /g/.

b. Geminate consonants occur except for /h/.

# 2 Vowel phonemes[19]

## 2.1 Inventory

**a. Short**

| | FRONT | CENTRAL | BACK |
|---|---|---|---|
| Close | i | | u |
| Close-mid | e | | o |
| Open -mid | | ə | |

**b. Long**

| | FRONT | CENTRAL | BACK |
|---|---|---|---|
| Open | | a: | |

**c. Nasal:**

| | FRONT | CENTRAL | BACK |
|---|---|---|---|
| Close | ĩ | | ũ |
| Close-mid | ẽ | | õ |
| Open-mid | ə̃ĩ | ə̃ | ə̃ũ |
| Open | | ã : | |

**d. Diphthongs:** /əi əu/

[19] Vowel length distinction is neutralized in Magahi as in Bhojpuri. Most vowels have slightly long realizations.

## 2.2 Distribution

Sufficient details not available.

# 3 Consonant allophones

## 3.1 Inventory and Distribution

a. [b] < /w/ and [ɟ] < /j/ occur word-initially.

# 4 Vowel allophones[20]

# 5 Syllable structure

## 5.1 Canonical syllable structure

(C) V (C)

## 5.2 Consonant clusters

Two-consonant clusters:

| | |
|---|---|
| Initial | : Nil |
| Final | : Nil |
| Medial | : General. |

Three-consonant clusters: Nil

**Reference:** Verma (2003)

[20] Vowels are reduced in length non-finally in unstressed positions.

# Mahl

**Ethnologue code:**
**Language classification:** Indo-Aryan, Southern Zone
**Alternate names:**
**Main region:** Minicoy island of the Lakshadweep islands (with 10 of 36 islands inhabited).

## 1 Consonant Phonemes

### 1.1 Inventory

| | Bilabial | Labiodental | Dental | Alveolar | Retr. | Palatal | Velar | Glottal |
|---|---|---|---|---|---|---|---|---|
| Plosive | p b | | t d | | ʈ ɖ | | k g | ʔ |
| Nasal | m | | n | | ɳ | | | |
| Trill | | | | r | | | | |
| Flap | | | | | ɽ | | | |
| Fricative | | f v | | s z | ʂ | | ɣ | h |
| Approx. | | | | | | j | | |
| Lat. Appr. | | | | l | ɭ | | | |
| Affricate | | | | | | ʧ ʤ | | |

### 1.2 Distribution

a. Consonants occur in general initially and medially, with the following restrictions:

   i. /ɖ ʔ ɳ ɣ/ do not occur initially.

   ii. Only /s ʔ/ occur finally.

b. The following consonants have geminates in the medial position: /p t d k m l/.

# 2 Vowel Phonemes

## 2.1 Inventory

a. **Short**

| | FRONT | CENTRAL | BACK |
|---|---|---|---|
| Close | i | | u |
| Close-mid | e | | |
| Open -mid | ɛ | | |
| Open | | a | ɒ |

b. **Long**

| | FRONT | CENTRAL | BACK |
|---|---|---|---|
| Close | i: | | u: |
| Close-mid | e: | | |
| Open | | a: | ɒ: |

## 2.2 Distribution

a. Vowels occur in all positions in words.

b. The following vowel sequences occur: /ei eu ai au ui ɒi/.

# 3 Consonant Allophones

## 3.1 Inventory

[ŋ] : /m/, /n/

## 3.2 Distribution

a. The bilabial and alveolar nasals /m/ and /n/ are neutralized word-finally, where they are realized as the velar nasal [ŋ]. In complex words, they emerge as either of the basic phonemes.

# 4 Vowel Allophones

## 4.1 Inventory and Distribution

**General:**

a. Short vowels are extra short before /ʔ/.

**Specific:**

a. /i iː/ have an optional /j/ on-glide word initially.

# 5 Syllable Structure

## 5.1 Canonical Syllable Structure[21]

(C) (C) V (Non-Initial)

(C) V(C) (General)

## 5.2 Consonant Clusters

Two-consonant clusters:

| | |
|---|---|
| Initial | : NIl |
| Final | : Nil. |
| Medial | : General. |

Three-consonant clusters : Nil

**Reference:** Joseph (1994).

[21] Word-medial geminate consonants occur as complex onsets, as well as Nasals and Stops. However, the data on N+S sequences are not clear.

# Maithili

**Ethnologue code:** ISO 639-3: mai
**Language classification:** Indo-Aryan, Eastern zone, Bihari
**Alternate names:** Maitli, Maitili, Methli, Tirahutia, Bihari, Apabhramsa
**Main region:** Bihar.

## 1 Consonant phonemes

### 1.1 Inventory

| | BILABIAL | DENTAL | ALV | POST-ALV | RETROFLEX | PALATAL | VELAR | GLOTTAL |
|---|---|---|---|---|---|---|---|---|
| Plosive | p b<br>p$^h$ b$^ɦ$ | t d<br>t$^h$ d$^ɦ$ | | | ʈ ɖ<br>ʈ$^h$ ɖ$^ɦ$ | | k g<br>k$^h$ g$^ɦ$ | |
| Nasal | m | | n | | (ɳ) | | | |
| Tap | | | ɾ | | | | | |
| Flap | | | | | (ɽ) | | | |
| Fricative | | | s | (ʃ) | (ʂ) | | | h |
| Approx | (w) | | | | | (j) | | |
| Lat Appr | | | l | | | | | |
| Affricate | | | | | | ʧ ʤ<br>ʧ$^h$ ʤ$^ɦ$ | | |

### 1.2 Distribution

a. Consonants occur in all positions, with the following restriction:

i. /ŋ/ does not occur initially.

b. Geminate consonants occur intervocalically. They are however in free variation with single consonants in this position.

| | | |
|---|---|---|
| /pətta/ | [ˈpətta] ~ [ˈpəta] | 'leaf' |
| /bərre/ | [ˈbərre] ~ [ˈbəre] | 'pimple' |

c. Productive free variation occurs between /w/ and /b/, and /j/ and /dʒ/ in common Maithili. Educated Maithili has /w/ and /j/ in these instances.

# 2 Vowel phonemes

## 2.1 Inventory

a. **Short**

| | FRONT | CENTRAL | BACK |
|---|---|---|---|
| Close | i | | u |
| Close-mid | e | ə | o |
| Open -mid | æ | | ɔ |
| Open | | a | |

b. **Nasal**

| | FRONT | CENTRAL | BACK |
|---|---|---|---|
| Close | ĩ | | ũ |
| Close-mid | ẽ | | õ |
| Open-mid | æ̃ | ə̃ | ɔ̃ |
| Open | | ã | |

## 2.2 Distribution

a. Both oral and nasal vowels occur in all positions.

b. Vowels occur in sequences of two and three. Two-vowel clusters occur in all positions-initial, medial and final. Three vowel clusters do not occur initially.

/ iau iəu əia əua uia /

The two vowel sequences, which are productive, give rise to surface diphthongs.

# 3 Consonant allophones

## 3.1 Inventory and distribution

a. [ɽ ɽʱ] < /ɖ ɖʱ/ occur inter-vocalically and word-finally, and freely vary with [ɾ ɾʱ].

# 4 Vowel allophones

## 4.1 Inventory

[æ̯] ~ [ ae̯ ] ~ [ ai̯] : /æ/

[ o ] ~ [əu̯ ] : /ɔ /

## 4.2 Distribution

a. /æ/ may be freely realized as [æ̯] ~ [ ae̯ ] ~ [ ai̯].

b. /ɔ/ may be freely realized as [ o ] or [əu̯ ].

# 5 Syllable structure

## 5.1 Canonical structure

(C) (C) V (C) (C).

## 5.2 Consonant clusters

Two-consonant clusters:

| | | |
|---|---|---|
| Initial | : | S + Son, /s/ + S; /s/ + Son, N + L L, /h/ + /r/. |
| Final | : | S + S; S + /s/, S + Son, /s/ + Son, Son + S, Son + /s/, Son + Son, Son + /h/ |
| Medial | : | General. |

Three-consonant clusters:

| | | |
|---|---|---|
| Initial | : | /str-, smr-/ |
| Medial | : | /-str-/ |
| Final | : | Nil. |

**Reference:** R. Yadav (1996, 2003)

# Mandeali

**Ethnologue code:** ISO 639-3: mjl
**Language classification:** Indo-Aryan, Northern zone, Western Pahari
**Alternate names:** Mandi, Pahari, Himachali
**Main region:** Himachal Pradesh, Mandi District.

## 1 Consonant Phonemes

### 1.1 Inventory

| | Bilabial | Dental | Alv. | Retroflex | Palatal | Velar | Glottal |
|---|---|---|---|---|---|---|---|
| Plosive | p b<br>$p^h$ $b^ɦ$ | t d<br>$t^h$ $d^ɦ$ | | ʈ ɖ<br>$ʈ^h$ $ɖ^ɦ$ | | k g<br>$k^h$ $g^ɦ$ | |
| Nasal | m | | n | | ɳ | | |
| Trill | | | r | | | | |
| Fricative | | | s | | ʃ | | h |
| Approx | w | | | | j | | |
| Lat Approx | | | l | ɭ | | | |
| Affricate | | | | | ʧ ʤ<br>$ʧ^h$ $ʤ^ɦ$ | | |

### 1.2 Distribution

a. Consonants occur in all positions, with the following restriction:
   i. /ɭ ɳ/ do not occur word-initially.
b. Most final consonants except /s h/ have a vocalic release.

# 2 Vowel Phonemes

## 2.1 Inventory

a. **Short**

| | FRONT | CENTRAL | BACK |
|---|---|---|---|
| Close | i | | u |
| Close-mid | e | | o |
| Open -mid | | ə | |
| Open | | a | |

b. **Long**

| | FRONT | CENTRAL | BACK |
|---|---|---|---|
| Close | i: | | u: |
| Close-mid | e: | | o: |
| Open-mid | | ə: | |
| Open | | a: | |

c. **Nasal:**

| | FRONT | CENTRAL | BACK |
|---|---|---|---|
| Close | ĩ ĩ: | | ũ ũ: |
| Close-mid | ẽ ẽ: | | õ õ: |
| Open-mid | | ə̃ ə̃: | |
| Open | | ã ã: | |

## 2.2 Distribution

a. Vowels occur in all positions. Their occurrence is less frequent initially than medially and finally.

b. Vowel sequences of two occur in all positions.

# 3 Consonant Allophones

## 3.1 Inventory

| | LABIO-DENTAL | RETROFLEX | GLOTTAL |
|---|---|---|---|
| Plosive | | | ʔ(h) |
| Tap/ Flap | | ɽ (ɖ)<br>ɽʱ (ɖʱ) | |
| Fricative | f(pʰ) | | |

## 3.2 Distribution

a. [f] < /pʰ] and [ʔ] < /h/ occur inter vocallically and finally.

b. [ɽ] < /ɖ/ and [ɽʰ] < /ɖʰ/ occur finally and medially when not preceded by a nasal or a geminate counterpart.

# 4 Vowel Allophones

## 4.1 Inventory

| | |
|---|---|
| [ɨ]: | /ə/ |
| [ɔ] [æ]: | /a/ |
| [ɔː] [æː]: | /aː/ |

## 4.2 Distribution

a. [ɨ] < /ə/ occurs in the unstressed syllables preceding stressed syllables of the structure CV:C, e.g., /kəta : b/ > [kɨ ˈ ta : b] 'book'.

b. [ɔ] < /a / occurs before /w/, e.g., /hawa/ > /hɔwa/ 'air'.

c. [ɔː] < /aː/ occurs after /w/, e.g., /kʰwaː ɳa/ > [kʰwɔ : ɳa]' to feed'.

d. [æ æː] < /a aː/ occur after a palatal consonant, e.g., /ʧamʧa/ > [ʧæamʧæ] 'spoon'; /kʰ əljaːr/ > [kʰɨljæːr] (a place name).

# 5 Syllable Structure

## 5.1 Canonical Syllable Structure

(C) (C) (C) V (C) (C)

## 5.2 Consonant Clusters

Two-consonant clusters:

Initial : (a) C + L/G; (b) C + h.
Final : (a) N + C; (b) –jr, -wɖ, -wr, -ws, -wɭ, -ss, -hɖ, -hn, -hr, -hl, -ɭd, -ɭh.
Medial : General.

Three-consonant clusters:

Initial : C + l/h + j. E.g., prj, mhj, etc.
Final : Nil.
Medial : General.

**Reference:** Ranganatha (1971)

# Marathi

**Ethnologue code:** ISO 639-3: mar
**Language classification:** Indo-Aryan, Southern zone
**Alternate names:** Maharashtra, Maharathi, Malhatee, Marthi, Muruthu
**Main region:** Maharashtra and adjacent states. Also spoken in Israel, Mauritius.

## 1 Consonant phonemes

### 1.1 Inventory

| | BILA-BIAL | LABIO-DENTAL | DEN-TAL | ALV | POST-ALV | RETRO-FLEX | PALA-TAL | VEL-AR | GLO-TTAL |
|---|---|---|---|---|---|---|---|---|---|
| Plosive | p b<br>p$^h$ b$^ɦ$ | | t d<br>t$^h$ d$^ɦ$ | | | ʈ ɖ<br>ʈ$^h$ ɖ$^ɦ$ | | k g<br>k$^h$ g$^ɦ$ | |
| Nasal | m | | | n | | ɳ | | (ŋ) | |
| Tap | | | | ɾ | | | | | |
| Fricative | | f v | | s | ʃ | ʂ | | | ɦ |
| Approx | w | | | | | | j | | |
| Lat Appr | | | | l | | ɭ | | | |
| Affricate | | | | | | | ʧ ʤ<br>ʧ$^h$ ʤ$^ɦ$ | | |

### 1.2 Distribution

a. Consonants occur in all positions, with the following exceptions:
   i. /ʧ$^h$ ʤ$^ɦ$/ do not occur finally.
   ii. /ɳ ɭ/ do not occur initially.

b. Geminates of the following consonants occur inter-vocalically: /p t k k$^h$ ʧ m n l r/.

c. /f/ occurs in loanwords.

# 2 Vowel phonemes

## 2.1 Inventory

a. **Short:**

| | FRONT | CENTRAL | BACK |
|---|---|---|---|
| Close | ɪ | | ʊ |
| Close-mid | e | | o |
| Open -mid | æ | ə | ɔ |
| Open | | a | |

b. **Long:**

| | FRONT | CENTRAL | BACK |
|---|---|---|---|
| Close | i : | | u : |
| Open | | a : | |

c. **Nasal:**

| | FRONT | CENTRAL | BACK |
|---|---|---|---|
| Close | | | ũ |
| Close-mid | ẽ | | |
| Open-mid | | ə̃ | |
| Open | | ã | |

d. **Diphthongs: /əi əu/**

## 2.2 Distribution

a. Vowel sequences occur in all positions. The following sequences are found: /ie iːe uo iːu ɪu iːuː/
b. Sequences such as /iːiː eiː euː aːi aɪ aːuː uiː/ are not found in simple or complex words. Across morpheme boundaries, they have an intervening /j/ or /w/.
c. /ɪ ʊ/ rarely occur word-finally.

d. /əi əu/ do not occur finally.

e. The nasalized vowels /ẽ ã/ may freely vary with their oral counterparts.

f. /ə̃ ũ/ occur before sibilants and liquids in words derived from Sanskrit: /hə̃ũs/ < /həms/ 'swan'.

# 3 Consonant allophones

## 3.1 Inventory

| | LABIO-DENTAL | ALVEOLAR | GLOTTAL |
|---|---|---|---|
| Fricative | f(pʰ) | | h(ɦ) |
| Affricate | | ts (ʧ)<br>ʣ (ʤ) | |

## 3.2 Distribution

a. [f] < /pʰ/ occurs word-finally.

b. [ts ʣ] < /ʧ ʤ/ occur before front vowels.

c. [h] < /ɦ/ occurs before voiceless consonants.

# 4 Vowel allophones

Inadequate details available.

# 5 Syllable structure

## 5.1 Canonical syllable structure

(C)(C)(C)V(C)

## 5.2 Consonant clusters

Two-consonant clusters:

Initial : (i) C + L/G; (ii) s + C; (iii) N + ɦ.

Final : Nil. (Only borrowed words from English have them.)

Medial : General.

Three-consonant clusters:

Initial : s + S + r

Final : Nil.

Medial : (i) N + S + r; (ii) -mbɖ- -ŋgɖ- -pl j- -mtʃj -; (iii) general, on account of word-formation.

**References:** Kelkar (1958), Pandharipande (1997)

# Nepali[22]

**Ethnologue code:** ISO 639-3: nep
**Language classification:** Indo-Aryan, Northern zone, Eastern Pahari
**Alternate names:** Nepalese, Gorkhali, Gurkhali, Khaskura, Parbatiya
**Main region: North Bengal, northeast India, Delhi.**

## 1 Consonant Phonemes

### 1.1 Inventory

| | Bilabial | | Dental | | Alveolar | Retroflex | | Palatal | | Velar | | Glottal |
|---|---|---|---|---|---|---|---|---|---|---|---|---|
| Stop | p | b | t | d | | ʈ | ɖ | | | k | g | |
| | (pʰ) | (bʱ) | tʰ | dʱ | | ʈʰ | ɖʱ | | | kʰ | gʱ | |
| Nasal | | m | | n | | | | | | | ŋ | |
| Trill | | | | | r | | | | | | | |
| Fricative | | | | | s | | | | | | | ɦ |
| Approx | | (w) | | | | | | | (j) | | | |
| Lat Approx | | | | | l | | | | | | | |
| Affricate | | | | | | | | ts | dz | | | |
| | | | | | | | | tsʰ | dzʱ | | | |

### 1.2 Distribution

a. Consonants occur in all positions, with the following restrictions:
   i. /ŋ/ does not occur initially (except in some onomatopoeic words).
   ii. The aspirated phonemes and /ɦ/ do not occur finally.

b. Geminate consonants, except of /ɦ ŋ/, occur in the medial position.

[22] The variety being described here is the eastern Nepali spoken by the largest number of speakers.

# 2 Vowel Phonemes

## 2.1 Inventory

a. **Short**

| | FRONT | CENTRAL | BACK |
|---|---|---|---|
| Close | i | | u |
| Close-mid | e | | o |
| Open-mid | | | ʌ |
| Open | | a | |

b. **Nasal**

| | FRONT | CENTRAL | BACK |
|---|---|---|---|
| Close | ĩ | | ũ |
| Close-mid | ẽ | | õ |
| Open-mid | | | ʌ̃ |
| Open | | ã | |

## 2.2 Distribution

a. All the vowels occur in all the positions.

b. Vowel sequences occur.

# 3 Consonant Allophones

## 3.1 Inventory

| | BILABIAL | ALVOLAR | RETROFLEX | VELAR |
|---|---|---|---|---|
| Nasal flap | | | ɽ̃ (ɳ) | |

| | | | | |
|---|---|---|---|---|
| Flap | m | | ɽ̃ (ɖ) | ŋ |
| Trill | | ɾ (r) | | |
| Fricative | ɸ(pʰ) β(bʱ) | | | x (kʰ) ɣ(gʱ) |

## 3.2 Distribution

a. The labial and velar fricative allophones [ɸ β x ɣ] < /pʰ bʱ kʰ gʱ/ occur in the intervocalic position in fast speech.

b. The tap rhotic allophone [ɾ] < /r/ occurs in non-initial position.

c. The retroflex flap allophone [ɽ] < /ɖ/ occurs when single and post-vocalic.

d. The nasal flap allophone [ɽ̃] < /ɳ/ occurs before a homorganic consonant and inter-vocalically.

# 4 Vowel Allophones

a. Vowels are breathy following aspirated stops, yielding breathy voiced allophones of the 6 oral and 5 nasal vowels: [i̤ e̤ ṳ o̤ ʌ̤ a̤ ĩ̤ ẽ̤ ṳ̃ ʌ̤̃ ã̤].

b. /ʌ/ has the rounded variants [ɞ ɔ] in the speech of different individuals.

# 5 Syllable Structure

## 5.1 Canonical syllable structure[23]

(C) (r/G) V (C)

[23] In finite verb forms, the combination of root and suffix may result in three consonant clusters word-medially; e.g. -ntʰj-, -rtʰ-.

## 5.2 Consonant clusters

Two-consonant clusters:

Initial : C+r/G

Final : Nil.

Medial : General.

Three-consonant clusters:

Medial : Restricted clusters in complex forms.

**References:** Khatiwada (2009), Acharya (1991), Riccardi (2002)

# Oriya

**Ethnologue code:** ISO 639-3: ori
**Language classification:** Indo-Aryan, Eastern zone
**Alternate names:** Uriya, Utkali, Odri, Odrum, Oliya, Vadiya, Yudhia
**Main region:** Orissa; West Bengal; Assam; Andhra Pradesh.

## 1 Consonant phonemes

### 1.1 Inventory

| | BILABIAL | DENTAL | ALV | RETRO-FLEX | PALATAL | VELAR | GLOTTAL |
|---|---|---|---|---|---|---|---|
| Plosive | p b<br>p$^{h}$ b$^{ɦ}$ | t d<br>t$^{h}$ d$^{ɦ}$ | | ʈ ɖ<br>ʈ$^{h}$ ɖ$^{ɦ}$ | | k g<br>k$^{h}$ g$^{ɦ}$ | |
| Nasal | m | n | | ɳ | | ŋ | |
| Trill | | | r | | | | |
| Fricative | | | s | | | | h |
| Approx | w | | | | j | | |
| Lat Approx | | | l | ɭ | | | |
| Affricate | | | | | t ʃ dʒ<br>ʧ ʧ$^{h}$ | | |

### 1.2 Distribution

a. Consonants occur in all positions, with the following restrictions:
   i. /ŋ ɳ ɭ/ do not occur initially.
   ii. /g$^{h}$ t$^{h}$ b$^{ɦ}$ j w/ do not occur finally.

b. Most Oriya words end in a vowel, except loan words, and in words used as imperative minor sentences.

c. Geminate consonants do not occur.

# 2 Vowel phonemes

## 2.1 Inventory

a. **Short**

| | FRONT | CENTRAL | BACK |
|---|---|---|---|
| Close | i | | u |
| Close-mid | e | | o |
| Open-mid | | | ɔ |
| Open | | a | |

b. **Nasal:**

| | FRONT | CENTRAL | BACK |
|---|---|---|---|
| Close | ĩ | | ũ |
| Close-mid | ẽ | | |
| Open-mid | ɛ̃ | ə̃ | ɔ̃ |
| Open | | ã | |

## 2.2 Distribution

a. Vowels occur in all positions.

b. /o/ does not have a nasal counterpart.

c. Contrast in vowel length is limited to a few words and to morphemic boundaries. The long vowels have been treated as sequences of identical vowels.

d. Vowel sequences of two occur in all positions:/iu ia ie uẽ ei/.

e. The following three vowel sequences are attested: /eia iao iai uai/.

# 3 Consonant allophones

## 3.1 Inventory

[ɽ] : / ɖ/

[ɽʰ] : / ɖʰ/

## 3.2 Distribution

a. [ɽ ɽʰ] < /ɖ ɖʰ/ occur inter-vocalically and in the Coda position.

# 4 Vowel allophones

## 4.1 Inventory

| | |
|---|---|
| [i ˑ ] [ ï ] : | / i / |
| [e ˑ ] [ ë] : | / e / |
| [u ˑ ] [ ü]: | / u / |
| [o ˑ ] [ ö] : / o̹] : | / o / |
| [a ˑ ] [a̹] : | / a / |

## 4.2 Distribution

a. Vowels have half length in monosyllables and the word-final position.

b. The centralized allophones of non-low vowels occur before retroflex consonants.

c. The raised allophones [ɔ̝ a̝] < /ɔa/ occur when followed by a high vowel in the following syllable.

# 5 Syllable structure

## 5.1 Canonical syllable structure

(C) (C) (C) V (N) (C)

## 5.2 Consonant clusters

Two-consonant clusters:

| | | |
|---|---|---|
| Initial | : | (i) C + L/G; (ii) s + C. |
| Final | : | N + C. |
| Medial | : | General. |

Three-consonant clusters:

| | | |
|---|---|---|
| Initial | : | /spr- str- smr-/ |
| Final | : | Nil |
| Medial | : | (i) N + C + r/j; (ii) s + C + r; (iii) r + C + j. |

**References**: Pattanayak (1968), Gauda (1989)

# Punjabi

**Ethnologue code:** ISO 639-3: pan
**Language classification:** Indo-Iranian, Indo-Aryan, Central zone, Panjabi
**Alternate names:** Punjabi, Gurumukhi
**Main region:** Punjab; Haryana; Rajasthan; Delhi.

## 1 Consonant Phonemes

### 1.1 Inventory

| | BILABIAL | LABIODENTAL | DENTAL | ALVEOLAR | POSTALV | RETR. | PALATAL | VELAR | UVULAR | GLOTTAL |
|---|---|---|---|---|---|---|---|---|---|---|
| Stop | p b<br>$p^h$ | | t d<br>$t^h$ | | | ʈ ɖ<br>$ʈ^h$ | | k g<br>$k^h$ | (q) | |
| Nasal | m | | n | | | ɳ | ɲ | ŋ | | |
| Trill | | | | r | | | | | | |
| Flap | | | | | | ɽ | | | | |
| Fricative | | (v) | | s (z) | ʃ | | | (x) (ɣ) | | h |
| Approx | w | | | | | | j | | | |
| Lat Appr | | | | l | | ɭ | | | | |
| Affricate | | | | | | | tʃ dʒ<br>$tʃ^h$ | | | |

### 1.2 Distribution

a. Consonants occur in all positions, with the following restrictions:
   i. / hjw / do not occur finally.
   ii. / l ɽ ɳ / do not occur initially.
   iii. / h / does not occur medially.

b. Geminates of the following consonants occur medially /p d t d ʈ ɖ ʧ ʤ k g m n l s w /, and of / k g t ʃ ʈ$^{h}$ / finally.

# 2 Vowel Phonemes

## 2.1 Inventory

a. **Short**

| | FRONT | CENTRAL | BACK |
|---|---|---|---|
| Close | i | | u |
| Open-mid | | ə | |

b. **Long**

| | FRONT | CENTRAL | BACK |
|---|---|---|---|
| Close | i: | | u: |
| Close-mid | e: | | o: |
| Open-mid | æ:[1] | | ɔ: |
| Open | | a: | |

c. **Nasal**

| | FRONT | CENTRAL | BACK |
|---|---|---|---|
| Close | ĩ: | | ũ: |
| Close-mid | ẽ: | | õ: |
| Open-mid | æ̃: | | ɔ̃: |
| Open | | ã : | |

[24] The vowel is below open-mid.

## 2.2 Distribution

1. Vowels occur in all positions, with the following restriction:
   a. / ɪ ʊ ə / do not occur finally.
   b. Sequences of two syllabic vowels occur in abundance. Sequences of three syllabic vowels are also found, e.g. /a:ia:./ 'came', /rəso:ia:/ 'cook$_N$', / ɟʊa:i: / 'son-in-law'.
   c. Short oral vowels do not have nasal counterparts.

# 3 Consonant allophones

Inadequate data, apart from those of nasal and lateral consonants.

# 4 Syllable structure

## 4.1 Canonical syllable structure[25]

(C) (C) V (C) (C)

## 4.2 Consonant clusters

Two-consonant clusters:

Initial : i) p/k/g/t/ʈ +r; ii) s+l; iii) p/t/k/ kʰ +j; iv) k/g/+ w

Final : General

Medial : General

Three-consonant clusters:

Initial : Nil

[25] Geminate consonants have syllabic division medially, e.g., /bətʃ.tʃa:/ 'child'. When followed by another consonant, however, syllabic consonants have the division after the geminate consonant, e.g., /ləgg.ɳa:/ 'to begin to'.

Final : Nil
Medial : N + S + ɽ/ɭ/r.

# 5 Suprasegmentals

## 5.1 Tone

**Tonemes:**

a. High: H ( ´ )

b. Low: L ( ` )

c. Mid: M (unmarked)

E.g., /kó:ɽa:/ 'leper'; / kò:ɽa: / 'horse'; / ko:ɽa: / 'whip'.

Reference: Bhatia (1997)

# Rathvi

**Ethnologue code:** ISO 639-3: rtw
**Language classification:** Indo-Aryan, Central zone, Bhil
**Alternate names:** Kohelia, Bal-La
**Main region:** Gujarati, Baroda and Panchmahals districts

## 1 Consonant phonemes

### 1.1 Inventory

| | Bila-bial | Labio-dental | Dental | Alv | Retro. | Pala-tal | Velar | Glo-ttal |
|---|---|---|---|---|---|---|---|---|
| Plosive | p b<br>pʰ bʱ | | t d<br>tʰ dʱ | | ʈ ɖ<br>ʈʰ ɖʱ | | k g<br>kʰ gʱ | |
| Nasal | m | | n | | ɳ | | | |
| Tap | | | | r | | | | |
| Flap | | | | | ɽ | | | |
| Fricative | | | | s | | | | h |
| Approx | | ʋ | | | | j | | |
| Lat Appr | | | | l | | | | |
| Affricate | | | | | | ʧ ʤ<br>ʧʰ ʤʱ | | |

## 1.2 Distribution

a. Consonants occur in all positions, with the following restriction:
   i. /ɳ ɽ j/ do not occur word-initially.

b. Geminates of the following consonants occur: /p t ʈ k tʃ m l ʋ/.

c. The following consonants are found to occur in free variation in a large number of lexical items.: t ~ tʰ, r ~ ɽ, b ~ bʱ, ɖ ~ ɽ, s ~ tʃʰ , s ~ ʃ.

# 2 Vowel phonemes

## 2.1 Inventory[26]

a. **Short**

| | FRONT | CENTRAL | BACK |
|---|---|---|---|
| Close | i | | u |
| Close-mid | e | ə | o |
| Open-mid | ɛ | a | ɔ |

b. **Long**

| | FRONT | CENTRAL | BACK |
|---|---|---|---|
| Close | i: | | u: |
| Close-mid | ɛ: | | ɔ: |
| Open | | a: | |

c. **Nasal:**

| | FRONT | CENTRAL | BACK |
|---|---|---|---|
| Close | ĩ | | ũ |
| Close-mid | ẽ | ə̃ | |
| Open-mid | ɛ̃ | ã | ɔ̃ |

## 2.2 Distribution

a. Vowels occur in all positions.

[26] The short vowel counterparts of the long vowels are higher in height than the long vowel counterparts.

b. Sequences of two vowels occur in all positions, with the following restrictions:

   i. Word-initially, only the sequence /oi/ is attested.
   ii. Word-medially, the sequences /əi ɔi ai/ are attested.
   iii. Word-finally a much larger number of sequences is attested.

c. The following vowels are found to occur in free variation in a number of lexical items: e ~ ɛ, o ~ ɔ,

# 3 Consonant allophones

a. [ʃ] < /s/ occurs before /i/.

# 4 Vowel allophones

**General:**
Length. All the vowels are longer in stressed syllables[27].

# 5 Syllable structure

## 5.1 Canonical syllable structure

(C) (G/r) V (C) (C)

## 5.2 Consonant clusters

Two-consonant clusters:

Initial : C+j/ʋ/r
Medial : General.
Final : k/n/r/j + C.

[27] Stress patterns of Rathvi are not described in the study.

Three-consonant clusters:

Initial : Nil.

Medial : General, $C_3$ must be one of the following: /l r ɽ j ʋ/.

Final : Nil.

**Reference:** Parakh (2000)

# Shina[28]

**Ethnologue code** ISO 639-3: scl
**Language classification:** Indo-Aryan, Northwestern zone, Dardic
**Alternate names:** Sina, Shinaki, Brokpa
**Main region (within India):** Jammu and Kashmir (Drass, Gurez, Kargil, Karkit Badgam and Ladakh valleys).

## 1 Consonant Phonemes

### 1.1 Inventory

| | BILABIAL | LABIODENTAL | DENTAL | ALV. | POST-ALV. | RETR. | PALATAL | VELAR | GLOTTAL |
|---|---|---|---|---|---|---|---|---|---|
| Plosive | p b<br>p$^h$ | | t d<br>t$^h$ | | | ʈ ɖ<br>ʈ$^h$ | | k g<br>k$^h$ | |
| Nasal | m | | | n | | ɳ | | ŋ | |
| Trill | | | | r | | | | | |
| Fricative | | | | s z | ʃ ʒ | ʐ | | x ɣ | h |
| Approx | | ʋ | | | | | j | | |
| Lat Appr | | | | l | | | | | |
| Affricate | | | ts<br>ts$^h$ | | | ʈʂ<br>ʈʂ$^h$ | ʧ ʤ<br>ʧ$^h$ ʤ$^ɦ$ | | |

[28] Shina has three main dialects: Astori, Gilgiti and Kohistani. The present description is of the Drasi variety of Astori, spoken around Ranabirpura. The main variety, Astori, as well as Gilgiti and Kohistani are spoken in the areas in Pakistan. Smidt and Kohistani (1998) is a detailed description of Kohistani Shina containing a larger set of consonant phonemes, including uvular sounds, aspirated voiced stops, aspirated alveolar lateral, and aspirated bilabial nasal.

## 1.2 Distribution

a. Consonants occur in all positions, with the following restriction:

   i. The following consonants do not occur finally /pʰ b tʰ d ʈʰ ɖ kʰ ɡ z ʒ ʐ x ɣ tsʰ ʤ ʤʱ/.

   ii. /ɳ ŋ/ do not occur initially.

b. Geminate consonants do not occur.

# 2 Vowel phonemes

## 2.1 Inventory

a. **Short**

| | FRONT | CENTRAL | BACK |
|---|---|---|---|
| Close | i | | u |
| Close-mid | e | | o |
| Open-mid | ɛ | ə | |
| Open | | a | |

b. **Long**

| | FRONT | CENTRAL | BACK |
|---|---|---|---|
| Close | iː | | uː |
| Close-mid | eː | | oː |
| Open-mid | ɛː | əː | ɔː |
| Open | | aː | |

c. **Nasal:**

| | FRONT | CENTRAL | BACK |
|---|---|---|---|
| Close | ĩː ĩ | | ũː ũ |

| | | | |
|---|---|---|---|
| Close-mid | ẽ: ẽ | | õ: õ |
| Open-mid | ɛ̃ : ɛ̃ | | |
| Open | | ã: ã | |

**Diphthongs:**

Oral: / ei ɛi ai ui oi au eə /

Nasal: / ẽĩ ɛ̃ĩ ãĩ ũĩ õĩ ãũ ẽə̃ /

## 2.2 Distribution

a. Vowels occur in all positions, with the following restriction:

   i. /ə ə : ɛ :/are not found to occur finally.

# 3 Consonant allophones

## 3.1 Inventory

| | Bilabial | Dental | Alveolar | Retroflex | Pre-Velar | Velar |
|---|---|---|---|---|---|---|
| Plosive | | | | | k̟ (k) ɡ̟(g) k̟ʰ(kʰ) | |
| Tap/ Flap | | | ɾ(r) | ɽ (ɖ) | | |
| Fricative | β(b) | ð(d) | | | | ɣ (g) |
| Approx | w(ʋ) | | | | | |

## 3.2 Distribution

a. The fricative allophones of the voiced stops [β ð ɣ] < /b d g/ occur intervocalically, and between a /r/ and a vowel.

b. The prevelar allophones of the velar plosives [ k̟ ɡ̟ k̟ʰ ] < / k g kʰ/ occur before high front vowels.

c. [ɽ] < /ɖ/ occurs intervocalically.
d. [ɾ ] < / r/ occurs between /b d g/ and a short vowel.
e. [w] < / ʋ / occurs before rounded vowels.

# 4 Vowel allophones

Data not available.

# 5 Syllable structure

## 5.1 Canonical syllable structure

(C)(r)V(C)

## 5.2 Consonant clusters

Two-consonant clusters:

Initial : C+r
Final : Nil
Medial : General.

Three-consonant clusters: Nil.

Medial : Restricted

# 6 Suprasegmentals

## 6.1 Stress

Stress is phonemic in Shina, e.g.,

| | |
|---|---|
| / ɖáŋo / 'high' | / ɖaŋó / 'bridge' |
| / áʐo / 'cloud, wet' | / aʐó / 'inside, in' |

## 6.2 Tone

Schmidt & Kohistani (1998) include two contrastive tones on long vowels. The description by Rajapurohit (1983) doesn't show any contrastive tone in the Drasi variety of Astori dialect.

**Reference:** Rajpurohit (1983)

# Sindhi

**Ethnologue code:** ISO 639-3: snd
**Language classification:** Indo-Aryan, Northwestern zone
**Alternate names:** Nil
**Main region:** Gujarat; Maharashtra; Rajasthan; Delhi.

## 1 Consonant phonemes

### 1.1 Inventory

| | Bilabial | Labiodental | Dental | Post-Alv | Retro. | Palatal | Velar | Uvular | Glottal |
|---|---|---|---|---|---|---|---|---|---|
| Plosive | p b<br>p$^{h}$ b$^{ɦ}$ | | t d<br>t$^{h}$ d$^{ɦ}$ | | ʈ ɖ<br>ʈ$^{h}$ ɖ$^{ɦ}$ | | k g | (q) | |
| Nasal | m | | n | | | ɲ | ŋ | | |
| Trill | | | r | | | | | | |
| Flap | | | | | ɽ | | | | |
| Fricative | f | | s z | ʃ | | | x ɣ | | h |
| Approx | | ʋ | | | | j | | | |
| Lat Appr | | | l | | | | | | |
| Affricate | | | | | | ʧ ʤ<br>ʧ$^{h}$ ʤ$^{ɦ}$ | | | |
| Implosive | ɓ | | | | ᶑ | ʄ | ɠ | | |

### 1.2 Distribution

a. Native words end in a vowel, so do a majority of borrowed words.
b. Gemination is rare.
c. /f z q x ɣ/ occur only in words of Perso-Arabic origin.

# 2 Vowel phonemes

## 2.1 Inventory

a. **Short**

| | FRONT | CENTRAL | BACK |
|---|---|---|---|
| Close | ɪ | | ʊ |
| Open-mid | | ə | |

b. **Long**

| | FRONT | CENTRAL | BACK |
|---|---|---|---|
| Close | i: | | u: |
| Close-mid | e: | | o: |
| Open-mid | (ɛ :) | | (ɔ :) |
| Open | | a: | |

c. **Nasal:**

| | FRONT | CENTRAL | BACK |
|---|---|---|---|
| Close | ĩ: ɪ̃ | | ũ: ʊ̃ |
| Close-mid | ẽ: | | õ: |
| Open-mid | (ɛ̃ :) | ə̃ | (ɔ̃ :) |
| Open | | ã: | |

## 2.2 Distribution

a. Vowels occur in all positions.

b. Sequences of two and three vowels occur in all positions.

c. /ɛ ɛ̃ ɔ ɔ̃ / occur rarely; they occur more frequently in borrowed items.

# 3 Consonant allophones

Data are not available.

# 4 Vowel allophones

Data are not available.

# 5 Syllable structure

## 5.1 Canonical syllable structure[29]

(C) V (C)

## 5.2 Consonant clusters

Two-consonant clusters:

Initial : Nil
Final : Nil
Medial : General.

Three-consonant clusters: Nil

**Reference:** Khubchandani (2003)

[29] Words of up to eight syllables may occur.

# Urdu[30]

Ethnologue code: ISO 639-3: urd
**Language classification:** Indo-Aryan, Central zone, Western Hindi, Hindustani
**Alternate names:** Islami, Undri, Urudu
**Main region:** Jammu and Kashmir and by Muslims and some Hindus in many parts of India; Dakhini dialect spoken in Andhra Pradesh, Karnataka, and Tamil Nadu.

## 1 Consonant Phonemes

### 1.1 Inventory

| | Bilabial | Labiodental | Dental | Alv. | Post-Alv | Retroflex | Palatal | Velar | Uvular | Glottal |
|---|---|---|---|---|---|---|---|---|---|---|
| Plosive | p b<br>pʰ bʱ | | t d<br>tʰ dʱ | | | ʈ ɖ<br>ʈʰ ɖʱ | | k g<br>kʰ gʱ | q | |
| Nasal | m | | | n | | | | (ŋ) | | |
| Nasal Flap | | | | | | ɽ̃ | | | | |
| Tap | | | | ɾ | | | | | | |
| Fricative | | f v | | s z | ʃ | | | x ɣ | | h |
| Approx | | ʋ | | | | | j | | | |
| Lat Appr | | | | l | | | | | | |
| Affricate | | | | | | | tʃ dʒ<br>tʃʰ dʒʱ | | | |

30 The sound structures of Urdu and Hindi are close to each other. The phonemic system differs in the addition of a plosive and two fricatives among consonants. The vowel phonemic system is identical. There are greater differences in the allophonic systems.

## 1.2 Distribution

a. Consonants occur in all positions, with the following restrictions:
   i. /ɽ̃ (ŋ)/ do not occur word-initially.
   ii. /ŋ/ tends to occur with /g/.

b. Geminate consonants occur except for the following: [bʱ ʃ h j]. A sequence of a long vowel followed by a consonant has the lexical alternant of a short vowel followed by a geminate consonant, e.g., /dərʋa:za:/ ~ /dərvəzza:/ 'door'.

c. In cases of free variation between fricatives and stops in words of Perso-Arabic origin, Urdu speakers show a preference for the fricatives.

# 2 Vowel phonemes

## 2.1 Inventory

a. **Short:**

| | FRONT | CENTRAL | BACK |
|---|---|---|---|
| Close | ɪ | | ʊ |
| Open-mid | | ə | |

b. **Long:**

| | FRONT | CENTRAL | BACK |
|---|---|---|---|
| Close | i: | | u: |
| Close-mid | e: | | o: |
| Open-mid | ɛ: (æ:) | | ɔ: |
| Open | | a: | |

c. **Nasal:**

| | FRONT | CENTRAL | BACK |
|---|---|---|---|
| Close | ĩ: ɪ̃ | | ũ: ʊ̃ |

| | | | |
|---|---|---|---|
| Close-mid | ẽ: | | õ: |
| Open-mid | ɛ̃: | ə̃ | ə̃ʊ̃ : |
| Open | | ã: | |

## 2.2 Distribution

a. Short vowels do not occur word-finally in Urdu, unlike in Sanskritized Hindi. However, in compound forms, short vowels occur, freely varying with [e] and [o], as in [dərdɪ](~[dərde]) + [dɪl] 'heartache', [əlla:hʊ]([əlla:ho] + [əkbər] 'god is great'.

b. In western Urdu, /e :/ is pronounced as /ɛ :/.

c. /æ:/ occurs in borrowed vocabulary from English. It does not contrast with /ɛ:/.

d. In cases of free variation between [e o] and /ɪ ʊ/ in exical items of Perso-Arabic origin, urdu speakers show a preference for [ɪ ʊ].

e. The Urdu /əʊ/ is phonetically different from the IPA /ɔ/ in having a fast rise from unrounded to rounded lip position , and from the open-mid central to close-mid back position.

# 3 Consonant allophones

## 3.1 Inventory

| | BILABIAL | DENTAL | ALV. | POST-ALV. | RETROFLEX | PALATAL | GLOTTAL |
|---|---|---|---|---|---|---|---|
| Nasal | m̤ (m) | | n̤ (n) | | | | |
| Trill | | r̪ (ɾ) | r ~ ɽ | r̠ (ɾ) | | | |
| Flap | | | | | ɽ (ɖ)<br>ɽʰ(ɖʰ) | | |
| Fricative | | | | | ʂ(s) | | ɦ(h) |
| Lat Appr | | | l̤ (l) | l̠ (l) | | | |

## 3.2 Distribution

**General:**

a. Consonants are lengthened before /j w r/. Aspirated plosives and affricates have their plosive parts lengthened, e.g., [p:ʰ t:ʃ] etc.

**Specific:**

a. [ɽ ɽʰ] < / ɖ ɖʰ/ occur between vowels, and in syllable Coda positions, except in loan-words.

b. [ m̤ n̤ l̤ ]< /m n l/ occur before /h/.

c. [ʂ̺ ] < /s / occurs before retroflex consonants.

d. The post-alveolar lateral allophone [l̟ ] < /l / occurs before retroflex consonants, e.g., [ ʊl̟ʈa:] < /ʊlʈa:/ 'inverted'.

e. [ɦ] < / h/ occurs non-finally.

f. The dental [r̪] and the post-alveolar [r̟] allophones of the tap /ɾ/ occur after dental and retroflex consonants. E. g., /tritija:/ 'the third day of the fortnight', /ɖrəm / 'drum'.

g. [r] and [ɽ] freely vary in many lexical items in Hindi-Urdu; in such cases Urdu speakers show a preference for [r], as in [ɣubba:ra:]' baloon'.

# 4 Vowel allophones

## 4.1 Inventory

[e] [ə] : /e :/

[əi̯]: /ɛ :/

[o :]: /o :/

[ə u̯]: /əo :/

[e] [ɐ]: /ə/

## 4.2 Distribution

a. [e] < /ə/ occurs when followed by /h/, and a vowel other than /ə a:/ in the next syllable.

b. [e o] < /e: o:/ occur before /h/, e.g., /ko : hra : / > [kohra : ] 'fog'; /me : hta : / > [mehta : ] (a last name)

c. [əi̯]: < /ɛ :/and [əu̯] < /ɔ:/ occur before vowels and semivowels, e.g., /bʰ ɛ j a : / > [bʰəija : ] 'brother' (mainly vocative).

d. Urdu shows a preference for nasalized vowels for the V + N sequences, as in /ʤəha:n/ > [ʤəhã:] 'world'

# 5 Syllable structure

## 5.1 Canonical syllable structure[31]

(C)(C)(C)V(C)(C)(C)

E.g., /ʃa:str/ 'learned book'; /stri:/ 'woman'.

## 5.2 Consonant clusters

Two-consonant clusters:

Initial : (i) C + L/G; (ii) s + C.
Final : general
Medial : general.

Three-consonant clusters:

Initial : /spr str smr/
Final : /str ntr ʂʈr rdr/
Medial : general.

**References:** Kelkar (1968), Gumperz and Naim (1960)

[31] The three consonant clusters are rare in Urdu speech , most of them are in borrowed vocabulary from Sanskrit and English.

# Urdu-Dakhani-Hyderabadi[32]

**Ethnologue code:** ISO 639-3: dcc
**Language classification:** Indo-Aryan
**Alternate names:** Dakhini Urdu, Dakhini.
**Main region:** Andhra Pradesh, Hyderabad

## 1 Consonant phonemes

### 1.1 Inventory

| | BILA-BIAL | LABIO-DENTAL | DEN-TAL | ALV. | POST-ALV. | RET. | PALA-TAL | VEL-AR | GLO-TTAL |
|---|---|---|---|---|---|---|---|---|---|
| Plosive | p b $p^h$ $b^{ɦ}$ | | t d $t^h$ $d^{ɦ}$ | | | ʈ ɖ $ʈ^h$ $ɖ^{ɦ}$ | | k g $k^h$ $g^{ɦ}$ | |
| Nasal | m | | | n | | ɳ | | (ŋ) | |
| Trill | | | | r | | | | | |
| Fricative | | f (v) | | s z | ʃ | | | x | h |
| Approx | | ʋ | | | | | j | | |
| Lat. Approx | | | | l | | | | | |
| Plosive | | | | | | | ʧ ʤ $ʧ^h$ $ʤ^{ɦ}$ | | |

[32] "The phonemic inventory of Hyderabadi Dakhini is nearly identical to that of standard Urdu. In a few cases the phonetic realization of a phoneme may differ; there is also some allophonic variation which is typically Dakhini. Phonetic realizations are supplied here for the vowels, and for sounds which show differences as compared with standard Urdu" (Schmidt 1981:17)

## 1.2 Distribution

a. Consonants occur in all positions, with the following restrictions:
   i. /ɳ h j/ do not occur word-initially.
   ii. /ŋ/ tends to occur before /g/, which may be deleted.
   iii. The aspirated phonemes do not occur finally.

b. Geminate consonants occur except for the following: [bʱ ʃ h j].

c. /x/ replaces standard Urdu /q/.

# 2 Vowel phonemes

## 2.1 Inventory

a. **Short:**

| | FRONT | CENTRAL | BACK |
|---|---|---|---|
| Close-Mid | ɪ | | ʊ |
| Mid | | ə | |

b. **Long:**

| | FRONT | CENTRAL | BACK |
|---|---|---|---|
| Close | i: | | u: |
| Mid | e: | | o: |
| Open | | a: | |

c. **Nasal:**

| | FRONT | CENTRAL | BACK |
|---|---|---|---|
| Close | ĩ: | | ũ: |
| Close-Mid | ɪ̃ | | ʊ̃ |
| Mid | ẽ: | ə̃ | õ: |
| Open | | ã: | |

## 2.2 Distribution

a. Vowels occur in all positions, with the following restriction:
   i. The short vowels do not occur finally.

b. Vowel sequences occur. E.g., /ba:oa:/ 'father'.

# 3 Consonant allophones[33]

## 3.1 Inventory

| | LABIO-DENTAL | RETROFLEX | PALATAL | VELAR | GLOTTAL |
|---|---|---|---|---|---|
| Flap | | ɽ (ɖ) | | | |
| Fricative | β (w) | | | ɣ (x) | ø (h) |
| Affricate | | | ʤ ~z | | |

## 3.2 Distribution

a. [ɽ] < /ɖ/ occurs inter-vocalically and finally.

b. [w] < /ʋ/ occurs following /ʊ/

# 4 Vowel allophones

## 4.1 Inventory

**General:**
Long vowels have allophones of half length word-finally.

[33] The approximant phonemes /j ʋ/ have non-syllabic allophones.
/j/: [i], [ɪ]; /w/: [ʊ], [u].

**Specific:**

[ʊ̯] : /ʊ/

[ɪ̯] : /ɪ/

## 4.2 Distribution

a. The non-syllabic vocalic allophones [ʊ̯] < /ʊ/ and [ɪ̯] < /ɪ/ occur medially or finally after /ɐ / or / ɐ̃ /.

# 5 Syllable structure

## 5.1 Canonical syllable structure

(C) (L/j) V (C)

## 5.2 Consonant clusters

Two-consonant clusters:

Initial : Obs + j/ɾ/l.

Final : Nil except in a few words borrowed from English

Medial : General.

Three-consonant clusters: Nil.

**Reference:** Schmidt (1981)

Chapter 4

# TIBETO-BURMAN

# Adi

**Ethnologue code:** ISO 639-3: adi
**Language classification:** Tibeto-Burman, North Assam, Tani
**Alternate names:** Abhor, Abor, Boga'er Luoba, Lhoba, Luoba
**Main region:** Arunachal Pradesh

## 1 Consonant Phonemes

### 1.1 Inventory

| | BILA-BIAL | LABIO-DENTAL | DEN-TAL | ALV. | POST ALV. | PALATAL | VELAR | GLOTTAL |
|---|---|---|---|---|---|---|---|---|
| Plosive | p b<br>pʰ | | t d<br>tʰ dʱ | | | | k g<br>kʰ | ʔ |
| Nasal | m | | | n | | | ŋ | |
| Trill | | | | r | | | | |
| Fricative | | f v | | s z | ʃ | | | h |
| Approx | w | | | | | j | | |
| Lat Appr | | | | l | | | | |
| Affricate | | | | ts | | ʧ ʤ<br>ʧʰ | | |

## 1.2 Distribution

a. Consonants occur in all positions, with the following restrictions:
   i. The following consonants do not occur in the final position: /p pʰ tʰ d dʱ g ʃ z s ʦ ʧ ʤ f v h w/.
   ii. The following consonants do not occur initially: /kʰ ʦ ʧ ʤ f v h w/.
   iii. The following consonants do not occur medially: / kʰ ʃ/.

b. Geminates of the following consonants occur inter-vocalically: /p b t d k s m n j/.

# 2 Vowel Phonemes

## 2.1 Inventory

**a. Short**

| | FRONT | CENTRAL | BACK |
|---|---|---|---|
| Close | i | ɨ ʉ | u |
| Close-mid | e | | o |
| Open-mid | ɛ | ə | ɔ |
| Open | | a | |

**b. Long**

| | FRONT | CENTRAL | BACK |
|---|---|---|---|
| Close | iː | ɨː | uː |
| Close-mid | eː | | oː |
| Open-mid | ɛː | əː | ɔː |
| Open | | aː | |

## 2.2 Distribution

a. Vowels occur in all positions, with the following restriction: /ɨ ʉ u/ do not occur initially.

b. Vowel sequences occur in all positions.

# 3 Consonant Allophones

Inadequate data available.

# 4 Vowel Allophones

Inadequate data available.

# 5 Syllable Structure

## 5.1 Canonical syllable structure

(C)V(C)

## 5.2 Consonant clusters

Two-consonant clusters:

Initial : Nil.
Final : Nil
Medial : General.

Three-consonant clusters:

Initial : Nil
Final : Nil
Medial : /-nts- -mdr-/; only two clusters attested.

# 6 Suprasegmentals

## 6.1 Tone

Tonemes:

a. Falling: HL ( ̀ )

b. Rising: LH ( ́ )

c. Falling-Rising: HLH (ˇ)

d. Rising-Falling: LHL (ˆ)

E.g., /takě/ 'split with axe', /takè/, 'six years', /také/ 'crab', /takê/ 'ginger'.

**Reference:** Suebplai (1986)

# Angami

**Ethnologue code:** ISO 639-3: njm
**Language classification:** Tibeto-Burman, Kuki-Chin-Naga
**Alternate names:** Gnamei, Ngami, Angamis, Tsoghami, Tsugumi, Monr, Tsanglo, Tendydie
**Main region:** Western Nagaland; Manipur.

## 1 Consonant Phonemes

### 1.1 Inventory

| | Bilabial | Labiodental | Alveolar | Post Alveolar | Palatal | Velar | Glottal |
|---|---|---|---|---|---|---|---|
| Plosive | p b<br>$p^{h}$ | | t d<br>$t^{h}$ | | | k g<br>$k^{h}$ | |
| Nasal | $\text{m̥}^{h}$ m | | $\text{n̥}^{h}$ n | | $\text{ɲ̊}^{h}$ ɲ | ŋ | |
| Trill | | | $\text{r̥}^{h}$ r | | | | |
| Fricative | | f v | s z | ʃ ʒ | | | h |
| Approx. | w | | | | j | | |
| Lateral Appr. | | | $\text{l̥}^{h}$ l | | | | |
| Affricate | pf bv<br>$pf^{h}$ | | ts dz<br>$ts^{h}$ | | tʃ dʒ<br>$\text{tʃ}^{h}$ | | |

### 1.2 Distribution

a. In native words, consonants do not occur word-finally.

b. Nasals can be syllabic.

c. Only /p $p^h$ k $k^h$/ occur with /r/ in a cluster, other consonants don't.

d. Geminate consonants do not occur.

# 2 Vowel Phonemes

## 2.1 Inventory

**a. Short**

| | FRONT | CENTRAL | BACK |
|---|---|---|---|
| Close | i | | u |
| Close-mid | e | | o |
| Open-mid | | ə | |
| Open | | a | |

**Diphthongs:**

The diphthongs have the second vowel position as more prominent than the first, also found for Ao-N. These are termed as Class II diphthongs for some other T-B languages that also have the more common class of the first vowel position being more prominent than the second, e.g., Liangmai and Mao-N.

i̯e i̯o (e̯o) ə̯i o̯u u̯o

## 2.2 Distribution

a. / e o/ do not occur initially.

b. Diphthongs carry one tone each, compared to vowel sequences, which have a tone on each vowel.

# 3 Consonant Allophones

## 3.1 Inventory

| | LABIO-DENTAL |
|---|---|
| Nasal | ɱ (m) |
| Fricative | f(p)<br>f(w)<br>v(w) |

## 3.2 Distribution

a. [m] < /ɱ/, [f] < /p/ occur before /ə/.

b. [f] < /w/ occurs before /ə/, when preceded by /k$^{h}$/: /k$^{h}$fə] < /k$^{h}$wə/.

c. [v] < /w/ occurs before /ə/, when preceded by /k g/.

# 4 Vowel Allophones

## 4.1 Inventory

[i] < /ə̯i/

[u] < /o̯u/

[ɛ] < /e/

[ə̥] < /ə/

[ɔ] < /o/

## 4.2 Distribution

a. [ə̥] < /ə/ occurs after /r/.

b. [ɛ] < /e/ and [ɔ] < /o/ occur word-finally.

c. [i] < /ə̯i/ and [u] < /o̯u/ are the free variants of the diphthong phonemes.

# 5 Syllable Structure

## 5.1 Canonical syllable structure

(C) (r)V/ C̩.

C̩ = syllabic consonant

## 5.2 Consonant clusters

Two-consonant clusters:

| | | |
|---|---|---|
| Initial | : | /pr/ /$p^h$r/ kr/ $k^h$r/ |
| Final | : | Nil. |
| Medial | : | Same as initial |

Three-consonant clusters:

| | | |
|---|---|---|
| Initial | : | Nil |
| Final | : | Nil |
| Medial | : | Nil. |

# 6 Suprasegmentals

## 6.1 Tones

a. High: H ($^1$)

b. Mid: M ($^2$)

c. Mid-Low: ML ($^3$)

d. Low: L ($^4$)

E.g.,

/$g^we^1$/ 'to bud;

/$g^we^2$/ 'to occupy;

/$g^we^3$/ 'to be thin';

/$g^we^4$/ 'physique'.

**References:** Giridhar (1980), Blankenship et. al. (1993)

# Ao-Naga

**Ethnologue code:** ISO 639-3: njo
**Language classification:** Tibeto-Burman, Kuki-Chin-Naga
**Alternate names:** Aorr, Paimi, Cholimi, Hatigoria, Uri, Ao
**Main region:** Northeastern Nagaland; Assam.

## 1 Consonant Phonemes

### 1.1 Inventory

| | BILABIAL | ALVEOLAR | RETROFLEX | PALATAL | VELAR | GLOTTAL |
|---|---|---|---|---|---|---|
| Plosive | p | t | | | k | ʔ |
| Nasal | m | n | | | ŋ | |
| Tap | | ɾ | | | | |
| Fricative | | s z | | | | h |
| Approx | w | | | j | | |
| Lat Appr | | l | | | | |
| Lat fricative | | | ɮ˙ | | | |
| Affricate | | | | tʃ | | |

### 1.2 Distribution

a. Consonants occur in all the positions, with the following restriction:
   i. /tʃ s z l/ do not occur finally.
   ii. /ʔ/ does not occur initially.

b. Geminate consonants of the following consonants occur intervocalically: /p k ʔ m n /.

# 2 Vowel Phonemes

## 2.1 Inventory

a. **Short**

| | FRONT | CENTRAL | BACK |
|---|---|---|---|
| Close | i | | ɯ u |
| Close-mid | e | | o |
| Open | | | ɑ |

**Diphthongs**[1]: /i̯e i̯o (e̯o) ə̯i o̯u u̯o/

## 2.2 Distribution

a. Vowels occur in all positions.

b. Vowel sequences do not occur. In word-formation, too, vowel sequences are avoided by either deleting a vowel or inserting a semi-vowel j or w. E.g., /ta+apú / > [tapú] 'don't blow'; /ta + imsa/ [tijimsa] 'don't melt'.

# 3 Consonant Allophones

## 3.1 Inventory

| | BILABIAL | ALVEOLAR | POST ALVEOLAR | PALATAL | VELAR |
|---|---|---|---|---|---|
| Plosive | pʰ (p)<br>b(p) | tʰ (t)<br>d(t) | | | kʰ (k)<br>g(k) |

[1] As also noted for Angami, all the vowels are represented as being of the pattern with the second vowel being more prominent than the first. However, this requires checking, as in such cases, the other T-B languages such as Liangmai, Paite and Wancho also have diphthongs with the first vowel as more prominent.

| | | | | | |
|---|---|---|---|---|---|
| Fricative | | | ʃ(s) | | |
| Affricate | | ts (tʃ) | | dʒ(tʃ) | |
| Approx. | | w(Ø) | | j(Ø) | |

## 3.2 Distribution

a. Aspirated voiceless plosives [ $p^h$ $t^h$ $k^h$] < /p t k/ occur word-initially.

b. Voiced stop allophones [b d g dʒ] < /ptk tʃ/ occur inter-vocalically or following a voiced sound.

c. [ts] < /tʃ/ occurs when followed by /ɯ/.

d. [ʃ] < /s/ occurs before /i/.

e. The front vowels /i i: e e:/ have a j-onglide [$^j$i $^j$i: $^j$e $^j$e:] and the vowels /u u: o o:/ have a w-onglide [$^w$u $^w$u: $^w$o $^w$o:] in words beginning with them.

# 4 Vowel Allophones

## 4.1 Inventory

[ẹ] [$^j$e]: /e /

[ʌ]: /ɑ/

[ɔ][$^w$o]: /o/

## 4.2 Distribution

a. [ẹ ]< /e/ occurs when flanked by tautosyllabic consonants.

b. [$^j$e $^w$o]< /e o/ occur word-initially.

c. [ɔ] < /o/ occurs when preceded or followed by velar consonants /k ŋ/.

d. [ʌ] < /ɑ/ occurs when accompanied by falling tone. /ɑ̀ŋó/ > [ʌ̀ŋɔ́] 'to see, find'. /mɑŋɑ̀/ [maŋʌ̀] 'to fly'.

# 5 Syllable Structure

## 5.1 Canonical syllable structure

(C) (ɬ) V (j/ʔ) (C).

## 5.2 Consonant clusters

Two-consonant clusters:

Initial : /pɬ̩- tɬ-/

Final : /-ɟp -ʔp/

Three-consonant clusters: Nil.

# 6 Suprasegmentals

## 6.1 Tone

Tonemes:

a. Rising: H ( ´ )
b. Falling: L ( ` )
c. Level: unmarked

E.g., /ápu/ 'blow', /àpu/ 'borrow', /apu/ bridge, ladder'

**Reference:** Gowda (1975)

# Apatani

**Ethnologue code:** ISO 639-3: apt
**Language classification:** Tibeto-Burman, North Assam, Tani
**Alternate names:** Apa
**Main region:** Arunachal Pradesh.

## 1 Consonant Phonemes

### 1.1 Inventory

| | BILABIAL | | ALVEOLAR | | PALATAL | | VELAR | | GLOTTAL |
|---|---|---|---|---|---|---|---|---|---|
| Plosive | p | b | t | d | | | k | g | |
| Nasal | | m | | n | | | | ŋ | |
| Trill | | | | r | | | | | |
| Fricative | | | s | | | | x | | h |
| Approx | | | | | | j | | | |
| Lat Appr | | | | l | | | | | |
| Affricate | | | | | tʃ | ʤ | | | |

### 1.2 Distribution

a. Consonants, except /m ŋ r l s/ do not occur word-finally.

b. Geminates do not occur.

# 2 Vowel Phonemes

## 2.1 Inventory

a. **Short**

| | FRONT | CENTRAL | BACK |
|---|---|---|---|
| Close | i | ɨ | u |
| Close-mid | e | | o |
| Open | | a | |

## 2.2 Distribution

a. Vowels occur in all positions.

b. Vowel sequences are found to occur, although not frequently.

c. Word-finally, /ɨ/ is deleted before consonant-initial morphemes. E.g., /amɨ/ + /sanɨ/ > [amsanɨ] 'mango tree'

# 3 Consonant Allophones

## 3.1 Inventory

| | BILABIAL | ALVEOLAR | PALATAL |
|---|---|---|---|
| Nasal | m (ŋ) | n (ŋ) | ɲ (ŋ)<br>ɲ (n) |
| Fricative | β (b) | | |

## 3.2 Distribution

a. [ɲ ] < / n/ occurs before palatal stops.

b. [m n ɲ] < / ŋ/ occur before homorganic stops.

# 4 Vowel Allophones

## 4.1 Inventory

[ɛ] : /e/

[a̟]: /a/

[ə] [ɯ]: /ɨ/

## 4.2 Distribution

a. [ɛ ] < /e /, [ a̟ ] < /a / occur in the first syllable of a word with /j/ as an Onset. E.g., [jɛso ] 'cane'.

b. [ə ] < / ɨ / occurs in the final syllable, before or after /r/, e.g.,: [kakər] 'look back', [tɨ rə] 'forehaead'

c. [ɯ ] < /ɨ/ occurs in final closed syllable before /ŋ/ or in a final open syllable.

# 5 Syllable Structure

## 5.1 Canonical syllable structure[2]

(C) (j) V (C)

## 5.2 Consonant clusters

Two-consonant clusters:

Initial : Only Cj- (pj- mj- etc.) are attested.

Final : Nil.

Medial : only –NC-, -rC-, -Cj- clusters are attested.

Three-consonant clusters:

Initial : Nil

[2] Monovocalic and monosyllabic words are quite common.

Final : Nil
Medial : Only –CCj- type are attested.

# 6 Suprasegmentals

## 6.1 Tone

Toneme:

a. Rising: LH ( ́ )
b. Falling: HL ( ̀ )
c. Level : M (unmarked)

E.g.,

/ámi/ 'cat', /àmi/ 'eye', / ami/ 'tail'.

**Reference:** Abraham (1985)

# Balti

**Ethnologue code:** ISO 639-3: bft
**Language classification:** Tibeto-Burman, Himalayish
**Alternate names:** Sbalt, Baltistani, Bhoti of Baltistan
**Main region:** Jammu and Kashmir.

## 1 Consonant Phonemes

### 1.1 Inventory

| | **BILAB.** | **LABIO-DENTAL** | **DENTAL** | **ALVEOLAR** | **ALVEO-PALATAL** | **PALATAL** | **VELAR** | **POST VELAR** | **UVU.** | **GL.** |
|---|---|---|---|---|---|---|---|---|---|---|
| Plosive | p b $p^h$ | | t d $t^h$ | t̠ d̠ $\underline{t}^h$ | | | k g $k^h$ | | q | |
| Nasal | m | | n | | | ɲ | ŋ | | | |
| Trill | | | | r | | | | | | |
| Fricative | | (f) | | s z | ʃ ʒ | | | x ɣ | | h |
| Approx | w | | | | | j | | | | |
| Lat Appr | | | | l | | | | | | |
| Affricate | | | ts $ts^h$ | | | tʃ ʤ $tʃ^h$ | | | | |

### 1.2 Distribution

a. All consonants occur initially and medially, with the following restriction:
   i. Semivowels, aspirated stops, and voiced stops do not occur word-finally.
b. Geminate consonants occur.

# 2 Vowel Phonemes

## 2.1 Inventory

a. **Short**

| | FRONT | CENTRAL | BACK |
|---|---|---|---|
| Close | i | | u |
| Close-mid | e | | o |
| Open | | a | |

b. **Long**

| | FRONT | CENTRAL | BACK |
|---|---|---|---|
| Close | i : | | u : |
| Close-mid | e : | | o: |
| Open | | a : | |

## 2.2 Distribution

a. The long vowels / e : / and / o : / do not occur initially.

b. The long vowels, except / i : / do not occur word-finally.

c. Vowel sequences do not occur.

# 3 Consonant Allophones

## 3.1 Inventory

| | DENTAL | ALVEOLAR | RETROFLEX |
|---|---|---|---|
| Nasal | n̪ (n̠) | | |
| Tap / Flap | | | ɽ (d̠) |
| Fricative | ð (d) | z (s) | ʂ (ʃ) |
| Lat Appr | | ɬ (l) | |

## 3.2 Distribution

a. [ð] < /d/ and [ɾ] < /(d̪ / occur inter-vocalically.
b. [ʂ] < /ʃ/ and [ɬ][3] < /l/ occur before consonants.

# 4 Vowel Allophones

## 4.1 Inventory

[i·] < /i/

[e·] < /e/

[ɛ] < /e/

[u·]< /u/

[o·] < /o/

[ɔ] < /o/

[a·] < /a/

[ʌ] < /a/

## 4.2 Distribution

a. Short vowels have half-length word-finally
b. Vowel lowering in [ɛ] < /e/ and [ɔ] < /o/ occurs word-initially.
c. [ʌ] < /a/ occurs word-medially.

# 5 Syllable Structure

## 5.1 Canonical syllable structure

(C)(C)(C)V(C)(C)

E.g., /zug/ 'end'; /zgru/ 'hunchback'; /bjaltʃʰoŋs/ 'wild animal'

---

[3] [ɬ] is a voiceless lateral fricative.

## 5.2 Consonant Clusters

Two-consonant clusters: Occur in all positions.

Inadequate data available for generalizations.

Three-consonant clusters: Occur initially and medially.

Inadequate data available for generalizations.

**References:** Rangan (1975), Sprigg (2002)

# Bantawa

**Ethnologue code:** ISO 639-3: bap
**Language classification:** Tibeto-Burman, Himalayish, Mahakiranti
**Alternate names:** Bantawa Rai, Bantaba, Bontawa, Bantawa Yüng, Bantawa Yong, Bantawa Dum, Kiranti
**Main region:** West Bengal, Sikkim, Assam. (Spoken mainly in Nepal.)

## 1 Consonant Allophones

### 1.1 Inventory

| | Bilabial | | Dental | | Alveolar | | Retroflex | | Palatal | | Velar | | Glottal |
|---|---|---|---|---|---|---|---|---|---|---|---|---|---|
| Plosive | p<br>pʰ | b<br>bʱ | t<br>tʰ | d<br>dʱ | | | ʈ<br>ʈʰ | ɖ<br>ɖʱ | | | k<br>kʰ | g<br>gʱ | ʔ |
| Nasal | m | | | | | n | | | | | | ŋ | |
| Trill | | | | | | r | | | | | | | |
| Fricative | | | | | s | | | | | | | | h |
| Appr | | w | | | | | | | | j | | | |
| Lat Appr | | | | | | l | | | | | | | |
| Affricate | | | | | | | | | tʃ<br>tʃʰ | ʤ<br>ʤʱ | | | |

### 1.2 Distribution

a. Consonants occur in all positions, with the following restrictions:
   i. /ʔ/ does not occur word-initially
   ii. Consonants other than /p ʈ k m n ŋ/ do not occur word-finally in native words.

b. Geminates of the following consonants are attested: /p b t d ʈ ɖ k g tʃ dʒ m n ŋ l / inter-vocalically.

# 2 Vowel Phonemes

## 2.1 Inventory

a. **Short**

| | FRONT | CENTRAL | BACK |
|---|---|---|---|
| Close | i | | ɯ u |
| Mid | e | ə | o |
| Open | | a | |

## 2.2 Distribution

a. Vowels occur in all the positions, with the following restriction:

   i. / ə / does not occur finally.

b. Sequences of two vowels occur with syllabic divisions between them.

# 3 Consonant Allophones

Inadequate data available.

# 4 Vowel Allophones

The front and the back vowels have long allophones word-finally.

# 5 Syllable Structure

## 5.1 Canonical syllable structure

(C) (G/l) V (C)

## 5.2 Consonant clusters

Two-consonant clusters:

Initial : C+j/w/l

Final : Nil

Medial : General.

Three-consonant clusters: Nil

**Reference:** Rai (1985)

# Bodo

**Ethnologue code:** ISO 639-3: brx
**Language classification:** Tibeto-Burman, Jingpho-Konyak-Bodo
**Alternate names:** Boro, Bodi, Bara, Boroni, Mechi, Meche, Mech, Meci
**Main region:** Assam; north West Bengal, Meghalaya

## 1 Consonant Phonemes

### 1.1 Inventory

| | Bilabial | Alveolar | Post alveolar | Palatal | Velar | Glottal |
|---|---|---|---|---|---|---|
| Plosive | p b | $t^h$ d | | | $k^h$ g | |
| Nasal | m | n | | | ŋ | |
| Trill | | r | | | | |
| Fricative | | | ʃ ʒ | | | h |
| Approx | w | | | j | | |
| Lat Approx | | l | | | | |

### 1.2 Distribution

a. Consonants occur in all positions, with the following restriction:
   i. / $p^h$ $t^h$ $k^h$ ʃ h/ do not occur word-finally or as codas.

b. Geminates of /n/ alone are attested word-medially.

# 2 Vowel Phonemes

## 2.1 Inventory

a. **Short**

| | FRONT | CENTRAL | BACK |
|---|---|---|---|
| Close | i | | ɯ |
| Close-mid | e | ə | o |
| Open | | a | |

## 2.2 Distribution

a. Vowels occur in all positions.

b. Vowel sequences do not occur.

# 3 Consonant Allophones

## 3.1 Inventory

| | BILABIAL | ALVEOLAR | POST ALVEOLAR | PALATAL | VELAR | GLOTTAL |
|---|---|---|---|---|---|---|
| Plosive | pˀ (b) p (b) | tˀ (d) t (d) | | | kˀ(g) k (g) | |
| Nasal | mˀ (m) | nˀ (n) | | | ŋˀ (ŋ) | |
| Tap / Flap | | ɾˀ (r) | | | | |
| Fricative | β(b) | sˀ (z) | ʃ(s) ʒ(z) | ç(s) | | ɦ(h) |
| Lat Approx | | lˀ (l) | | | | |
| Affricate | pʰ ɸ (pʰ) | tʰ θ (tʰ) | | ʤ (z) | kʰx (kʰ) | |

### 3.2 Distribution

a. [pʰɸ tʰθ kʰx ] < /pʰ tʰ kʰ/ occur syllable initially before /i o u/ with or without intervening /r l n/.

b. [pˀ tˀ kˀ mˀ nˀ ŋˀ sˀ lˀ ɾˀ] occur word-finally in short syllable with Tone 1.

c. [p t k] occur syllable-finally in other than Tone 1 syllables.

d. [β] occurs between high vowels in rapid speech.

e. [ʒ] occurs initially before /i e/ and non-initially before /u o ə/.

f. [ç] occurs before /i e/ and advanced allophones of /a/ in Tone 1.

g. [ʃ] occurs before /u o/ and back allophones of /ə a/.

h. [ɦ]/ /h/ occurs in Tone 3 syllables.

## 4 Vowel Allophones

### 4.1 Inventory

| | |
|---|---|
| [i·] [ĭ̥] [i̞ː][i̟] [e·] [eː]: | /i/ |
| [e·] [ĕ̥] [e̞ː] [e̟] [ɛ] [ɛː]: | /e/ |
| [ɯ·] [ɯ̥̆] [ɯ̞ː][ɯ̟] [o̯]: | /ɯ/ |
| [ŏ̥] [ɔ·] [o̟] [ɔː]: | /o/ |
| [ə·] [ə̥̆] [ə̞][ə̟] [əː]: | /ə/ |
| [a·] [ḁ̆] [a̟][aː]: | /a/ |

### 4.2 Distribution

a. [i· e· ɯ· ɔ· ə· a·] occur in stressed syllables associated with Tone 2.

b. [i̞ː e̞ː ɯ̞ː ɔː ə̞ː aː] are opener (and retracted) varieties, associated with Tone 3.

c. [ĭ̥ ĕ̥ ɯ̥̆ ŏ̥ ə̥̆ ḁ̆] are extra short vowels that are also voiceless occurring in unstressed syllables.

d. [i̟ e̟ ɯ̟ o̟ ə̟ a̟] are advanced varieties associated with Tone 1.

e. [eˑ e:] < /i/ and [ɛˑ ɛ:]< /e/ occur in closed syllables.

f. [i̯ e̯] </j /, and [u̯ o̯ ] < /w/ occur after /a e/ and /o i/ respectively.

# 5 Syllable Structure[4]

## 5.1 Canonical syllable structure

Initial: (C)(L/n/m) V (C)

Non-initial: C V (C)

## 5.2 Consonant clusters

Two-consonant clusters:

| | |
|---|---|
| Initial | : C+ l/r/n/m |
| Final | : /rd/ |
| Medial | : general. |

Three-consonant clusters:

| | |
|---|---|
| Initial | : Nil |
| Final | : Nil |
| Medial | : permitted Onset and Coda segments |

# 6 Suprasegmentals

## 6. Tone

Bodo has four levels of tone[5], which mark each syllable. A tone has vowel length, stress, voice quality, presence of glottal check, pitch register and pitch contour as its phonetic correlates, as given below:

[4] Syllables without onsets occur word-initially, but not medially.

[5] Vijaykrishnan (p. c.) informs me that in a study carried out by a researcher at English and Foreign Languages University, Hyderabad, Bodo has been found to have only two tonemes. Clearly the tones of Bodo need careful investigation.

| Tone | Length | Voice-Quality | Pitch Register | Pitch Range | Vowel Quality |
|---|---|---|---|---|---|
| 0 | Extra-short | Voiceless and tendency to whisper | Dependent on /123/ | Dependent on /123/ | Centralized and more lax |
| 1 | Short and glottal check/ or long or extra-long or extra-long and no gl. Check | Clear | High | Lever or Rising | Closer and tense |
| 2 | Half-long without glottal check | Clear | Mid | Lever or Falling | Neutral as to closeness and tenseness |
| 3 | Long without gl. Check | Breathy | Low | Falling | Opener and lax |

E.g., /$^{1}$bar/ 'jump, /$^{2}$bar/ 'wind', /$^{3}$bar/ ' bloom'.

**Reference:** Bhattacharya (1977)

# Byangsi[6]

**Ethnologue code:** ISO 639-3: bee
**Language classification:** Tibeto-Burman, Himalayish, Tibeto-Kanauri
**Alternate names:** Byangkho Lwo, Byanshi, Byansi, Bhotia, Byangkhopa, Jaba, Saukas, Shaukas, Rang
**Main region:** Uttaranchal,

## 1 Consonant Phonemes

### 1.1 Inventory

| | Bilabial | Dental | Alveolar | Post Alveolar | Retroflex | Palatal | Velar | Glottal |
|---|---|---|---|---|---|---|---|---|
| Plosive | p b<br>p$^h$ (d$^ɦ$) | t d<br>t$^h$ (d$^ɦ$) | | t$^{>}$ d$^{>}$<br>t$^{h>}$ (d$^{ɦ>}$) | | | k g<br>k$^h$ | |
| Nasal | m̥ m | | n̥ n | | | ɲ | ŋ | |
| Trill | | r̥ r | | | (ɽ) | | | |
| Flap | | | | | | | | |
| Fricative | | | s | ʃ | | | | h |
| Approx | w | | | | | j | | |
| Lat. Appr | | | l̥ l | | | | | |
| Affricate | | | ʦ ʥ<br>ʦ$^h$ | | | ʧ ʤ<br>ʧ$^h$ ʤ$^ɦ$ | | |

[6] The description in S. R. Sharma (2007), on which the present sketch is based, differs on many points from Trivedi (1991) and from D. D. Sharma (1989). S. R. Sharma takes those points for discussion. The latter's 'preaspirated' nasals are treated here as voiceless nasals.

## 1.2 Distribution

a. Consonants occur in all positions, with the following restriction:
   i. Aspirated stops /$p^h$ $t^h$ $t^{h>}$ $k^h$ h/, voiced stops /d $d^>$ ʤ g/, and approximants /w j/ do not occur finally.

b. Geminates for /p t  k s m n/ are attested to occur inter-vocalically.

# 2 Vowel Phonemes

## 2.1 Inventory

a. **Short**

| | FRONT | CENTRAL | BACK |
|---|---|---|---|
| Close | i | ɨ | ɯ u |
| Close-mid | e | | o |
| Open-mid | ɛ | | ɔ |
| Open | | a | |

b. **Long**

| | FRONT | CENTRAL | BACK |
|---|---|---|---|
| Close | i: | | u: |
| Open | | a: | |

c. **Nasal:** Nasal vowels are found to occur erratically. However, there are no minimal pairs to establish their phonemic status vis-à-vis oral vowels.

## 2.2 Distribution

a. Vowels occur in all positions, with the following restriction:
   i. /e ɛ o ɯ/ do not occur initially[7].

[7] Trivedi (1991) notes that /e o/ do not occur in lexical morphemes, but only in grammatical morphemes in the dialect he has analyzed.

ii. /ɛ ɔ / have a low functional load.
iii. The contrast between /e/ and /ɛ/ and /o/ and / ɔ/ is neutralized in closed syllables.

b. The following two vowel sequences are found to occur: /ai au ui ue ua uo/.

# 3 Consonant and Vowel Allophones

Adequate data unavailable.

# 4 Vowel Allophones

Adequate data unavailable.

# 5 Syllable Structure

## 5.1 Canonical syllable structure

(C)(C)V(C)

## 5.2 Consonant clusters

Two-consonant clusters:

Initial : (a) S/F/N + j; (b) S/F + w, (c) S + r

Final : Nil

Medial : General.

Three-consonant clusters: Nil

Note: (a) is the commonest in occurrence, (c) occurs only in non-initial syllables.

# 6 Tones

Tonemes:

a. Falling HL ( ` )

b. Rising LH ( ´ )

c. Level M (unmarked)

E.g. /ʧò/ lake', /ʧó/ 'spoon'; /ga: / 'paddy', /gá:/ 'wound' (<IA)

**Reference:** Sharma (2007)

# Chaudangsi

**Ethnologue code:** ISO 639-3: cdn
**Language classification:** Tibeto-Burman, Himalayish, Tibeto-Kanauri
**Alternate names:** Chaudans Lo, Chanpa Lo, Bangba Lo, Tsaudangsi, Bangbani, Saukas, Shaukas
**Main region:** Uttaranchal.

## 1 Consonant Phonemes[8]

### 1.1 Inventory

| | Bilabial | Labiodental | Dental | Alv. | Retroflex | Palatal | Velar | Glottal |
|---|---|---|---|---|---|---|---|---|
| Stop | p b<br>pʰ bʱ | | t d<br>tʰ dʱ | | ʈ ɖ<br>ʈʰ ɖʱ | | k g<br>kʰ gʱ | |
| Nasal | m<br>ʰm | | | n<br>ʰn | ɳ | | ŋ | |
| Trill | | | | r<br>ʰr | | | | |
| Flap | | | | | ɽ | | | |
| Fricative | | | | s | | ɕ | | h |
| Appr | w<br>ʰw | | | ɹ | | j<br>ʰj | | |
| Lat Appr | | | | l<br>ʰl | | | | |
| Affricate | | | ts<br>tsʰ | | | ʧ ʤ<br>ʧʰ ʤʱ | | |

[8] /ʰm ʰn ʰr ʰj ʰw ʰl/ are described as "preaspirated sounds" (Krishnan 2001:408)

## 1.2 Distribution

a. Consonants occur in all positions, with the following restrictions:
   i. Consonants other than /pt k s ç m n ŋ l r/ do not occur word-finally.
   ii. Aspirated consonants except /kʰ/ do not occur medially.
   iii. /ɳ ɽ / do not occur initially.

b. Geminates of the following consonants are attested: /p t d ʈ k tʃ m n l r/

# 2 Vowel Phonemes[9]

## 2.1 Inventory

a. **Short**

| | FRONT | CENTRAL | BACK |
|---|---|---|---|
| Close | ɪ | | ɯ |
| Mid | | ə | |
| Open-mid | ɛ | | ɔ |

b. **Long**

| | FRONT | CENTRAL | BACK |
|---|---|---|---|
| Close | iː | | uː |
| Mid | eː | | oː |
| Open | | aː | |

## 2.2 Distribution

a. Vowels occur in all the positions, with the following restrictions:
   i. / ɪ ɯ ɛ ɔ / do not occur initially.
   ii. / ɪ ɯ / do not occur finally.

b. Vowel sequences occur with syllabic divisions between them.

[9] The distinction of short and long vowels is inferred from the description, in which the long vowels have not been transcribed with the length notation, [ : ].

# 3 Consonant Allophones

## 3.1 Inventory

| | BILABIAL | DENTAL | RETR | VELAR |
|---|---|---|---|---|
| Stop | b(p) | d(t) | ɖ (ʈ) | g(k) |

## 3.2 Distribution

a. The voiced allophones [b d ɖ g] of the voiceless plosives /p t ʈ k/ occur after voiced plosives and inter-vocalically.

# 4 Vowel Allophones

Inadequate data available.

# 5 Syllable Structure

## 5.1 Canonical syllable structure

(C) (G) V (C)

## 5.2 Consonant clusters[10]

Two-consonant clusters:

Initial : C+G
Final : Nil
Medial : General.

Three-consonant clusters: Nil

**Reference:** Krishan (2001a)

[10] The first consonant is among those permitted to occur initially.

# Chokri

**Ethnologue code:** ISO 639-3: nri
**Language classification:** Tibeto-Burman, Kuki-Chin-Naga
**Alternate names:** Eastern Angami, Chakrima Naga, Chakru, Chokri, Chakhesang
**Main region:** Nagaland, Phek District.

## 1 Consonant Phonemes

### 1.1 Inventory

| | Bilabial | Labiodental | Dental | Alv | Alv. Pal. | Palatal | Velar | | Glottal |
|---|---|---|---|---|---|---|---|---|---|
| Plosive | p b<br>pʰ | | | t d<br>tʰ | | | k g<br>kʰ | | |
| Nasal | m̥ m | ɱ | n̥ n | | | ɲ | ŋ | | |
| Trill | | | r̥ r | | | | | | |
| Tap | | | | ɾ | | | | | |
| Fricative | β | v | | s z | ʃ ʒ | | ɣ | χ ʁ | h |
| Approx | w | | | ɹ̥ ɹ | | j | | | |
| Lat. Appr | | | | l̥ l | | | | | |
| Affricate | pf | | | ʦ ʣ<br>ʦʰ | | ʧ ʤ<br>ʧʰ | | | |

### 1.2 Distribution

a. Consonants do not occur word-finally, with the following restriction:
   i. Syllabic consonants are found to occur word-finally on account of loss of a following vowel. If the following vowel is tone bearing then the syllabic consonant may be tone-bearing too.

b. Geminate consonants do not occur.

# 2 Vowel Phonemes

## 2.1 Inventory

**a. Short**

| | FRONT | CENTRAL | BACK |
|---|---|---|---|
| Close | i | ɨ | u |
| Close-mid | e | | o |
| Open | | a | |

## 2.2 Distribution

a. Vowels occur in all positions.

b. Diphthongs do not occur. [ Marrison (1967) mentions [ei] and [ou] as diphthongs, which don't appear in the present study.]

c. Vowel sequences do not occur intra-morphemically. Across morphemes, they are heterosyllabic.

d. There are instances of "linking vowels" reported. In one case, a linking vowel is found to precede the morpheme [no$^{3}$ ], when "used as a topicalizer or suspensive marker "; the vowel in this case is identical with the preceding vowel, e.g., /pa$^{4}$ no$^{3}$/ > [pa$^{4}$ a no$^{3}$] 'emerge +SUSP'.

# 3 Consonant Allophones

## 3.1 Inventory

| | BILABIAL | LABIODENTAL | ALVEO PALATAL | PALATAL | VELAR | UVULAR |
|---|---|---|---|---|---|---|
| Plosive | | | | | | q(k)<br>q$^{h}$ (k$^{h}$) |
| Nasal | | ɱ (m) | | ɲ (n) | ŋ (n) | |

| | | | | | | |
|---|---|---|---|---|---|---|
| Fricative | β (b) | | ʃ (s)<br>ʒ(z) | | ɣ(g)<br>ɣ (ɹ) | ʁ(ɹ) |
| Affricate | | pf (p$^{h}$) | tʃ (ts)<br>dʒ (dz)<br>tʃ$^{h}$ (ts$^{h}$) | | | |

## 3.2 Distribution

a. [β]< /b/ occurs word-initially before high, back unrounded vowel [ɯ]< /u/.

b. [pf] </p$^{h}$/ occurs before high central vowel /ɨ/.

c. [tʃ] < /ts/, [dʒ] < /dz/, [ʒ] < /z/, [ɲ] < /n/ occur before high front vowel /i/.

d. [ʃ] < /s/ occurs before word-medial high, front vowel /i/.

e. [ɱ] < /m/ occurs before high, back vowel /u/.

f. [ŋ] < /n occurs between two high back vowels.

g. [ɣ] ~[g]< /g/, [q] ~ [k] < /k/, [q$^{h}$]~ k$^{h}$] < /k$^{h}$/, [tʃ$^{h}$] ~ [ts$^{h}$] < /ts$^{h}$/, [ɣ] ~ [ɻ] < /ɻ/ [ʁ] ~ [ɻ]< /ɻ/, [χ]~[ ɹ̥] < / ɹ̥ / are in free variation.

h. Syllabic consonants occur on account of the loss of a following vowel, e.g., /məbo$^{4}$/ >[ m̩b o$^{4}$ ] 'kiss', / mədi$^{4/}$ > [ m̩di$^{4}$ ] > [n̩di$^{4}$ ]'to lose'. [The data contain tone-bearing syllabic consonants too, which may be on account of the loss of tone-bearing vowels, e.g [ʒi$^{3}$ ŋ̍$^{3}$] 'that' [k$^{h}$ r̩`$^{3}$.ki$^{2}$ ] 'window'.]

# 4 Vowel Allophones

## 4.1 Inventory

[ə] < /ɨ/

[ɛ] ~ /e/

[ɔ] ~ /o/

[ɯ] ~ /u/

## 4.2 Distribution

a. [ə] < /ɨ/ occurs when non-tone-bearing.

b. [ ɛ] ~ /e/, [ɔ] ~ /o/, [ɯ] ~ /u/ are in free variation.

c. Tone-bearing vowels can be deleted, leading to syllabic consonants.

# 5 Syllable Structure

## 5.1 Canonical syllable structure

$(<C_1>)\ (<C_2>)V/\underset{|}{C}$

Cond.: (i) If $C_1$ is general, $C_2$ is /r/; (ii) if $C_2$ is general, $C_1$ is /h/.

## 5.2 Consonant clusters

Two-consonant clusters:

| | |
|---|---|
| Initial | : hC-, Cr-. |
| Final | : Nil. |
| Medial | : Same as initial |

Three-consonant clusters: Nil

# 6 Suprasegmentals

## 6.1 Tone

Tonemes:

a. High: H $(^1)$

b. High- Mid: M1 $(^2)$

c. Low-Mid: M2 $(^3)$

d. Low: L $(^4)$

E.g .,

/pu$^1$/ 'fat', / pu$^2$/ 'bridge', /pu$^3$/ '(s)he', /pu$^4$/ 'one'.

**Reference:** Bielenberg and Nienu (2001)

# Darma[11]

**Ethnologue code:** ISO 639-3: drd
**Language classification:** Sino-Tibetan, Tibeto-Burman, Himalayish, Tibeto-Kanauri
**Alternate names:** Darimiya, Darmani, Saukas, Shaukas
**Main region:** Uttaranchal.

## 1 Consonant Phonemes

### 1.1 Inventory

| | Bilabial | Dental | Alveolar | Palatal | Velar | Glottal |
|---|---|---|---|---|---|---|
| Stop | p b<br>pʰ | t̪ d̪<br>t̪ʰ | | | k g<br>kʰ | |
| Nasal | m<br>ʱm | | n<br>ʱn | | ŋ | |
| Trill | | | r<br>ʱr | | | |
| Fricative | | | s | ç | | h |
| Appr | w<br>ʱw | | ɹ | j<br>ʱj | | |
| Lat Appr | | | l<br>ʱl | | | |
| Affricate | | | t̪s d̪z<br>t̪sʰ | ʧ ʤ<br>ʧʰ | | |

[11] The description of Derma in Krishan (2001), on which the present sketch is based, has many points of difference with the description in Willis (2007).

## 1.2 Distribution

a. Consonants occur in all positions, with the following restriction:
   i. Consonants other than / p t k m n ŋ l r j / do not occur word-finally

b. Geminates are not attested.

# 2 Vowel Phonemes

## 2.1 Inventory

a. **Short**

| | FRONT | CENTRAL | BACK |
|---|---|---|---|
| Close | | | ɯ |
| Mid | | ə | |
| Open-mid | ɛ | | ɔ |

b. **Long vowels**

| | FRONT | CENTRAL | BACK |
|---|---|---|---|
| Close | iː | | uː |
| Mid | eː | | oː |
| Open | | aː | |

## 2.2 Distribution

a. Vowels occur in all the positions, with the following restriction:
   i. / ɛ ɔ ɯ / do not occur initially.

b. Vowel sequences occur with syllabic divisions between them.

c. Sequences of long vowels are rare. When they do occur the first vowel is shortened.

# 3 Consonant Allophones

## 3.1 Inventory

| | BILABIAL | DENTAL | VELAR |
|---|---|---|---|
| Stop | b (p) | d (t) | g (k) |

## 3.2 Distribution

a. The voiced allophones [**b d g**] of the voiceless plosives /**p t k**/ occur after voiced plosives and inter-vocalically.

# 4 Vowel Allophones

Insufficient data available.

# 5 Syllable Structure

## 5.1 Canonical syllable structure

(C) (j) V (C)

## 5.2 Consonant clusters

Two-consonant clusters:

Initial : C+j

**Note:** in two or three lexical items, /r/ and /w/ also occur as the second member.

Final : Nil

Medial : General.

Three-consonant clusters: Nil

# 6 Suprasegmentals

## 6.1 Tone[12]

Tonemes:

a. Rising: LH ( ´ )

b. Falling: HL ( ` )

c. Level : M (unmarked)

E.g., /lá / 'moon', /là/ 'rock', /la/ 'hand'

/ ró/ 'flat basket', /rò/ 'hungry (person)', /ro/ 'bone'.

**Reference:** Krishan (2001b)

[12] On account of a long period of contact with Hindi, the language is loosing tonal contrasts in lexical items.

# Dimasa

**Ethnologue code:** ISO 639-3: dis
**Language classification:** Sino-Tibetan, Tibeto-Burman, Jingpho-Konyak-Bodo, Konyak-Bodo-Garo, Bodo-Garo, Bodo
**Alternate names:** Dimasa Kachari, Hills Kachar
**Main region:** Assam, North Cachar District and Cachar Hills, Karbi Anglong, Nagaon districts; Nagaland, Haflong District; Meghalaya, Mizoram.

## 1 Consonant Phonemes

### 1.1 Inventory

| | Bilabial | Alveolar | Post-Alv. | Palatal | Velar | Glottal |
|---|---|---|---|---|---|---|
| Plosive | p b | | ṭ ḍ | | k g | |
| Nasal | m | n | | | ŋ | |
| Trill | | r | | | | |
| Fricative | | s z | | | | h |
| Approx | w | | | j | | |
| Lat Appr | | l | | | | |

### 1.2 Distribution

a. Consonants occur in all positions, except the following:
   i. /b d g s z h j w/ do not occur word-finally.
   ii. /ŋ/ does not occur word-initially.

b. Geminates do not occur.

# 2 Vowel Phonemes

## 2.1 Inventory

a. **Short**

| | FRONT | CENTRAL | BACK |
|---|---|---|---|
| Close | ɪ | | ʊ |
| Open-mid | ɛ | ə | ɔ |
| Open | | a | |

b. **Diphthongs: /ei ai oi ui əo ao eo/**

## 2.2 Distribution

a. Vowels occur in all positions, with the following restrictions:
   i. /i/ does not occur word-initially.
   ii. /ə/ does not occur word-finally.

b. Vowel sequences do not occur; all occurrences of vowel sequences are diphthongs, with the second vowel non-syllabic.

# 3 Consonant Allophones

## 3.1 Inventory

| | BILABIAL | ALVEOLAR | PALATAL |
|---|---|---|---|
| Plosive | $p^h$ (p) | $t^h$ (t) | $k^h$ (k) |
| Affricate | | ts (s)<br>d(z) | |

## 3.2 Distribution

a. [$p^h$ $t^h$ $k^h$ ] < / p t k/ occurs in the syllable onset position.

b. [ ts d] < /s z/ occur before the high vowels /i u/.

# 4 Vowel Allophones

## 4.1 Inventory

[i]: /ɪ/

[e] : /ɛ/

[u]: /ʊ/

[o]: /ɔ/

## 4.2 Distribution

a. [i e u o] < /ɪ ɛ ʊ ɔ / occur in word-final position.

# 5 Syllable Structure

## 5.1 Canonical syllable structure[13]

$(<C>_1)\ (<L>_2)\ V\ (C)$

Cond.: If $< >_{2,}$ then $< >_1$ = S/m/s.

[13] Monovocalic words are not attested. A monosyllabic word must have either an onset or a coda.

## 5.2 Consonant clusters

Two-consonant clusters:

Initial : S/m/s + L.

Final : Nil.

Medial : General.

Three-consonant clusters:

Initial : Nil

Final : Nil

Medial : N + S/s + L, with a syllable division following N.

# 6 Suprasegmentals

## 6.1 Tone

Tonemes:

a. High: H ( ́ )
b. Low: L ( ̀ )

E.g., /tú/ 'to sleep', /tù/ ' to wear'; /kám/ 'sit', /kàm/ 'burn.

**Reference:** Singha (2007)

# Gallong

**Ethnologue code:** ISO 639-3: adl
**Language classification:** Tibeto-Burman, North Assam, Tani
**Alternate names:** Adi-Gallong, Adi-Galo, Gallong, Galong, Lare-Galo
**Main region:** Arunachal Pradesh, West Siang, East Siang, Dibang Valley (south), Lohit (east), Changlang (northeast), and some in Upper Subansiri (west) districts.

## 1 Consonant Phonemes[14]

### 1.1 Inventory

| | Bilabial | Dental | Alveolar | Palatal | Velar | Glottal |
|---|---|---|---|---|---|---|
| Plosive | p b | t d | | | k g | ʔ |
| Nasal | m | | n | ɲ | ŋ | |
| Trill | | r | | | | |
| Fricative | | | s | | | h |
| Approx | | | | j | | |
| Affricate | | | | ʧ ʤ | | |

### 1.2 Distribution

a. Consonants occur in all positions, with the following restriction:

i. /ŋ/ does not occur finally.

[14] 1. The alveolars /t d n/ may be realized as dentals in some varieties.

2. /s/ may be realized as alveolar or as alveo-palatal in different varieties.

# 2 Vowel Phonemes

## 2.1 Inventory

a. **Short**

| | FRONT | CENTRAL | BACK |
|---|---|---|---|
| Close | i | ɨ | u |
| Close-mid | e œ | | |
| Open-mid | | | ɔ |
| Open | | a | |

b. **Long:**

| | FRONT | CENTRAL | BACK |
|---|---|---|---|
| Close | iː | | uː |
| Open-mid | | | ɔː |
| Open | | aː | |

## 2.2 Distribution

a. Vowels occur in all positions.

b. Sequences of two vowels occur, resulting in surface diphthongs : /ao ɔo eo au/.

# 3 Consonant Allophones

## 3.1 Inventory

| | BILABIAL | ALVEOLAR | PALATAL | VELAR |
|---|---|---|---|---|
| Plosive | b (p) | d (t) | | g (k) |
| Nasal | m (p, b) | n (t, d) | | ŋ (k, g) |

| | | | | |
|---|---|---|---|---|
| Trill | | r (ɾ) | | |
| Approx | | | j (ɾ) | |

## 3.2 Distribution

a. The voiced allophones [ b d g ] < /p t k/ occur before voiced consonants.

b. The nasal homorganic allophones of plosives, [m ] < /p b/, [n] < /t d/, and [ŋ] < /k g/ occur before nasals.

# 4 Vowel Allophones

Allophonic details not available.

# 5 Syllable Structure

## 5.1 Canonical syllable structure

(C)V(C)

## 5.2 Consonant clusters[15]

Two-consonant clusters:

Initial : Nil
Final : Nil
Medial : General

Three-consonant clusters: Nil

**Reference:** Dasgupta (1963)

[15] The medial clusters are on account of word-formation. There are no intra-morphemic clusters in Gallong.

# Galo

**Ethnologue code:** ISO 639-3: adl
**Language classification:** Tibeto-Burman, North Assam, Tani
**Alternate names:** Adi-Gallong, Adi-Galo, Gallong, Galong, Lare-Galo
**Main region:** Arunachal Pradesh, West Siang, East Siang, Dibang Valley (south), Lohit (east), Changlang (northeast), and some in Upper Subansiri (west) districts.

## 1 Consonant Phonemes

### 1.1 Inventory

| | BILABIAL | DENTAL | ALVEOLAR | PALATAL | VELAR | GLOTTAL |
|---|---|---|---|---|---|---|
| Plosive | p b | t | d | | k g | |
| Nasal | m | n | | ɲ | ŋ | |
| Trill | | r | | | | |
| Fricative | | s | | | | ɦ |
| Approx | | | | j | | |
| Lat Approx | | l | | | | |
| Affricate | | | | ʤ | | |

### 1.2 Distribution

a. Consonants occur in all positions, with the following restriction:
   i. /ɦ ɲ j / do not occur word-finally.
b. All consonants except /ɦ ɲ j/ have geminates in the medial position.

# 2 Vowel Phonemes

## 2.1 Inventory

a. **Short**

| | FRONT | CENTRAL | BACK |
|---|---|---|---|
| Close | i | ɨ | u |
| Close-mid | e | | o |
| Open-mid | ɛ | | ɔ |
| Open | | a | |

b. **Long:**

| | FRONT | CENTRAL | BACK |
|---|---|---|---|
| Open | | | ɒː |

## 2.2 Distribution

a. Vowels occur in all positions, with the following restrictions:
   i. /i/ does not occur after /ɲ ŋ/.
   ii. /u/ does not occur after /ɲ/.
b. Sequences of two vowels occur commonly, with syllable division between them.

# 3 Consonant Allophones

Allophonic data are not available.

# 4 Vowel Allophones

Allophonic data not available.

# 5 Syllable Structure

## 5.1 Canonical syllable structure

(C) V (C)

### 5.2 Consonant clusters

Two-consonant clusters:

Initial : Nil

Final : Nil.

Medial : Geminates of all consonants except /ɦ ɲ j/

Three-consonant clusters:

Initial : Nil

Final : Nil

Medial : -mmg-, -nnl-, -nkk-, -ntk-, -rdn-, -dtk-

**References:** Gandhi (1978)

# Lare Galo[16]

**Ethnologue code:** ISO 639-3: adl
**Language classification:** Tibeto-Burman, North Assam, Tani
**Alternate names:** Adi-Gallong, Adi-Galo, Gallong, Galong, Lare-Galo
**Main region:** Arunachal Pradesh, West Siang, East Siang, Dibang Valley (south), Lohit (east), Changlang (northeast), and some in Upper Subansiri (west) districts.

## 1 Consonant Phonemes

### 1.1 Inventory

| | Bilabial | | Dental | | Alveolar | | Palatal | | Velar | | Glottal |
|---|---|---|---|---|---|---|---|---|---|---|---|
| Plosive | p | b | t | d | | | | | k | g | ʔ |
| Nasal | | m | | | | n | | ɲ | | ŋ | |
| Trill | | | | r | | | | | | | |
| Fricative | | | | | s | | | | | | h |
| Approx | | | | | | | | j | | | |
| Affricate | | | | | | | ʧ | ʤ | | | |

### 1.2 Distribution

a. Consonants occur in all positions, with the following restriction:

   i. Consonants other than /p k m n r/ do not occur morpheme-finally and word- finally.

b. All consonants except /ɦ ɲ j/ have geminates in the medial position.

[16] The Galo described here is the Lare dialect spoken in Darii and Baahar villages of the West Siang district of Arunachal Pradesh.

# 2 Vowel Phonemes

## 2.1 Inventory

a. **Short**

| | FRONT | CENTRAL | BACK |
|---|---|---|---|
| Close | i | ɨ | u |
| Mid | e | ə | o |
| Open | | a | |

b. **Diphthongs:** Surface vowel sequences occur frequently; those that are qualitatively distant are likely to be diphthongs: /**ai au ui oi**/. Definite evidence in favour of these being diphthongs or monophthongs is not available.

## 2.2 Distribution

a. Vowels occur in all positions, with the following restrictions:

   i. /**e ɨ a**/ do not occur word-finally.

b. Sequences of vowels occur.

# 3 Consonant Allophones

a. Adjacent stops agree in voicing, leading to voiceless stops /**p t ʧ k**/ having voiced allophones [**b d ʤ g**/, and vice versa on the surface.

b. Vowel initial words have a glottal stop in the beginning.

c. [**w ɰ**] occur on the surface across morphemes that end and begin with vowels; [**w**] occurring with the first morpheme ending in /**u o**/, and [**ɰ**] occurring with the first morpheme ending in /**ɨ**/.

# 4. Vowel Allophones

a. All the vowels are realized longer in open syllables.

b. /o ə u/ have breathy allophones [o̤ ə̤ṳ], heard also with a following [ɦ], in syllables with high tones.

# 5 Syllable Structure

## 5.1 Canonical syllable structure[17]

**a. The root morpheme:**

Root morphemes have the following canonical syllable structure:

(C) V ($C_F$/ Vi), where $C_F$ = a permitted coda consonant, and Vi = the second vowel position of a diphthong. The root morphemic syllable is maximally bimoraic.

**b. The phonological word:**

The phonological word has the following expanded canonical syllable:

(C) V (Vi) (C), where any consonant can occur in the coda position (on account of word internal sandhi and related word-phonological processes. The word-phonological syllable can be trimoraic.

## 5.2 Consonant clusters[18]

Two-consonant clusters:

Initial : Nil

Final : Nil.

Medial : General.

Three-consonant clusters: Nil.

[17] "In short, what we seem to find in modern Galo is an emergent restructuring of "syllable" in response to an overall shift of focus from "syllable" to "word" as the basic organizational unit in Galo phonology." (Post 2007: 146)

[18] Consonant clusters in the medial position are found at the phonological word level.

# 6 Tones

Tonemes:

High: H ( ´ )

Falling: HL ( ` )

E.g., [hɨɨ́nam] 'to urinate', [hɨɨ̀nam] 'to plug/ clamp'

**References:** Post (2007)

# Garo

**Ethnologue code:** ISO 639-3: grt
**Language classification:** Tibeto-Burman, Jingpho-Konyak-Bodo
**Alternate names:** Garrow, Mande
**Main region:** Meghalaya; west Assam.

## 1 Consonant Phonemes

### 1.1 Inventory

| | Bilabial | Dental | Alveolar | Palatal | Velar | Glottal |
|---|---|---|---|---|---|---|
| Plosive | p b | t d | | | k g | ʔ |
| Nasal | m | | n | | ŋ | |
| Trill | | | r | | | |
| Fricative | | | s | | | h |
| Approx | w | | | | | |
| Lateral Appr | | | (l) | | | |
| Affricate | | | | ʧ ʤ | | |

### 1.2 Distribution

a. Words must begin with a consonant, with the following restrictions:
   i. /ŋ l ʔ/ do not occur initially. /l/ is found only in borrowed forms.
   ii. /b d g ʧ ʤ h r w/ occur only word-initially.
   iii. /b d g s h w ʧ ʤ/ do not occur word-finally.
   iv. /ʔ/ can co-occur with /m n ŋ l/ at the end of a syllable. (Its position however is difficult to assign, since it "seems to occur right in the middle of the nasal or the lateral.").
   v. Geminates occur inter-vocalically

# 2 Vowel Phonemes

## 2.1 Inventory

a. **Short**

| | FRONT | CENTRAL | BACK |
|---|---|---|---|
| Close | i | | u |
| Open-mid | e | | o |
| Open | | a | |

b. **Diphthongs:** /ai au oi ei ui/

## 2.2 Distribution

a. Vowels occur in all positions.

b. Sequences of two or three vowels occur frequently. Up to four vowel sequences are attested, e.g., /aiao/ 'gracious'. Vowel sequences and diphthongs are distinguished with the presence and absence respectively of a glottal stop between the vowel positions.

# 3 Consonant Allophones

## 3.1 Inventory

| | BILABIAL | DENTAL | ALVEOLAR | VELAR | GLOTTAL |
|---|---|---|---|---|---|
| Plosive | p˺ (p)<br>pʰ (p) | t˺ (t)<br>tʰ (t) | | k˺ (k)<br>kʰ (k) | ʔ (Ø) |
| Approx | | | r (l) | | |

## 3.2 Distribution

a. The aspirated allophones [$p^h$ $t^h$ $k^h$] < /p t k/ occur in the onset position of a syllable.
b. The unreleased allophones [p˺ t˺ k˺] < /p t k/ occur in the coda-position of a syllable, which may be assigned non-automatically. (See the note on syllable structure below.)
c. In certain dialects, /l/, found mostly in non-native vocabulary, may be substituted by /r/.
d. A glottal stop in inserted between two syllabic vowels.

# 4 Vowel Allophones

## 4.1 Inventory

[ə ] < / i /

## 4.2 Distribution

a. [ə ] < / i/ occurs in syllables closed by consonants other than /ʔ/.

# 5 Syllable Structure[19]

## 5.1 Canonical syllable structure

($C_1$) ($C_2$) ($C_3$) V (ʔ) (C)

Cond.: (i) If $C_3$, then $C_1$ = s, $C_2$ = p/k;

(ii) If not $C_3$, then either (a) $C_1$ = s, $C_2$ = p/t/k or (b) $C_1$ = Obs, $C_2$ = r.

(iii) If ʔ, then the following C = N/r

[19] Syllabification in Garo reflects morphological structure. "Thus [$k^h$a$t^h$a] 'word' and [$k^h$at˺a] 'run' are in contrast. The obvious phonological interpretation of this situation is to distinguish these words by the position of the syllable boundry (sic): /ka-ta/ 'word'; /kat-a/ 'run'

## 5.2 Consonant clusters

Two-consonant clusters:

| | |
|---|---|
| Initial | : a. s + p/t/k; b. Obs + /r/ |
| Final | : ? + N/r |
| Medial | : General |

Three-consonant clusters:

| | |
|---|---|
| Initial | : spr-, str-, skr- |
| Final | : Nil |
| Medial | : General. |

**References:** Burling (1981)

# Hmar

**Ethnologue code:** ISO 639-3: hmr
**Language classification:** Tibeto-Burman, Kuki-Chin-Naga_
**Alternate names:** Hamar, Mhar, Hmari
**Main region:** Manipur; Mizoram; Assam.

## 1 Consonant Phonemes

### 1.1 Inventory

| | Bila-bial | Labio-dental | Den-tal | Alv | Retr | Pala-tal | Velar | Glottal |
|---|---|---|---|---|---|---|---|---|
| Plosive | p b<br>$p^h$ | | t d<br>$t^h$ | | ʈ ɖ<br>$ʈ^h$ | | k<br>$k^h$ | |
| Nasal | m | | n | | | | ŋ | |
| Tap | | | | ɾ | | | | |
| Fricative | | f v | | s z | | | | h |
| Lat. Appr | | | | l | | | | |
| Affricate | | | | | | tʃ | | |

### 1.2 Distribution

a. Consonants occur in all positions, with the following restrictions:

   i. /$p^h$ b $t^h$ d $ʈ^h$ ɖ $k^h$ f v (s) z/ do not occur in the final positions.

   ii. /z/ does not occur medially.

b. Germinates are not attested.

# 2 Vowel Phonemes

## 2.1 Inventory

**a. Short**

| | FRONT | CENTRAL | BACK |
|---|---|---|---|
| Close | i | | u |
| Close-mid | e | | |
| Open-mid | | ɐ | ɔ |

**b. Long:**

| | FRONT | CENTRAL | BACK |
|---|---|---|---|
| Close | i: | | u: |
| Close-mid | e: | | o: |
| Open-mid | | | ɔ: |
| Open | | a: | |

## 2.2 Distribution

a. Vowels occur in all positions.

b. /a/ and /a:/ are mostly in free variation in the final position.

c. /o:/ often freely alternates with /ou/ and /uo/.

d. Sequences of two and three syllabic vowels occur frequently.

e. /ɔ ɔ:/ are phonetically realized in the position between Half close and half-open [ɔ̝ ɔ̝].

# 3 Allophones

Data not available.

# 4 Syllable Structure

## 4.1 Canonical syllable structure

(C) V (C)

Note: Limited Onset clusters occur, as stated in 4.2

## 4.2 Consonant clusters

Two-consonant clusters:

Initial : t1-, h + L/m
Final : nil
Medial : general

Three-consonant clusters:

Initial : Nil
Final : Nil
Medial : Coda + Onset sequence.

# 5 Suprasegmentals

## 5.1 Tone[20]

Tonemes:

Rising : H (´)
Falling : L (`)
Level : unmarked

e.g. /bú / 'rice', /bù / 'nest'.

**Reference:** Dutta-Baruah & Bapui (1996)

[20] All the three tones may be present in any position. There is a general tendency, however, for the rising and falling tones to go with the main verb and the auxiliary verbs. Other elements very often carry the level tone. The verbs in isolation may be pronounced with the level tone.

# Kabui

**Ethnologue code:** ISO 639-3: nkf
**Language classification:** Tibeto-Burman, Kuki-Chin-Naga
**Alternate names:** Inpui, Kabui, Kapwi, Koboi, Kubai, Kabui Naga
**Main region:** Manipur, Senapati, Tamenglong, Imphal districts; Nagaland, near Dimapur.

## 1 Consonant Phonemes

### 1.1 Inventory

| | BILABIAL | DENTAL | ALV. | PALATAL | VELAR | GLOTTAL |
|---|---|---|---|---|---|---|
| Plosive | p b<br>$p^h$ | t d<br>$t^h$ | | | k g<br>$k^h$ | |
| Nasal | m | n | | | ŋ | |
| Trill | | | r | | | |
| Fricative | | | s | | | h |
| Approx | w | | | j | | |
| Lat. Appr | | | l | | | |
| Affricate | | | | tʃ dʒ | | |

### 1.2 Distribution

a. Consonants occur in all positions, with the following restrictions:
   i. /$p^h$ b $t^h$ d $k^h$ g d ʒ s hl r/ do not occur finally. /l r/ occur finally only in borrowed words.
   ii. /w j/ occur rarely initially.
   iii. /l/ and /r/ occur in free variation word initially in native words.
   iv. /p t k m n ŋ/ have geminates inter-vocalically.

# 2 Vowel Phonemes

## 2.1 Inventory

a. **Short**

| | FRONT | CENTRAL | BACK |
|---|---|---|---|
| Close | i | | u |
| Close-mid | e | | o |
| Open-mid | | ə | |
| Open | | a | |

b. **Long:**

| | FRONT | CENTRAL | BACK |
|---|---|---|---|
| Open-mid | | ə : | |

## 2.2 Distribution

a. Vowels occur in all positions, with the following restrictions:
   i. /əː/ occurs only medially before /k/ and /ŋ/.
   ii. /e o/ occur finally only in complex forms.
   iii. / ə/ occurs finally after /t n h/.
b. Vowel sequences do not occur.

# 3 Consonant Allophones

## 3.1 Inventory

a. [ t̲ ] < / t /

## 3.2 Distribution

a. [ t̲ ] < / t / occurs word-finally.

# 4 Vowel Allophones

## 4.1 Inventory

[ ə̝ ] : /ə/
[ ɪ̯ ] : / j/
[ ʊ̯ ]: /w /

## 4.2 Distribution

a. The higher mid central vowel allophone [ ə̝ ] < /ə/ occurs after /j w/, e.g. /tjə́ŋ/ > [t ɪ̯ ə̝́ ŋ/ 'ant', /gwəj/ > [gʊ̯ ə̝ ɪ̯] 'cattle'.

b. [ɪ̯] < /j/ and [ʊ̯] < / w/ occur (a) between a consonant and /ə/, and (b) finally, after /ə/. [ɪ̯] occurs also finally after /o/ and /u/.

# 5 Syllable Structure

## 5.1 Canonical syllable structure

(C)(G)V(C)

## 5.2 Consonant clusters

Two-consonant clusters:

Initial : C+j/w ; e.g., /rjek/ 'to lick', /swaŋ/ 'to cook'.
Final : Nil
Medial : General

Three-consonant clusters:

Initial : Nil
Final : NIl
Medial : C+C+j/w e.g., /muksjəm/ 'to share ink'/ləŋkjək/ 'a piece of thread', /pəkdwək/ 'to escape'

**Reference:** Tiwari (1971)

# Kangri

**Ethnologue code:** ISO 639-3: xnr
**Language classification:** Indo-European, Indo-Iranian, Indo-Aryan, Northern zone, Western Pahari
**Alternate names:** Kangra-Dogri, Pahari, Pahari Kangri
**Main region:** Himachal Pradesh, Kangra, Hamirpur, Una districts.

## 1 Consonant Phonemes

### 1.1 Inventory

| | Bilabial | Dental | Alveolar | Retro-flex | Pal. - Alv. | Velar | Glottal |
|---|---|---|---|---|---|---|---|
| Plosive | p b<br>$p^h$ | t d<br>$t^h$ | | ʈ ɖ<br>$ʈ^h$ | | k g<br>$k^h$ | |
| Nasal | m | n | ɳ | | | | |
| Trill | | | r | | | | |
| Flap | | | | ɽ | | | |
| Fricative | | | s | | | | |
| Approx | w | | | | j | | |
| Lat Appr | | | l | ɭ | | | |
| Affricate | | | | | tʃ dʒ<br>$tʃ^h$ | | |

### 1.2 Distribution

a. Consonants occur in all positions, except the following:

   i. A coda consonant is voiced ('lenis') when preceded by a vowel with a tone.

ii. /ɳ ɭ ɽ/ occur rarely word-initially.
iii. /j w/ do not occur word-finally.

b. /n/ and /l/ are in free variation in a lot of lexical items.

c. Geminates of all consonants except the following six occur inter-vocalically: /r ɽ ɭ ɳ j w/.

# 2 Vowel Phonemes

## 2.1 Inventory

a. **Short**

| | FRONT | CENTRAL | BACK |
|---|---|---|---|
| Close | ɪ | | ʊ |
| Close-mid | e | | o |
| Open-mid | | ɐ | |

b. **Long:**

| | FRONT | CENTRAL | BACK |
|---|---|---|---|
| Close | iː | | uː |
| Close-mid | eː | | oː |
| Open | | aː | |

c. **Nasal:**

| | FRONT | CENTRAL | BACK |
|---|---|---|---|
| Close | ɪ̃ ĩː | | ʊ̃ ũː |
| Close-mid | ẽ ẽː | | õ õː |
| Open-mid | | ɐ̃ | |
| Open | | ãː | |

## 2.2 Distribution

a. Vowels occur in all positions.

b. Vowel sequences of two occur with considerable frequency; sequences of up to five vowels have been attested.

# 3 Consonant Allophones

a. Glottal stops are found to occur initially when accompanied by HLH tones in words beginning with an 'h' that are borrowings from Indo-Aryan languages.

# 4 Vowel Allophones

## 4.1 Inventory

**General:**

Shortened vowels.

**Specific:**

[ɨ]: /ɪ/

[ʉ]: /ʊ/

[ə]: /ɐ/

## 4.2 Distribution

**General:** Vowels are shortened before geminate consonants.

**Specific:**

a. [ɨ ʉ ə] < /ɪ ʊ ɐ/ occur before retroflex sonorants and geminate consonants.

# 5 Syllable Structure

## 5.1 Canonical syllable structure[21]

(C) (C) V (C)

## 5.2 Consonant clusters

Two-consonant clusters:

Initial : CC[22]
Final : Nil.
Medial : General.

Three-consonant clusters: Nil.

# 6 Suprasegmentals

## 6.1 Tone

Tonemes:

a. (High) Falling: HL ( ` )
b. Falling-Rising: HLH ( ˇ )
c. Level: M (unmarked)

Note: i. The HL tone can occur anywhere; however, in a sequence of vowels, it occurs on the first vowel.

ii. As mentioned above, the HLH tone is accompanied by an allophonic glottal catch in the word-initial position in words that begin with [h] in borrowings from Indo-Aryan languages.

E.g., /é/ 'this one', /ě/ 'BE 3 per. PL, M.), /e/ 'this'.

**Reference:** Chauhan (1992)

---

[21] Final consonant clusters are found in some borrowed English words, as[sərʈ]

[22] The general CC- initial clusters have some exceptions that do not crucially affect the generalization.

# Karbi[23]

**Ethnologue code:** ISO 639-3: mjw
**Language classification:** Tibeto-Burman, Mikir
**Alternate names:** Mikir, Mikiri, Manchati, Karbi Karbak, Arleng Alam, Nihang, Puta
**Main region:** Assam; Arunachal Pradesh; Meghalaya.

## 1 Consonant Phonemes

### 1.1 Inventory

| | BILABIAL | LABIO-DENTAL | ALV. | PALATAL | VELAR | GLOTTAL |
|---|---|---|---|---|---|---|
| Plosive | p b<br>$p^h$ $b^{ɦ}$ | | t d<br>$t^h$ $d^{ɦ}$ | | k g<br>$k^h$ $g^{ɦ}$ | |
| Nasal | m | | n | | ŋ | |
| Trill | | | r | | | |
| Fricative | | | | | | h |
| Approx | | ʋ | | j | | |
| Lat. Appr | | | l | | | |
| Affricate | | | | ʦ ʥ<br>$ʦ^h$ | | |

### 1.2 Distribution

a. Consonants occur in all positions, with the following restrictions:
   i. /$g^h$ ʔ/ do not occur word-medially
   ii. /$p^h$ $t^h$ $k^h$ $g^{ɦ}$/ do not occur word-finally

[23] The description is of the dialect spoken in the Mikir Hills area, which is considered as the standard Karbi.

b. Geminate consonants do not occur intra-morphemically. Across morphemes, they may be optionally reduced to single consonants.

# 2 Vowel Phonemes

## 2.1 Inventory

a. **Short**

| | FRONT | CENTRAL | BACK |
|---|---|---|---|
| Close | i | | u |
| Close-mid | e | | o |
| Open | | a | |

## 2.2 Distribution

a. Vowels occur in all positions.
b. Vowel sequences only occur across morphemes. Even across morphemes, when the vowels / i/ or /a/ occur adjacent to /i/ or /a/ they are deleted as the first in the sequence, e.g., /pa + iŋŋi/ > [piŋŋi] 'make someone sit'.

# 3 Consonant Allophones

## 3.1 Inventory

| | BILABIAL | ALVEOLAR | PALATAL | VELAR |
|---|---|---|---|---|
| Plosive | b (p) | d (t) | | g (k) |
| Fricative | | | | x (~h) |
| Affricate | | | tʃ (ts)<br>dʒ (dz)<br>tʃʰ (tsʰ) | |

## 3.2 Distribution

a. The palatal affricate allophones [tʃ tʃ$^{h}$ dʒ]</ts ts$^{h}$ ʥ / occur before the front vowels / i e /

b. [x] freely varies with /h/ in certain lexical items.

c. [ b d g ] < / p t k / occur before voiced sounds.

# 4 Vowel Allophones

## 4.1 Inventory

[ɪ]: /i/

[ɛ]: /e/

[ə] [ɑ]: /a/

[ɔ]: /o/

[ʊ]: /u/

[u̯]: /ʋ/

[i̯]: /j/

## 4.2 Distribution

a. [ɪ] < /i /, [ʊ] < /u/ occur non-finally in words.

b. [ɛ] < /e /, [ɔ] < /o/ occur in closed syllables.

c. [ə] < /a/ occurs non-finally in polysyllabic words.

d. [ɑ] < /a/ occurs in non-final closed syllables or after velar and glottal stops in closed monosyllabic words.

e. [u̯] < /ʋ/, [i̯] < /j/ occur after vowels.

# 5 Syllable Structure

## 5.1 Canonical syllable structure

(C)(L/j) V (C)

## 5.2 Consonant clusters

Two-consonant clusters:

Initial : C + r/l/j

Final : Nil.

Medial : general

Three-consonant clusters:

Initial : Nil

Final : Nil

Medial : C+C+l/r

# 6 Suprasegments

## 6.1 Tone

Toneme:

High: H ( ´ )
Low: L ( ` )
Level: unmarked

E.g.: /pí/ 'what'
/pì/ 'give'
/pi/ 'a piece of cloth used to piggyback a child'

**Reference:** Jeyapaul (1987)

# Khezha[24]

**Ethnologue code:** ISO 639-3: nkh
**Language classification:** Tibeto-Burman, Kuki-Chin-Naga
**Alternate names:** Kezami, Khezhama, Khezha
**Main region:** Eastern Nagaland, Kohima District, Khezhakhonoma, Phek District.

## 1 Consonant Phonemes

### 1.1 Inventory

| | Bilabial | Labio-dental | Apico-alveolar | Palatal | Velar | Glottal |
|---|---|---|---|---|---|---|
| Plosive | p b<br>$p^h$ | | t d<br>$t^h$ | | k<br>$k^h$<br>$k^w$<br>$k^{hw}$ | |
| Nasal | m<br>$m^ɦ$ | | n<br>$n^ɦ$ | | ŋ | |
| Trill | | | r<br>$r^ɦ$ | | | |
| Fricative | | f v | s z | ç ʝ | | h ɦ |
| Approx | w<br>$w^ɦ$ | | | j | | |
| Lat Approx | | | l<br>$l^ɦ$ | | | |
| Affricate | pf bv<br>$pf^h$ | | ts ʣ<br>$ts^h$ | ʧ ʤ<br>$ʧ^h$ | | |

[24] Apico-alveolar and 'Fronto-alveolar' (Kapfo 2004:77) distinction is without a contrastive value, so all are being treated as alveolar.

## 1.2 Distribution

a. All consonants occur initially and medially in words. Consonants do not occur word-finally.

b. Geminate consonants do not occur in the language.

# 2 Vowel Phonemes

## 2.1 Inventory

a. **Short**

| | FRONT | CENTRAL | BACK |
|---|---|---|---|
| Close | i | | u |
| Close-mid | e | | o |
| Open-mid | | ə ɞ | |
| Open | | a | |

## 2.2 Distribution

a. Vowels occur in all positions, with the following restriction:

   i. /u o ə ɞ/ do not occur in the initial position.

b. Sequences of vowels /ie io iu ia / occur medially. These sequences and /ei ai/ occur finally.

c. Word- initially vowel sequences do not occur. These sequences are treated as sequences in the absence of evidence for them to be treated as diphthongs.

# 3 Consonant Allophones

## 3.1 Inventory

| | LAMINO-ALVEOLAR | PALATAL |
|---|---|---|
| Nasal | | ɲ (n)<br>ɲʰ (nʱ) |
| Trill | r̥ (r) | |

## 3.2 Distribution

a. The palatal nasal allophones of the apico-alveolar nasals occur before high front and open-mid vowels.

b. The voiceless lamino-alveolar fricativised trill allophone occurs before bilabial and apico-alveolar voiceless stops.

# 4 Vowel Allophones

## 4.1 Inventory

[ɨ]: /i/

## 4.2 Distribution

The high central allophone of the high front vowel occurs before another vowel.

# 5 Syllable Structure

## 5.1 Canonical syllable structure[25]

(C) (w/r) V

## 5.2 Consonant clusters[26]

Two-consonant clusters:

Initial : C + w/r

Final : Nil.

Medial : (m +C)

Three-consonant clusters: Nil

# 6 Suprasegmentals

## 6.1 Tone

Three levels of contrastive tones are found:

H ( ´ ) : só 'repeat' (V)

L ( ` ) : sò 'count', 'bribe' (V)

M (unmarked) : so 'drink' (V)

## 6.2 Distribution

a. Every syllable has a tone.

b. There is rule governed morphophonemic variation in the placement of tone on account of word-formation (see Kapfo 2004: 97-99).

---

[25] 1. The second consonant is restricted to /w/ or /r/.

2. Words of up to six open syllables are found. A majority of words are disyllabic.

[26] The medial clusters with m+C are found in fast speech pronunciations of words with the morpheme -mi, a connective.

# 7 Allotones

## 7.1 Inventory

H: HM

L: LM

## 7.2 Distribution

a. HM occurs following Mid and Low tones
b. LM occurs following high tone and between mid tones.

**Reference**: Kapfo (2005)

# Kinnauri

**Ethnologue code:** ISO 639-3: cik
**Language classification:** Tibeto-Burman, Himalayish, Tibeto-Kanauri
**Alternate names:** Chitkuli, Chitkhuli, Tsíhuli, Tsitkhuli, Kinnauri, Kanauri, Thebarskad
**Main region:** Himachal Pradesh.

## 1 Consonant Phonemes

### 1.1 Inventory

| | Bilabial | Labiodental | Dental | Alv. | Alveo-Palatal | Retro. | Palatal | Velar | Glottal |
|---|---|---|---|---|---|---|---|---|---|
| Plosive | p b $p^h$ | | t d $t^h$ | | | ʈ ɖ ʈ$^h$ | | k g $k^h$ | |
| Nasal | m | | n | | | ɳ | | ŋ | |
| Trill | | | r | | | | | | |
| Fricative | | f v | | s z | ʃ ʒ | ʂ ʐ | | | h |
| Approx | w | | | | | | j | | |
| Lat Approx | | | | l | | ɭ | | | |
| Affricate | | | | | | | tʃ ʤ tʃ$^h$ | | |

### 1.2 Distribution

a. Consonants occur in all positions, with the following restrictions:
   i. /$p^h$ d$^ɦ$ ɖ tʃ$^h$ / do not occur initially.
   ii. /p b $t^h$ ʈ$^h$ $k^h$ tʃ$^h$ v z ʐ h ɳ w j/ do not occur finally.

b. The following consonants have geminates in the medial position: /t l m ɳ/. Occasionally, /t/ freely varies with /dd/.

# 2 Vowel Phonemes

## 2.1 Inventory

a. **Short**

| | FRONT | CENTRAL | BACK |
|---|---|---|---|
| Close | i | ɨ | u |
| Close-mid | e | | o |
| Open-mid | ɛ | ə | ɔ |
| Open | | a | |

b. **Long**

| | FRONT | CENTRAL | BACK |
|---|---|---|---|
| Close | i: | | u: |
| Close-mid | e: | | o: |
| Open-mid | ɛ: | | |
| Open | | a: | |

c. **Nasal**

| | FRONT | CENTRAL | BACK |
|---|---|---|---|
| Close | ĩ ĩ: | ɨ̃ | ũ ũ: |
| Close-mid | ẽ ẽ: | | õ õ: |
| Open-mid | ɛ̃ ɛ̃: | ə̃ | ɔ̃ |
| Open | | ã ã: | |

## 2.2 Distribution

a. Vowels occur in all positions, with the following restrictions:
   i. /ɨ ə/ do not occur initially.
   ii. /ɔ/ occurs only medially.

b. The short vowels, except /ə ɨ ɔ/ have long counterparts.

c. All the vowels have nasal counterparts.

d. Vowel sequences of two occur frequently.

# 3 Consonant Allophones

## 3.1 Inventory

[k>]: /k/

[g>]: /g/

## 3.2 Distribution

a. Limited details on allophonic alternants are available. The post-velar allophones of the velar stops [k> g<] < /k g/ occur before /j/ either immediately or in the following syllable.

# 4 Vowel Allophones

## 4.1 Inventory

Data on allophonic alternants not available.

# 5 Syllable Structure

## 5.1 Canonical syllable structure

(C) (C) V (C) (C)

## 5.2 Consonant clusters

Two-consonant clusters:

Initial : sk-, kr-, pr-.

Final : -ts, -ns, -ṭk, -kṭ.

Medial : General.

Three-consonant clusters:

Initial : Nil.

Final : Nil

Medial : -ndr-, -ŋkn-, -npr-.

**Reference:** Sharma (1988)

# Kiranti-Koints

**Ethnologue code:** None
**Language classification:** Tibeto-Burman, Himalayish, Kiranti_
**Alternate names:** Not available
**Main region:** Sikkim

## 1 Consonant Phonemes

### 1.1 Inventory

| | BILABIAL | DENTAL | ALV. | RETRO | PALATO ALV | PALATAL | VELAR | GLOTTAL |
|---|---|---|---|---|---|---|---|---|
| Plosive | p b pʰ | t d tʰ | | ʈ ɖ | | | k g kʰ | ʔ |
| Nasal | m | | n | | | | ŋ | |
| Trill | | | r | | | | | |
| Fricative | | | s | | ʃ | | | h |
| Approx | w | | | | | j | | |
| Lat. Appr | | | l | | | | | |
| Affricate | | | ʦ ʤ | | | | | |

### 1.2 Distribution

a. Consonants occur in all positions, with the following restriction:

   i. /h j w / do not occur word-finally.

b. Geminates of the following consonants occur inter-vocalically: /p b t k ʦ s m n l/.

# 2 Vowel Phonemes

## 2.1 Inventory

a. **Short**

| | FRONT | CENTRAL | BACK |
|---|---|---|---|
| Close | i | | u |
| Close-mid | | | o |
| Open-mid | ɛ | ə | |
| Open | | a | |

b. **Diphthongs :** /ai ɛi əi oi ui au ɛu əu iu əɛ/

c. **Nasal**

| | FRONT | CENTRAL | BACK |
|---|---|---|---|
| Close | ĩ | | ũ uĩ |
| Close-mid | | | õ õi |
| Open-mid | ɛ̃ ɛ̃: | ə̃ əĩ | |
| Open | | ã ãi | |

## 2.2 Distribution

a. All the vowels occur in all positions.

b. Sequences of vowels occur.

# 3 Consonant Allophones

## 3.1 Inventory

| | ALVEOLAR | RETRO |
|---|---|---|
| Nasal | $n^{ɦ}$ ~ n | |
| Trill | ($r^{ɦ}$) ~ r | ɽ (<r) |
| Lat. Appr | ($l^{ɦ}$) ~l<br>ɫ (<l) | |

## 3.2 Distribution

a. The alveolar sonorants /n l r/ have free variant allophones [$n^{ɦ}$ $l^{ɦ}$ $r^{ɦ}$] in some of the varieties.

b. [ɫ] < /l/ occurs in the coda position, especially as a first member of a geminate /ll/.

# 4 Vowel Allophones

Adequate data are not available.

# 5 Syllable Structure

## 5.1 Canonical syllable structure[27]

(C) (L/j) V (C)

---

[27] Words of a maximum number of four syllables are attested. Most polysyllables are complex or compound words.

## 5.2 Consonant clusters

Two-consonant clusters:

Initial : C + L/j

Final : Nil

Medial : General.

Three-consonant clusters: Nil

**References:** Rapacha (2006)

# Kokborok

**Ethnologue code:** ISO 639-3: trp
**Language classification:** Tibeto-Burman, Jingpho-Konyak-Bodo
**Alternate names:** Tripuri, Tipura, Usipi Mrung, Tripura, Kakbarak, Kokbarak
**Main region:** Assam; eastern Tripura.

## 1 Consonant Phonemes

### 1.1 Inventory

| | BILABIAL | LABIODENTAL | DENTAL | ALVEOLAR | PALATAL | VELAR | GLOTTAL |
|---|---|---|---|---|---|---|---|
| Plosive | p b p$^h$ | | t d t$^h$ | | | k g k$^h$ | |
| Nasal | m | | n | | | ŋ | |
| Trill | | | | r | | | |
| Fricative | | | | s | | | h |
| Approx | w | | | | j | | |
| Lat Appro | | | | l | | | |
| Affricate | | | | | tʃ ʤ tʃ$^h$ | | |

### 1.2 Distribution

a. Consonants occur in all positions, with the following restrictions:
   i. /p$^h$ b t̠$^h$ d k$^h$ g s h tʃ tʃ$^h$ ʤ/ do not occur word-finally.
   ii. /ŋ/ does not occur word-initially

b. The alveolar stops freely vary with dental stops.

# 2 Vowel Phonemes

## 2.1 Inventory

a. **Short**

| | FRONT | CENTRAL | BACK |
|---|---|---|---|
| Close | i | | ʊ |
| Open-mid | ɛ | ə | ɔ |
| Open | | a | |

## 2.2 Distribution

a. All the vowels occur in all the positions.

b. Vowel sequences do not occur morpheme-internally: they, however, occur across morpheme boundaries.

c. Nasal vowels are found to occur only in two words: [hĩ] `Yes', [ĩhĩ] `No'.

# 3 Consonant Allophones

## 3.1 Inventory

| | DENTAL | POST ALVEOLAR |
|---|---|---|
| Fricative | | ʃ (~tʃʰ) |
| Affricate | ts~s(tʃ)<br>dz (ʤ) | |

## 3.2 Distribution

a. [ts dz] < / tʃ dʒ / occur before non-front vowels. In this position they freely vary with [tʃ dʒ].

b. The alveolar affricate allophone [ts] < /tʃ/ freely varies with /s/ in many words.

# 4 Vowel Allophones

## 4.1 Inventory

[e]: /ɛ/

[u]: /ʊ/

[o]: /ɔ/

[ɯ]: /ə/

[i̯]: /j/

[u̯]: /w/

## 4.2 Distribution

a. [ɯ] < /ə/ occurs in monosyllables and between consonants and is never followed by /ə/ or /a/ in the following syllable.

b. [e] < /ɛ/ is always followed by /a/ in the following syllable.

c. [u] < /ʊ/ occurs after a bilabial consonant and word-finally.

d. [o] < /ɔ/ occurs before or after /j/ and word-finally.

e. [i̯ u̯] < /j w/ occur when adjacent to a vowel.

# 5 Syllable Structure

## 5.1 Canonical syllable structure

(C)V(C)

Mono-morphemic words are usually of CVC structure.

## 5.2 Consonant clusters

Two-consonant clusters:

Initial : Nil

Final : Nil

Medial : Hom N+C

Three-consonant clusters: Nil

**Reference:** Pai (1976)

# Koren

**Ethnologue code:** ISO 639-3: nkd
**Language classification:** Sino-Tibetan, Tibeto-Burman, Kuki-Chin-Naga, Naga, Zeme
**Alternate names:** Koirng, Kolren, Koren, Kwoireng, Liangmai, Liangmei, Liyang, Liyangmai, Lyengmai, Quoireng
**Main region:** Manipur, Senapati District, Saikul and Kangpokpi subdivisions

## 1 Consonant Phonemes

### 1.1 Inventory

| | Bilabial | Labiodental | Dental | Alv. | Post-Alv | Palatal | Velar | Glottal |
|---|---|---|---|---|---|---|---|---|
| Plosive | p b<br>pʰ | | t d<br>tʰ | | | | k (g)<br>kʰ | ʔ |
| Nasal | m | | | n | | ɲ | ŋ | |
| Trill | | | | r | | | | |
| Fricative | | (f) | | s z | ʃ | | | h |
| Approx | w | | | | | j | | |
| Lat. Appr | | | | l | | | | |
| Affricate | | | | l | | ʧ ʤ | | |

### 1.2 Distribution

a. Consonants occur in all positions except the following:

i. / pʰ tʰ kʰ ʧ b d s z ʃ h w / do not occur word-finally.

b. Geminates of the following consonants occur word-medially: /p t k m n ŋ r l/.

c. /f g/ are marginal phonemes found in borrowed items.

# 2 Vowel Phonemes

## 2.1 Inventory

a. **Short**

| | FRONT | CENTRAL | BACK |
|---|---|---|---|
| Close | i | | u |
| Close-mid | e | | o |
| Open-mid | | ə | |
| Open | | a | |

b. **Long**

| | FRONT | CENTRAL | BACK |
|---|---|---|---|
| Close | iː | | uː |
| Close-mid | eː | | oː |
| Open | | aː | |

**Diphthongs :** /iu io ia ie iu uo uə ui ou oi ei ai/

**Triphthongs:**[28] /uoi uia uəi/.

---

[28] a. The diphthongs and the triphthongs are differentiated from sequences of two and three vowels, respectively, on the basis of syllable divisibility, insertion of vocalic glides, and word-stress placement. The diphthongs and triphthongs are considered phonetically indivisible by the native speaker. The sequences can have optional glide insertion between the vowels. And, the word-stress placement on final heavy syllables helps distinguish the sequences in final closed syllables as single vowels or as vowel sequences. If a single vowel, the stress falls on the first vowel position, if a sequence of vowels, the stress falls on the last vowel position.

b. Koren presents a case of wide-spread vocalic symbolism in the language, where the vowels /i e u o/ stand for separate sets of semantic shades of shapes, sizes, amount, degree, etc.

## 2.2 Distribution

a. All the vowels occur in all positions.

b. Across morphemes, sequences of vowels have either glide insertion or deletion of the first vowel, e.g. [əti əni] > [ətijəni] 'he said'; [əru əra:n] > [ərura:n] 'bones and others'.

# 3 Consonant Allophones

## 3.1 Inventory

| | ALVEOLAR | POST ALVEOLAR | PALATAL |
|---|---|---|---|
| | | | ʤ ~ (j) |
| Fricative | v ~ (w) | ʒ ~ (z) | ħ ~ (h) |

## 3.2 Distribution

a. The variant allophones of the fricatives are used for emphasis. The conditioning for the allophones is thus pragmatic here.

b. /j / ~/ʤ / variation exists in a lot of lexical items.

# 4 Vowel Allophones

Adequate data are not available.

# 5 Syllable Structure

## 5.1 Canonical syllable structure[29]

**Monosyllables:** (C) (Son) V (C) (C) (C)

**Polysyllables:** (C) (Son) V (C) (C)

**Condition for Codas:** (i) If two consonants, then either Son+ Son/Obs, or Obs + Son, (ii) If three consonants, then N+S+C.

## 5.2 Consonant clusters

Two-consonant clusters:

Initial : C+ Son.
Final : Son+ Son/Obs, Obs + Son
Medial : General.

Three-consonant clusters:

Final (in monosyllables): N+S+C.
Medial: permitted codas + onsets in complex words.

# 6 Suprasegmentals

## 6.1 Tones

Tonemes:

High (H): ( ´ )

Low (L): ( ` )

Mid: (M) (Unmarked)

E.g., /athíŋ/, 'swollen', /athìŋ/ 'wood', /athiŋ/ 'to hinder, block'

**Reference:** Zeite and Pandey (2007).

[29] Words of a maximum number of four syllables are attested. Most polysyllables are complex or compound words.

# Ladakhi

**Ethnologue code:** ISO 639-3: lbj
**Language classification:** Tibeto-Burman, Himalayish, Tibeto-Kanauri
**Alternate names:** Ladaphi, Ladhakhi, Ladak, Ladwags
**Main region:** Jammu and Kashmir: Ladakh District.

## 1 Consonant Phonemes

### 1.1 Inventory

| | Bilabial | Dental | Alv | Post-Alv | Retr | Palatal | Velar | Glottal |
|---|---|---|---|---|---|---|---|---|
| Plosive | p b<br>$p^h$ | t d<br>$t^h$ | | | ʈ ɖ<br>$ʈ^h$ | | k g<br>$k^h$ | |
| Nasal | m | n | | | | ɲ | ŋ | |
| Trill | | | r | | | | | |
| Fricative | | | s z | ʃ ʒ | ʂ ʐ | | | h |
| Approx | w | | | | | j | | |
| Lat. Appr | | | l<br>$l^ɦ$ | | | | | |
| Affricate | | | ts dz<br>$ts^h$ | | | ʧ ʤ<br>$ʧ^h$ | | |

### 1.2 Distribution

a. Consonants occur in all positions, with the following restriction:
   i. Consonants other than /p t k m n ŋ s r l/ do not occur finally in words.
b. Geminates do not occur.

# 2 Vowel Phonemes

## 2.1 Inventory

a. **Short**

| | **FRONT** | **CENTRAL** | **BACK** |
|---|---|---|---|
| Close | i | | u |
| Close-mid | e | | o |
| Open-mid | | ə | |

## 2.2 Distribution

a. All vowels occur in all positions.

b. Vowel sequences do not occur.

# 3 Consonant Allophones

## 3.1 Inventory

| | **BILABIAL** | **DENTAL** | **ALVEOLAR** | **VELAR** |
|---|---|---|---|---|
| Plosive | | | | k˃ (k) |
| Trill | | | r̥ (r) | |
| Fricative | β (b) | ð (d) | | ɣ (g) |
| Lat Appr | | | l̥ (l) | |

## 3.2 Distribution

a. [β ð ɣ] </ /b d g/ occur (i) after /r/ initially in words, (ii) as onsets in medial syllables, following vowels or / r l n ɲ ŋ/. The allophones are in free variation.

b. [ k˃] < /k/ occurs finally.

c. [ r̥ l̥] < /r l / occur initially in clusters before a voiceless consonant.

# 4 Vowel Allophones

## 4.1 Inventory

| | |
|---|---|
| [ẹ]: | /e / |
| [ ọ ] : | /o / |
| [a ] [ɑ ] : | / ə/ |
| [i ˑ]: | /i/ |
| [u ˑ]: | /u/ |

## 4.2 Distribution

a. [ẹ ọ a] < /e o ə/ occurs initially and medially.

b. [ɑ] < /ə / occurs finally.

c. The vowels /i u/ are longer in the final position.

# 5 Syllable Structure

## 5.1 Canonical syllable structure

(C) (C) (C)V(C) (C)

## 5.3 Consonant clusters

Two-consonant clusters:[30]

Initial : (i) r/l + Plosive/affr. (ii) s/ʂ + Pl/N;

[30] 1. Syllabic onsets /btʃ kʃ ks gɲ bd bʒ rg brg/ are permitted after open syllables in numerals.

2. Syllabic onsets /mt mk mts/ occur medially after open syllables in certain compounds.

(iii) z + Pl; (iv) Pl/N + j.

Final : (i) s + k/p/m/j/s ; (ii) Plosive/Nasal + **s**;

(iii) (rare) t/n/r/l/ + s.

Medial : General.

Three-consonant clusters:

Initial : skj-, rgj-, s̺kj-

Final : Nil.

Medial : General.

**Reference:** Koshal (1979a, 1979b)

# Lepcha

**Ethnologue code:** ISO 639-3: lep
**Language classification:** Tibeto-Burman, Himalayish, Tibeto-Kanauri
**Alternate names:** Lapche, Rong, Rongke, Rongpa, Nünpa
**Main region:** Sikkim; north West Bengal

## 1 Consonant Phonemes

### 1.1 Inventory

| | Bilabial | Labiodental | Dental | Alv. | Postalv. | Retroflex | Palatal | Velar | Glottal |
|---|---|---|---|---|---|---|---|---|---|
| Stop | p b | | t d | t̠ d̠ | | ʈ ɖ | | k g | |
| Nasal | m | | n | | | | ɲ | ŋ | |
| Trill | | | | r | | | | | |
| Fricative | | f v | | s z | ʃ ʒ | | | | h |
| Approx. | | | | | | | j | | |
| Lat Appr. | | | | l | | | | | |
| Affricative | | | ts dz | | | | dʒ | | |

### 1.2 Distribution

a. Consonants occur in all positions, with the following restriction:

   i. The aspirated plosives/$p^h$ $t^h$ $k^h$/, the voiced velar plosive /g/, the affricates /ts dz dʒ/, the fricatives / f v s z ʃʒ h/, the palatal nasal /ɲ/, and the approximant /j/ do not occur finally. (Only /p t k m n ŋ r l/ occur finally in words.)

b. Geminates of the following consonants occur medially: /b t k m n ŋ l/.

# 2 Vowel Phonemes

## 2.1 Inventory

a. **Short:**

| | FRONT | CENTRAL | BACK |
|---|---|---|---|
| Close | i | | ɯ u |
| Mid | e | ə | ɤ o |
| Open-mid | ɛ | | ɔ |
| Open | | a | |

b. **Long:**

| | FRONT | CENTRAL | BACK |
|---|---|---|---|
| Close | i: | | ɯ: u: |
| Mid | e: | ə: | ɤ: o: |
| Open-mid | ɛ: | | ɔ: |
| Open | | a: | |

c. **Nasal:**

| | FRONT | CENTRAL | BACK |
|---|---|---|---|
| Open-mid | | | ɔ̃ ɔ̃: |
| Open | | ã: | |

## 2.2 Distribution

a. All the vowels occur in all the positions.

b. Vowel sequences occur with syllabic divisions between them.

# 3 Consonant allophones

## 3.1 Inventory

| | BILABIAL | DENTAL | ALVEOLAR | PALATAL | VELAR |
|---|---|---|---|---|---|
| Stop | b (p) | d (t) | | | g (k) |
| Lat Appr | | | l̥ (l) | | |
| Affricate | | | | tʃ$^h$ (s) | |

## 3.2 Distribution

a. The voiced allophones [b d g] of the voiceless plosives /p t k/ occur before voiced plosives.

b. The voiceless allophone [l̥] of the lateral phoneme /l/ occurs following /h/.

c. The aspirated voiceless palatal affricate allophone [tʃ$^h$] of the voiceless alveolar fricative phoneme /s/ occurs following /n/ and /t/.

# 4 Vowel allophones

Insufficient data available.

# 5 Syllable structure

## 5.1 Canonical syllable structure

(C) (C) (C) V (C)

## 5.2 Consonant clusters

Two-consonant clusters:[31]

Initial : C + L/j/h, s + d

Final : Nil

Medial : Geminates and General.

Three-consonant clusters: Nil

Initial : C+L+j/h

Medial : C+L+j/h

Final : Nil

Four-consonant clusters:

Initial : Nil

Medial : Some clusters occur with the following restriction: the final consonant is /j/ and the third consonant is l/r/h.

Final : Nil

# 6 Suprasegmentals

## 6.1 Tone[32]

Tonemes:

a. Low-Rising: LH ( ´ )

b. High-Falling: HL ( ` )

c. Level: unmarked

E.g., /kú / 'image', /kù / 'costly

/út/ 'a kind of lizard', /ùt/ 'falling of hair.

/kekyò/ 'barley'

**Reference:** Sinha (1966)

[31] The following consonants do not occur as the first member: /n ɲ dz dʒ ʃ ʒ j/.

[32] Sinha (1966) does not contain examples of monosyllabic words with level tone.

# Liangmai

**Ethnologue code:** ISO 639-3: njn
**Language classification:** Sino-Tibetan, Tibeto-Burman, Kuki-Chin-Naga, Naga, Zeme
**Alternate names:** Kacha, Liangmai, Liangmei, Liyang, Lyangmay, Lyengmai
**Main region:** Nagaland, Kohima District, Jhaluke, Paren, Medzephima blocks.

## 1 Consonant phonemes

### 1.1 Inventory

| | Bilabial | Labio-dental | Alveolar | Post-alveolar | Palatal | Velar | Glottal |
|---|---|---|---|---|---|---|---|
| Plosive | p b | | t d $t^h$ | | | k g $k^h$ | |
| Nasal | m | | n | | | ŋ | |
| Fricative | | f | s z | | | | h |
| Approx | w | | | ɹ | j | | |
| Lat Approx | | | l | | | | |
| Affricate | | | ʦ | | | | |

### 1.2 Distribution

a. Consonants in Liangmai occur in all positions, with the following restrictions:

   i. Only the following sounds occur syllable- and word- finally: /p t k m n ŋ/.

b. Geminate consonants do not occur.

# 2 Vowel phonemes

## 2.1 Inventory

a. **Short**

| | FRONT | CENTRAL | BACK |
|---|---|---|---|
| Close | i | | u |
| Open-mid | ɛ | | ɔ |
| Open | | a | |

b. **Diphthongs**

The language has nine diphthongs, which can be classified into two types, Class I and Class II, according to whether the first or the second is relatively more prominent. This distinction is crucial to the placement of tones in syllables: the prominent vowel position is the tonic.

Class I diphthongs(first member strong): /ai̯ iu̯ au̯ ui̯ ɔi̯/.

Class II diphthongs (second member strong): /i̯a i̯o i̯e ɔ̯a/

## 2.2 Distribution

a. The vowels occur in medial and final positions, with the following restrictions:

   i. The vowel /a/ occurs also in the initial position in words; there is one instance each for the occurrence of /i/ and /u/ initially in words.

b. While all the monophthongs occur in both closed and open syllables, most diphthongs occur in open syllables. The diphthongs /i̯a i̯e ɔ̯a/ occur in closed syllables with a nasal in the coda position, and a Low tone.

c. Vowel sequences do not occur, i.e. sequences of monophthongs and/or diphthongs do not occur.

# 3 Consonant allophones

## 3.1 Inventory

**General:**

a. Non-labial consonants are palatalized before /e æ/.

**Specific:**

| | BILABIAL | ALVEOLAR | POST-ALVEOLAR | VELAR |
|---|---|---|---|---|
| Plosive | b(p) | d (t) | d̙ (t) | g(k) |

## 3.2 Distribution

a. The voiced plosive allophones [b d g] < /p t k/ occur inter-vocalically.

b. The post-alveolar voiced plosive allophone [d̙] < /t/ occurs before /ɹ/

# 4 Vowel allophones

## 4.1 Inventory

**General:**

a. Vowels are lengthened word-finally.

**Specific:**

| | |
|---|---|
| [ə], [ɐ], [a ː] | : /a/ |
| [wa] | : /u̯a/ |
| [ja] | : /i̯a/ |

## 4.2 Distribution

a. The raised low vowel allophone [ɐ] < /a/ occurs in closed syllables.

b. The approximant allophone occurs when the first vowel position in a diphthong is high and less prominent than the second vowel position.

# 5 Syllable structure

## 5.1 Canonical syllable structure

(C) V (C)

Note: The optionality of the onset consonant is restricted to the vowel /a/. The occurrence of onsetless syllables with other vowels, as noted above in the footnotes, has been attested for the following: /í/ 'I' and /upū/ 'box', /àm/ 'mango'. The latter two are borrowings from Manipuri and Assamese.

## 5.2 Consonant clusters

Two-consonant clusters:

Initial : Nil

Final : Nil.

Medial : Coda + Onset sequences[33].

Three-consonant clusters: Nil

# 6 Tone

**Tonemes:**

High (H): ( ´ )

[33] Medial clusters have syllable divisions between them in deliberate speech., e.g./ tat/ 'go' + /jè/ 'PAST' > [tɐt.jè :] 'went', *[tɐ.tjè˙], [tɐt.tjè :]. In fast speech, the second consonant may be elided accompanied by a consequent voicing of the intervocalic consonant, in favour of cluster reduction: [tɐdè :] < [tɐtè :].

Low (L): ( ` )

Mid: (M) (Unmarked)

E.g. /pa´/, /pà/, /pa/

**Reference:** Wichamdinbo and Pandey (2009)

# Limbu

**Ethnologue code:** ISO 639-3: lif
**Language classification:** Sino-Tibetan, Tibeto-Burman, Himalayish, Mahakiranti, Kiranti, Eastern
**Alternate names:** Yakthung Pan
**Main region:** Limbuwan (preferred term for the Limbu area), Eastern hills, east of Arun River; Koshi zone, Dhankuta, Sankhuwasabha, Terhathum, Dhankuta.

## 1 Consonant Phonemes

### 1.1 Inventory

| | Bilabial | Dental | Alv. | Post-Alv. | Retroflex | Palatal | Velar | Glottal |
|---|---|---|---|---|---|---|---|---|
| Stop | p b<br>pʰ (bʱ) | t (d)<br>tʰ | | | (ʈ) (ɖ)<br>(ʈʰ) (ɖʱ) | | k (g)<br>kʰ | ʔ |
| Nasal | m | n | | | (ɳ) | | ŋ | |
| Trill | | | r | | | | | |
| Fricative | | | s | | | | | ɦ |
| Approx. | w | | | | | j | | |
| Lat Appr. | | | l | | | | | |
| Affricate | | | | ts˃ dz˃<br>(tsʰ˃) | | | | |

### 1.2 Distribution

a. Consonants occur in all positions, with the following restrictions:
   i. /b r ʔ ŋ/ do not occur word-initially in native words. /ʔ ŋ/ occur as onsets word-internally in native words. In loan words, all the other phonemes (including the marginal ones) occur word-initially.
   ii. /k r s ɦ ts˃/ do not occur as codas word-finally and internally.

b. Geminates of consonants occur inter-vocalically; Inadequate data available; geminates of /k l/ have been attested.

# 2 Vowel Phonemes

## 2.1 Inventory

a. **Short**

| | FRONT | CENTRAL | BACK |
|---|---|---|---|
| Close | i | | u |
| Mid | | ə | |
| Open-mid | ɛ | ɐ | ʌ |

b. **Long**

| | FRONT | CENTRAL | BACK |
|---|---|---|---|
| Close | i: | | u: |
| Mid | e· | | o· |
| Open-mid | ɛ: | ɐ : | ʌ: |

## 2.2 Distribution

a. All the vowels occur in all the positions.
b. Vowel sequences occur with syllabic divisions between them.

# 3 Consonant allophones

## 3.1 Inventory

**General:** A glottal stop [ʔ] is inserted word-initially before a vowel, and inter-vocalically.

**Specific:** As below.

| | **Bilabial** | **Dental** | **Alveolar** | **Palatal** | **Velar** |
|---|---|---|---|---|---|
| Plosive | $p^{ʔ}$(p) b(p)<br>p(t) $b^{ɦ}$($p^{h}$) | $t^{ʔ}$ (t) d(t) | | | $k^{ʔ}$ (k) g(k)<br>$g^{ɦ}$($k^{h}$) |
| Nasal | | | | | ŋ (m) |
| Trill | | | r(l) | | |
| Approx | (w)(b) | | | | |
| Lat approx | | | $^{ʔ}$l (t)<br>l(m,n,ŋ) | | |
| Affricate | | | | $tʃ^{h}$(s) ʤ(tʃ) | |

## 3.2 Distribution

a. The voiced stop allophones [b d g ʤ $b^{ɦ}$ $d^{ɦ}$ $g^{ɦ}$] of the voiceless plosives /p t k ʧ $p^{h}$ $t^{h}$ $k^{h}$/ occur following a nasal, a glottal stop or inter-vocalically.

b. The glottalized voiceless plosive allophones {$p^{ʔ}$ $t^{ʔ}$ $k^{ʔ}$] < /p t k/, with simultaneous glottalization, occur in the coda position.

c. The aspirated voiceless palatal affricate allophone [$tʃ^{h}$] of the voiceless alveolar fricative phoneme /s/ occurs following /n/ and /t/.

d. [$^{ʔ}$l] </t/ occurs before /l/.

e. [r] < /l/ occurs in the onset position within the word and in the beginning in clitics.

f. The optional approximant allophone [w] < /b/ occurs following a nasal or inter-vocalically.

g. [l] < /m n ŋ/ occurs before /l/.

h. [ŋ] < /m/ occurs before /ŋ/.

# 4 Vowel allophones

## 4.1 Inventory

[ɪ] : /i/

[ɷ·] : /o·/

## 4.2 Distribution

a. The lowered allophones [ɪ] < /i/ and [ɷ·] < /o·/ occur before a nasal.

# 5 Syllable structure

## 5.1 Canonical syllable structure

(C (G)) V/N̩ (C)

## 5.2 Consonant clusters

Two-consonant clusters:

Initial : C + G

Final : Nil

Medial : Geminates and General.

Three-consonant clusters: Nil

**Reference:** van Driem (1987)

# Lotha

**Ethnologue code:** ISO 639-3: njh
**Language classification:** Tibeto-Burman, Kuki-Chin-Naga
**Alternate names:** Chizima, Choimi, Hlota, Kyong, Lhota, Miklai, Tsindir, Lutha, Lotha, Tsontsii
**Main region:** Nagaland, west central, Workha District.

## 1 Consonant phonemes

### 1.1 Inventory

| | Bilabial | Labio-dental | | Alv. | Post-alveolar | Palatal | Velar | Glottal |
|---|---|---|---|---|---|---|---|---|
| Plosive | p b<br>$p^h$ | | t<br>$t^h$ | | | | k<br>$k^h$ | |
| Nasal | m<br>$m^ɦ$ | | | n<br>$n^ɦ$ | | ɲ<br>$ɲ^ɦ$ | ŋ<br>$ŋ^ɦ$ | |
| Trill | | | | r<br>$r^ɦ$ | | | | |
| Fricative | | f v | | s z | ʃ ʒ | | | h |
| Approx | w | | | | | j | | |
| Lat Approx | | | | l<br>$l^ɦ$ | | | | |
| Affricate | pɸ bv | | | ts<br>$ts^h$ | | tʃ<br>$tʃ^h$ | | |

### 1.2 Distribution

a. Consonants occur in all positions, with the following restriction:
   i. Consonants other than /p t k v s m n ŋ j/ do not occur finally.
b. Geminates do not occur.

# 2 Vowel phonemes

## 2.1 Inventory

a. **Short**

| | FRONT | CENTRAL | BACK |
|---|---|---|---|
| Close | i | | u |
| Close-mid | e | | o |
| Open-mid | | ə | |
| Open | | a | |

## 2.2 Distribution

a. Vowels occur in all positions, with the following restriction:

   i. /ə/ does not occur initially in words.

b. Sequences of vowels occur.

# 3 Consonant allophones

## 3.1 Inventory

[d]: /t/
[g]: /k/

## 3.2 Distribution

a. [d] < /t/ occurs after nasals.

b. [g] < /k/ occurs medially when flanked by voiced sounds., e.g., / tekrə̀/ [tegrə̀] 'honey bee'.

# 4 Vowel allophones

## 4.1 Inventory

| | |
|---|---|
| [ɪ] [$^{j}$i :]: | /i/ |
| [ʊ] : | /u/ |

## 4.2 Distribution

a. [i:] < /i/ occurs with a palatal onglide word-initially.

b. [ɪ ʊ] < /i u/ occur when preceded by an onset in the first syllable with the Falling tone.

c. The phonetic realization of vowels depends on their tonal association in a majority of cases.

# 5 Syllable structure

## 5.1 Canonical syllable structure

(N)(C)V(C)

E,g., /à/ 'I'; /nrə́ / 'earth quake'; /mp$^{h}$əv/ 'to hide'

## 5.2 Consonant clusters

Two-consonant clusters:

| | |
|---|---|
| Initial | : N + C |
| Final | : Nil. |
| Medial | : General. |

Three-consonant clusters: Not attested

# 6 Suprasegmentals

## 6.1 Tone

Tonemes:

Lotha has three contour tonemes:

High (H): ( ´ )

Low (L): ( ` )

Mid: (M) (Unmarked)

E.g. /vá/ 'go ahead (Imp.)', /và/ 'stitch (Imp.)', /va/

## 6.2 Distribution

Any of the three tones can occur on any of the syllables.

**References:** Acharya (1975)

# Magar

**Ethnologue code:** ISO 639-3: mgp
**Language classification:** Sino-Tibetan, Tibeto-Burman, Himalayish, Mahakiranti, Kham-Magar-Chepang-Sunwari, Magar
**Alternate names:** Magari, Manggar
**Main region:** Gandaki zone, Tanahu District, east of Bagmati River, central mountains, Okhaldhunga, Taplejung, Bhojpur, Dhankuta, Chainpur, Terhathum, Ilam, and Letang are main centers

## 1 Consonant Phonemes

### 1.1 Inventory

| | Bilabial | Apico alveolar | Post-alv. | Palatal | Velar | Glottal |
|---|---|---|---|---|---|---|
| Plosive | p b<br>$p^{h}$ $b^{ɦ}$ | t d<br>$t^{h}$ $d^{ɦ}$ | | | k g<br>$k^{h}$ $g^{ɦ}$ | |
| Nasal | m | n | | | ŋ | |
| Trill | | r | | | | |
| Fricative | | | ʃ | | | h |
| Approx | w | | | j | | |
| Lat Appr | | l | | tʃ ʤ<br>$tʃ^{h}$ $ʤ^{ɦ}$ | | |

### 1.2 Distribution

a. Consonants occur in all positions, with the following restriction:
   i. In native vocabulary, aspirated consonants, voiced stops, and /h/ do not occur word-finally. In borrowed words, / $p^{h}$ $t^{h}$ $k^{h}$ ʧ ʤ d/ are found to occur finally.

b. Geminates of the following consonants occur inter-vocalically: /t d ʧ ʤ k g ʃ m n l r/.

# 2 Vowel Phonemes

## 2.1 Inventory

a. **Short**

| | FRONT | CENTRAL | BACK |
|---|---|---|---|
| Close | ɪ | | ʊ |
| Close-mid | e | | o |
| Open-mid | | (ə) | |
| Open | | a | |

## 2.2 Distribution

a. Vowels occur in all positions. /ə/ occurs only in borrowed words.

b. Sequences of two vowels occur medially and finally in native vocabulary, with the following restrictions:
   i. /e/ does not occur as a second member
   ii. /a a/ sequence does not occur.

# 3 Consonant Allophones

## 3.1 Inventory (General allophones excluded)

| | BILABIAL | DENTAL | ALVEOLAR | RETROFLEX | PALA-TAL | VELAR | GLO-TTAL |
|---|---|---|---|---|---|---|---|
| Plosive | | | | | | | ʔ(k, ø) |
| Trill | | | r̥(r) | | | | |
| Tap/ Flap | | | | ɽ(ɖ) | | | |
| Fricative | ɸ(pʰ) | θ(tʰ) β(b) | | | | x(kʰ) | |
| Affricate | | | ts(tʃ) d(dʒ) | | | | |

## 3.2 Distribution

**General:**

a. Apico-alveolar, palatal and velar consonants are palatalized before front vowels.

**Specific:**

a. [ts dz] < /tʃ dʒ / before front vowels.
b. [ɸ θ x] < /$p^h$ $t^h$ $k^h$/ occur word-finally in borrowed words.
c. [ɾ] < / ɖ / occurs between vowels, and in syllable Coda positions in borrowed words.
d. [i̯ ] < /j/ occurs before /u/.
e. [r̥] < /r/ occurs word-finally.
f. [ʔ] < /k/ occurs optionally word-finally.
g. [ʔ] is inserted between two identical vowels.

# 4 Vowel Allophones

## 4.1 Inventory

| | |
|---|---|
| [u<]: | /u/ |
| [o<]: | /o/ |
| [ɛ]: | /e/ |
| [ʊ]: | /u/ |
| [a<]: | /a/ |
| [j]: | /ø/ |
| [w]: | /ø/ |
| [i̯]: | /j/ |

## 4.2 Distribution

**General:**

a. Vowels are breathy before intervocalic /h/ and aspirated consonants.

**Specific:**

a. [j] is inserted between a front vowel /i e/ and /a/; word-initially, it is optionally inserted as an on-glide before a front vowel.

b. [w] is inserted between a back vowel /u o/ and /a/; word-initially, it is optionally inserted as an on-glide before a back vowel.

c. The back vowels /u o/ are fronted [u< o<] following a palatal approximant /j/.

d. The vowels /e u/ are lowered [ɛ ʊ] in the final open or closed syllable.

e. The low vowel /a/ is considerable fronted (and raised) in non-final open syllables.

# 5 Syllable Structure

## 5.1 Canonical Syllable Structure

(C) (G) V (C)

## 5.2 Consonant Clusters

Two-consonant clusters:

Initial : C + j/w

Final : Nil

Medial : general.

Three-consonant clusters: Nil

**Reference:** Subba (1972)

# Manchad

**Ethnologue code:** ILO 639-3: lae.
**Language classification:** Tibeto-Burman, Himalayish, Tibeto-Kanauri.
**Alternate names:** Manchati, Manchad, Patni, Chamba, Chamba Lahuli, Lahuli, Swangla, Changsapa Boli
**Main region:** Lahul Valley, Pattan, Chamba-Lahul, and lower Mayar valley.

## 1 Consonant phonemes

### 1.1 Inventory

| | Bilabial | Dental | Alveolar | Retroflex | Palatal | Velar | Glottal |
|---|---|---|---|---|---|---|---|
| Stop | p b<br>tʰ bʱ | t d<br>tʰ dʱ | | ʈ ɖ<br>ʈʰ ɖʱ | | k g<br>kʰ gʱ | |
| Nasal | m<br>mʱ | | n<br>nʱ | ɳ | | | |
| Trill | | | r<br>rʱ | | | | |
| Flap | | | | ɽ<br>ɽʱ | | | |
| Fricative | | | s z | ʂ | ɕ | | h |
| Appr | w | | | | j | | |
| Lat Appr | | | l<br>lʱ | | | | |
| Affricate | | | ts ʥ<br>tsʰ | | ʧ ʤ<br>ʧʰ ʤʱ | | |

## 1.2 Distribution

a. Consonants occur in all positions, with the following exceptions:
   i. /ɳ ɭ ɽ / do not occur word-initially.
   ii. Voiceless and aspirated plosives /p pʰ bʱ/ and /ɽʱ w j/ do not occur finally in native words. In borrowed words, however, the plosives may occur in the final position.
   iii. The voiced aspirates are mostly found in loanwords from Indo-Aryan, which are on the increase.

b. All consonants except the fricatives /s z ʂ ç h/ and glides /w j/ have geminates that contrast with non-geminates inter-vocalically.

# 2 Vowels

## 2.1 Inventory

a. **Short:**

| | FRONT | CENTRAL | BACK |
|---|---|---|---|
| Close | i | | u |
| Close-mid | e | | o |
| Open-mid | | ə | |
| Open | | | ɑ |

b. **Nasal:**

| | FRONT | CENTRAL | BACK |
|---|---|---|---|
| Mid | ẽ | | õ |
| Open | | ã | |

## 2.2 Distribution

a. Vowels occur in all positions.

b. Sequences of two syllabic vowels are common, with the exception that /ə/ doesn't occur as the second member.

# 3 Consonant allophones

## 3.1 Inventory

The following general classes of allophones occur:

a. Devoiced

b. Deaspirated

c. Palatalized

d. Pre-glottalized

e. High Falling Tone due to Tonogenesis.

## 3.2 Distribution

a. Voiced stops are devoiced in the Coda position, e.g, [tup] < /tub/ 'fist', [jaktʃiː] < /jagtʃi/ 'to lick'.

b. Aspirated sounds are deaspirated in the Coda position, e.g., [d$^{ɦ}$obri : ] < / /d$^{ɦ}$ob$^{ɦ}$ri/ 'enough', [ məɽ] < /məɽ$^{ɦ}$ / 'corpse'.

c. Consonants are palatalized before /e/, e.g., [k$^{j}$etri : ] < /ketri/ 'to say'.

d. Voiced stops, especially / d g / are preglottalized in the Coda position, e.g., /t$^{h}$aʔkt ʃ i : ] < /t$^{h}$agt ʃ i / 'to break'

e. Loss of final /h/ leads to high Falling tone, e.g., [ gò ]< /goh/ 'hill'.

# 4 Vowel allophones

## 4.1 Inventory

| | |
|---|---|
| [i : ]: | /i/ |
| [ɛ] [$^{j}$e] [e : ]: | / e / |
| [u : ] : | /u/ |
| [ɔ] [ o : ]: | / o / |
| [e] [ɐ] [ə :]: | /ə/ |
| [a : ] : | /a/ |

## 4.2 Distribution

a. Vowels are lengthened in final open syllables in disyllabic and longer words.

b. [ɛ ɔ] < /e o / occur before nasal consonants; [ə] < /a/ occurs before velar nasals.

c. [e] < /ə/ occurs before /i/, e.g., [kei] < / kəi/ 'by you'.

# 5 Syllable Structure

## 5.1 Canonical syllable structure

(C) (G/r) V (C) (C)

## 5.2 Consonant Clusters

Two-consonant clusters:

Initial : C + G/r
Final : -nz, -nd, -rp$^h$,-st.
Medial : General.

Three-consonant clusters:

Initial : Nil.

Final : Nil.

Medial : /-rpj-, -mɖr-, -ŋɖr-, -ŋgz-, -ŋgs-, -kʈʰr-. (N + S + j/r/s/z)

**Reference:** Sharma (1982)

# Mao-Naga[34]

**Ethnologue code:** ISO 639-3: nbi
**Language classification:** Tibeto-Burman, Kuki-Chin-Naga
**Alternate names:** Mao, Spowama, Sopvoma, Maikel, Memi, Sopfomo, Emela
**Main region:** Northwest Manipur, Senapati District; Nagaland.

## 1 Consonant phonemes

### 1.1 Inventory

| | Bilabial | Labio-dental | Alveo-lar | Psot-alveolar | Palatal | Velar | Glottal |
|---|---|---|---|---|---|---|---|
| Plosive | p b<br>pʰ | | t̠ d̠<br>t̠ʰ | | | k g<br>kʰ | |
| Nasal | m | | n | | | ŋ | |
| Trill | | | r̥ r | | | | |
| Fricative | | f v | s z | ʃ ʒ | | (x) | h |
| Approx | (w) | | | | j | | |
| Lat Approx | | | l | | | | |
| Affricate | pf bv | | ts ʥ | | ʧ ʤ | | |

### 1.2 Distribution

a. Consonants do not occur word-finally.

b. Any single consonant can occur initially and medially, with the following restrictions:

[34] Special sounds: (i ) syllabic voiced bilabial plosive [ b̩ ]; (ii) 'a co-articulated segment of a voiceless trill and a voiceless glottal fricative': [h͜r̥]. The sound is being included here as [r̥], leaving it for further examination.

i. [$t^h$] occurs medially, and in that position, can freely vary with [ $\underline{t}^h$].
ii. /pf/ occurs only before /i o u/.
iii. /bv/ occurs only before /ɨo/.
iv. /ts/ occurs only before /ɨ/
v. /dz/ occurs only before /ɨ e/.

# 2 Vowel phonemes

## 2.1 Inventory

a. **Short**

| | FRONT | CENTRAL | BACK |
|---|---|---|---|
| Close | i | ɨ | u |
| Close-mid | e | | o |
| Open | | a | |

b. **Diphthongs:**

Intra-morphemic:

Class I (first member strong): / əi̯ ou̯/

Class II (second member strong): /i̯u ə̯i ə̯u ə̯e/

Inter-morphemic:

Class I: / ae̯ ao̯ ue̯ oe̯ ie̯/

## 2.2 Distribution

a. Vowels occur in all positions, with the following restriction:

/e u ɨ/ do not occur initially.

b. The inter-morphemic diphthongs / ae̯ ao̯ ue̯ oe̯ ie̯/ may interact with morphology. The second vowel may be desyllabified (or undergo synaeresis). E.g., /ta-e/ > [tae̯] 'go-past' 'went'

i. / ta-e/ > [ta-e] 'go-progr', 'is/was going'.

c. Sequences of two vowels occur.

# 3 Consonant allophones

## 3.1 Inventory and distribution

Syllabic consonants occur. List of these is not provided. As an example, [b̩ ] < /b/, as in [toab̩le] < /toa bəi̯le/ ‘I chose to eat’.

# 4 Vowel allophones

## 4.1 Inventory

| | |
|---|---|
| [ɪ]: | /i̯/ |
| [ɨ̈]: | /ɨ/ |
| [ʊ] [ɔ]: | /o/ |
| [ɛ]: | /e/ |

## 4.2 Distribution

a. [ɪ ʊ] < /i u/ occur word-initially.

b. [ɛ ɔ] < /e o/ occur word-finally.

c. [ɨ̈] is a free variant of /ɨ/

# 5 Syllab!e structure

## 5.1 Canonical syllable structure

$(<C>_{1})(<r>_{2})V$

Condition: If $_{2}$, then $_{1}$ is / p $p^{h}$ k $k^{h}$/.

## 5.2 Consonant clusters

Two-consonant clusters:

Initial : pr-, $p^h$r-, kr-, $k^h$r-

Final : Nil.

Medial : Same as initial

Three-consonant clusters:

# 6 Suprasegmentals

## 6.1 Tone[35]

High : H ( ́ )
Mid-High : M1 ( ̌ )
Mid-Low : M2 ( ̄ )

Low: L ( ̀)

E.g.,

/ōdó/ 'art, technique of politeness'

/ōdǒ/ 1) 'show/ splurge'; 2) 'Isn't that so?' (a tag question); 3) ' trick' etc.

/ōdō/ 1) 'paddy field' 2) 'notch, step, layer'

/ōdò/ 'field ridge'

/ōt^hǐhópə̀i̯/ 'younger sister'

**Reference:** Giridhar (1994)

[35] Tone in Mao-Naga has grammatical function, too. E.g., /mōzɨ̄/ 'to urinate'; /mōzɨ́ / 'urine'.

# Maring

**Ethnologue code:** ISO 639-3: nng
**Language classification:** Tibeto-Burman, Kuki-Chin-Naga
**Alternate names:** Khoibu, Khoibu Maring
**Main region:** Manipur, southeast, Laiching, Chandel District.

## 1 Consonant phonemes

### 1.1 Inventory

| | BILABIAL | LABIO-DENTAL | DENTAL | ALV. | PRE-PALATAL | PALATAL | VELAR | GLOTTAL |
|---|---|---|---|---|---|---|---|---|
| Stop | p b<br>$p^h$ | | t d<br>$t^h$ | | | | k<br>$k^h$ | |
| Nasal | m | | n | | | | ŋ | |
| Trill | | | | r | | | | |
| Fricative | | | | | ś | | | h |
| Appr | w | | | | | j | | |
| Lat Appr | | | | l̥ l | | | | |
| Affricate | | | | | tʃ | | | |

### 1.2 Distribution

a. Consonants occur in all positions, with the following restriction:

   i. /$p^h$ $t^h$ $k^h$ b d g tʃ h/ do not occur finally.

b. Geminate consonants except / p t k m n ŋ l w j / occur in the medial position.

# 2 Vowel phonemes

## 2.1 Inventory

a. **Short**

| | FRONT | CENTRAL | BACK |
|---|---|---|---|
| Close | i | | u |
| Mid | e | ə | o |
| Open | | a | ɑ |

## 2.2 Distribution

a. All the vowels occur in all the positions.

b. The following vowel sequences occur with syllabic divisions between them: /i.u i.e i.a e.ə e.u a.u/.

# 3 Consonant allophones

Allophonic data on consonants and vowels are not available.

# 4 Syllable structure

## 4.1 Canonical syllable structure

$(<C>_1)\ (<C>_2)\ V\ (C)$

Cond.: (i) If $C_1$ is Pl, then $C_2$ is L/G, (ii) If $C_1$ is /s/, then $C_2$ is p/t.

## 4.2 Consonant clusters

Two-consonant clusters:

Initial : P + L/G, sp, st

Final : Nil

Medial : General.

Three-consonant clusters:

Initial : Nil

Final : Nil

Medial : A limited number occur, with the restriction that the third consonant is one of the following: /r l w m/

# 5 Suprasegmentals

## 5.1 Tone[36]

Tonemes:

a. Rising: H ( ´ )

b. Falling: L ( ` )

E.g., /á/ 'this', / à / 'he/she'

/mə́khú/ 'a (kind of) basket', /mə̀khù/ 'cough'

**Reference:** Ningomba (1978)

[36] On the basis of the description in Ningomba (1978) tone in Maring is predictable. Rising tone occurs only flowing the voiceless lateral consonant. The falling tone occurs elsewhere. The facts need attestation.

# Mishmi

**Ethnologue code:** ISO 639-3: mxj
**Language classification:** Tibeto-Burman, North Assam, Tani_
**Alternate names:** Kaman, Mishmi, Miji, Miju
**Main region:** Assam; Arunachal Pradesh, Lohit District.

## 1 Consonant phonemes

### 1.1 Inventory

| | Bilabial | Labio-dental | Alveolar | Palatal | Velar | Glottal |
|---|---|---|---|---|---|---|
| Plosive | p b<br>$p^h$ | | t d<br>$t^h$ | | k g<br>$k^h$ | |
| Nasal | m | | n | | ŋ | |
| Trill | | | r | | | |
| Fricative | | | s z | | | h |
| Approx | w | | | j | | |
| Lat Approx | | | l | | | |
| Affricate | | | ts ʥ<br>$ts^h$ | | | |

### 1.2 Distribution

a. Consonants occur in all positions, with the following restrictions:

i. / p b m k g ŋ /, and / l / in borrowed words.
ii. /ʔ/ do not occur word-finally.

b. Geminate consonants do not occur. Identical consonants due to word-formation are reduced to single consonants.

# 2 Vowel phonemes

## 2.1 Inventory

a. **Short:**

| | FRONT | CENTRAL | BACK |
|---|---|---|---|
| Close | i | ɨ | u |
| Close-mid | e | | o |
| Open | | a | |

b. **Long:**

| | FRONT | CENTRAL | BACK |
|---|---|---|---|
| Close | i : | ɨ : | u : |
| Close-mid | e : | | o : |
| Open | | a : | |

c. **Nasal:**

| | FRONT | CENTRAL | BACK |
|---|---|---|---|
| Close | | | |
| Close-mid | ẽ | | õ |
| Open | | ã | |

## 2.2 Distribution

a. Vowels occur in all positions, with the following restriction:
   i. The mid vowels /ə e o/ do not occur in syllables with a nasal consonant in the coda position.

b. Sequences of syllabic vowels occur medially and finally. Identical vowels are kept separate with a glottal stop insertion, e.g., /eẽ)/ > [eʔẽ)]. The following sequences have been found:

   Medial: /eẽ iẽ ɨu õa ɨi/

   Final: / áà aà /

# 3 Consonant allophones

## 3.1 Inventory

| | Bilabial | Alveolar | Velar |
|---|---|---|---|
| Plosive | $p^w$ (p)<br>b̥ (b)<br>$b^w$ (b) | d̥ (d) | g̊ (g) |
| Nasal | | | ŋ: (ŋ) |

## 3.2 Distribution

a. [b̥ d̥ g̊] < / b d g / occur word-finally.

b. [$p^w$ $b^w$ ] < / p b / occur before short mid front vowels/e ẽ/.

c. The lengthened allophone of the velar nasal [ŋˑ] < /ŋ/ occurs as the Coda of a syllable carrying Rising-Falling tone, e.g., /nâŋ/ > [ nâŋ: ] 'smell'.

# 4 Vowel allophones

## 4.1 Inventory

| | |
|---|---|
| [i ˑ] [ˀi]: | /i / |
| [ e ˑ] [ˀe]: | /e / |
| [ a ˑ] [ ˀa] [ɐ]: | /a / |
| [ o ˑ] [ˀo] : | / o/ |
| [u ˑ] [ ˀu]: | /u / |
| [ɯ]: | /ɨ/ |

## 4.2 Distribution

a. Short vowels are lengthened in syllables carrying Rising-Falling tone. Nasal vowels remain short.

b. Vowels in the word-initial position and as the second member in asequence of two are preglottalized.

c. [ɐ] < /a/ occurs in a non-initial syllable carrying a Rising tone.

d. [ɯ] </ɨ/ occurs in a syllable with level tone.

# 5 Syllable structure

## 5.1 Canonical syllable structure

(C)(L/G) V $(<j>_{1})$ $(<C>_{2})$

Cond. If both 1 and 2, then 2= k/g/ŋ.

## 5.2 Consonant clusters

Two-consonant clusters:

Initial : C + L/G
Final : -jk, -jg, -jŋ.
Medial : general

Three-consonant clusters:

Initial : Nil
Final : Nil
Medial : (a) C+C+l/r/w/j; (b) j+C+C.

# 6 Suprasegments

## 6.1 Tone[37]

**Tonemes:**

a. Rising: LH ( ´ )

b. Falling: HL ( ` )

c. Rising-Falling: LHL ( ˆ )

d. Level: unmarked

**Allotones:**

a. Low Rise [ LM ] < / LH / : Rising tones have low rise if the preceding syllable carries a Falling tone, e.g., /kàtsígt jan / 'scorpion'.

b. High Fall [ H'L ] < / HL / : Falling tones have a high fall if the preceding syllable carries a Rising tone.. e.g., / támè / 'wild boar'.

**Reference:** Sastry (1984)

[37] All the tones have a mid-rise in normal contexts.

# Mizo

**Ethnologue code:** ISO 639-3: lus
**Language classification:** Tibeto-Burman, Kuki-Chin-Naga
**Alternate names:** Lushai, Lusei, Lushei, Lukhai, Lusago, Sailau, Dulien, Duhlian Twang, Lusai, Hualngo, Whelngo
**Main region:** Mizoram; Assam; Manipur; Nagaland; Tripura.

## 1 Consonant phonemes

### 1.1 Inventory

| | Bilabial | Labio-dental | Dental | Alveolar | Palatal | Velar | Glottal |
|---|---|---|---|---|---|---|---|
| Plosive | p b<br>tʰ | | t d<br>tʰ | t̠ d̠<br>t̠ʰ | | k<br>kʰ | ʔ |
| Nasal | m<br>m̥ʰ | | | n̠<br>n̠̊ʰ | | ŋ<br>ŋ̊ʰ | |
| Trill | | | | r<br>r̥ʰ | | | |
| Fricative | | f v | | s z | | | h |
| Approx | w | | | | j | | |
| Lat Appr | | | | l<br>l̥ʰ | | | |
| Affricate | | | | ts<br>tsʰ | | | |

### 1.2 Distribution

a. Consonants occur in all positions, with the following restrictions:
   i. Only /p t ʈ k ʔ m n ŋ l r w j/ occur word-finally or in the coda position:

ii. Nasals in the Coda position are preceded by short vowels.
iii. /ʔ j w/ do not occur in the beginning or in the middle as Onsets.

b. Geminates of consonants do not occur.
c. As a single segment in the Coda position, /ʔ/ has extra Low tone in non-derived forms.

# 2 Vowel phonemes

## 2.1 Inventory

a. **Short**

| | FRONT | CENTRAL | BACK |
|---|---|---|---|
| Close | i | | u |
| Close-mid | e | | o |
| Open | | a | |

b. **Diphthongs**

ai au ɔu ɔi ei eu ia ua

## 2.3 Distribution

a. Vowels occur in all positions.
b. Vowels have tonal associations. For example, vowels with L tone are pronounced short, and vowels with H, LH or HL tones are pronounced long.
c. Vowel sequences occur commonly.

# 3 Consonant allophones

## 3.1 Inventory

| | PALATAL | GLOTTAL |
|---|---|---|
| Plosive | | ʔ (p, t, k) |
| Fricative | ʃ (~s)<br>ʒ (~z) | |

## 3.2 Distribution

a. [ ʃ Z ] freely vary with /s z/.

b. [ʔ] < /p t k/ occurs in the coda position.

c. [ʔ] is added to / r l / ending forms leading to tone depression to extra low tone (5): e.g.

1 1 5
/bar/ [ba: r] > [bar] 'to stuff something into one's mouth'

4 4 5
/pel/ [pe:l] > [pel] 'to pass'

# 4 Vowel allophones

## 4.1 Inventory

[i:] [ĭ]: /i/

[e:] [ĕ]: /e/

[u:] [ŭ]: /u/

[o:] [ŏ]: /o/

[a:] [ă]: /a/

### 4.2 Distribution

a. Vowels are lengthened in open syllables.

b. Vowels are shortened before /ʔ/.

## 5 Syllable structure

### 5.1 Canonical syllable structure

(C)V(C)

### 5.2 Consonant clusters

Two-consonant clusters:

Initial : Nil<br>
Final : C+ /ʔ/ (C=/p t ʈ k m n ŋ l r w j/)<br>
Medial : $C_1 + C_2$ ($C_1$ = /p t ʈ k ʔ m n ŋ l r/)<br>
($C_2$ = all consonants except /ʔ w j/)

Three-consonant clusters: Nil.

## 6 Suprasegmentals

### 6.1 Tone

Tonemes:

There are four register tonemes in Lushai/ Mizo:

High: H<br>
Low: L<br>
Falling-Rising: L-H<br>
Rising-Falling: H-L

E.g.: H L

/lei/ 'slanting' /lei/ 'bridge'

| LH | HL |
|---|---|
| / pǎ / 'mushroom' | / pâ /'father' |

## 6.2 Distribution

All tones have an allotone, extra low tone EL (5), which normally occurs on syllables with /ʔ/ in the coda position.

**References:** Fanai (1992), Changte (1986), Bright (1957)

# Monpa

**Ethnologue code:** ISO 639-2: sit
**Language classification:** Tibeto-Burman, Himalayish, Mahakiranti.
**Alternate names:** Monba, Mompa, Monpa, Momba, Menba, Khamba
**Main region:** Arunachal Pradesh, Tawang and Kameng districts.

## 1 Consonant phonemes

### 1.1 Inventory

| | Bilabial | Dental | Alveolar | Post-alv. | Palatal | Velar | Glottal |
|---|---|---|---|---|---|---|---|
| Plosive | p b<br>pʰ | t d<br>tʰ | | | | k g<br>kʰ | |
| Nasal | m | | n | | ɲ | ŋ | |
| Trill | | | r | | | | |
| Fricative | | | s z<br>zʰ | ʃ | | | h |
| Approx | w | | | | j | | |
| Lat Approx | | | l | | | | |
| Lat Fricative | | | ɮ | | | | |
| Affricate | | | ʦ ʣ | | tʃ ʤ<br>tʃʰ | | |

### 1.2 Distribution

a. Consonants occur in all positions, with the following restriction:

i. Only / p k m n s/ occur finally.

# 2 Vowel phonemes

## 2.1 Inventory

a. **Short**

| | FRONT | CENTRAL | BACK |
|---|---|---|---|
| Close | i | | u |
| Close-mid | e | | o |
| Open-mid | | ɐ | |

## 2.2 Distribution

a. Vowels occur in all positions.

b. Vowel sequences occur in two's, often realized distinctly, but sometimes as diphthongs, in which case "the first of the pair is modified into a front or short, sometimes indistinct vowel".

# 3 Consonant allophones

## 3.1 Inventory

| | BILABIAL | DENTAL | PALATAL | VELAR |
|---|---|---|---|---|
| Plosive | p (b) | t (d) | | k (g) |
| Affricate | | | tʃ (ʤ) | |

## 3.2 Distribution

a. The voiceless stop allophones [ p t k tʃ ] < / b d g ʤ/ occur word-finally.

# 4 Vowel allophones

## 4.1 Inventory

| | |
|---|---|
| [ i : ] : | / i/ |
| [e : ] : | / e/ |
| [ a : ]: | / ɐ/ |
| [ o : ] [ ö ]: | / o/ |
| [ u : ] [ ü ]: | / u/ |

## 4.2 Distribution

a. The vowels / e o / are lower than the cardinal vowels.

b. Vowels are lengthened in open syllables. The lengthened allophone [aː] of the low vowel / ɐ / is lower than the short allophone.

c. The advanced mid-vowel allophones [ö ü] < /o u/ occur when the following consonant is elided, e.g., [wö] < /wod/ , [ʃü] < / ʃug/ .

# 5 Syllable structure

## 5.1 Canonical syllable structure[38]

(C) (C) V (C) (C)

## 5.2 Consonant clusters

Two-consonant clusters:

| | |
|---|---|
| Initial | : Only S + r, p + s are attested. |
| Final | : Only -ŋk, -ŋp are attested. |
| Medial | : General |

Three-consonant clusters: Nil.

---

[38] Onsets and codas are of limited combinations.

# 6 Suprasegmentals

## 6.1 Tone

Tonemes:

Rising: H ( ´ )
Level: Unmarked.

E.g.,

/kʰú / 'dog, / kʰu/ 'rice'; /ŋgá / 'fish' , / ŋga/ 'full'.

**Reference:** Das Gupta (1968)

# Padaam

**Ethnologue code:** None (a variety of Adi)
**Language classification:** Tibeto-Burman, Tani, Adi.
**Alternate names:** Abor
**Main region:** Arunachal Pradesh

## 1 Consonant phonemes

### 1.1 Inventory

| | BILABIAL | DENTAL | ALVEOLAR | PALATAL | VELAR | GLOTTAL |
|---|---|---|---|---|---|---|
| Plosive | p b | t d | | | k g | |
| Nasal | m | | n | ɲ | ŋ | |
| Trill | | | r | | | |
| Fricative | | | s | | | (~h) |
| Approx | | | | j | | |
| Lat Approx | | | l | | | |
| Affricate | | | | ʤ | | |

### 1.2 Distribution

a. Consonants occur in all positions, with the following restriction:
   i. /s h ɲ / do not occur in the final position.

b. /s/ is in free variation with /h/ in all positions.

c. /g/ and / ʤ / are in free variation before long front vowels /i: e:/.

d. Geminate consonants occur on the surface. Many of them result from total assimilation across forms in complex words.

# 2 Vowel phonemes

## 2.1 Inventory

a. **Short**

| | FRONT | CENTRAL | BACK |
|---|---|---|---|
| Close | i | ɨ | u |
| Close-mid | e | | o |
| Open-mid | | ə | |
| | | a | |

b. **Long**

| | FRONT | CENTRAL | BACK |
|---|---|---|---|
| Close | iː | ɨː | uː |
| Close-mid | eː | | oː |
| Open-mid | | əː | |
| Open | | aː | |

c. **Diphthongs:** /ɨa  ua ai əi oi/

## 2.2 Distribution

a. Vowels occur in all positions, with the following restrictions:
   i. /oi/ does not occur initially
   ii. /əi oi/ do not occur finally.

b. Vowel sequences of different heights occur occasionally.

c. Vowel sequences across forms are avoided, except when both forms are bound forms.

d. Sequences of long and short vowels are not found in any form.

# 3 Allophones

Data not available.

# 4 Syllable structure

## 4.1 Canonical syllable structure[39]

(C) V (C)

## 4.2 Consonant clusters

Two-consonant clusters:

Initial : Nil

Final : Nil

Medial : General.

Three-consonant clusters:

**Reference:** Tayeng (1983)

[39] 1. Words of up to five syllables may occur.

2. The final consonant is restricted to /ʔ/.

# Paite

**Ethnologue code:** ISO 639-3: pck
**Language classification:** Tibeto-Burman, Kuki-Chin-Naga, Kuki-Chin, Northern.
**Alternate names:** Haithe, Paite, Paithe, Parte, Zoukam
**Main region:** Assam; Manipur, Churachandpur District, Khuga Valley, Copur Bazar; Mizoram, Aizawl District, Champhai Subdivision, 20 villages; Tripura. (Also in Myanmar.)

## 1 Consonant phonemes

### 1.1 Inventory

| | BILABIAL | LABIO-DENTAL | DENTAL | ALVEOLAR | PRE-PALATAL | VELAR | GLOTTAL |
|---|---|---|---|---|---|---|---|
| Plosive | p b<br>$p^h$ | | t d<br>$t^h$ | | | k g | ʔ |
| Nasal | m | | | n | | ŋ | |
| Fricative | | f v | | s z | | x | h |
| Approx | | | | (ɹ) | | | |
| Lat Appr | | | | l | | | |
| Affricate | | | ts | | (tʃ˂) (ʤ˂) | | |

### 1.2 Distribution

a. Consonants occur in all positions, except the following:
   i. /$p^h$ b $t^h$ d g ts (ʧ˂) (ʤ˂) f v z x h/ do not occur word- finally, when preceded by a monophthong; /s/ occurs rarely in that position.
   ii. Following a diphthong, only /ʔ/ occurs word-finally.

iii. /ʔ/ does not occur word-initially and inter-vocalically, that is, in the onset position.

iv. (/ɹ/) and /l/ are in free variation, with /l/ having wider distribution.

b. Geminates of the following consonants occur inter-vocalically: /ptkm nŋl/.

# 2 Vowel phonemes

## 2.1 Inventory

a. **Short**

| | FRONT | CENTRAL | BACK |
|---|---|---|---|
| Close | ɪ | | ʊ |
| Close-mid | e | | o |
| Open | | a | |

a. **Long**

| | FRONT | CENTRAL | BACK |
|---|---|---|---|
| Close | iː | | uː |
| Close-mid | eː | | |
| Open | | a | |

b. **Diphthongs:**

Considering the relative prominence of the vowel positions in a diphthong, the diphthongs can be divided into two types[40]:

i. **Primary** (with the first vowel more prominent than the second): /əɪaɪeɪoɪʊɪeʊəʊaʊ/

ii. **Secondary** (with the second vowel more prominent than the first): /i̯au̯a/.

iii. **Triphthongs:** /ɪaɪʊaʊɪaʊ/

[40] See also the descriptions of Liangmai and Wancho.

## 2.2 Distribution

a. Vowels occur in all positions, with the following restrictions:

   i. /ə/ does not occur word-finally.

   ii. Following /ts/, /i/ occurs most commonly, while /ʊə a/ do not occur.

b. Vowel sequences occur with considerable frequency, with some restrictions on the occurrence of the second vowel.

# 3 Consonant allophones

[l̥]: /l/

[l̥] < /l/ occurs before a glottal stop, [l̥ʔ] < /lʔ/

# 4 Vowel allophones

Vowels are lengthened if accompanied by a Rising (LH) tone,

# 5 Syllable structure

## 5.1 Canonical syllable structure

(C) V (C) (C)

## 5.2 Consonant clusters

Two-consonant clusters:

| | |
|---|---|
| Initial | : Nil |
| Final | : lʔ, -nn. |
| Medial | : General. |

Three-consonant clusters:

Initial : Nil
Final : Nil
Medial : lʔ + C.

# 6 Suprasegmentals

## 6.1 Tone

Tonemes:

Paite has three tonemes:
a. Rising: LH
b. Falling: HL
c. Mid: M

## 6.2 Allotones

The following allotones are found to occur regularly in Paite (Moi 2013):

a. M > Low-mid (LM) occursbefore (i) a glottal stop coda, and (ii) in infinitive forms derived from a verbal, nominal or adjectival stem.

b. LH > i. HL occurs in Infinitive forms derived from a verbal, nominal or adjectival stem.

  ii. M occurs in Infinitive forms derived from a verbal, nominal or adjectival stem, when there is either an insertion of a glottal stop /ʔ/ finally (e.g. zuɪ-$_{V}$> zuɪʔ-$_{INF}$ 'follow'), or a change from a nasal to a homorganic plosive (e.g. en-$_{V}$ > en–$_{INF}$ 'look')

c. HL > i. M occurs inInfinitive forms derived from a verbal, nominal or adjectival stem, with a change from a final /m/ to /p/ (e.g. tum-$_{V}$ > tup-$_{INF}$ 'try')

  ii. LH occurs in Infinitive forms derived from a verbal, nominal or adjectival stem, with the insertion of a final /t/ or /k/ (e.g. bia-$_{V}$ > biak-$_{INF}$ 'propitiate/ appease', xia-$_{V}$ > xiat-$_{INF}$ 'fall dow')

**References: Singh (2006), Moi (2013)**

# Phom

**Ethnologue code:** ISO 639-3: nph
**Language classification:** Tibeto-Burman, Jingpho-Konyak-Bodo
**Alternate names:** Phom, Phon, Tamlu Naga, Chingmengu, Tamlu
**Main region:** Northeastern Nagaland.

## 1 Consonant phonemes[41]

### 1.1 Inventory

| | BILABIAL | ALVEOLAR | POST-ALV. | RETRO | PALATAL | VELAR | GLOTTAL |
|---|---|---|---|---|---|---|---|
| Plosive | p b<br>pʰ | t d<br>tʰ | | | | k g<br>kʰ | ʔ |
| Nasal | m | n | | | ɲ | ŋ | |
| Fricative | | | ʃ | ʐ | | | h |
| Approx | w | | | | j | | |
| Lat Approx | | l | | | | | |
| Affricate | | | | | ʧ | | |

### 1.2 Distribution

a. Consonants occur in all positions, with the following restrictions:
   i. Only the following sounds occur syllable- and word- finally: /p t k ʔ m n ŋ/.
   ii. /p t k ʔ/ do not occur syllable-and word-initially.
   iii. Consonants do not occur after diphthongs.

[41] Burling and Phom (1998) have the symbol /ʒ/ instead of /ʐ/. Our choice is based on the description of this sound as being close to a rhotic, and pronounced with the tongue drawn far back. /ʐ/ is used for a sound of the a similar description in other Sino-Tibetan languages, including standard Chinese [ʐaŋ] 'to assist'.

b. /w/ occurs only before /o ɔ/.
c. /ʐ/ does not occur before /o ɔ/.

# 2 Vowel phonemes[42]

## 2.1 Inventory

a. **Short**

| | FRONT | CENTRAL | BACK |
|---|---|---|---|
| Close | i | | ɯ u |
| Close-mid | e | ɘ | o |
| Open-mid | ɛ | | ɔ |
| Open | æ | a | |

**Diphthongs:**
/aɪ ʌɪ aɯ ɛɯ aʊ oɪ/

## 2.2 Distribution

a. Vowels occur in all positions.
b. Diphthongs occur in open syllables, except for one type of closed syllable, with a glottal stop, /ʔ/.

# 3 Consonant allophones

## 3.1 Inventory

| | BILABIAL | ALVEOLAR | VELAR |
|---|---|---|---|
| Plosive | p : (p) | t : (t) | k : (k) |

[42] I have used ə for ʌ in the source description, on the basis of the phonetic description given in it and the closest IPA symbol for it. On the same grounds, I have also used different symbols for the diphthongs, /aɪ ʌɪ ɛɯ aʊ oɪ/ for /ay ʌy aɯ aw oy/.

## 3.2 Distribution

a. A voiceless plosive at the end of a syllable (or word) can be geminated before a syllable initial /h/. (Before a vowel, a syllable final nasal can also be geminated, but the generalization is not clear in the source description, since non-geminate forms exist in that environment.)

# 4 Vowel allophones

## 4.1 Inventory

[ɪ]: /i/

[ɐ][ə̝]: /a/

## 4.2 Distribution

**General:**

a. Vowels are noticeably shorter in closed syllables than in open syllables.

**Specific:**

a. [ɪ] < /i/ occurs in open syllables and before /ʔ/.

b. [ɐ] < /a/ occurs before /mp/.

c. [ə̝] < /a/ occurs in open syllables and before a syllable-final /n/ or /t/.

# 5 Syllable structure

## 5.1 Canonical syllable structure

(C) V (C)

## 5.2 Consonant clusters

Two-consonant clusters:

Initial : Nil

Final : Nil.

Medial : General.

Three-consonant clusters: Nil

# 6 Suprasegmentals

## 6.1 Tone[43]

High: H (1)
Mid: M (2)
Falling (Mid): ML (3)

E.g.,

/ʃə¹/ 'enter', /ʃə³ / 'insert'

/ʃe²/ 'rot', /ʃe³/ 'cause to rot'.

**Reference:** Burling and Phom (1998)

[43] Apart from lexical tone, tone is used in word-formation, as indicated by the above examples.

# Purki

**Ethnologue code:** None
**Language classification:** Tibeto-Burman, Himalayish, Tibeto-Kinnauri.
**Alternate names:** Not available.
**Main region:** Ladakh.

## 1 Consonant Phonemes

### 1.1 Inventory

| | BILABIAL | LABIODENTAL | DENTAL | ALVEOLAR | POST-ALV. | PALATAL | VELAR | UVULAR | GLOTTAL |
|---|---|---|---|---|---|---|---|---|---|
| Plosive | p b $p^h$ | | t̪ d̪ $t̪^h$ | t d $t^h$ | | | k g $k^h$ | q | |
| Nasal | m | | | n | | ɲ | ŋ | | |
| Trill | | | | r | | | | | |
| Fricative | | (f) | | s z | ʃ ʒ | | x ɣ | χ | h |
| Approx | w | | | | | j | | | |
| Lat Approx | | | | l | | | | | |
| Affricate | | | | ts dz | | ʧ ʤ $ʧ^h$ | | | |

### 1.2 Distribution

a. Consonants occur in all positions, with the following restriction:

   i. Only /p t k q m n ŋ l r/ occur word-finally. (That is, fricatives, affricates, aspirated and voiced plosives and /ɲ h j / do not occur word-finally.)

# 2 Vowel Phonemes

## 2.1 Inventory

a. **Short**

| | FRONT | CENTRAL | BACK |
|---|---|---|---|
| Close | i | | u |
| Close-mid | e | | o |
| Open | | a | |

b. **Long**[44]

| | FRONT | CENTRAL | BACK |
|---|---|---|---|
| Close | i: | | u: |
| Close-mid | e: | | o: |
| Open | | a: | |

## 2.2 Distribution

a. Vowels occur in all positions, with the following restrictions:

   i. Only the long vowels /i : a : / occur word-initially.

   ii. The long vowel phonemes /i : e : a : o : u: / do not occur finally.

b. Sequences of vowels beginning with any of the short vowels occur; e.g. ai, eu, io, ui, ou, oe, oa.

44 The author (p. c.) has expressed doubts about the validity of his analysis of Purki with phonemic vowel length distinction. The topic needs investigation.

# 3 Consonant Allophones

## 3.1 Inventory

| | DENTAL | ALVEOLAR | RETROFLEX |
|---|---|---|---|
| Tap / Flap | | | ɽ (ḏ) |
| Fricative | ð (d) | | ʂ (ʃ) |
| Lat Appr | | ɬ (l) | |

## 3.2 Distribution

a. [ð] < /d/ and [ɽ ] < / ḏ / occur inter-vocalically.

b. [ʂ] < /ʃ/ occurs before a consonant.

c. [ɬ] < / l / occurs before voiceless consonants morpheme-internally.

# 4 Vowel Allophones

## 4.1 Inventory

[i ˑ]: /i/

[u ˑ]: /u/

[e ˑ] [ɛ]: /e/

[o ˑ] [ɔ]: /o/

[a ˑ] [ʌ]: /a/

## 4.2 Distribution

a. The half-long vowel allophones of short vowels occur in the final position.

b. The low mid allophones [ɛ ɔ] < /e o/ occur when the following syllable has the low central vowel /a aː/.

c. [ʌ] < /a/ occurs medially and finally.

# 5 Syllable Structure

## 5.1 Canonical syllable structure[45]

(C) (C) (C) V (C) (C)

## 5.2 Consonant clusters

Two-consonant clusters:

Initial : i) S+G/L; ii) F+S/N/G/L; iii) N+G; iv) L+S/F;
v) r + O + Approx

Final : i) N+homS; ii) Fr+S; iii) N+F; r+ S.

Medial : General.

Three-consonant clusters: Not attested

**Reference:** Rangan (1979)

45 It is common for words to have an onset with a single consonant.

# Raji

**Ethnologue code:** ISO 639-3: jnl
**Language classification:** Tibeto-Burman, Himalayish, Tibeto-Kanauri
**Alternate names:** Dzanggali, Janggali, Jangali, Jhangar, Raut,
**Main region:** Uttaranchal, Pithoragarh District.

## 1 Consonant Phonemes

### 1.1 Inventory

| | BILABIAL | LABIODENTAL | DENTAL | ALV. | POST-ALV. | RETROFLEX | PALATAL | VELAR | GLOTTAL |
|---|---|---|---|---|---|---|---|---|---|
| Stop | p b<br>pʰ bʱ | | t d<br>tʰ dʱ | | | ʈ ɖ<br>ʈʰ ɖʱ | | k g<br>kʰ gʱ | |
| Nasal | m<br>mʱ | | | n<br>nʱ | | ɳ | | ŋ | |
| Trill | | | | r<br>rʱ | | | | | |
| Flap | | | | | | ɽ | | | |
| Fricative | | | | s | | | | x | h |
| Appr | w | | | ɹ | | | j<br>jʱ | | |
| Lat Appr | | | | l<br>lʱ | | | | | |
| Affricate | | | | | | | ʧ ʤ<br>ʧʰ ʤʱ | | |

### 1.2 Distribution

a. Consonants occur in all positions with the following restrictions:
   i. Aspirated consonants do not occur word-finally.

ii. /mʱ nʱ rʱ jʱ / do not occur medially.
iii. /ɳ ŋ w / do not occur initially.

b. Geminates of the following consonants are attested: /p b t d ʈ tʰ ɖ.k kʰ g tʃ dʒ s m n l /

# 2 Vowel Phonemes

## 2.1 Inventory

a. **Short**

| | FRONT | CENTRAL | BACK |
|---|---|---|---|
| Close | i | | u |
| Close-mid | e | ə | o |
| Open-mid | ɛ | | |
| Open | | a | |

b. **Nasal**

| | FRONT | CENTRAL | BACK |
|---|---|---|---|
| Close | ĩ | | ũ |
| Close-mid | ẽ | ə̃ | õ |
| Open-mid | ɛ̃ | | |
| Open | | ã | |

## 2.2 Distribution

a. Vowels occur in all the positions, with the following restrictions:
   i. /e ɛ/ do not occur initially.
   ii. /ɪ ɯ/ do not occur finally.

b. Sequences of two and three vowels occur with syllabic divisions between them.

# 3 Consonant Allophones

## 3.1 Inventory

| | BILABIAL | DENTAL | RETR | PALATAL | VELAR |
|---|---|---|---|---|---|
| Stop | b(p) | d(t) | ɖ(ʈ)<br>ɽ(ɖ) | | g(k) |
| Fricative | | | | ç (s) | |
| Approx | o(w) | | | | |

## 3.2 Distribution

a. The voiced allophones [b d ɖ g] of the voiceless plosives /p t ʈ k/ occur after voiced plosives and inter-vocalically.

b. The retroflex flap allophone [ɽ] of the stop /ɖ/ occurs inter-vocalically.

c. The voiceless palatal fricative allophone [ç ] of the alveolar fricative /s/ occurs before /i j/.

d. The vocalic allophone /o/ of the bilabial approximant /w/ occurs in intervocalic and final positions.

# 4 Vowel Allophones

## 4.1 Inventory and distribution[46]

[ɪ] : /i/

[ʊ] : /u/

[ɔ] : /o/

[46] The lower allophones [ɪ ʊ ɔ] of the vowels /i u o/ are attested, but their environments have not been specified in the reference.

# 5 Syllable Structure

## 5.1 Canonical syllable structure

(C) (j) V (C)

## 5.2 Consonant clusters

Two-consonant clusters:[47]

Initial : C+j

Final : Nil

Medial : General.

Three-consonant clusters: Nil

**Reference:** Krishan (2001c)

[47] The first consonant is among those permitted to occur initially.

# Rangpo Bhāsā

**Ethnologue code:** ISO 639-3: rnp
**Language classification:** Sino-Tibetan, Tibeto-Burman, Himalayish,
**Alternate names:** "Manchhi Bhassa", "Marchha", "Marchha Pahari", Rangkas, Rangpa, Rang Po Bhasa, "Tolchha"
**Main region:** Uttaranchal, Chamoli district, Joshimath Tahsel, Niti valley,

## 1 Consonant Phonemes

### 1.1 Inventory

| | BILA-BIAL | DEN-TAL | ALVE-OLAR | POST-ALV. | RETR-OFLEX | PALA-TAL | VELAR | GLOT-TAL |
|---|---|---|---|---|---|---|---|---|
| Plosive | p b<br>$p^h$ $b^ɦ$ | t d<br>$t^h$ $d^ɦ$ | | | ʈ ɖ<br>$ʈ^h$ $ɖ^ɦ$ | | k g<br>$k^h$ $g^ɦ$ | ʔ |
| Nasal | m<br>$m^ɦ$ | n<br>$n^ɦ$ | | | ɳ | ɲ | ŋ | |
| Trill | | | r<br>$r^ɦ$ | | | | | |
| Tap / Flap | | | | | ɽ<br>$ɽ^ɦ$ | | | |
| Fricative | | s | | ʃ | ʂ | | | h |
| Approx | w | | | | | j | | |
| Lat Appr | | | l<br>$l^ɦ$ | | ɭ | | | |
| Affricate | | | | | | tʃ dʒ<br>$tʃ^h$ $dʒ^ɦ$ | | |

## 1.2 Distribution

a. Consonants occur in all positions, with the following restrictions:
   i. / ɳ ɽ / do not occur initially.
   ii. Aspirated consonants and the palatal glide, /pʰ bɦ tʰ dʱ ʈʰ ɖʱ tʃʰ dʒʱ gʱʰ mʱ nʱ rʱ lʱ j/ do not occur finally.

b. There is free variation between /pʰ/ ~ [ɸ], /s/ ~ [ʃ], /l/ ~ [lʲ].

# 2 Vowel Phonemes

## 2.1 Inventory

a. **Short**

| | FRONT | CENTRAL | BACK |
|---|---|---|---|
| Close | i | | u |
| Close-mid | | ə | |
| Open | | a | ɑ |

b. **Long**

| | FRONT | CENTRAL | BACK |
|---|---|---|---|
| Close | iː | | uː |
| Close-mid | eː | | oː |
| Open-mid | ɛː | | ɔː |
| Open | | aː | |

c. **Nasal**

| | FRONT | CENTRAL | BACK |
|---|---|---|---|
| Close | ĩː | | ũː |
| Close-mid | ẽː | | õː |
| Open-mid | ɛ̃ː | ə̃ | ɔ̃ː |
| Open | | ãː | |

## 2.2 Distribution

a. Vowels occur in all positions, with the following restriction:

   i. Long vowels occur only before single consonants.

b. The following vowel sequences occur: /əi ai a:i ɔi oi u:i au ou u:a/.

c. There is free variation between /ə/~/ʌ/, /e:/~[e:$^{ə}$], /o:/ ~ [o:$^{ə}$]

# 3 Consonant Allophones

## 3.1 Inventory

**General:**

a. Consonants in the onset position in the second syllable tend to get lengthened.

**Specific:**

[ɭ] : /l/

[ɹ] : /r/

[ü :] [ö :] :/w/

## 3.2 Distribution

a. [ɭ] < /l/ occurs before an immediately following retroflex consonant or after a following vowel.

b. [ɹ] < /r/ occurs before a retroflex after the following vowel.

c. [ü:] < /w/ occurs following /j/ and before a non-low vowel, usually /i/.

d. [ö :] < /w/ occurs following /j/ and a low front vowel /ɛ/.

# 4 Vowel Allophones

## 4.1 Inventory and distribution

**General:**

a. Vowels are lengthened finally in monosyllables.

b. Vowels are half-long finally in disyllables.

# 5 Syllable Structure

## 5.1 Canonical syllable structure

(C)(G/r)V(C)(C)

## 5.2 Consonant clusters

Two-consonant clusters:

Initial : C + r/w/j

Final : -limited (details not clear)

Medial : General.

Three-consonant clusters: Nil

Initial : Nil.

Final : Nil.

Medial : -rpj-, -mɖr-, -ŋɖr-, -ŋgz-, -ŋgs-, -kʈʰr-.

**Reference:** Zoller (1983)

# Rawang[48]

**Ethnologue code:** ISO 639-3: raw
**Language classification:** Tibeto-Burman, Nungish
**Alternate names:** Nung Rawang, Ganung-Rawang, Hkanung, Numg, Krangku, Taron, Kiutze, Ch'opa, Chiutse
**Main region:** Arunachal Pradesh, Assam. (Mainly spoken in Myanmar.)

## 1 Consonant Phonemes

### 1.1 Inventory

| | Bilabial | Labiodental | Alveolar | Postalv | Retr | Palatal | Velar | Glottal |
|---|---|---|---|---|---|---|---|---|
| Plosive | pʰ b | | tʰ d | | | | kʰ g | ʔ |
| Nasal | m | | n | | | | ŋ | |
| Flap | | | | | ɽ | | | |
| Fricative | | | s | ʃ | | | | h |
| Approx | w | | | | | j | | |
| Lat Approx | | | l | | | | | |
| Affricate | | | ts ʥ | | | ʧ ʤ | | |

### 1.2 Distribution

a. Consonants occur in all positions, with the following restrictions:

i. All the consonant phonemes occur initially, except /ʔ/.
ii. Only the following sounds occur finally: /p t k ʔ m n ŋ r l/.

48 Rawang is spoken in both India and Myanmar. The dialect being described is from the Matwang dialect in Myanmar.

# 2 Vowel Phonemes

## 2.1 Inventory

a. **Short**

| | FRONT | CENTRAL | BACK |
|---|---|---|---|
| Close | i | ɨ | u |
| Close-mid | e | | o |
| Open-mid | | ɔ | |
| Open | | a | |

## 2.2 Distribution

a. The vowels /i e a ə ɨ o u/ contrast in open syllables.

b. Rawang being an agglutinating language, vowels when occurring adjacently may coalesce. As they carry tones (with the exception of /ə/), the contour tones on them indicate syllable boundaries.

# 3 Consonant Allophones

## 3.1 Inventory

| | BILABIAL | LABIO-DENTAL | DENTAL | VELAR |
|---|---|---|---|---|
| Plosive | p/ᵐb(b) | | t/ⁿd(d) | k/ᵑ g(g) |
| Fricative | | v(w) | | |

## 3.2 Distribution

a. Voiced plosives have prenasalized variants [ᵐb ⁿd ᵑg] as well as voiceless unaspirated free variants [p t k].

b. [v] freely varies with [w] word-initially.

# 4 Vowel Allophones

a. All the vowels have corresponding long allophones [i: e: ɨ: ə : a : u : o :], that are morphologically and phonologically predictable. They occur in an open syllable, when followed by the final suffix /-i/ 'let's' or /-í/, the relational suffix of cause, means.

# 5 Syllable Structure

## 5.1 Canonical syllable Structure:

(C) V (C)

Cond.: Word-final consonants are also coda consonants.

## 5.2 Consonant clusters

Two-consonant clusters:

Initial: Nil

Final: Nil

Medial: Coda+ Onset consonants.

Three-consonant clusters: Nil

# 6 Suprasegmentals

## 6.1 Tone

Toneme:

Rawang has three levels of register tonemes:

1. High: H / ´ /

2. Low: L / ` /

3. Mid: M (unspecified)

E.g. /rú/ 'to be struck or bitten by a snake'; /rù/ 'to be poisoned'; /ru/ 'to write'

In addition to the three levels of contrastive tone, Rawang has a Neutral tone, which occurs on non-final open syllables with the vowel /ə/.

Contrastive tone does not occur also when any of the seven vowels is followed by the three stops /p t k/.

Contour tones occur as a result of two syllabic vowels coming together:

L H L M<br>
E.g., [a: ŋ. gi ˥ mbo :. e] 'He is wearing (it, hat)' <

/ aŋ gi mbo e /

**Reference:** Morse (1988)

# Sema–Naga[49]

**Ethnologue code:** ISO 639-3: nsm
**Language classification:** Tibeto-Burman, Kuki-Chin-Naga
**Alternate names:** Sema, Simi, Sumi
**Main region:** Central and southern Nagaland

## 1 Consonant Phonemes

### 1.1 Inventory

| | Bilabial | Labio-dental | Alve-olar | Pala-tal | Velar | Post-Velar | Glot-tal |
|---|---|---|---|---|---|---|---|
| Plosive | p b<br>pʰ | | t d<br>tʰ | | k g<br>kʰ | q<br>qʰ | |
| Nasal | m<br>mʱ | | n<br>nʱ | | ŋ | | |
| Fricative | | f | s z | | x ɣ | | h |
| Approx | w | | | j | | | |
| Lat Approx | | | l<br>lʱ | | | | |
| Affricate | | | | ʧ | | | |

### 1.2 Distribution

a. Consonants have the following restriction:
   i. Consonants, except / w j /, do not occur word-finally.

[49] Sreedhar 1980 analyses aspirated voiceless consonants as clusters of unaspirated consonants and /h/. They are treated here as phonemes. One of the reasons is that they behave like single phonemes instead of clusters of phonemes. For example, an allophonic process of /n/ palatalization, that palatalizes /n/ before /i/, takes place irrespective of /h/ being present or absent.

b. Geminates of the following consonants occur inter-vocalically: /d s l w j/.

# 2 Vowel Phonemes

## 2.1 Inventory

a. **Short**

| | FRONT | CENTRAL | BACK |
|---|---|---|---|
| Close | i | ɨ | u |
| Close-mid | e | | o |
| Open | | a | |

## 2.2 Distribution

a. Vowels occur in all positions.

b. Vowel sequences of two identical (except e ə) and non-identical vowels are found to occur.

# 3 Consonant Allophones

## 3.1 Inventory

| | LABIO-DENTAL | DENTAL | ALVEO-LAR | ALVEO-PALATAL | PALATAL | VELAR |
|---|---|---|---|---|---|---|
| Plosive | | | t̲ (t)<br>d̲ (d) | | | k˃ (k)<br>g˃ (g) |
| Fricative | v(w) | | | ʒ(z) | | |
| Affricate | | ʦ (ʧ) | | | ʤ (∞) | |

## 3.2 Distribution

a. The alveolar allophones of the dental plosives [t̠ d̠] < /t d/ occur before front vowels.

b. [ts] < /ʧ/ occurs before central vowels.

c. [ʒ] < /z/

d. [ʤ ]< /ꝏ/ occurs before /o/.

e. [v] < / w/ occurs before front vowels.

f. [ɲ] < /n/ occurs before /i/.

# 4 Vowel Allophones

## 4.1 Inventory

| | |
|---|---|
| [ɯ] [ɯ̣]: | /ɨ/ |
| [ɛ]: | /e/ |
| [ɔ]: | /o/ |
| [ə][ɐ] [ɐ]: | /a/ |
| [u̯]: | /w/ |

## 4.2 Distribution

a. [ ɯ ɯ̣ ] < /ɨ /

b. [ ɛ ] < /e/ and [ə] < /a/ occur before /j/.

c. [ ɔ ]: < /o/ occurs after fricative consonants.

d. [ ɐ ] < /a/ occurs before a consonant other than / wjŋ/.

e. [ ɐ̣ ] < /a / occurs before / ŋ/

f. [ u̯ ] < /w/ occurs before back vowels.

# 5 Syllable Structure

## 5.1 Canonical syllable structure

(C) (C) V (g)

## 5.2 Consonant clusters

Two-consonant clusters:

Initial : m + C, p/k/G/ + l, kj-, tr-, ŋk-.

Final : Nil

Medial : General

Three-consonant clusters: Nil

# 6 Suprasegmentals

Sreedhar (1980) does not discuss tones in Sema-Naga, although the lexical items are marked for tones. Mainly three tonemes are assumed: High ( ´ ), Low ( ` ) and Mid (unmarked).

There is no description of tone in Sema-Naga.

**References:** M. V. Sreedhar (1980)

# Spiti

**Ethnologue code:** ISO 639-3: spt
**Language classification:** Tibeto-Burman, Himalayish, Tibeto-Kanauri
**Alternate names:** Piti Bhoti
**Main region:** Himachal Pradesh, Lahul-Spiti District.

## 1 Consonant Phonemes

### 1.1 Inventory

| | BILABIAL | DENTAL | ALV | POST-ALV | RETR | PALATAL | VELAR | GLOTTAL |
|---|---|---|---|---|---|---|---|---|
| Plosive | p b<br>pʰ (bʱ) | t d<br>tʰ (dʱ) | | | ʈ ɖ<br>ʈʰ (ɖʱ) | | k g<br>kʰ (gʱ) | ʔ |
| Nasal | m | | n | | (ɳ) | ɲ | ŋ | |
| Trill | | r | | | | | | |
| Tap | | | ɾ | | | | | |
| Fricative | | | s z | ʃ ʒ | ʂ | | | h |
| Approx | w | | | | | j | | |
| Lat Approx | | | l | | (ɭ) | | | |
| Affricate | | | ʦ ʣ<br>ʦʰ | | | ʧ ʤ<br>ʧʰ (ʤʱ) | | |

## 1.2 Distribution

a. Consonants occur in all positions, with the following restrictions:
   i. /ɳ ɽ/ do not occur initially.
   ii. Only nasals /m n ɳ ɲ ŋ/ and liquids /l ɾ/ occur finally.
   iii. Semivowels /w j/ freely vary with /u i/ respectively; /w/ may also vary with /m/.

b. Geminates do not occur.

c. Voiced aspirated stops occur mostly in the word-initial position in both words of Indo-Aryan and Tibeto-Burman origin, and are found to freely vary with their unaspirated counterparts.

# 2 Vowel Phonemes

## 2.1 Inventory

a. **Short**

| | FRONT | CENTRAL | BACK |
|---|---|---|---|
| Close | i | | u |
| Close-mid | e | | o |
| Open-mid | | (ə) | |
| Open | | | ɑ |

## 2.2 Distribution

a. All the vowels occur in all positions.

b. Vowel sequences of two occur in all positions.

# 3 Consonant Allophones

## 3.1 Inventory

| | BILABIAL | DENTAL | ALVEOLAR | PALATAL | VELAR | GLOTTAL |
|---|---|---|---|---|---|---|
| Plosive | p(b) b(p) bʱ(b) | t(d) d(t) dʱ(d) | | | k(g) g(k) gʱ(g) | ʔ (d, g) |

| Nasal | m$^{ɦ}$(m) | n$^{ɦ}$(n) | | ɲ$^{ɦ}$(ɲ) | ŋ$^{ɦ}$(ŋ) | |
|---|---|---|---|---|---|---|
| Tap | | | ɾ$^{ɦ}$(ɾ) | | | |
| Lateral Appr. | | | l$^{ɦ}$(l) | | | |
| Affricate | | | | dʒ (ʧ)<br>dʒ$^{ɦ}$ (ʤ) | | |

## 3.2 Distribution

a. Aspirated allophones of voiced stops, nasals, and liquids, [ b$^{ɦ}$ d$^{ɦ}$ g$^{ɦ}$ dʒ$^{ɦ}$ m$^{ɦ}$ n$^{ɦ}$ ɲ$^{ɦ}$ ŋ$^{ɦ}$ l$^{ɦ}$ ɾ$^{ɦ}$ ] < / b d g dʒ m n ɲ ŋ l ɾ /, occur word-initially.

b. [ p t k tʃ ] < /b d g dʒ/ occur in the word-final position.

c. [ʔ] < /d g/ occurs in the word-final position before pause (i.e., phrase finally).

d. [b d g dʒ] < / p t k tʃ/ occur following a nasal consonant.

# 4 Vowel Allophones

## 4.1 Inventory

[ɛ ] ~ : / e/

[ɔ ] ~ : / o/

[ə]: / a/

## 4.2 Distribution

a. [ə] < /a/ occurs in closed syllables.

b. [ɛ] ~ /e/ and [ɔ]~/o/ in mono-syllables or in the final syllables of polysyllables.

# 5 Syllable Structure

## 5.1 Canonical syllable structure

$(<C>_1)(<G>_2)V(C)$

Cond.: If 2 then, 1= Obs/L.

## 5.2 Consonant clusters

Two-consonant clusters:

Initial : Obs/L + G

Final : Nil

Medial : General.

Three-consonant clusters:

Initial : Nil.

Final : Nil

Medial : As permitted in the initial and final positions of the word.

**References:** S. R. Sharma (1979), D. D. Sharma (1989)

# Stod/Tod

**Ethnologue code:** ISO 639-3: sbu
**Language classification:** Tibeto-Burman, Himalayish, Tibetan, Central
**Alternate names:** Stod, Tod, Tod-Kad, Stod-Kad, Lahul Bhoti
**Main region:** Himachal Pradesh, Lahul Region, Stod, Khoksar, and upper Mayar valleys.

## 1 Consonant Phonemes

### 1.1 Inventory

| | Bilabial | Dentał | Alv | Post-alv | Retr. | Palatal | Velar | Glottal |
|---|---|---|---|---|---|---|---|---|
| Plosive | p b<br>(pʰ) (bʱ) | t d<br>tʰ (dʱ) | | | ʈ ɖ<br>ʈʰ ɖʱ | | k g<br>kʰ gʱ | |
| Nasal | m | | n | | | ɲ | ŋ | |
| Trill | | | r | | | | | |
| Fricative | | | s z | ʃ ʒ | | | | h |
| Approx | w | | | | | j | | |
| Lat Appr | | | l | | | | | |
| Affricate | | | | ts dz<br>tsʰ | | ʧ ʤ<br>ʧʰ (ʤʱ) | | |

### 1.2 Distribution

1. Voiced aspirates occur mainly in loan-words from Indo-Aryan, and are often replaced by unaspirated counterparts. On the other hand, there are instances of native forms having unaspirate voiced plosives varying with aspirated counterparts, e.g., /da/ ~ /dʱa/ 'arrow', /gʱa/ ~ /gu/ 'nine'.
2. Consonants occur in all positions, with the following restriction:

i. Only nasals, liquids, and voiced plosives /m n ŋ l r b d/ occur finally. Borrowed words can also have /g dʒ/ in the final position in rare instances.

3. Geminates are not found.
4. The glottal stop has restricted occurrence. It occurs either finally or before a velar stop.

# 2 Vowel phonemes

## 2.1 Inventory

a. Short

| | FRONT | CENTRAL | BACK |
|---|---|---|---|
| Close | i | | u |
| Close-mid | e | | o |
| Open-mid | | ə | |
| Open | | | ɑ |

## 2.2 Distribution

1. Vowels occur in all positions.
2. Vowel sequences occur in all combinations.

# 3 Consonant allophones

## 3.1 Inventory

| | BILABIAL | DENTAL | PALATAL | VELAR |
|---|---|---|---|---|
| Plosive | p   bʱ(b) | t, ˀd, dʱ (d) | ʧ   ʤ<br>ʤʱ   (ʤ) | k, ˀk, ʔ, gʱ, ɤ<br>(g)<br>x (k, g) |

## 3.2 Distribution

1. There is a tendency for consonants to be palatalized before the front vowels /i e/.
2. Voiced stops are devoiced in the final coda position: [p t k ʧ]< /b d g ʤ/.
3. Dental and velar plosives are pre-glottalized in the final coda position: [ˀt ˀk] < /t k/.
4. Voiced stops are aspirated word-initially: [bʱ dʱ gʱ ʤʱ] < /b d g ʤ/.
5. [x] < /kʰ/ occurs word-initially, or, in common with [k ɤ] < /k g/ intervocalically or in the coda position.

# 4 Vowel allophones

## 4.1 Inventory

General: Long vowels

Specific:

[ɛ]: /e/

[ɔ]: /o/

[e]: /i/

## 4.2 Distribution

1. Vowels are lengthened in final accented syllables: [iː eː aː əː oː uː].
2. [ɛ ɔ]< /e o/ occur before nasal consonants or the glottal stop.
3. [e] < /i/ occurs before /i/.

# 5 Syllable structure

## 5.1 Canonical syllable structure

(C)(G/r)V(C)

## 5.2 Consonant clusters

Two-consonant clusters:

| | | |
|---|---|---|
| Initial | : | C+ G/r |
| Final | : | Nil. |
| Medial | : | General |

Three-consonant clusters: Nil.

**Reference:** Sharma (1989)

# Tamang[50]

**Ethnologue code:** ISO 639-3: taj
**Language classification:** Sino-Tibetan, Tibeto-Burman, Himalayish, Tibeto-Kanauri, Tibetic, Tamangic
**Alternate names:** "Bhotia", Ishang, Murmi, Sei.
**Main region:** northeast, east, and south. Most districts east, Outer-Eastern in Janakpur zone, east Sindhupalchowk, Ramechhap, Dolakha districts. Central-Eastern in Bagmati zone

## 1 Consonant Phonemes

### 1.1 Inventory

| | Bilabial | Dental | Retroflex | Pre-palatal | Palatal | Velar | Glottal |
|---|---|---|---|---|---|---|---|
| Stop | p<br>pʰ | t<br>tʰ | ʈ<br>ʈʰ | | | k<br>kʰ | |
| Nasal | m | n | | | | ŋ | |
| Fricative | | s | | | | | h |
| Trill | | r | | | | | |
| Approx. | (w) | | | | (j) | | |
| Lat Appr. | | l | | | | | |
| Affricate | | | | ʧ˂<br>ʧʰ˂ | | | |

### 1.2 Distribution

a. Consonants occur in all positions, with the following restrictions:

[50] The variety described here is of Eastern Tamang

i. Consonants other than /p t k m n ŋ l r (s)/ do not occur word finally.

b. Geminate consonants do not occur.

# 2 Vowel Phonemes

## 2.1 Inventory

a. **Short**

| | FRONT | CENTRAL | BACK |
|---|---|---|---|
| Close | i | | u |
| Mid | e | | o |
| Open | | a | |

b. **Long**

| | FRONT | CENTRAL | BACK |
|---|---|---|---|
| Close | i : | | u : |
| Mid | e : | | o : |
| | | a : | |

## 2.2 Distribution

a. Vowels occur in all the positions, with the following restrictions:

i. Long vowels occur mainly in initial open syllables.

b. Sequences of two and three vowels (/iau uai iua : /) occur; if the first vowel is /i/ or /u/, it is desyllabified.

# 3 Consonant Allophones

**General:**

a. Voiceless stops are lax between vowels.

b. Approximants [j w] < /i u/ are pronounced when the vowels occur before another vowel.

# 4 Vowel Allophones

**General:** Vowels are pronounced breathy before /h/.

# 5 Syllable Structure

## 5.1 Canonical syllable structure

(C (L/G)) V (C)

## 5.2 Consonant clusters

Two-consonant clusters:

| | |
|---|---|
| Initial | : C+L/G |
| Final | : Nil |
| Medial | : General |

Three-consonant clusters: NIl

# 6 Suprasegmentals

## 6.1 Tone

**Tonemes:**

High Falling: HL

Mid-High level: M1

Mid-Low level: M2

Low Falling (in a monosyllable)
or Falling-Rising-Falling (in a disyllable): ML/ MLM

**References:** Mazaudon (2003), Taylor (1969).

# Tangsa

**Ethnologue code:** ISO 639-3: nst
**Language classification:** Tibeto-Burman, Jingpho-Konyak-Bodo
**Alternate names:** Cham Chang, Rangpan, Tangsa, Tasey
**Main region:** Southeastern Arunachal Pradesh, Changlang District, Eastern Hills, Tirap River valley and Namchik area; Assam.

## 1 Consonant Phonemes

### 1.1 Inventory

| | Bilabial | Dental/ Alveolar | Palatal | Velar | Phar | Glottal |
|---|---|---|---|---|---|---|
| Plosive | p b<br>$p^h$ | t d<br>$t^h$ | | k<br>$k^h$ | | ʔ |
| Nasal | m | n | | ŋ | | |
| Tap | | ɾ | | | | |
| Fricative | β | s | ç | x | (ʕ) | h |
| Approx | | | | | | |
| Lat Appr | | l | | | | |
| Affricate | | ts | tʃ dʒ | | | |

### 1.2 Distribution

a. Consonants occur in all positions, with the following restrictions:

   i. /b ʔ/ do not occur in the initial position.
   ii. /ʔ/ does not occur in the medial position.
   iii. /$p^h$ b $t^h$ d tʃ dʒ $k^h$ β s x h ʕ ɾ/ do not occur in the final position. (This leaves only /p t k ʔ m n ŋ ç l/ occurring in the final position.)

# 2 Vowel Phonemes

## 2.1 Inventory

a. **Short**

| | FRONT | CENTRAL | BACK |
|---|---|---|---|
| Close | i | | u |
| Close-mid | e | | o |
| Open-mid | | | ɔ |
| Open | | a | |

b. **Long**

| | FRONT | CENTRAL | BACK |
|---|---|---|---|
| Open | | | ɒ: |

## 2.2 Distribution

a. Vowels occur in all positions, with the following restriction:

   i. /a o̜/ do not occur in the initial position.

b. Sequences of vowels occur.

# 3 Consonant Allophones

a. Approximant allophones [w j] occur as free variants of /β ɟ/ in all positions except when preceded by a consonant or in compounds.

# 4 Vowel Allophones

Data not available.

# 5 Syllable Structure

## 5.1 Canonical syllable structure

(C) V (C)

## 5.2 Consonant clusters

Two-consonant clusters:

Initial : Nil

Final : Nil.

Medial : General.

Three-consonant clusters: Nil

**Reference:** Bandhopadhyaya (1980)

# Tarao

**Ethnologue code:** ISO 639-3: tro
**Language classification:** Tibeto-Burman, Kuki-Chin-Naga
**Alternate names:** Tarao, Tarau, Taraotrong
**Main region:** Manipur: Chandel and Ukhrul Districts.

## 1 Consonant Phonemes[51]

### 1.1 Inventory

| | Bilabial | Labio-dental | Dental | Alveolar | Palatal | Velar | Glottal |
|---|---|---|---|---|---|---|---|
| Plosive | p b pʰ | | | t d tʰ | | k (g) kʰ | |
| Nasal | m | | n | | | ŋ | |
| Trill | | | | r | | | |
| Tap | | | | ɾ | | | |
| Fricative | | | | s | | | h |
| Approx. | w | | | | j | | |
| Lat Appr | | | | l | | | |
| Affricate | | | | ts | | ʧ ʤ | |

### 1.2 Distribution

a. Consonants occur in all positions, with the following restrictions:
   i. /g/ occurs only medially, and rarely, being a borrowing from Manipuri and Bengali.
   ii. Only /p t k m n ŋ l r/ occur finally.

[51] Singh lables the lateral and the trill as palatal, but uses the alveolar symbols for both. Since palatal trill and lateral are of rare occurrence in that region, and no description of the sounds as palatal is provided, I am including them here as alveolar trill and lateral. Singh also has palatal plosives /c ɟ/ and a voiceless palatal affricate /ʧ/. I have confirmed that these are in fact palatal and alveolar affricates /ʧ ʤ ts/.

# 2 Vowel Phonemes

## 2.1 Inventory

a. **Short**

| | FRONT | CENTRAL | BACK |
|---|---|---|---|
| Close | i | | u |
| Close-mid | e | | o |
| Open-mid | | ə | |
| Open | | a | |

## 2.2 Distribution

a. Vowels occur in all positions, with the exception of /o/ occurring word-initially.
b. Vowel sequences of two are found to occur.

# 3 Allophones

Data on allophones are not available.

# 4 Syllable Structure

## 4.1 Canonical syllable structure

(C)(L)V(C)

## 4.2 Consonant Clusters

Two-consonant clusters:

Initial : C+ L

Final : Nil

Medial : General.

Three-consonant clusters:

Initial : Nil

Final : Nil

Medial : Only the following: -ntr-, -ŋtl-, -ntʰl-.

**Reference:** Singh (2002)

# Thaadou

**Ethnologue code:** ISO 639-3: tcz
**Language classification:** Tibeto-Burman, Kuki-Chin-Naga
**Alternate names:** Thadou, Thado-Ubiphei, Thado-Pao, Kuki, Kuki-Thado, Thaadou Kuki
**Main region:** Assam; Manipur, Chandel District; Nagaland, Kohima District; Mizoram, northeast Tripura.

## 1 Consonant phonemes

### 1.1 Inventory

| | Bilabial | Labio-dental | Alveolar | Palatal | Velar | Glottal |
|---|---|---|---|---|---|---|
| Plosive | p b<br>pʰ | | t d<br>tʰ | | k g<br>kʰ | ʔ |
| Nasal | m | | n | | ŋ | |
| Fricative | | v | s | | (x) | h |
| Approx | w | | | j | | |
| Lat Approx | | | l | | | |
| Lat fricative | | | ɬ | | | |
| Affricate | | | ts | | | |

### 1.2 Distribution

a. Consonants occur in all positions, with the following restriction:

   i. The voiceless aspirated stops, voiced stops, and fricatives /pʰ b tʰ d kʰ g ɬ ts s x h / do not occur finally. (That is, only the nasals, the voiceless unaspirated stops and the laterals occur finally.)

b. Geminates of /n m/ occur inter-vocalically.

# 2 Vowel phonemes

## 2.1 Inventory

a. **Short**

| | FRONT | CENTRAL | BACK |
|---|---|---|---|
| Close | i | | u |
| Mid | e | ə | o |
| Open | | a | |

## 2.2 Distribution

a. Vowels occur in all positions, with the following restriction:
   i. /a/ does not occur finally.
b. Vowel sequences occur. The first member always carries the tone, and the second member tends to get desyllabified, leading to surface diphthongs.

# 3 Consonant allophones

## 3.1 Inventory and distribution

a. [ʔ] < /k/ occurs in the coda position.
b. [z] < /ʤ/ occurs initially and inter-vocalically.

# 4 Vowel allophones

## 4.1 Inventory

[i̯] : /i/
[u̯] : /u/
[o̯] : /o/

## 4.2 Distribution

a. The desyllabified allophones [i̯ u̯ o̯] < /i u o/ occur as the second member in a sequence and are less prominently pronounced than the second member.

# 5 Syllable structure

## 5.1 Canonical syllable structure

(C)V(C)

## 5.2 Consonant clusters

Two-consonant clusters:

Initial : Nil

Final : Nil

Medial : Coda ( /p t (k) m n ŋ l/) + Onset

Three-consonant clusters: Nil

# 6 Suprasegmentals

## 6.1 Tone

Tonemes:

High: H ( ́ )
Rising: LH ( ̌ )
Low: L ( ̀ )

Examples: [sá] 'meat', [sǎ] 'fat', [sà] 'thick, to build'

**References:** Thirumalai (1972), Gibbon, Pandey, Haokip and Bachan (2009)

# Standard Tibetan[52]

**Ethnologue code:** ISO 639-3: bod
**Language classification:** Sino-Tibetan, Tibeto-Burman, Himalayish, Tibeto-Kanauri, Tibetic, Tibetan, Central
**Alternate names:** Bhotia, Dbus, Dbusgtsang, Phoke, Tibetan, U, Wei, Weizang, Zang
**Main region:** Tibet, Sichuan, Qinghai. Also in Bhutan, India, Nepal, Norway, Switzerland, Taiwan, United States.

## 1 Consonant Phonemes

### 1.1 Inventory

| | Bilabial | Dental | Retroflex | Pal.-Alv. | Palatal | Velar | Glottal |
|---|---|---|---|---|---|---|---|
| Plosive | p<br>p$^h$ | t<br>t$^h$ | ʈ<br>ʈ$^h$ | | c<br>c$^h$ | k<br>k$^h$<br>k$^j$<br>k$^{hj}$ | ʔ |
| Nasal | m | n | | | ɲ | ŋ | |
| Fricative | | s | | ʃ | | | h |
| Trill | | r̥ r | | | | | |
| Approx. | w | | | | j | | |
| Lat Appr. | | l̥ l | | | | | |
| Affricate | | ts<br>ts$^h$ | (tʂ)<br>(tʂ$^h$) | tʃ$^<$<br>tʃ$^{h<}$ | | | |

[52] Tibetan is spoken by a relatively large community in India, settled in various parts. The present description is of the Standard Tibetan of the Lhasa variety. It differs in a few segmental and suprasegmental features from Classical Tibet (see e.g. Delancey 2003).

## 1.2 Distribution

a. Consonants occur in all positions, with the following restrictions:
   i. Consonants other than /p k m ŋ / do not occur syllable-finally.

b. Geminate consonants do not occur.

# 2 Vowel Phonemes

## 2.1 Inventory[53]

**a. Short:**

| | FRONT | CENTRAL | BACK |
|---|---|---|---|
| Close | i | | u |
| Close-mid | e | | o |
| Open-mid | | | (ɔ) |
| Open | | a | |

**b. Long:**

| | FRONT | CENTRAL | BACK |
|---|---|---|---|
| Close | i : | | u : |
| Close -mid | e : | | o : |
| | | a : | |

**c. Nasal:**

| | FRONT | CENTRAL | BACK |
|---|---|---|---|
| Close | ʏ̃ : | | ũ : |
| Close-mid | ø̃ : | | õ : |
| Open | ɶ̃ : | ɐ̃ : | |

[53] The oral long vowels in Standard Tibetan have resulted from the loss of coda */r l/, all the nasal vowels, which are also long, have resulted from the loss of a coda */n/, the rounded front vowels, both oral and nasal have resulted from the loss of a coronal coda */d s n l/.

## 2.2 Distribution

a. All the vowels occur in all the positions.

b. Vowel sequences occur with syllabic divisions between them.

# 3 Consonant allophones

## 3.1 Inventory

**General:** A glottal stop [ʔ] is inserted word-initial before a vowel, and inter-vocalically.

**Specific:** As below.

| | Bilabial | Dental | Alveolar | Palatal | Velar | Glottal |
|---|---|---|---|---|---|---|
| Plosive | b(p)<br>p̌ʰ (pʰ) | d(t)<br>ťʰ (tʰ) | | | g(k)<br>ǩʰ (kʰ) | ʔ (ø) |
| Affricate | | | | ʤ(ʧ) | | |

## 3.2 Distribution

a. The voiced stop allophones[b d g ʤ] of the voiceless unaspirated stops /p t k ʧ/ and the weakly aspirated allophones [p̌ʰ ťʰ ǩʰ ʧ̌ʰ] of the voiceless aspirated stops / pʰ tʰ kʰ ʧʰ/ occur in syllables with low tone.

b. The glottal stop [ʔ] is inserted word-initially in the absence of a consonant.

# 4 Vowel allophones

## 4.1 Inventory

**General:** Standard Tibetan shows vowel harmony of the feature [+high] that applies bidirectionally: "vowels are raised in any word which contains an underlying high vowel....within compounds and from affixes to stems in high vowel and vice versa" (DeLancey 2003: 271)

**Specific:**

[ɐ], [ə] : /a/
[ɔ] : /o/
[ɛ] : /e/

## 4.2 Distribution

a. The lowered allophones [ɪ] < /i/ and [ɷ·] < /o·/ occur before a nasal.
b. The raised allophones [ə ɔ ɛ] < /a o e/ occur in closed syllables (apart from the result of vowel harmony).

# 5 Syllable structure

## 5.1 Canonical syllable structure[54]

**Non-Final:** (C) V (ʔ)

Cond.: The glottal stop coda occurs if the V is a short vowel.

**Word-Final:** (C) V (p/m/ŋ)[55]

## 5.2 Consonant clusters

Two-consonant clusters: Nil

[54] V here, as for the entire book stands for all vowels, unless specified otherwise. The V here includes (i) /V:/, which results from the loss of coda /r l/ for the main five vowels, and of the coda /d s/ for the rounded front vowels, (ii) ṽ :, which results from the loss of a coda /n/.

[55] The velar nasal in the coda occurs optionally.

# 6 Suprasegmentals

## 6.1 Tone

Tonemes:

High: H

Low or Falling: L/ML

**Note:** The contrast between the two tones is manifested in the first syllable of a word. The Falling contour of a low tone alternates with a glottal stop.

**References:** DeLancey (2003), Hodge (2003).

# Wancho

**Ethnologue code:** ISO 639-3: nnp
**Language classification:** Tibeto-Burman, Jingpho-Konyak-Bodo
**Alternate names:** Wancho, Banpara Naga, Joboka
**Main region:** Assam; Nagaland; southeastern Arunachal Pradesh.

## 1 Consonant phonemes

### 1.1 Inventory

| | Bilabial | Dental | Alveolar | Post-Alv | Palatal | Velar | Glottal |
|---|---|---|---|---|---|---|---|
| Plosive | p b<br>pʰ | | t d<br>tʰ | | | k (g)<br>kʰ | ʔ |
| Nasal | m | | n | | | ŋ | |
| Fricative | β | | s z | ʃ ʒ | | | h |
| Approx | w | | | | j | | |
| Lat Appr | | | l | | | | |
| Affricate | | ts | | | tʃ | | |

### 1.2 Distribution

a. Consonants occur in all positions, with the following restrictions:
   i. Only the following sounds occur syllable- and word-finally: /p t k ʔ m n ŋ/.
   ii. /ʔ/ does not occur syllable-and word-initially.
   iii. Consonants do not occur after most diphthongs, especially after / aʊ aɪ ʌɪ ʊ̯i/.

# 2 Vowel phonemes

## 2.1 Inventory

a. **Short**[56]

| | FRONT | CENTRAL | BACK |
|---|---|---|---|
| Close | i | | ɯ u |
| Close-mid | e | | o |
| Open-mid | | ə | |
| Open | | a | |

b. **Nasal**[57]

| | FRONT | CENTRAL | BACK |
|---|---|---|---|
| Open | | ( ã ) | |

**Diphthongs:**

Considering the relative prominence of the vowel positions in a diphthong, the diphthongs can be divided into two types[58]:

i. **Primary** (with the first vowel more prominent than the second): /aɪ̯ əɪ̯ aʊ̯/

ii. **Secondary** (with the second vowel more prominent than the first): i̯e i̯a ʊ̯i ʊ̯a ʊ̯o

## 2.2 Distribution

a. Vowels occur in all positions.

[56] /ə/ has been used here for /ʌ/ in the source description, on the basis of the phonetic description given in it and the closest IPA symbol for it, as for Phom. On the same grounds, different symbols have been used for the diphthongs, /aI əI aʊ ji i̯e i̯a ʊ̯i ʊ̯a ʊ̯o/ for /ay ʌy aw yi ye ya wi wa wo/.

[57] In the speech of Wancho described here there is one instance of a nasal vowel occurring in one word. But other dialects of Wancho have been found to have nasal vowels.

[58] See also the descriptions of Liangmai and Paite.

b. Some of the diphthongs occur only in open syllables, especially /aɪ əɪ aʊ ji ʊ̯i/.
c. Syllables lacking an onset have either /a/ or /o/ as the nucleus.

# 3 Consonant allophones

The glottal stop is epenthesized before a vowel initial syllable, which occurs rather infrequently.

# 4 Vowel allophones

## 4.1 Inventory

[ö]: /o/

## 4.2 Distribution

a. [ö] < /o/ occurs before syllable-final / m p/.

# 5 Syllable structure

## 5.1 Canonical syllable structure

(C)V (C).

## 5.2 Consonant clusters

Two-consonant clusters:

Initial : Nil

Final : Nil.

Medial : General.

Three-consonant clusters: Nil

# 6 Suprasegmentals[59]

## 6.1 Tone[60]

Tonemes:

The tonemes are as follows:

High: H ( ´ )
Falling (High): HL ( ` )
Low: L (unmarked)

E.g.,

/ku̯óm/ 'we', /ku̯om/ 'us'
/átʃi̯èn/ 'shake' (V.I. ) /átʃién/ (bounce (a baby)'

**Reference:** Burling and Wangsu (1998)

[59] Tones occurring in monosyllables in Wancho differ according to whether they occur in (a) "unstopped mono syllables" ("i.e., open syllables and syllables closed with /-m –n -ŋ/)" or stopped monosyllables. The latter are of two types, (b) one (stopped Syllable-I), ending in /p t k/, and (c) two (stopped syllable-II), ending in /ʔ/. There are three types of tonal contrast in (a)type monosyllables, two-types of tonal contrast in (b) type monosyllables, and single tone used in (c) type monosyllable.

Of the three tonemes given below, 1 is the commonest, the Low tone is very low.

Combinations of tones occur in disyllabic words.

[60] Apart from lexical tone, tone is used in word-formation, as indicated by the above examples.

# Zo

**Ethnologue code:** ISO 639-3: zom
**Language classification:** Sino-Tibetan, Tibeto-Burman, Kuki-Chin-Naga, Kuki-Chin, Northern
**Alternate names:** Jou, Kuki Chin, Zau, Zome, Zomi, Zou
**Main region:** Primarily Chin state: Tonzang, Hakha, and Teddim townships; Sagaing Division: Kalay, Khampat, and Tamu townships. Also in India.

## 1 Consonant phonemes

### 1.1 Inventory

| | Bilabial | Labio-dental | Alveolar | Velar | Glottal |
|---|---|---|---|---|---|
| Plosive | p b<br>pʰ | | t d<br>tʰ | k g<br>kʰ ~ (x) | |
| Nasal | m | | n | ŋ | |
| Fricative | | v | s | | h |
| Lat Appr | | | l̥ l | | |
| Affricate | | | ts ʤ | | |

### 1.2 Distribution

a. Consonants occur in all positions, with the following restrictions:
   i. /b d g k pʰ tʰ kʰ ts dz v s l̥/ do not occur root- and word-finally. (I.e., Only /p t h l m n ŋ/ occur in the final position in roots and words.)
   ii. Geminates of the consonants /p t h l m n ŋ/ occur in compound words across root morphemes.

b. /kʰ/ varies freely with /x/ everywhere.

# 2 Vowel phonemes

## 2.1 Inventory

a. **Short**

| | FRONT | CENTRAL | BACK |
|---|---|---|---|
| Close | i | | u |
| Mid | e | | o |
| Open-mid | | ə | |

b. **Long**

| | FRONT | CENTRAL | BACK |
|---|---|---|---|
| Close | i : | | u: |
| Mid | e: | | o : |
| Open | | a: | |

c. **Diphthongs:** /ia ie iu ei eu e:u ai a:i au a:u oi ɔ : i u : i uo: ou ua ui/

d. **Triphthongs:** /uoɪ uou /

The diphthongs and the triphthongs have been analyzed as single vowels, as they occur in root forms. As vowel sequences, the word forms are analyzable as compounds. For example, /né : u/ 'small, tiny' and /né :+u/ 'eat + Hon.'. The difference between diphthongs and vowel sequences is also manifested in the tonal realizations. In the case of a diphthong or a triphthong, the tone starts on the first vowel and ends with a peak on the second or the third vowel. But in the case of the vowel sequence, the tone is completed on the first vowel, if it is a sequence of two vowels or on the second vowel, if it is a sequence of a diphthong and a monophthong.

## 2.2 Distribution

a. Vowels occur everywhere, with the following restrictions:

i. /o o :/ freely vary with /ɔ ɔ :/, especially in the case of the long vowels.

# 3 Consonant allophones

## 3.1 Inventory

[ṭ]; /t/

[ḍ]: /d/

[ṭʰ]: /tʰ/

[ʔ]: /h/

[x]: ~/kʰ/

## 3.2 Distribution

a. The voiceless unaspirated alveolar plosives /t tʰ d/ have post-alveolar realizations [ṭ ṭʰ ḍ] before the back vowels /u u : o o :/, e.g.

b. The voiceless glottal fricative /h/ is realized as the glottal stop [ʔ] in the coda position, e.g. /pé : h/ > [pé : ʔ] 'flat, plain'.

c. /kʰ/ freely varies with /x/.

# 4 Vowel allophones

## 4.1 Inventory

[w]: /u/

[j]: /i/

## 4. 2 Distribution

a. The diphthongs beginning with the back vowels and the front vowels are realized respectively as [w ] and [j] in fast speech, e.g.

# 5 Syllable structure

While considering the syllable structure of Zo, it becomes apparent that for generalizations to hold, it is necessary to assume that the word phonology must be divided into two types, root phonology and word phonology. Such a division is well-motivated, as noted for some other Tibeto-Burman languages, e.g. Lare Galo (Post 2007). The two-level word phonological analysis applies for languages that have monosyllabic roots. Most of these languages also have constraints on the occurrence of consonants in the onset and coda positions. When the root forms come together in word formation, medial consonant clusters are permitted, which are otherwise not possible in monosyllabic roots. In most languages, as also in Zo, as shown below, the medial clusters do not violate the constraints on the onsets and codas in monosyllables. Apart from the emergence of medial clusters, there is also a change in the realizations of the tones in adjacent syllables, giving rise to 'downstepping' or 'upstepping', as the case may be.

## 5.1 Canonical syllable structure

($C_1$) V ($C_2$)

Cond.: $C_2$= /p t h l m n ŋ/.

## 5.2 Consonant clusters

Two-consonant clusters:

Initial: Nil
Final: Nil

Medial: C1C2, where C1 is the permitted coda in monosyllables (i.e. /p t h l m n ŋ/),

and C2 is any consonant, with syllable division between them. E.g. /po : lpi/

'...'/, təŋva : l/ '...', and /mənna : / '...'.

# 6 Suprasegmentals

## 6.1 Tone

Tonemes:

Zo roots have three tonemes:

Rising : LH ( ´ )
Falling: HL ( ` )
Level: M (unmarked)

E.g. /$k^h$ám/ 'intoxicated, drunken', /$k^h$àm/ '$block_V$', /$k^h$am/ '$block_V$'.

**Reference:** Mangkang and Pandey (2009)

Chapter 5

# TAI-KADAI

## Khampti-Tai

**Ethnologue code:** ISO 639-3: kht
**Language classification:** Tai-Kadai, Kam-Tai, Tai, Southwestern, Nortwest.
**Alternate names:** Kham-Tai, Hkamti, Khampti, Khamti Shan, Khantis, Tai Khamti
**Main region:** Assam; Arunachal Pradesh.

## 1 Consonant Phonemes

### 1.1 Inventory

| | BILABIAL | DENTAL | ALV. | PALATAL | VELAR | GLOTTAL |
|---|---|---|---|---|---|---|
| Plosive | p<br>$p^h$ | t<br>$t^h$ | | | k<br>$k^h$ | ʔ |
| Nasal | m | n | | | ŋ | |
| Trill | | | r | | | |
| Fricative | | | s | | | h |
| Approx | w | | | j | | |
| Lat. Appr | | | l | | | |
| Affricate | | | ts | | | |

## 1.2 Distribution

a. Consonants occur in all positions.

Inadequate details available.

# 2 Vowel Phonemes

## 2.1 Inventory

a. **Short**

| | FRONT | CENTRAL | BACK |
|---|---|---|---|
| Close | i | ɨ | ɯ u |
| Close-mid | e | | o |
| Open-mid | ɛ | | ɔ |
| Open | | a | |

## 2.2 Distribution

a. Vowels occur in all positions, with the following restriction:

   i. /ɛ ɔ/ have restricted occurrence morpheme-finally.

b. Vowel sequences occur, giving rise to diphthongs on the surface.

# 3 Consonant Allophones

## 3.1 Inventory

[ŋ˂]: /ŋ/

[q] : /k/

[x] : /kʰ/

## 3.2 Distribution

a. The pre-velar allophone of the velar nasal, [ŋ˂] < /ŋ/ occurs before /i j/.

b. The uvular allophone of the voiceless velar plosive, [q] < /k/, occurs in the coda position.

c. The velar fricative allophone of the voiceless aspirated velar plosive, [x] < /kʰ/ occurs as a free variant.

# 4 Vowel Allophones

## 4.1 Inventory

**General:**

a. Long vowels.

b. Half-long vowels.

**Specific:**

| | |
|---|---|
| [ i̯ ] [j]: | /i/ |
| [ u̯ ] [w] : | /u/ |
| [ɯ̯ ] : | /ɯ/ |
| [e:] : | /ɛ/ |
| [o:] : | /ɔ/ |
| [i:] : | /e/ |
| [u:] : | /o/ |

## 4.2 Distribution

a. The high vowels have long allophones, [i: ɯ: u:] < /i ɯ u/, in open syllables, and half-long allophones [i ˑ ɯ ˑ u ˑ ] in closed syllables.

b. The mid vowels have raised long allophones [i: e: u: o:] < /e ɛ o ɔ/ in open syllables, and non-raised half-long allophones [eˑ ɛˑ oˑ ɔˑ/ < /e ɛ o ɔ/ in closed syllables.

c. The high vowels have non-syllabic allophones [i̯ ɯ̯ u̯] < /i ɯ u/ following vowels, leading to surface diphthongs.

d. The glide allophones of high front and high rounded back vowels, [j w] < /i u/, occur before vowels.

# 5 Syllable Structure

## 5.1 Canonical syllable structure

(C) (L/G) V (C)

## 5.2 Consonant clusters

Two-consonant clusters:

Initial : C+L/G
Final : Nil.
Medial : General.

Three-consonant clusters: Nil.

# 6 Suprasegmentals

## 6.1 Tone

Tonemes:

a. High: H (1)
b. Low: L (3)
c. High-Falling: (13)
d. Low-Rising: LH (31)
e. Low with creaky voice: (30)

**Reference:** Weidert (1977)

# Turung[1]

**Ethnologue code:** ISO 639-3: try
**Language classification:** Tai-Kadai, Kam-Tai, Be-Tai, Tai-Sek, Tai, East Central, Northwest
**Alternate names:** Tai Turung, Tailung, Tairong
**Main region:** Assam, Golaghat District, Titabar; Karbi Anglong.

## 1 Consonant Phonemes

### 1.1 Inventory

| | BILABIAL | DENTAL/ ALVEOLAR | PRE-PALATAL | PALATAL | VELAR | GLOTTAL |
|---|---|---|---|---|---|---|
| Plosive | p b<br>$p^h$ | t d<br>$t^h$ | | | k g<br>$k^h$ | ʔ |
| Nasal | m | n | | ɲ | ŋ | |
| Fricative | | s | | | | h |
| Lat Appr | | l | | | | |
| Approx | w | ɹ | | j | | |
| Affricate | | | ʧ< ʤ< | | | |

### 1.2 Distribution

a. Consonants occur in all positions, except the following:
   i. Consonants other than / p t k ʔ m n ŋ / do not occur word-finally.

b. Geminate consonants do not occur.

c. [f] and [ɸ] are free variants of /$p^h$/, especially in the speech of the young.

[1] The data are based on the speech of the Turung community, called Tai Turung or Tairong, of about 1200 people in seven villages distributed in three districts of upper Assam, namely, Golaghat, Jorhat and Karbi Anglong.

# 2 Vowel Phonemes

## 2.1 Inventory

a. **Short**

| | FRONT | CENTRAL | BACK |
|---|---|---|---|
| Close | i | | u |
| Mid | e | ə | o |
| Open | | a | |

b. **Long**[2]

| | FRONT | CENTRAL | BACK |
|---|---|---|---|
| Close | iː | | uː |
| Mid | eː | | oː |
| Open | | aː | |

c. **Diphthongs**: diphthongs such as /ai au/ occur; full data not available.

d. **Syllabic consonants**[3]: /m̩ n̩ ŋ̩/

## 2.2 Distribution

a. Vowels occur in all positions, with the following restrictions:
   i. /ə/ occurs in stressed syllables.

b. Vowel sequences do not occur.

# 3 Consonant Allophones

Data not available.

[2] Long vowels contrast with short vowels marginally.

[3] The syllabic consonants can carry tones; they also function as morphemes.

# 4 Vowel Allophones

Data not available.

# 5 Syllable Structure

## 5.1 Canonical syllable structure[4]

(C) (ɹ) V (C)

## 5.2 Consonant clusters

Two-consonant clusters:

Initial : Cr-
Final : Nil.
Medial : Nil[5].

Three-consonant clusters: Nil

# 6 Suprasegmentals

## 6.1 Tone

Tonemes:

a. Falling: HL ( ` )
b. Rising-Falling: LHL ( ^ )
c. Level: M (Unmarked)

**Reference:** Morey (2005)

---

[4] Phonetically, loss of vowels in adjacent words may give rise to compound forms with complex codas and onsets as optional variants, e.g.[[ l ə] [juŋ]] 'finger' is realized as [ləjuŋ] ~ [lijuŋ]~ [ljuŋ].

[5] Most lexical items are monosyllabic, and thus have no medial clusters. However, phonetically, compound forms have medial consonant clusters, which are a combination of permitted codas (voiceless plosives and non-palatal nasals); e.g.[[ $p^hi^2$] [ mə] [$lu^1$]] 'bruise' is realized as [$p^h$îmlú].

Chapter 6

# THE ANDAMAN GROUP

## Great-Andamanese[1]

**Ethnologue code:** ISO 639-3: anq
**Language classification:** Andaman group
**Main region:** Andaman Islands (Rutland Island, South Andaman Island, Middle Andaman Island, west coast, 70 square km reserve).

## 1 Consonant Phonemes

### 1.1 Inventory

| | BILABIAL | DENTAL | ALVEOLAR | RETRO-FLEX | PALATAL | VELAR |
|---|---|---|---|---|---|---|
| Plosive | p b $p^h$ | t d $t^h$ | | ʈ ɖ $ʈ^h$ | | k $k^h$ |
| Nasal | m | | n | | ɲ | ŋ |
| Trill | | | r | ɽ | | |
| Fricative | ɸ β | | s | | | (x) |
| Approx | w | | | | j | |
| Lat Appr | | | l | | | |
| Affricate | | | | | tʃ dʒ | |

[1] The Andamanese population has been reported to have been only 26.

## 1.1 Distribution

a. Consonants occur in all positions, with the following restrictions:

   i. / b tʰ d ɸ s ɖ / do not occur finally.

   ii. /w/ does not occur initially

b. The following consonants have geminates word-medially: /t ʈ c k n m ɲ ŋ ɸ /.

c. Lexically-conditioned free variation is found between the following pairs: x ~ kʰ, x ~k, ¸ ɸ ~ b, ʈ ~ t, c ~ s.

# 2 Vowel Phonemes

## 2.1 Inventory

a. **Short**

| | FRONT | CENTRAL | BACK |
|---|---|---|---|
| Close | i | | u |
| Close-mid | e | | o |
| Open-mid | ɛ | | ɔ |
| Open | | a | |

b. **Long**[2]

| | FRONT | CENTRAL | BACK |
|---|---|---|---|
| Close | iː | | uː |
| Close-mid | eː | | oː |
| Open-mid | ɛː | | ɔː |
| Open | | a : | |

[2] Some of the long vowels, especially /eː ɛː uː oː/ have been established on the basis of sub-minimal pairs.

## 2.2 Distribution

a. Vowels occur in all positions, with the following restriction:
   i. The long vowels /eː ɛː uː oː/ do not occur initially.

b. Vowel sequences do not occur.

# 3 Consonant Allophones

## 3.1 Inventory

| | ALVEOLAR | POST ALVEOLAR | RETROFLEX | VELAR |
|---|---|---|---|---|
| Nasal | | n˃(n) | | |
| Trill | | r˃(r) | | |
| Flap | | | ɽ (ɖ) | |
| Fricative | | ʃ(s) | | x(~kʰ) |
| Approx | | l˃(l) | | |
| Lat Appr | lʷ(~β) | | | |

## 3.2 Distribution

a. /n r ɖ l/ have post-alveolar allophones [n˃ r˃ ɽ˃ l˃] respectively in the inter-vocalic position.
b. /β/ freely varies with [lʷ] in most contexts, and occasionally with [l].
c. /kʰ/ freely varies with [x].
d. /s/ is realized as [ʃ] before a high front vowel.

# 4 Vowel Allophones

## 4.1 Inventory

[ ɪ ] [ʲi ]: /i/

[ʲe ]: /e/

[ʲɛ]: /ɛ/

[ə ]: /a/

[ɯ ]: /u/

## 4.2 Distribution

a. Front vowels have a j-onglide word-initially.

b. [ɯ ] < /u/ occurs in open syllables when preceded by /b/ or /l/ in the onset.

c. [ə ] < /a/ occurs when preceded or followed by /j/.

# 5 Syllable Structure

## 5.1 Canonical syllable structure[3]

(C) (C) V (C) (C)

## 5.2 Consonant clusters

Two-consonant clusters:

Initial : mj-, ɲj-

Final : -jp.

Medial : General.

Three-consonant clusters: Nil.

**References:** Abbi (2013), Manoharan (1989).

[3] Initial and final clusters are minimal.

# Jarawa

**Ethnologue code:** ISO 639-3: anq
**Language classification:** Andamanese, South Andamanese
**Alternate names:** Nil
**Main region:** Andaman Islands (Rutland Island, South Andaman Island, Middle Andaman Island, west coast, 70 square km reserve).

## 1 Consonant Phonemes

### 1.1 Inventory[4]

| | Bilabial | Labiodental | Alveolar | Post Alveolar | Retro | Palatal | Velar | Uvular | Glottal |
|---|---|---|---|---|---|---|---|---|---|
| Plosive | p b | | t d<br>tʰ | | ʈ ɖ<br>ʈʰ (ɖʱ) | | k g<br>kʰ | (q) | (ʔ) |
| Nasal | m | | n | | | ɲ | ŋ | | |
| Trill | | | r | | | | | | |
| Flap | | | | | ɽ | | | | |
| Fricative | ɸ | (f) (v) | (s) | (ʃ) | | | | | h |
| Approx | w | | | | | j | | | |
| Lat Appr. | | | l | | ɭ | | | | |
| Affricate | | | | | | ʧ ʤ<br>ʧʰ | | | |

[4] The consonants in parentheses are from Senkuttuvan (2000).

## 1.2 Distribution

a. Consonants occur in all positions, with the following restrictions:

   i. /g (ʔ) ɳ ɲ r ɽ f s w ts tʃ / do not occur initially.

   ii. / t$^h$ ʈ ʈ$^h$ ɖ (ɖ$^ɦ$) ʧ ʧ$^h$ (q) (ʔ) ɲ ɽ ɭ (f) (v) s ʃ j (ts) tʃ/ do not occur finally.

b. Geminates of the following consonants occur inter-vocalically: /p b t ʈ ɖ k g m ɲ ɽ/.

# 2 Vowel Phonemes

## 2.1 Inventory[5]

a. **Short**

| | FRONT | CENTRAL | BACK |
|---|---|---|---|
| Close | i | | u |
| Close-mid | | ɨ | |
| Mid | e | | o |
| Open | | a | |

b. **Long**

| | FRONT | CENTRAL | BACK |
|---|---|---|---|
| Close | i: | | u: |
| Close-mid | e: | | o: |
| Open | | a: | |

[5] Abbi (2007) lists some other vowels on the surface. For lack of contextual data, it is difficult to determine their phonemic status. Some of those surface vowels, e.g. [ɛ ɔ] appear to be allophones on Senkuttuvan's account.

## 2.2 Distribution

a. Vowels occur in all positions.

b. Vowel sequences occur with glide insertion between them.

# 3 Consonant Allophones

## 3.1 Inventory

Adequate data are not available.

# 4 Vowel Allophones

## 4.1 Inventory

| | |
|---|---|
| [ iˑ ] | : /i/ |
| [ ɛˑ ] | : /e/ |
| [ọ], [ ɔ: ] | : /o/ |
| [aˑ ], [ɐ] | : /a/ |

## 4.2 Distribution

a. The half-long allophones [iˑ ɛˑ aˑ] < /i e a/ and the lowered allophones [ ɔ: ] < /o/ occur in the final position.

b. [ọ] < /o/ and [ɐ] < /a/ occur in the medial position.

# 5 Syllable Structure

## 5.1 Canonical syllable structure

(C)V(C)

## 5.2 Consonant clusters

**Two**-consonant clusters:

Initial : Nil

Final : Nil.

Medial : -nm-, pd-, -ṭb-, -ṭk-, -fv-, -nb-, -sj-, and HN + S.

Three-consonant clusters: Nil.

**References:** Kumar (2010), Senkuttuvan (2000).

# Onge

**Ethnologue code:** ISO 639-3: oon
**Language classification:** Andamanese, South Andamanese
**Alternate names:** Ong
**Main region:** Southern Andaman Islands, Dugong Creek and South Bay islands.

## 1 Consonant Phonemes

### 1.1 Inventory[6]

| | BILABIAL | DENTAL | ALVEOLAR | RETRO-FLEX | PALATAL | VELAR | GLOTTAL |
|---|---|---|---|---|---|---|---|
| Plosive | (p) b | t d | | ʈ ɖ | | k g | |
| Nasal | m | | n | | ɲ | ŋ | |
| Fricative | | | | | | | (h) |
| Trill | | | r | | | | |
| Approx | w | | | | j | | |
| Lat Appr | | | l | (ɭ) | | | |
| Affricate | | | | | ʧ ʤ | | |

### 1.2 Distribution

a. Consonants occur in all positions, with the following restrictions:

   i. /l ɭ/ do not occur initially
   
   ii. Consonants other than / k m n ɲ ŋ w ɭ / do not occur finally.

[6] The inventory in Dasgupta and Sharma (1982) does not include the retroflex lateral /ɭ/ and the fricative /h/ found in Abbi (2006). The latter sound is reported to occur once only. Abbi (2006) reports absence of /p/.

# 2 Vowel Phonemes

## 2.1 Inventory

**a. Short**

| | FRONT | CENTRAL | BACK |
|---|---|---|---|
| Close | i | (ɨ) | u |
| Close-mid | e | | ɤ o |
| Open-mid | ɛ | ə | ɔ |
| Open | | a | |

## 2.2 Distribution

a. Vowels occur in all positions.

b. Vowel sequences occur.

# 3 Allophones

Data not available.

# 4 Syllable Structure

## 4.1 Canonical syllable structure

(C)V(C)

## 4.2 Consonant clusters

Two-consonant clusters:

Initial : Nil

Final : Nil

Medial : Restricted: -N+S-, -S+w-, -bb-.

Three-consonant clusters: Nil.

**References:** Abbi (2006), Dasgupta and Sharma (1982)

Chapter 7

# CONTACT VARIETIES

# Bishnupuria[1]

**Ethnologue code:** ISO 639-3: bpy
**Language classification:** Indo-Aryan, Eastern zone, Bengali-Assamese
**Alternate names:** Bishnupria, Manipuri
**Main region:** Assam, Cachar, Northern Tripura.

## 1 Consonant Phonemes

### 1.1 Inventory

| | BILABIAL | DENTAL | ALV. | POST ALV. | RETRO. | PALATAL | VELAR | GLOTTAL |
|---|---|---|---|---|---|---|---|---|
| Plosive | p b<br>p$^{h}$ b$^{ʔ}$ | t d<br>t$^{h}$ d$^{ʔ}$ | | | ʈ ɖ<br>ʈ$^{h}$ ɖ$^{ʔ}$ | | k g<br>g$^{ʔ}$ | |
| Nasal | m | n | | | | | ŋ | |
| Trill | | | r | | | | | |
| Fricative | ɸ | | s | ʃ | | | | ɦ |
| Appr | w | | | | | j | | |
| Lat Appr | | | l | | | | | |
| Affricate | | | | | | tʃ dʒ<br>dʒ$^{ʔ}$ | | |

[1] Bishnupuriya is a contact variety that has arisen out of a contact between Assamese, Bengali and Manipuri, and is spoken predominantly in Cachar district of Assam and in Manipur.

## 1.2 Distribution

a. Consonants occur in all positions, with the following restrictions:
   i. /ŋ/ does not occur initially.
   ii. The aspirated phonemes and /h/ do not occur finally.

b. Geminates of consonants other than / tʃ dʒ h ŋ / occur inter-vocalically.

# 2 Vowel Phonemes

## 2.1 Inventory

a. **Short**

| | FRONT | CENTRAL | BACK |
|---|---|---|---|
| Close | i | | u |
| Mid | e | | o |
| Open-mid | ɛ | | ɔ |
| Open | | a | ɑ |

**Diphthongs:** / ei ai ɑu ɔi ɔu /

## 2.2 Distribution

a. All the vowels occur in all the positions.

b. Vowel sequences occur.

# 3 Consonant Allophones

## 3.1 Inventory

| | BILABIAL | DENTAL | POST-ALV | RETRO-FLEX | PALA-TAL | VELAR | GLOTTAL |
|---|---|---|---|---|---|---|---|
| Plosive | p(b, p$^h$)<br>b(p) | t(d, t$^h$)<br>d(t) | | ʈ(t, ʈ$^h$)<br>ɖ(t)<br>ʈ(d) ɖ(d) | | k(g, k$^h$)<br>g(k) | |
| Fricative | | s(ʃ) | ʃ(ɦ) | ʂ(ʃ) | | | h(ɦ) |
| Affricate | | ts(ʧ / ʤ) | | | ʧ(t) ʤ(t) | | |

[ o̯ ] : /w/

[ e̯ ] : /j/

## 3.2 Distribution

**General:**

a. Voiced plosives, affricate and fricative become voiceless ([p t ʈ k tʃ h] < /b d ɖ g ʤ ɦ/)word-finally.

b. Aspirated plosives are de-aspirated word-finally and before a consonant.

**Specific:**

a. The Voiceless bilabial plosive /p/ is voiced [b] before voiced plosives.

b. The voiced bilabial plosive /b/ is devoiced [p] when followed by voiceless plosives or a sonorant.

c. The voiceless dental plosive /t/ is realized as

   i. Voiced alveolar plosive[d] when followed by /d/ or /g/
   
   ii. Voiceless palatal affricate [ʧ] and voiced palatal affricate [ʤ] when followed by /ʧ/ and /ʤ/ respectively
   
   iii. Voiceless retroflex plosive [ʈ] and voiced retroflex plosive [ɖ] when followed by /ʈ ʈ$^h$/ and /ɖ/ respectively.

d. The voiced dental plosive /d/ is devoiced when followed by a consonant other that a voiced plosive.

e. The voiceless velar plosive /k/ is voiced obligatorily before /g/ and optionally before other voiced plosives.

f. The voiced velar plosive /g/ becomes voiceless [k] when followed by voiceless obstruents or a sonorant.

g. The voiced and voiceless palatal affricates /tʃ dʒ/ become voiceless dental affricate /ts/ word-finally and before a consonant.

h. The voiceless post- alveolar fricative /ʃ/ becomes a retroflex [ʂ] or dental fricative [s] before a retroflex or dental sound.

i. The labial and palatal approximants become non-syllabic vocoids [o̯] and [e̯] intervocalically and word-finally.

j. The voiced glottal fricative becomes voiceless post-alveolar fricative before a voiceless post-alveolar fricative.

# 4 Vowel Allophones

Allophonic data on vowels are not available.

# 5 Syllable Structure

## 5.1 Canonical syllable structure[2]

(C) V (C)

## 5.2 Consonant clusters

Two-consonant clusters:

Initial : Nil
Final : Nil
Medial : General.

[2] Sinha (1968) does not discuss syllable structure and consonant clusters. The generalizations given here are based on the data in that work.

Three-consonant clusters: Nil

**Reference:** Sinha (1981[1968])

# Diu Indo-Portugese

**Ethnologue code:** None
**Language classification:** Creole, Portugese-based.
**Alternate names:** Purtagez da diw ('Portugese of Diu'), Ling tort ('twisted language'), Purtagez
barat ('cheap Portuguese'), Purtagez kebrad ('broken Portugese'), Ling da trap ('ragged tongue').
**Main region:** Diu island

## 1 Consonant Phonemes

### 1.1 Inventory

| | Bilabial | | Labio-dental | | Alveolar | | Pal. - Alv. | | Palatal | | Velar | |
|---|---|---|---|---|---|---|---|---|---|---|---|---|
| Plosive | p | b | | | t | d | | | | | k | g |
| Nasal | | m | | | | n | | | | | | ŋ |
| Trill | | | | | | r | | | | | | |
| Fricative | | | f | v | s | z | ʃ | (ʒ) | | | | |
| Approx | | w | | | | | | | | j | | |
| Lat Appr | | | | | | l | | | | | | |
| Affricate | | | | | | | | | ʧ | ʤ | | |

### 1.2 Distribution

a. Consonants occur in all positions, except the following:
   i. /ŋ/ does not occur word-initially.
b. /ʒ/ occurs only in free variation with /ʤ/in some lexical items. /ʃ/ and /tʃ/, however, contrast as well as occur in free variation in some lexical items.
c. Geminates do not occur.

# 2 Vowel Phonemes

## 2.1 Inventory

a. **Short**[3]

| | FRONT | CENTRAL | BACK |
|---|---|---|---|
| Close | i | | u |
| Open-mid | e | (ə) | o |
| Open-mid | ɛ | | ɔ |
| Open | a | | |

b. **Diphthongs:** /iw ew ɛw aw ej ɛj əj aj ɔj oj uj/

c. **Nasal**

| | FRONT | CENTRAL | BACK |
|---|---|---|---|
| Close | ĩ | | ũ |
| Open-mid | ẽ ẽj | | õ õj |
| Open | ã<br>ãj ãw | | |

## 2.2 Distribution

a. Vowels occur in all positions, with the following restrictions:
   i. /ə/ does not occur in stressed syllables.
   ii. /e ɛ/ and /o ɔ / are not found to contrast in height in unstressed syllables, in which position usually the Close-mid vowels occur.

b. Vowel sequences occur. Phonetically, vowels in a sequence tend to have an intervening palatal or labial-velar glide approximant following front or back vowels, respectively.

[3] The infrequently occurring /ə/ is a vowel occurring between Close-mid and Open-mid positions

# 3 Consonant Allophones

**General:** Obstruents are devoiced word-finally, giving rise to surface systematic allophones [p t k f s ʧ ] < /b d g v z ʤ/.

**Specific:** a. [ɰ] < /ŋ/ occurs in the intervocalic position.

b. [ɾ] < /r/ occurs in non-initial positions in the word.

# 4 Vowel Allophones

## 4.1 Inventory

[e]: /ɛ/

[o] : /ɔ/

[ɐ]: /a/

## 4.2 Distribution

a. [e o ɐ] < / ɛ ɔ a/ occur in unstressed syllables.

# 5 Syllable Structure

## 5.1 Canonical syllable structure

(C) (L) V (L) (C)

## 5.2 Consonant clusters

Two-consonant clusters:

Initial : O+L

Final : L+O
Medial : General.

Three-consonant clusters:

Initial : Nil
Final : Nil
Medial : Insufficient details available.

**Reference:** Cardoso (2009)

# Halbi[4]

**Ethnologue code:** None
**Language classification:** Inod-Aryan, Eastern zone, Oriya
**Alternate names:** Bastari, Halva, Halabi, Halvi, Mahari, Mehari
**Main region:** Madhya Pradesh, Chattisgarh, Andhra Pradesh, Orissa and Maharashtra

## 1 Consonant Phonemes

### 1.1 Inventory

| | BILA-BIAL | LABIO-DENTAL | DEN-TAL | ALVE-OLAR | RETR. | PALA-TAL | VELAR | GLOTTAL |
|---|---|---|---|---|---|---|---|---|
| Plosive | p b<br>$p^{h}$ $b^{ɦ}$ | | t d<br>$t^{h}$ $d^{ɦ}$ | | ʈ ɖ<br>$ʈ^{h}$ $ɖ^{ɦ}$ | | k g<br>$k^{h}$ $g^{ɦ}$ | |
| Nasal | m<br>($m^{ɦ}$) | | n<br>($n^{ɦ}$) | | | | ŋ | |
| Trill | | | | r<br>($r^{ɦ}$) | | | | |
| Fricative | | | | s | | | | h |
| Approx. | | ʋ | | | | j | | |
| Lat. Appr. | | | | l<br>($l^{ɦ}$) | | | | |
| Affricate | | | | | | tʃ dʒ<br>$tʃ^{h}$ $dʒ^{ɦ}$ | | |

[4] The variety being described here is spoken in Narayanpur tehsil (Chhotedonger and Sonapal villages) of Bastar district in Madhya Pradesh.

## 1.2 Distribution

a. Consonants occur in all positions, with the following restrictions:
   i. /pʰ mʱ nʱ lʱ rʱ/ do not occur word-finally; most aspirated consonants occur rarely in the word-final position.
   ii. /ŋ ʋ j/ do not occur word-initially.

b. The aspirated nasals and liquids have limited occurrence in the language.

c. /p b t ʈ k g l r/ have geminates in the intervocalic position; the geminates of /p ʈ r / occur more frequently than others.

# 2 Vowel Phonemes

## 2.1 Inventory

a. **Short**

| | FRONT | CENTRAL | BACK |
|---|---|---|---|
| High | i | | u |
| Mid | e | ɘ | o |
| Low | | a | |

## 2.2 Distribution

a. Vowels occur in all positions, with the following restriction:
   i. /ə/ does not occur initially in words.

2. Vowels sequences occur; the sequences /**iu eu au ei ai ui**/ are attested.

# 3 Consonant Allophones

Data not available.

# 4 Vowel Allophones

Data not available.

# 5 Syllable Structure

## 5.1 Canonical syllable structure[5]

(C) V (N) (C)

## 5.2 Consonant clusters

Two-consonant clusters:

Initial: Nil
Final: N+SH
Medial: General.

Three-consonant clusters:

Initial: Nil
Final: Nil
Medial: N+SH+C

**References:** Kanshikar (1972)

[5] Kanshikar (1972) mentions one word, /gja:n/ 'knowledge' with a word-initial onset cluster.

# Indian English (Hindi)[6]

**Ethnologue code:** None
**Language classification:** a Second language variety of English, a non-native variety of English, a variety of New Englishes.
**Alternate names:** (Names of non-standard varieties of English in India include Babu English, Butler English, and Hinglish. The variety being described is an educated variety of English in India.)
**Main region:** U.P, M.P, Bihar, Chattisgarh, Jharkhand, Delhi.

## 1 Consonant Phonemes

### 1.1 Inventory

| | BILA-BIAL | LABIO-DENTAL | DEN-TAL | ALVE-OLAR | POST-ALV. | RETRO-FLEX | PALA-TAL | VEL-AR | GLO-TTAL |
|---|---|---|---|---|---|---|---|---|---|
| Plosive | p b (b$^{ɦ}$) | | t$^{h}$ d | | | ʈ ɖ (ɖ$^{ɦ}$) | | k g (g$^{ɦ}$) | |
| Fricative | | f | | s z | ʃ | | | | h |
| Nasal | m | | | n | | | | ŋ | |
| Tap | | | | ɾ | | | | | |
| Lat. Appr. | | | | l | | | | | |
| Approx. | | ʋ | | | | j | | | |
| Affricate | | | | | | | ʧ ʤ | | |

**Note:** a. The phoneme / ʋ/ is phonetically different from the native English (NE) phoneme /v/ of which it is a substitute, but the former is a Novel segment.

[6] This is a variant of General Indian English, spoken by Second Language users of English with Hindi as their mother tongue. The term 'General Indian English' was first used by Bansal (1974) as the standard variety devoid of regional features, and based on the output of standard pronunciations of English across the country. The term is controversial in its present use.

b. /z/ and /ʒ/ have merged into /z/, there being no post-alveolar voiced fricative in the Filter.

c. The following phonemes have different phonetic qualities from the segments in NE: / tʰ d ʈ ɖ ɾ in place of /θ ð t d ɹ / respectively.

d. The following phonemes with restricted occurrence have been added without corresponding consonants in NE: /bʱ/ as in *abhor*, /ɖʱ/ as in *adhere*, and /gʱ/ as in *ghost*. These consonants are based on the orthographic representations of the words in which they occur.

## 1.2 Distribution

a. The consonant phonemes occur in all positions with the following restrictions:

   i. /ɾ/ optionally does not occur before consonants and word-finally. The optional deletion of /ɾ/ is restricted to the word domain. If dropped finally, it does not surface, even when the following word begins with a vowel, e.g. /də ɾivə iz floiŋ/ The river is flowing.

   ii. Word-medially, /ŋ/ always occurs with a following /g/, e.g. /siŋ/ sing, but /siŋgiŋ/ singing.

b. Geminate consonants occur within morphemes, e.g., innate /inne:t/, happy /hæppi:/, as well as across morphemes, e.g. illegal /illi:gəl/ vunnatural /ənnætʃ ʊ rr ə l/.

# 2 Vowel Phonemes

## 2.1 Inventory

a. **Short**

| | FRONT | CENTRAL | BACK |
|---|---|---|---|
| Close | i | | u |
| Close-mid | e | ə | |

b. **Long**

| | **FRONT** | **CENTRAL** | **BACK** |
|---|---|---|---|
| Close | i: | | u: |
| Close-mid | e: | | o: |
| Open-mid | ɛ: | | ɔ: |
| Open | | a: | |

c. **Diphthongs**[7]

/ai au ɔe/

## 2.2 Distribution

a. The monophthongs /e: o:/ correspond to NE diphthongs /ei əu/.

b. The long /ɔ:/ and the short /ɔ/ of NE have the same vowel quality in HE.

c. /æ:/ is realized as [ɛ:] in most instances.

d. The long and short close vowels /i: i u: u/ are closer in quality than in NE.

e. The vowel /o:/ occurs in place of /əu/ or /ɔ:/ in many cases, as in *go*, *court*, *force*, etc. in place of /ə/.

f. In most of those positions where full vowels have reduced vowel alternants in native English, such as in the underlined vowels in *phot<u>o</u>graph* / *photogr<u>a</u>phy*, *<u>o</u>ppose*/ *opp<u>o</u>site*, the full vowels occur. In non-alternating cases, /ə/ occurs, e.g. *<u>a</u>ttack, driv<u>e</u>r*, etc.

# 3 Consonant Allophones

## 3.1 Inventory and distribution

a. Consonant Gemination: Consonants are geminated before /j w ɾ/, e.g., [biʈ ʈ wi:n] *between*, [mæʈ ʈ ɾik] *matric*, [sekkjo: ɾ] *secure*.

[7] In Hindi English, and most varieties of Indian English all other surface diphthongs are vowel sequences, as shown in Pandey (1982).

b. Alveolar Nasal Assimilation: The alveolar nasal is assimilated in place to the following stop, e.g. [pæ̃ɳ ʈ] *pant,* [ʈ̃iɲdʒ] *tinge.*

c. Retroflex stop Assimilation: Retroflex stops have alveolar allophones following alveolar fricatives /s z/ , e.g. [best] *best*, [re:zd] *raised.*

d. Certain NE consonantal postlexical processes are absent in HE, e.g., l-Velarization, and Aspiration.

# 4 Vowel Allophones

## 4.1 Inventory and distribution

a. Vowel Nasalization: Vowels are nasalized preceding or following a nasal, e.g. [nõ:] *No*, [nɔ̃ʈ] not, [nẽʋəɾ] *never.*

b. Word-finally [a:] occurs commonly in place of the NE [ə], [pu:nã:] *[pu:nə] *Poona.*

c. /ə/ is optionally deleted in unstressed syllables flanked by a preceding stressed syllable, and followed by another syllable, following a general Schwa Deletion process in Hindi (Pandey 1990), e.g. [militri:] *military*, [sekkretri:] *secretary.*

d. Unlike in many varieties of NE, vowel length is insensitive to the voiced/voiceless distinction in the following environment. Thus /ai/ in *rice* and *rise* is not differentiated in terms of length in its allophonic manifestations in the words.

# 5 Syllable Structure

## 5.1 Canonical syllable structure

(C)(C)(C)V(C)(C)(C)(C)

## 5.2 Consonant clusters

Two-consonant clusters:

Initial : (i) C+L/G; (ii) s+C.
Final : general
Medial : general.

Three-consonant clusters:

Initial : /spr str smr/
Final : C+C+s/z/t/d/θ
Medial : general.

Four-consonant clusters:

Initial: Nil
Medial: general
Final: lfθs, -mpts, -kst/θs (as in native English)

**References:** Bansal and Harrison (1974), Balasubramanian (1981), Pandey (2005)

# Nagamese[8]

**Ethnologue code:** ISO 639-3: nag
**Language classification:** Creole, Assamese based
**Alternate names:** Naga Pidgin, Naga-Assamese, Naga Creole Assamese
**Main region:** Nagaland, especially Kohima District, Dimapur Subdivision; bordering areas of Arunachal Pradesh

## 1 Consonant Phonemes

### 1.1 Inventory[9]

| | BILABIAL | ALVEOLAR | POST ALVEOLAR | PALATAL | VELAR | GLOTTAL |
|---|---|---|---|---|---|---|
| Plosive | p b<br>$p^h$ ($b^ɦ$) | t d<br>$t^h$ ($d^ɦ$) | | | k g<br>$k^h$ ($g^ɦ$) | |
| Nasal | m | n | | | ŋ | |
| Trill | | r | | | | |
| Fricative | | s (z) | ʃ | | | h |
| Approx | w | | | j | | |
| Lat. Appr | | l | | | | |
| Affricate | | | | ʧ ʤ<br>$ʧ^h$ $ʤ^ɦ$ | | |

[8] The name 'Nagamese' is found preferable to 'Naga- Pidgin' on account of the presence of a large number of grammatical elements in the language. Nagamese speech has "reflexes" of tones found in the mother tongue Naga languages, but they are not systematic here.

[9] Boruah (1993) has a larger number of consonant phonemes, not included in Sridhar (1985). These are the voiced aspirated stops and the voiced alveolar fricative, given in parentheses in the chart.

## 1.2 Distribution

a. Consonants occur in all positions, with the following restriction:

   i. /ʧ s z l ] do not occur finally.

b. Geminates of the following consonants occur inter-vocalically: /p k ʔ m n/.

# 2 Vowel Phonemes

## 2.1 Inventory

a. **Short**

| | FRONT | CENTRAL | BACK |
|---|---|---|---|
| Close | i | | u |
| Close-mid | e | | o |
| Open-mid | | ɞ | |
| Open | | a | |

**Diphthongs:** /i̯e i̯o (e̯o) ə̯i o̯u u̯o/

## 2.2 Distribution

a. Vowels occur in all positions.

b. Vowel sequences do not occur. In word-formation, too, vowel sequences are avoided by either deleting a vowel or inserting a semi-vowel j or w. E.g., /ta + apú />[tapu] 'don't blow'; /ta + imsa/ [tijimsa] 'don't melt'.

# 3 Consonant Allophones

## 3.1 Inventory

| | **Bilabial** | **Alveolar** | **Post Alveolar** | **Palatal** | **Velar** |
|---|---|---|---|---|---|
| Plosive | p$^{h}$(p)<br>b(p) | t$^{h}$ (t)<br>d(t) | | | k$^{h}$(k)<br>g(k) |
| Fricative | | | ʃ(s) | | |
| Lat. Appr | | ts (ʧ) | | ʤ (ʧ) | |

## 3.2 Distribution

a. Aspirated voiceless plosives [p$^{h}$ t$^{h}$ k$^{h}$] < /ptk/ occur word-initially.

b. Voiced stop allophones [b d g ʤ] < /ptk ʧ/ occur inter-vocalically or following a voiced sound.

c. [ts] < /ʧ/ occurs when followed by /ɯ/.

d. [ʃ] < /s/ occurs before /i/.

# 4 Vowel Allophones

## 4.1 Inventory

| | |
|---|---|
| [ i̞ ]: | /i/ |
| [ e̞ ] [$^{j}$e]: | /e / |
| [ ə̞ ]: | /ə/ |
| [ ʌ ]: | /ɑ/ |
| [ ɔ ][$^{W}$o ]: | /o/ |

## 4.2 Distribution

a. [i̞ e̞ ə̞] < /i e ə / occur when flanked by tautosyllabic consonants, i.e. in closed syllables.

b. [ʲe ʷo] < /e o/ occur word-initially.

c. [ɔ] < / o/ occurs when preceded or followed by velar consonants /k ŋ/

d. [ʌ] < /ɑ/ occurs when accompanied by falling tone. / ɑ̀ŋó / > [ ʌ̀ŋɔ́] 'to see, find'. / mɑŋɑ̀ / [ maŋʌ̀ ] 'to fly'.

# 5 Syllable Structure

## 5.1 Canonical syllable structure

a. (C)(C)V (C)

b. (C)V (C) (C)

Note: A consonant cluster can occur either "in the onset or in the coda and not in both" (Sridhar 1985:61).

## 5.2 Consonant clusters

Two-consonant clusters:

Initial : (i) Pl + r/l/j; (ii) s + C (data on restrictions not available).
Final : n + d/j/s; j + dʒ/s; w + r/n; st; mb.
Medial : general (except /s z/ do not occur as $C_1$).

Three-consonant clusters:

Initial: Nil
Final: Nil
Medial: -ŋgl-, -ŋkʰj-, -mbl-, -nsj-, -ntj-, -jstʰ-, -ktr-.

**References:** Sreedhar (1974), Boruah (1993).

# Urdu-Dakhani (Tamil)[10]

**Ethnologue code:** None
**Language classification:** Urdu-based contact variety.
**Alternate names:** Not known
**Main region:** Tamil Nadu.

## 1 Consonant Phonemes

### 1.1 Inventory

| | BILABIAL | LABIODENTAL | DENTAL | ALVEOLAR | RETROFLEX | PRE-PALATAL | PALATAL | VELAR | GLOTTAL |
|---|---|---|---|---|---|---|---|---|---|
| Stop | p b (pʰ) (bʱ) | | t d (tʰ) (dʱ) | | ʈ ɖ (ʈʰ) (ɖʱ) | | | k g (kʰ) (gʱ) | |
| Nasal | m | | | n | ɳ | | | | |
| Tap | | | | r | | | | | |
| Fricative | | (f) | | s (z) | ʂ | ʃ< | | | h |
| Appr | | ʋ | | | | | j | | |
| Lat Appr | | | | l | ɭ | | | | |
| Affricates | | | | | | | ʧ ʤ (ʧʰ) (ʤʱ) | | |

### 1.2 Distribution

a. Consonants occur in all positions, with the following restrictions:

   i. The aspirated phonemes / pʰ ɖʱ ɟʱ gʱ mʱ nʱ lʱ rʱ jʱ / do not occur medially and finally.

[10] A variety of Urdu with features from Tamil, more like a mixed language than a dialectal variety.

ii. The aspirated phonemes /tʰ dʱ ʈʰ cʰ kʰ/ do not occur medially.
iii. / ŋ ɭ / do not occur initially and medially.
iv. /ŋ/ does not occur initially

b. Geminate consonants occur inter-vocalically, with the exception of /h/ and aspirated consonants.

# 2 Vowel Phonemes

## 2.1 Inventory

a. **Short**

| | FRONT | CENTRAL | BACK |
|---|---|---|---|
| Close | ɪ | | u |
| Open-mid | ɛ | | ɔ |
| Open | | ɐ | |

b. **Long**

| | FRONT | CENTRAL | BACK |
|---|---|---|---|
| Close | i: | | u: |
| Mid | e: | | o: |
| Open | | a: | |

c. **Nasal**

| | FRONT | CENTRAL | BACK |
|---|---|---|---|
| Close | ĩ: ɪ̃ | | ũ: ʊ̃ |
| Open-mid | ẽ: | | ɔ̃ õ: |
| Open | | ɐ̃ ã: | |

## 2.2 Distribution

a. Vowels occur in all positions, with the following restrictions:
   i. The short vowels do not occur finally.

b. Vowel sequences do not occur.

# 3 Consonant Allophones

## 3.1 Inventory[11]

| | Bilabial | Retr |
|---|---|---|
| Flap | | ɽ (ɖ) |
| Approx | w (ʋ) | |

## 3.2 Distribution

a. [ɽ] < /ɖ/ occurs inter-vocalically and finally.

b. [w] < /ʋ/ occurs following /ʊ/

# 4 Vowel Allophones

## 4.1 Inventory

**General:**

Long vowels have allophones of half length word-finally.

**Specific:**

[ ʊ̯ ] : /ʊ/

[ ɪ̯ ] : /ɪ/

[11] The approximant phonemes /j ʋ/ have non-syllabic allophones.

### 4.2 Distribution

a. The non-syllabic vocalic allophones [ʊ̯] < /ʊ/ and [ ɪ̯ ] < /ɪ/ occur medially or finally after /ɐ/ or /ɐ̃) /.

## 5 Syllable Structure

### 5.1 Canonical syllable structure

(C) (L/j) V (C)

### 5.2 Consonant clusters

Two-consonant clusters:

Initial : Obs + L/j.
Final : Nil except in a few words borrowed from English
Medial : General.

Three-consonant clusters: Nil.

**Reference:** Mohiddin (1980)

# Vaagri Boli

**Ethnologue code:** ISO 639-3: vaa
**Language classification:** Indo-Aryan, Unclassified
**Alternate names:** Narakureavar, Narikkorava, Kuruvikkaran, Karikk-orava, Hakkipikkaru, Haki Piki, Guvvalollu, Shikarijanam, Rattiyan, Marattiyan, Wogri Boli
**Main region:** Tamil Nadu (Arcot District).

## 1 Consonant Phonemes

### 1.1 Inventory

| | Bila-bial | Labio-dental | Den-tal | Retr | Pal-Alv. | Pal | Velar | Uvu-lar | Glo-ttal |
|---|---|---|---|---|---|---|---|---|---|
| Plosive | p b<br>$p^h$ $b^ɦ$ | | t d<br>$t^h$ $d^ɦ$ | ʈ ɖ<br>$ʈ^h$ $ɖ^ɦ$ | | | k g<br>$k^h$ $g^ɦ$ | | |
| Nasal | m<br>$m^ɦ$ | | n<br>$n^ɦ$ | ɳ | | ɲ | ŋ | | |
| Trill | | | r<br>$r^ɦ$ | | | | | ʀ | |
| Flap | | | | ɽ | | | | | |
| Fricative | | | s z | | | | | | h |
| Approx | | ʋ | | | | j | | | |
| Lat. Approx. | | | l<br>$l^ɦ$ | ɭ | | | | | |
| Affricates | | | | | | tʃ dʒ<br>$tʃ^h$ $dʒ^ɦ$ | | | |

## 1.2 Distribution

a. Consonants occur in all positions, with the following restrictions:
   i. /ɳ ɲ ŋ ɭ/ do not occur initially.
   ii. /pʰ bʱ tʰ ɟʱ nʱ/ do not occur medially.
   iii. /dʱ ʈʰ ɖ ɖʱ cʰ kʰ gʱ z/ do not occur finally.

b. All consonants except / bʱ dʱ ɖʱ ɟʱ gʱ l ɭ r ɽ rʱ mʱ ɳ ʀ h ʋ s z / can be geminated inter-vocalically.

# 2 Vowel Phonemes

## 2.1 Inventory

**a. Short**

| | FRONT | CENTRAL | BACK |
|---|---|---|---|
| Close | i | ɨ | u |
| Close-mid | e | | o |
| Open | | a | |

**b. Long**

| | FRONT | CENTRAL | BACK |
|---|---|---|---|
| Close | i: | | u: |
| Close-mid | e: | | o: |
| Open | | a: | |

**c. Nasal**

| | FRONT | CENTRAL | BACK |
|---|---|---|---|
| Close | ĩ: | | u ũ: |
| Close-mid | ẽ ẽ: | | õ: |
| Open | | ã ã: | |

## 2.2 Distribution

a. Vowels occur in all positions, with the following restrictions:
  i. /ĩ: ẽ ẽ: ã õ: ɨ/ do not occur initially.
  ii. /ẽ: ũ: / do not occur medially.
  iii. /a ã o ũ:/ do not occur finally.

b. Vowel sequences do not occur.

# 3 Consonant Allophones

## 3.1 Inventory and distribution

a. [t] < /ʈ/ occurs initially and finally.

b. [ɽ]< /ɖ/ occurs in the intervocalic position, and after a consonant other than /ɳ/.

c. The approximants have vocalic allophones, as described in section 4 below.

# 4 Vowel Allophones

## 4.1 Inventory

| | |
|---|---|
| [ i̯ ] | /j/ |
| [ u̯ ] | :/ʋ/ |
| [ ɪ ] | : /i/ |
| [ ɛ ] | : /e/ |
| [ ɛ :] | : /e:/ |
| [ ɐ ] | : /a/ |
| [ ʊ ] | : /u/ |

## 4.2 Distribution

a. The non-syllabic vocalic allophones of the approximants occur finally and before a segment.

b. The lowered allophones [ɪ ɛ ʊ] < /i e u/ and the raised allophone [ɐ] < /a/ occur medially in words.

c. The long lowered allophone [ɛ:] < /e:/ occurs after /b/.

# 5 Syllable Structure

## 5.1 Canonical syllable structure[12]

(C) (C) V (C)

## 5.2 Consonant Clusters

Two-consonant clusters:

Initial : mr-, kj-, -g-.
Final : Nil
Medial : General

Three-consonant clusters:

Initial: Nil
Medial: -prj-, -mnd-, -ndr-, -ŋgl-, -ŋg]-.

**Reference:** Varma (1970).

[12] Words of up to seven syllables are found to occur.

Chapter 8

# HISTORICAL VARIETIES

## Old Tamil

**Ethnologue code:** Not given
**Language classification:** Dravidian, southern zone
**Alternate names:** Sangam Tamil
**Main region:** Tamil Nadu, Karnataka, Kerala
**Historical period:** 1 A. D.

### 1 Consonant Phonemes

#### 1.1 Inventory

| | BILABIAL | DENTAL | ALVEOLAR | RETROFLEX | PAL.-ALV. | PALATAL | VELAR |
|---|---|---|---|---|---|---|---|
| Stop | p | t | t̲ | ʈ | | | k |
| Nasal | m | n | n̲ | ɳ | | ɲ | (ŋ) |
| Tap | | | ɾ | | | | |
| Approx | w | | | ɻ | | j | |
| Lat Appr | | l | | ɭ | | | |
| Affricate | | l | | | tʃ | | |

## 1.2 Distribution

a. Consonants occur in all positions, with the following restrictions:
   i. /l ŋ/ and the alveolar and retroflex consonants do not occur in the initial position.
   ii. /ɲ ŋ/ and the stops do not occur in the final position.

# 2 Vowel Phonemes

## 2.1 Inventory

a. **Short**

| | FRONT | CENTRAL | BACK |
|---|---|---|---|
| Close | i | | u |
| Close-mid | e | | o |
| Open | | a | |

b. **Long**

| | FRONT | CENTRAL | BACK |
|---|---|---|---|
| Close | iː | | uː |
| Close-mid | eː | | oː |
| Open | | aː | |

## 2.2 Distribution

a. Vowels occur in all positions, with the following restriction:
   i. They do not occur after /ŋ/ and /j/ word-medially.

b. Sequences of vowels occur within a morpheme, leading to surface realizations as diphthongs. Across morphemes, a glide /j/ or /w/ is inserted between adjacent vowels.

# 3 Consonant Allophones

## 3.1 Inventory and distribution

/j/ does not occur in the position between a short vowel and a stop as an approximant. In that position, an obstruent sound, called 'aytam'], occurs. However, the sound there is claimed to be an obstruent. The obstruent is interpreted as an allophone of a ProtoDravidian laryngeal /H/ (Krishnamurti (1997), which had restricted distribution. Alternatively, it has been interpreted as an allophone of /j/, on the grounds that /h/ does not occur anywhere else in the language.

# 4 Vowel Allophones

Data not available.

# 5 Syllable Structure

## 5.1 Canonical syllable structure[1]

Word Initial: (C) V (C)

Non-initial: ($C_1$) ($C_1$) V (C)

Note: $C_1$ $C_1$ are gemínate consonants.

## 5.2 Consonant clusters

Two-consonant clusters:

Initial : Nil

Final : Nil.

Medial : $C_1$ $C_1$, N+S.

[1] a. The coda consonant is found to be a Son.
b. Word-initially there are no clusters. The clusters occur medially.

Three-consonant clusters:

Initial : Nil

Final : Nil

Medial : Restricted, e.g. Son+S+S (e.g. /wa: ɻkkai/ 'living')

**References:** Lehmann (1998)

# Old Telugu

**Ethnologue code:** Not given
**Language classification:** Dravidian, Central zone.
**Alternate names:** Nil
**Main region:** Andhra Pradesh.
**Historical Period:** 1000 A. D.

## 1 Consonant Phonemes

### 1.1 Inventory

| | BILABIAL | LABIODENTAL | DENTAL | ALVEOLAR | RETROFLEX | PALATAL | VELAR | GLOTTAL |
|---|---|---|---|---|---|---|---|---|
| Stop | p b (p$^{h}$) (b$^{ɦ}$) | | t d (t$^{h}$) (d$^{ɦ}$) | | ʈ ɖ (ʈ$^{h}$) (ɖ$^{ɦ}$) | | k g (k$^{h}$) (g$^{ɦ}$) | |
| Nasal | m | | n | | ɳ | | ŋ | |
| Fricative | | | | s | (ʂ) | (ʃ) | | h |
| Tap | | | | ɾ | | | | |
| Trill | | | | r | | | | |
| Approx | w | | | | ɻ | j | | |
| Lat Approx | | | | l | ɭ | | | |
| Affricate | | | | | | ʧ ʤ (ʧ$^{h}$) (ʤ$^{ɦ}$) | | |

### 1.2 Distribution

a. Consonants occur in all positions, with the following restrictions:

   i. /ɳ ŋ ɭ j/ do not occur in the initial position.

ii. /w/ does not occur before /u o/ and the stops do not occur in the final position.

b. Aspirated stops, retroflex and palatal fricatives (in parentheses above) were introduced into Old Telugu through borrowings from Old Indo-Aryan.

# 2 Vowel Phonemes

## 2.1 Inventory

a. **Short**

| | FRONT | CENTRAL | BACK |
|---|---|---|---|
| Close | i | | u |
| Close-mid | e | | o |
| Open | | a | |

b. **Long**

| | FRONT | CENTRAL | BACK |
|---|---|---|---|
| Close | i: | | u: |
| Mid | e: | | o: |
| Open | | a: | |

## 2.2 Distribution

**Note:** "In poetry ai and au are treated, on the one hand, as monosyllables rhyming with long vowels, and on the other, as disyllables (viz., ayi, avu) rhyming with VCV sequences. This is applicable only to the diphthongs belonging to the native element." (Krishnamurti 1962:2) In Sanskrit loanwords, the diphthongs are treated as monosyllabic.

# 3 Consonant Allophones

## 3.1 Inventory

a. The phoneme /ɻ/ came to be allophonic with /d/ and /ɾ/ in complementary environments by "the literary period of the elevent century".

b. The distinction between /r/ and /ɾ/ also came to be lost "during the early literary period".

c. [ʦ ʥ]< /ʧ ʤ/ before back vowels

# 4 Vowel Allophones

Data not available.

# 5 Syllable Structure

## 5.1 Canonical syllable structure

(C) (r) V (C)

## 5.2 Consonant clusters

Two-consonant clusters:

Initial : Pl / m/w/s + r

Final : Nil.

Medial : General.

Three-consonant clusters: Nil

**References:** Krishnamurti (1961), Ramanarasimhan (1998)

# Pali

**Ethnologue code:** ISO 639-3: pli
**Language classification:** Indo-Aryan, Middle Indo-Aryan.
**Alternate names:** Nil
**Main region:** Northern India

## 1 Consonant Phonemes

### 1.1 Inventory

| | BILABIAL | LABIODENTAL | DENTAL | ALVEOLAR | RETROFLEX | PALATAL | VELAR | GLOTTAL |
|---|---|---|---|---|---|---|---|---|
| Stop | p b<br>p$^{h}$ b$^{ɦ}$ | | t d<br>t$^{h}$ d$^{ɦ}$ | | ʈ ɖ<br>ʈ$^{h}$ ɖ$^{ɦ}$ | | k g<br>k$^{h}$ g$^{ɦ}$ | |
| Nasal | m | | | | ɳ | | | |
| Tap | | | | ɾ | | | | |
| Fricative | | | s | | | | | h |
| Approx | | ʋ | | | | j | | |
| Lat Appr | | | | l | ɭ<br>ɭ$^{ɦ}$ | | | |
| Affricate | | | | | | ʧ ʤ<br>ʧ$^{h}$ ʤ$^{ɦ}$ | | |

### 1.2 Distribution

a. Consonants occur initially and medially.

b. Geminates of all consonants except /ɾ/ and /h/ are found medially.

# 2 Vowel Phonemes[2]

## 2.1 Inventory

a. **Short**

| | FRONT | CENTRAL | BACK |
|---|---|---|---|
| Close | i | | u |
| Open-mid | | ə | |

b. **Long**

| | FRONT | CENTRAL | BACK |
|---|---|---|---|
| Close | i: | | u: |
| Close-mid | e: | | o: |
| Open | | a: | |

c. **Nasal**

| | FRONT | CENTRAL | BACK |
|---|---|---|---|
| Close | ĩ | | ũ |
| Open | | ã : | |

## 2.2 Distribution

Vowels occur in all positions, with the following restrictions:

a. Long vowels do not occur before clusters and geminates.

b. Vowel sequences occur.

[2] i. The Sanskrit syllabic approximant /ɹ̩/ developed into /i u a/ and /l̩/ developed into /u/ unpredictably. These vowels have various other sources.

# 3 Consonant Allophones

Data not available.

# 4 Vowel Allophones

## 4.1 Inventory and distribution

The medial vowels /e: o:/ are pronounced short non-finally.

# 5 Syllable Structure

## 5.1 Canonical syllable structure

Finally: (C) V / NV

Non-finally (C) V (C)

**Note:** a. A Pāli syllable does not have more than two morae. Two morae are found in syllables with (a) a short oral vowel followed by a consonant, or (b) a long oral vowel, or (c) a short nasal vowel.

b. There are innumerable cases of contraction of syllables from Sanskrit to Pāli.

c. Pāli also has added syllables in Sanskrit words on account of 'sʋarabhakti', the addition of a vowel in non-permissible clusters within a syllable.

d. The Sanskrit h + C clusters have undergone metathesis in Pāli. Thus, hn, hm, hɳ, hj, hʋ have become nh, mh, ɳh jh, ʋh respectively. The clusters nh, mh, ɳh are also derived from sn, sm, sɳ through change of /s/ to /h/ following nasals and metathesis.

## 5.2 Consonant clusters

Two-consonant clusters:

Initial : Nil

Final : Nil.

Medial : Geminates, N+C.

Three-consonant clusters: Nil

**Reference:** Geiger (2000)

# Prakrit[3]

**Ethnologue code:** ISO- 639-3 psu
**Language classification:** Indo-Aryan, Middle period
**Alternate names:** Sauraseni, Paisaci (both different varieties of Prakrit)
**Main region:** Western, Central, and Eastern India.

## 1 Consonant Phonemes

### 1.1 Inventory

| | Bilabial | Dental | Alveolar | Retroflex | Palatal | Velar | Glottal |
|---|---|---|---|---|---|---|---|
| Stop | p b<br>$p^{h}$ $b^{ɦ}$ | t d<br>$t^{h}$ $d^{ɦ}$ | | ʈ ɖ<br>$ʈ^{h}$ $ɖ^{ɦ}$ | c ɟ<br>$c^{h}$ $ɟ^{ɦ}$ | k g<br>$k^{h}$ $g^{ɦ}$ | |
| Nasal | m | | | ɳ | | | |
| Tap | | ɾ | | | | | |
| Fricative | | s | | | | | h |
| Approx | w | | | | | | |
| Lat appr | | | l | | | | |

### 1.2 Distribution

a. Consonants occur initially and medially, with the following restrictions:
   i. /ʈ/ does not occur in the initial position; /$ʈ^{h}$ ɖ $ɖ^{ɦ}$ / occur rarely in the initial position.
   ii. /$t^{h}$ ʈ $ʈ^{h}$ $k^{h}$/ does not occur in the medial position.

b. Only /m/ occurs in the final position.

c. Geminates of all consonants except /ɾ/ and /h/ are found medially.

[3] The description is based on Hāla's text entitled *Sattasai.*

# 2 Vowel Phonemes

## 2.1 Inventory

a. **Short**

| | FRONT | CENTRAL | BACK |
|---|---|---|---|
| Close | i | | u |
| Open-mid | | ə | |

b. **Long**

| | FRONT | CENTRAL | BACK |
|---|---|---|---|
| Close | i: | | u: |
| Close-mid | e: | | o: |
| Open | | a: | |

## 2.2 Distribution

a. Vowels occur in all positions, with the following restrictions:
   i. /u/ does not occur in the initial position.
   ii. Long vowels do not occur before clusters and geminates.

b. Vowel sequences occur.

# 3 Consonant Allophones

Data not available.

# 4. Vowel Allophones

## 4.1 Inventory and distribution

The medial vowels /e: o:/ are pronounced short before geminates and clusters.

# 5 Syllable Structure

## 5.1 Canonical syllable structure

a. Final: (C) V (m)

b. Non-final: (C) V (C)

## 5.2 Consonant clusters

Two-consonant clusters:

Initial : Nil

Final : Nil.

Medial : Geminates, N + C.

Three-consonant clusters: Nil

**References:** Ananthanarayana (1973)

# Sanskrit-Classical

**Ethnologue code:** ISO639-2: san
**Language clasiification:** Indo-European, Indo-Iranian, Vedic Sanskrit, Classical Sanskrit.
**Alternate names:** Nil
**Main region:** Western India, Northern India and parts of southern India.

## 1 Consonant Phonemes[4]

### 1.1 Inventory

| | Bila-bial | Labio-dental | Den-tal | Alv. | Post Alv. | Retr-oflex | Pala-tal | Velar | Phar | Glo-ttal |
|---|---|---|---|---|---|---|---|---|---|---|
| Stop | p b<br>pʰ bʱ | | t d<br>tʰ dʱ | | | ʈ ɖ<br>ʈʰ ɖʱ | | k g<br>kʰ gʱ | | |
| Nasal | m | | n | | | ɳ | ɲ | ŋ | | |
| Trill | | | r | | | | | | | |
| Fricative | | | s | ʃ | ʂ | | | | ħ | h |
| Appr | | ʋ | | | | | j | | | |
| Lat Appr | | | l | | | | | | | |
| Affricate | | | | | | | tʃ dʒ<br>tʃʰ dʒʱ | | | |

### 1.2 Distribution

a. Consonants occur in all positions, with the following restrictions:
   i. /ɳ ŋ/ do not occur initially.
   ii. /ŋ ɲ tʃʰ/ do not occur medially.

[4] Certain sounds with specific names in the grammatical tradition have varied phonetic descriptions, such as the 'anuswāra' (nasalization) and 'ayogaʋāha' (segments dependent on other segments in articulation, presumably, allophones).

iii. All aspirated plosives and palatal consonants /ʧ ʤ ɲ j/ do not occur finally, before obstruents and prepausally.

b. Geminate consonants except /kʰ pʰ/ occur medially

# 2 Vowel Phonemes

## 2.1 Inventory

a. **Short**

| | FRONT | CENTRAL | BACK |
|---|---|---|---|
| Close | i | | u |
| Open-mid | | ə | |

b. **Long**

| | FRONT | CENTRAL | BACK |
|---|---|---|---|
| Close | i: | | u: |
| Mid | e: | | o: |
| Mid | æ: | | ɒ : |
| Open | | a: | |

c. Syllabic vocoid consonants: / ɹ̩, l̩ /

## 2.2 Distribution

a. All the vowels occur in all the positions.

b. Vowel sequences do not occur within words. They may occur across words, if the word-final consonant is deleted.

# 3 Consonant Allophones

## 3.1 Inventory

| | **BILABIAL** | **DENTAL** | **RETRO-FLEX** | **PALA-TAL** | **VELAR** |
|---|---|---|---|---|---|
| Plosive | ~b (ʋ) | $d^{ɦ}$ (t/$t^{h}$) | ʈ (Ø) | | k(Ø)<br>$k^{h}$ (ʂ) |
| Nasal | | | ɳ (n) | | |
| Fricative | | | ʂ (s) | | |
| Affricate | | | | ʤ(j) | |

## 3.2 Distribution

**General:**

a. Consonants (except r n) optionally geminate when preceded by a vowel and followed by another consonant.

b. Word-final stops assimilate in voicing to the following segment.

**Specific:**

a. /j ʋ / are optionally pronounced as [ɟ b ] word-initially in some dialects in certain traditions.

b. [$k^{h}$] < /ʂ/ in certain traditions except when followed by velar stops.

c. [ʂ] < /s/ occurs when preceded by a vowel other than /ə a:/ or a velar stop within a word.

d. [ɳ] < /n/ occurs when preceded by / ɹ̩ ɹ̩: r ʂ / with an optionally intervening vowel, ɦ, j, ʋ, a velar or labial stop or a combination of these.

e. [d] </t/ or /$t^{h}$/ occurs when preceded by a voiced aspirated stop / $b^{ɦ}$ $d^{ɦ}$ $g^{ɦ}$ /.

f. [t ʈ k] are optionally inserted between a /n ɳ ŋ/ respectively and a sibilant.

g. /r/ released before a consonant with an anaptyctic vowel (called 'sʋarabhakti').

# 4 Vowel Allophones

## 4.1 Inventory

| | |
|---|---|
| [ j ], [ i j ] | : /i/ |
| [ʋ], [uʋ] | : /u/ |
| [r] | : /ɹ̩/ |
| [e] | : /e:/ |
| [o] | : /o:/ |
| [əi] | : /æ:/ |
| [əu] | : /æɒ:/ |

## 4.2 Distribution

**General:**

a. An extra-short anaptyctic vowel is found with the release of /r/ before a consonant.

**Specific:**

a. [j] < /i/ /i:/, [ʋ] < /u/ /u:/ and [r] < /ɹ̩ / occur before dissimilar vowels.·

b. [i j] < /i/ /i:/ and [uʋ] < /u/ /u:/ occur in certain grammatical contexts.

c. [e o] < /e: o:/ occur in certain recitation traditions.

d. [əi] ~ /æ:/, [əu] ~ /æɒ: /are reported to occur in certain dialects. As allophones, [əi] < /æ:/, [əu]</æɒ:/ occur before semivowels.

# 5 Syllable Structure

## 5.1 Canonical syllable structure

(C) (C) (C) V (r) (C)

## 5.2 Consonant clusters[5]

Two-consonant clusters:

Initial : (i) C+L/G; (ii) s+C, (iii) ps-, kʃ-
Final : -rC
Medial : general.

Three-consonant clusters:

Initial : spr-, str-, smr-.
Medial : general
Final : Nil

# 6 Suprasegmentals

## 6.1 Tone

Tonemes:

High: H ('udātta')
Low: L ('anudātta')
High-Low: HL ('sʋarita')

## 6.2 Allophones

a. 'Extra high' < 'High' occurs following a Low tone.

b. 'Extra low' < 'Low' occurs preceding a High or High-Low tone.

c. 'High' < 'Low' occurs following a High-Low tone, but not if followed by a High or High-Low tone.

**Reference:** Cardona (2003)

[5] Sanskrit allows many specific consonant clusters in the medial position. These are being assumed to come under the category 'general' as mentioned here. Note that the trill /r/ should not be confused with the syllabic /r̥/ in Sanskrit, a possible source of misinterpretation of facts regarding consonant clusters in Sanskrit.

# Bibliography

Abbi, A. (2006). *Endangered languages of the Andaman Islands*. Munich: Lincom Europa.

Abbi, A. (2013). *A grammar of the Great Andamanese language: an ethnolinguistic study*. Leiden: Brill.

Acharya, J. (1991). *A descriptive grammar of Nepali and an analyzed corpus*. Washington, D. C.: Georgetown University.

Acharya, K. P. (1975). *Lotha phonetic reader*. Mysore: Central Institute of Indian Languages.

Almeida, M. (1989). *A description of Konkani*. Panaji: Thomas Stephens Konkani Kendra.

Ananthanarayana, H. S. (1973). *A Prakrit reader – a linguistic introduction – based on selections from Hālas Sattasaī*. Mysore: Central Institute of Indian Languages.

Andres, S. (1977). *A description of Muria Gondi phonology and morphology with a transformational account of the morpho-phonological processes employed*. Ph. D. dissertation. Pune: Deccan College Post-graduate & Research Institue.

Asher, R. E. & Kumari. T. C. (1997). *Malayalam*. London/New York: Routledge.

Ashirvadam, K. (1992). *The structure of Didayi, an Austro-Asiatic language*. Ph. D. dissertation. Hyderabad: Osmania University.

Bahri, U. S. (1969). Phonology of Dogri. *Pakha Sanjam (Patiala)* 1. 75-107.

Bahri, U. S. (2001). *Dogri: Phonology and grammatical sketch*. New Delhi: Bahri Publications.

Balakrishnan, R. (1976). *Phonology of Kodagu with vocabulary*. Annamalainagar: Annamalai University.

Balakrishnan, R. (1999). *Badaga*: A Dravidian Language. Annamalainagar: Annamalai University.

Balasubramaniam, T. (1981, rpt 1995). *A textbook of English phonetics for Indian students*. Macmillan.

Bandyopadhyay, S.K. (1980). *Linguistic analysis of Tangsa: A Tibeto-Burman language*. Ph. D. thesis. University of Delhi.

Bansal, R. K. and Harrison, J. B. (1974). *Spoken English for India*. New Delhi: Orient Longman.

Bardhan, S. K. (1999) *A phonological study of Chakma and English*. Ph. D. dissertation. Hyderabad: CIEFL

Baruah, B. K. (1993). *The language of Nagaland*. Delhi: Mittal Publication.

Bhaskararao, P. (1972–80). *Konekor Gadaba: A Dravidian language*. Pune: Deccan College Post-Graduate and Research Institute.

Bhat, D. N. S. (1967). *Descriptive analysis of Tulu*. Pune: DCPGRI.

Bhat, R. (1987). *A descriptive study of Kashmiri*. Delhi: Amar Prakashan.

Bhatia, T. K. (1997). *Punjabi: A cognitive-descriptive grammar*. London/ New York: Routledge.

Bhattacharya, P. C. (1977). *Descriptive analysis of Boro language*. Gauhati: University of Guwahati Press.

Bhattacharya, S. (1956). *Ollari: A Dravidian speech*. Delhi: Dept. of Anthropology. GOI.

Biligiri, H. S. (1965). *Kharia: Phonology, grammar and vocabulary*. Poona: Deccan College Postgraduate and Research Institute.

Blankenship, B. (1993). Phonetic structures of Khonoma Angami. *Linguistics of Tibeto-Burman Area* **16.2**. 69–88. *et al.*

Braine, J. C. (1970). *Nicobarese grammar (Car dialect)*. Ph.D. thesis. Barkeley: University of California.

Braine, J. C. (1970). *Nicobarese grammar (Car dialect)*. Ph.D. thesis. Barkeley: University of California.

Bright, W. (1957b). Alternations in Lushai. *Indian Linguistics* **18.**

Bright, W. (1958). *Colloquial Kannada*. Poona: DC.

Burling, R. & Wangsu, M. (1999). Wancho phonology and word list. *Linguistics of Tibeto-Burman Area* **21**. 43–71.

Burling, R. (1981). Garo spelling and Garo phonology. *Linguistics of Tibeto-Burman Area* **6.1**. 61–81.

Burling, R. and Phom, L.A. (1998). Phom phonology and word list. *Linguistics of the Tibeto-Burman Area* **21.2**: 13–42

Burrow, T. & Bhattacharya, S. (1970). *The Pengo language. Grammar, texts, and vocabulary*. Oxford: Clarendon Press.

Burrows, L. (1980 [1915]) *The grammar of the Ho language: An eastern Himalayan dialect*. New Delhi: Cosmo Publications.

Cardona, G. (2003). Sanskrit. In Cardona, G. & Jain, D. (eds.), *The Indo-Aryan*

Cardoso, H. C. (2009). The Indo-Portugese language of Diu. Ph. D. thesis. Unoiversiteit van Amsterdam. Uttrecht: LOT

Chandrashekhar, A. (1970). The phonemes of Garhwali. *Indian Linguistics* **31.3**. 80-5.

Chauhan, A. R. (1992). *The Kangri central Subsystems (A structural description)*. Shimla: Himachal Academy of Arts, Culture and Languages.

Chhangte, L. (1986). *A preliminary grammar of the Mizo language*. MA dissertation. Arlington: University of Texas.

Christdas, P. (1988). *The phonology and morphology of Tamil*. Ph.D. dissertation, Ithacca: Cornell University.

Cook, W. A. (1965). *A descriptive analysis of Mundari, a study of the structure (Hasada dialect)*. University Microfilm. Michigan: Ann Arbor.

Das Gupta, K. (1963). *An introduction to the Gallong language*. Shillong: North-East Frontier Agency.

Das Gupta, K. (1968). *An introduction to Central Monpa*. Shillong: North-East Frontier Agency.

Das, A. R. (1972). *A study on the Nicobarese language*. Calcutta: ASI.

Das, A. R. (1972). *A study on the Nicobarese language*. Calcutta: ASI.

Das, S. K. (1973). *Structure* of *Malto*. Annamalainagar: Annamalai University.

Dasgupta, D. (1976). *Linguistic studies in Juang, Kharia*. Calcutta: Anthropological Survey of India.

Dasgupta, P. & Sharma, S. R. (1982). *A handbook of Onge language*. Calcutta: Archaeological Survey of India.

De, S. (1996). Santal vowel phonemes. *Journal of the Anthropolgical Survey of India* **45**. 57–71.

DeLancey, S. (2003). Lhasa Tibetan. In Thurgood, G & Lapolla, R. (eds). 270–88.

Driem, G. van (1987). *A grammar of Limbu*. Berlin: Mouton de Gruyter.

Dutta-Baruah, P. N. & Bapui, V. L. T. (1996). *Hmar grammar*. Mysore: Central Institute of Indian Languages.

Ebert, K. H. (1996). *Kodava*. München: Lincom Europa.

Ekka, F. (1985). *Kurux phonetic reader*. Mysore: Central Institute of Indian Languages.

Emeneau, M. B. (1955). *Kolami: A Dravidian language*. Berkeley: University of California Press.

Emeneau, M. B. (1970). Kodagu vowels. *Journal of American Oriental Society* **90.** 145-58.

Emeneau, M. B. (1979). Toda vowels in non-initial syllables. *Bulletin of the School of Oriental and African Studies* **42.** 225–34. [Repr. in Emeneau 1994: 275–86.]

Emeneau, M. B. (1984). *Toda grammar and texts*. Philadelphia: American Philosophical Society

Fanai, L. T. (1992). *Some aspects of the lexical phonology of Mizo and English: An autosegmental approach*. Ph.D. dissertation. Hyderabad: CIEFL.

Ferguson, C. & Chowdhury, M. (1960). The phonemes of Bengali. *Language* **36.** 22–59.

Gandhi, D. P. (1978). *Structural sketch of Galo language*. Ph.D. dissertation. Delhi: University of Delhi

Gaud, D. S. (1980). *Gadaba.* Bhubaneshwar: Tribal and Research Insitute.

Gauda, D. (1989). *A study of the Ganjami dialect of Oriya*. Ph.D. dissertation. Poona: UP, Deccan College Post-Graduate and Research Institute.

Geiger, W. (2000). *A Pāli Grammar.* Translated into English by Ghosh, B. Revised and edited by Norman, K. R. Oxford: The Pali Text Society.

Ghai, V. K. (1991). *Studies in phonetics and phonology*. New Delhi: Ariana Publishing House.

Ghosh, T. (1996). *Bangla phonology*. M. Phil. dissertation. Hyderabad: CIEFL.

Giridhar, P. P. (1980). *Angami grammar.* Mysore: Central Institute of Indian Languages.

Giridhar, P. P. (1994). *Mao Naga grammar.* Mysore: Central Institute of Indian Languages.

Goswami, G. (1989). *Kisan*. Bhubaneshwar: Tribal and Research Institute.

Goswami, G. C. (1966). *An introduction to Assamese phonology*. Poona: DC.

Gowda, K. S. G. (1975). *Ao grammar*. Mysore: Central Institute of Indian Languages.

Gumperz, J. J. & Naim, C. M. (1960). Formal and informal standards in the Hindi regional language area. *International Journal of American Linguistics* **26 (3)**. 92-118.

Gusain, L. (2000). *Bagri.* München: Lincom Europa. [Languages of the World/Materials, 384]

Hodge, S. (2003). *An introduction to classical Tibetan.* Bernard: Orchid Press.

Indira, R. (1976). *A descriptive analysis of Kadar.* Ph.D. dissertation. Poona: DC.

Israel, M. (1979). *A grammar of the Kuvi language.* Trivandrum: DLA.

Jeyapaul, V. Y. (1987). *Karbi grammar.* Mysore: Central Institute of Indian Languages.

Joy, J. (1994). *Mahl: A descriptive analysis.* Ph.D. dissertation. Poona: UP.

Kanshikar, C. (1972). *A descriptive analysis of Halbi: An Indo-Aryan language.* Ph.D. dissertation. Poona: UP.

Kapfo, K. (1992). *A descriptive analysis of Khezha.* Ph.D. dissertation. Mysore: University of Mysore.

Kaul, D. (2012). *Phonetics and phonology of word prosody in Dogri.* M. Phil. Dissertation. New Delhi: Jawaharlal Nehru University.

Kelkar, A. R. & Trishal, P. N. (1964). Kashmiri word phonology: A first sketch. *Anthropological Linguistics* **6.1.** 13–22.

Kelkar, A. R. (1958). *The phonology and morphology of Marathi.* Ph.D. dissertation. Ithacca: Cornell University.

Kelkar, A. R. (1968). *Studies in Hindi-Urdu* **1**. Poona: DC.

Khatiwada, R. (2007). Nepalese retroflex stops: A static palatography study of the inter and intra-speaker variability. *Proceedings of the Interspeech 2007.* Antwerpen. Belgium. 1422–1425.

Khatiwada, R. (2009). Nepali. *Journal of International Phonetic Association* **39.3**. 373–380

Khubchandani, L. M. (2003). Sindhi. In Cardona, G. & Jain, D. (eds.), *The Indo-Aryan Languages.* London, New York: Routledge (Routledge Language Family Series). 622–58

Klaiman, M. H. (1987). Bengali. Comrie, B. (ed.), *The worlds major languages.* London/Sydney: Croom Helm. 490–513.

Koshal, S. (1979). *Ladakhi grammar.* Delhi: Motilal Banarasidas.

Krishan, S. (2001a). Sketch of Chaudangsi grammar. Nagano, Y. & Lapolla, R. (eds.), *New research on Zhangzhung and related Himalayan languages*, Osaka: National Museum of Ethnology ( [Bon Studies 3, Senri Ethnological Reports No. 19), 401–448.

Krishan, S. (2001b). Sketch of Darma grammar. Nagano, Y. & Lapolla, R. (eds.), *New research on Zhangzhung and related Himalayan languages.* Osaka: National Museum of Ethnology ([Bon Studies 3, Senri Ethnological Reports No. 19). 347–400.

Krishan, S. (2001c). A sketch of Raji grammar. In Nagano, Y. and LaPolla, R. J. (eds.), *New Research on Zhangzhung and Related Himalayan Language*. Osaka: National Museum of Ethnology. 449–501.

Krishnamurti, Bh. (1961). *Telugu verbal bases*. Bereley: University of California Press.

Krishnamurti, Bh. (1998). Telugu. Steever, S. B. (ed.), *The Dravidian Languages*. London and New York: Routledge. 202–240.

Kulkarni, S. B. (1976). *Bhili of Dangs*. Poona: DC.

Kumar, P. (2010). *A descriptive and typological study of Jarawa*. Ph. D. thesis, Jawaharlal Nehru University, New Delhi, and Max-Planck Institute, Leipzig.

*languages*. Oxford/New York: Routledge. 104–160.

Lehmann, T. (1998) Old Tamil. In Steever, S. A. (ed.), *The Dravidian languages*. London, N. Y.: Routledge. 75–99.

Macphail, R. M. (1983, [1953]). *An introduction to Santhali*. Parts I and II. Calcutta: Firma KLM Pvt. Ltd.

Mahapatra, S. (1994) *Parenga*. Bhubaneshwar: Tribal and Research Institute.

Maheswaran, C. (1989). *A descriptive study of the Kui language*. Ph.D. dissertation. Annamalainagar: Annamalai University.

Mallikarjun, B. (1998). *A descriptive analysis of Yerava*. Mysore: Central Institute of Indian Languages

Mangkang, P. & Pandey, P. (2009). Word-phonology of Zo. Ms. Centre for Linguistics, Jawaharlal Nehru University, New Delhi.

Manoharan, S. (1989). *A descriptive and comparative study of Andamanese language*. Calcutta: ASI.

Matson, D. M. (1964). *A grammatical sketch of Juang, a Munda language*. Ph. D. dissertation (University Microfilms). Ann Arbor: University of Wisconsin.

Mazaoudon, M. (2003). Tamang. In Thurgood, G & Lapolla, R. (eds). 289–314.

Mistry, P. J. (1999). Gujarati phonology. In Kaye, S. A. (ed.), *Phonologies of Asia and Afrika*. Winoa Lake IN: Eisenbrauns. 653–73.

Modi, B. V. (1983). *Some issues in the phonology of Gujarati*. Ph.D. dissertation. Baroda: M. S. University of Baroda.

Mohanan, K. P. & Mohanan, T. (1984) Lexical phonology of the consonant system in Malayalam. *Linguistic Inquiry* **15.4**. 575–602.

Mohiddin, S. K. (1980). *Dakhani Urdu*. Annamalinagar: Annamalai Univeristy

Moi, Niangliang. (2013). *Word Phonology of Paite*. M. Phil. Dissertation. New Delhi: Centre for Linguistics, Jawaharlal Nehru University.

Morey, S. (2005). *The Tai languages of Assam: A grammar and texts*. Canberra: Australian National University. [Pacific Linguistics, 565.]

Morse, S. A. (1988). A short update on Rawang phonology. *Linguistics of Tibeto-Burman Area* **11.2**. 120–32.

Nagaraja, K. S. (1999). *Korku language grammar, text and vocabulary*. Tokyo: Institute for the Study of Languages and Culture of Asia and Afrika. Tokyo University of Foreign Studies

Nara, T. & Bhaskararao, P. (eds.) (2002). *Toda texts*. (Endangered languages of the Pacific Rim Series. A3- 005). Osaka.

Natanasabapathy, S. (1986). Intonation patterns in Tamil. In Rajapurohit, B. B. (ed.), *Acoustic studies in India*. Mysore: Central Institute of Indian Languages. 92–97

Natarajan, G. V. (1985). *Abhujhamaria grammar*. Mysore: Central Institute of Indian Languages.

Nayar, P. V. R. (1971). Phonological treatment of nasal articulation in Malayalam – A polysystemic approach. Agesthelingam, S. & Valentine, E. (eds.), *Proceedings*

Ningomba, M. S. (1978). *Descriptive grammar of Maring*. Ph.D. dissertation. Poona: UP, Deccan College Post-Graduate and Research Institute

Ohala, M. (1983). *Aspects of Hindi phonology*. Delhi: Motilal Banarsidass.

Osada, T. (1992). *A reference grammar of Mundari*. Tokyo: Tokyo University of Foreign Studies.

Pai, P. (1976). *Kokborok grammar*. Mysore: Central Institute of Indian Languages.

Pandey, P. K. (1985). *Word accentuation in Hindustani in relation to word accents in English and Hindustani*. Ph.D. dissertation. Pune: DC.

Pandey, P. K. (1989). Syllable-dependent processes in Mundari. Paper presented at the *Seminar on phonetics and phonology of Austro-Asiatic languages*. Mysore: Central Institute of Indian Languages. [http://www.academia.edu/4776663/Syllable-based Processes in Mundari.....]

Pandey, P. K. (1990). Hindi schwa deletion. *Lingua* 82: 277–311.

Pandey, P. K. (2005). Second language varieties have a life of their own. [Invited paper for Festschrift volume entitled *Essays on Adegbija* edited by Demola Jolayemi (2005, unpublished)]. http://www.academia.edu/4776266/Second Language Varieties Have a Life of Their Own-Hindi English

Pandharipande, R. V. (1997). *Marathi*. London/New York: Routledge.

Pandit, P. B. (1975). A grammatical sketch of Gujarati. In Mitra, A. & Nigam, R. C. (eds.), *Grammatical sketches of Indian languages with comparative vocabulary and texts*. Census of India: GOI. 109–30.

Parakh, M. (2000). *Segmental phonology of Rathvi*. M. A. dissertation. Vadodara: Department of Linguistics. The M. S. University of Baroda.

Pattanayak, D. P. (1966). *A controlled historical reconstruction of Oriya, Assamese, Bengali and Hindi*. Hague/Paris.

Perialwar, R. (1979). *Phonology of Irula with vocabulary*. Annamalainagar: Annamalai University.

Peterson, J. (2006). *Kharia: A South Munda language, Volume I: Grammatical analysis,* Habilitationsschrift: Universität Osnabrück. [Also http://www.ling.uni-osnabrueck.de/uploads/Peterson/Grammar main body.pdf.].

Rabel, Lili (1961) *Khasi: A language of Assam*. Baton Rouge: Louisiana State University Press.

Radhakrishnan, R. (1981). *Nancowry word, phonology, morphology and roots of a Nicobarese language*. Canada: Linguistics Research Institute.

Rai, N. K. (1985). *A descriptive study of Bantawa*. Ph.D. dissertation. Poona: UP, Deccan College Post-Graduate and Research Institute.

Raina, S.N. (1990). *Kashmiri for non-Kashmiries: Learning and teaching problems*. Patiala: Gopi Publications.

Rajapurohit, B. B. (1983). *Shina phonetic reader*. Mysore: Central Institute of Indian Languages.

Ramachandrarao, V. (1986b). *The sound system of Remo*. M. Phil. dissertation. Hyderabad:

Ramanaiah, M. V. (1982). *Ave: A tribal Dravidian speech (phonology, morphology and lexicon)*. M. Phil. dissertation. Hyderabad: Osmania University.

Ramasvami, N. (1982). *Brokstat grammar*. Mysore: Central Institute of Indian Languages.

Ramaswami, N. (1975). *Brokstat phonetic reader*. Mysore: Central Institute of Indian Languages.

Ramaswami, N. (1989). *Bhumij Grammar*. Mysore: Central Institute of Indian Languages.

Rangan, K. (1975). *Balti phonetic reader*. Mysore: Central Institute of Indian Languages.

Rangan, K. (1979). *Purki grammar*. Mysore: Central Institute of Indian Languages.

Ranganatha, M. R. (1971). *Survey of Mandeali and Kului in Himachal Pradesh*. New Delhi: Census of India.

Rao, C. R. (1987). *A generative approach to Telugu phonology*. M.Phil. dissertation. Hyderabad: Osmania University

Rapacha, Lal (2006). *A descriptive grammar of Kiranti-Koints*. Ph. D. thesis. Centre for Linguistics, Jawaharlal Nehru University, New Delhi.

Reddy, B. R. (1986). Syllable-based grammatical rules: A note on the Manda plural formation. Paper presented at the *National seminar on syllable in phonetics and phonology*. Hyderabad: Osmania University.

Reddy, J. (1979). *Kuvi grammar*. Mysore: Central Institute of Indian Languages.

Reddy, K. N. & Reddy, B. R. (1986). Constraints on consonant combination in Manda. *Osmania Papers in Linguistics* **12**. 36-57.

Reddy, K. N. (forthcoming) *An outline of Telugu segmental phonology*.

Riccardi, T. (2003). Nepali. Cardona, G. & Jain, D. (eds.), *The Indo-Aryan Languages*. London, New York: Routledge (Routledge Language Family Series). 538-80.

Rohra, S. K. (1966). Descriptive Analysis of Kacchi. Ph. D. thesis. University of Poona.

Schiffman, H. F. (1999). *A reference grammar of spoken Tamil*. Cambridge: CUP.

Schmidt, R. L. (1981). *Dakhini Urdu: History and structure*. New Delhi: Bahri Publications.

Senkuttuvan, R. (1982). *The language of the Jarawa (phonology)*. Calcutta: Anthropological Survey of India.

Sharma, D. D. (1982) *A descriptive analysis of Pattani (a dialect of Lahul)*. Hoshiarpur: V. V. B. Institute. Punjab University.

Sharma, D. D. (1989). *Tibeto-Himalayan languages of Uttarakhand-Part I*. Delhi: Mittal Publication.

Sharma, J. C. (1979). *Gojri phonetic reader*. Mysore: Central Institute of Indian Languages.

Sharma, S. R. (1979). Phonological structure of Spiti. *Linguistics of Tibeto-Burman Area* **4.2**. 83-110.

Sharma, S. R. (2007). *Byangsi grammar and vocabulary*. Pune: Deccan College Post-Graduate and Research Institute.

Sharma, S. U. (1972). *Phonology and morphology of Jaunsari*. Ph.D. dissertation. Delhi: University of Delhi.

Sharma, S. U. (1990). *A linguistic study of Jaunsari*. New Delhi: Creative.

Shastri, G. D. P. (1984). *Mishmi phonetic reader.* Mysore: Central Institute of Indian Languages.

Shetty, R. T. (1978). *Koraga grammar.* Ph.D. dissertation. Poona: UP, Deccan College Post-Graduate and Research Institute.

Shreedhar, M. V. (1976). *Sema phonetic reader.* Mysore: Central Institute of Indian Languages.

Singh, J. D. (1970). *A descriptive grammar of Bangru.* Haryana: Kurukshetra University.

Singh, N. S. (2006). *Paite language.* New Delhi: Mittal Publications.

Singha, D. Kh. (2007). *An introduction to Dimasa phonology.* Guwahati: DVS Publishers.

Sinha, K. P. (1981[1968]). *The Bishnupriya Manipuri language.* Calcutta: Firma K. L. M.

Sinha, N. K. (1975). *Mundari grammar.* Mysore: Central Institute of Indian Languages.

Sinha, P. (1966). *A descriptive grammar of Lepcha.* Ph.D. dissertation. Poona: UP.

Sinisa, S., Ladefoged, P. & Bhaskararao, P. (1996). The trills of Toda. *Journal of International Phonetic Association* **26.1**. 1–21.

Smirnov, I. A. (1975). *The Lahndi language.* Moscow: Nanka.

Sprigg, R. K. (1967).Balti-Tibetan verb syllable finals, and a prosodic analysis, *Asia Major*, new series. **13**. 1–2, 187–201.

Sreedhar, M. V (1980). *Sema Grammar.* Mysore: Central Institute of Indian Languages

Sreedhar, M. V. (1974). *Naga Pidgin: A Socio-linguistic Study of Inter-lingual Communication Pattern in Nagaland.* Mysore: CIIL.

Sridhar, S. N. (1990). *Kannada.* London/New York: Routledge.

Steever, S. A. (1998). Malto. Steever, S. A. (ed.), *The Dravidian languages.* London, N. Y. : Routledge. 357–87.

Steever, S. A. (1998). Malto. Steever, S. A. (ed.), *The Dravidian languages.* London, N. Y. : Routledge. 357–87.

Subba, S. (1972). *Descriptive analysis of Magar: A Tibeto-Burman language.* Ph.D. dissertation. Pune: Deccan College Post-Graduate and Research Institute.

Subbaiah, G. (1986). *Kota phonetic reader.* Mysore: Central Institute of Indian Languages.

Subrahmanyam, P. S. (1974). *An introduction to modern Telugu.* Annamalainagar: Annamalai University.

Suebplai, P. S. (1986). *Phonetic description of Adi language.* MA dissertation. Delhi: University of Delhi.

Suresh, J. (1984) *Grammar of Ho*. Calcutta: Language Division.

Suresh, J. (1986). *Grammar of Santhali.* Calcutta: Language Division.

Tayeng, A. (1983). *A phrase book in Padam*. Itanagar: Director of Research, Govt of Arunachal Pradesh.

Taylor, D. (1969). Tamang phonemic summary. *Tibeto-Burman phonemic summaries* 7. Kathmandu: Summer Institute of Linguistics and Tribhuvan University.

Thirumalai, M. S. (1972). *Thaadou phonetic reader.* Mysore: Central Institute of Indian Languages.

Tiwari, S. K. (1971). *Descriptive grammar of Kabui.* Ph.D. dissertation. Poona: UP, Deccan College Post-Graduate and Research Institute.

Trail, R. L. (1968). *Lamani: Phonology, grammar and lexicon.* Ph.D. dissertation. Poona: UP.

Tyler, S. A. (1969). *Koya: An outline grammar (Gomma dialect).* Berkeley: University of California Press.

Varma, G. S. (1970). *Vaagri Boli: An Indo-Aryan language*. Annamalainagar: Annamalai University [Publications no. 21.]

Vasanthakumari, T. (1989). *Generative phonology of Tamil.* Delhi: Mittal Publications.

Verma, M. K. (2003). Bhojpuri. Cardona, G. & Jain, D. (eds.), *The Indo-Aryan Languages*. London, New York: Routledge (Routledge Language Family Series). 515–37.

*Verma*, S. (2003). Magahi. Cardona, G. & Jain, D., *The Indo-Aryan Languages*. London: Routledge, Corzon. 498–514

Wali, K. & Koul, O. N. (1997). *Kashmiri: A cognitive-descriptive grammar.* London/NY: Routledge.

Wichamdinbo & Pandey, P. K. (2009). Word-phonology of Liangmai: A sketch. Ms. Centre for Linguistics. Jawaharlal Nehru University, New Delhi.

Yadav, R. (1996). *A reference grammar of Maithili.* Delhi: Munshiram Manoharlal Publishers.

Yadav, R. (2003). Maithili. Cardona, G. & Jain, D. (eds.), *The Indo-Aryan languages*. London, New York: Routledge (Routledge Language Family Series). 477-97.

Zeite, L. & Pandey, P. K. (2007). A sketch of the word phonology of Koren. Ms. Centre for Linguistics, J. N. U., New Delhi.

Zide, N. H. (1960). *Korku phonology and morphophonemics*. Ph.D. dissertation. Philadelphia: University of Pennsylvania.

Zollar, C. P. (1983). *Die sprache der Rang Pas von Garhwal (Rang PO Bha:sa) grammatik, texte, wortterbuch*. Wiesbaden: Otto Harrassowitz.

Zvelebil, K. V. (1971). Irula vowels. *Indo-Iranian Journal* **13.2**. 113–22.